I'm a Terminal Cancer Patient

BUT I'M FINE

THIRTY-EIGHT-YEAR-OLD AUTHOR OF EROTIC MANGA HAS COLON CANCER

(TRUE) STORY AND ART BY

Hilnama

I'm a terminal cancer patient, but I'm fine.

contents

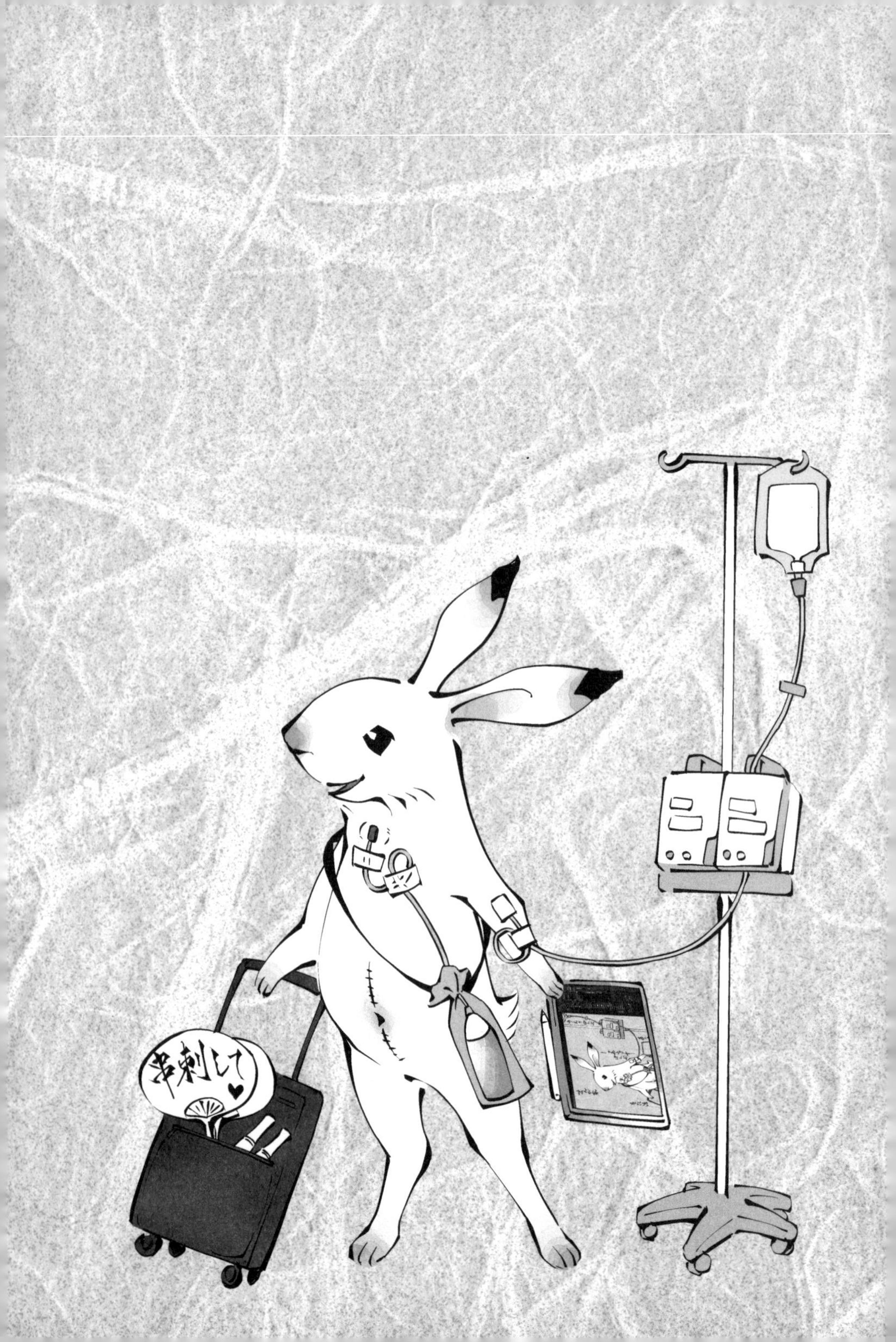
串刺して♥

The Story of how I thought I had a Stomachache when I went to the hospital, but it was Terminal Cancer.

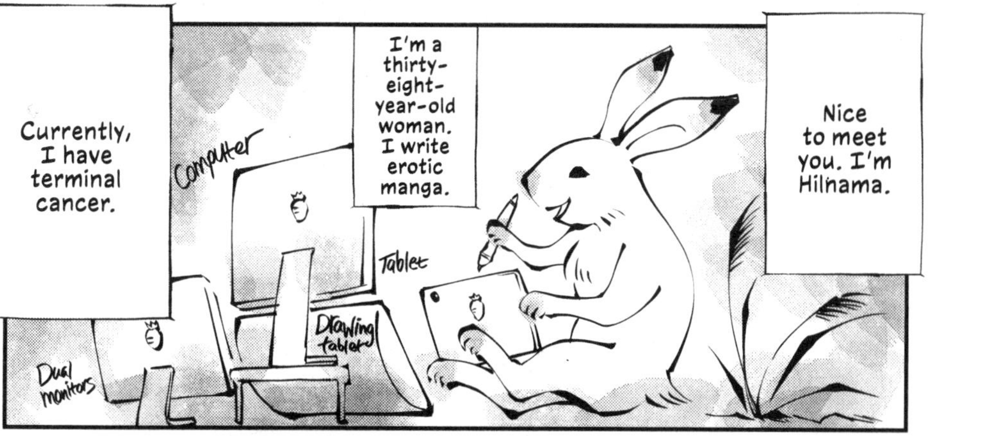

Nice to meet you. I'm Hilnama.
I'm a thirty-eight-year-old woman. I write erotic manga.
Currently, I have terminal cancer.
Computer
Tablet
Drawing tablet
Dual monitors

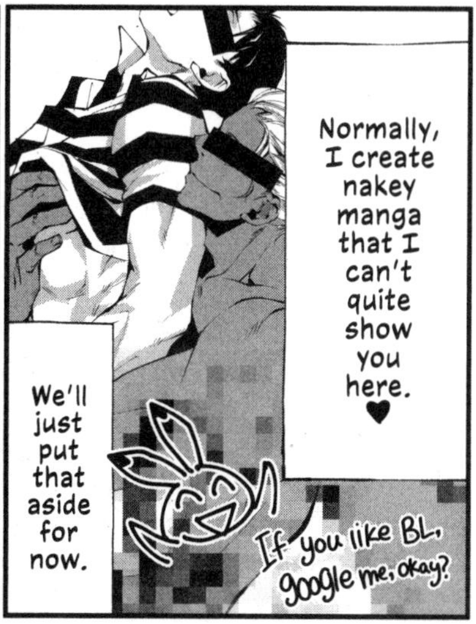

Normally, I create nakey manga that I can't quite show you here. ♥
We'll just put that aside for now.
If you like BL, google me, okay?

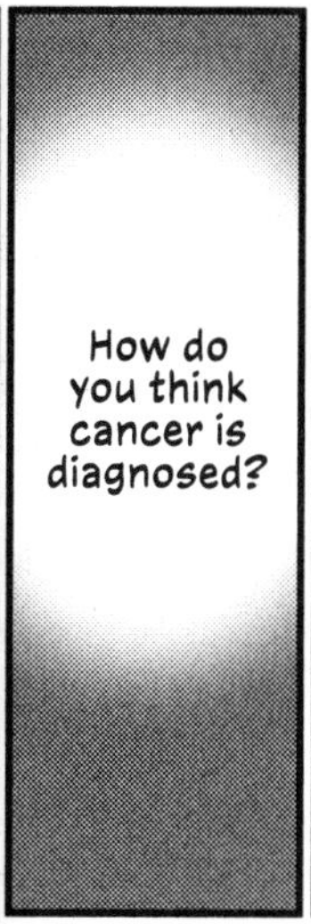

How do you think cancer is diagnosed?

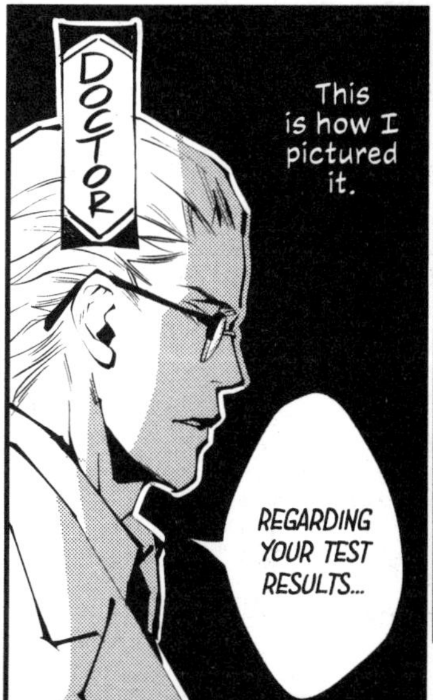

This is how I pictured it.
DOCTOR
REGARDING YOUR TEST RESULTS...

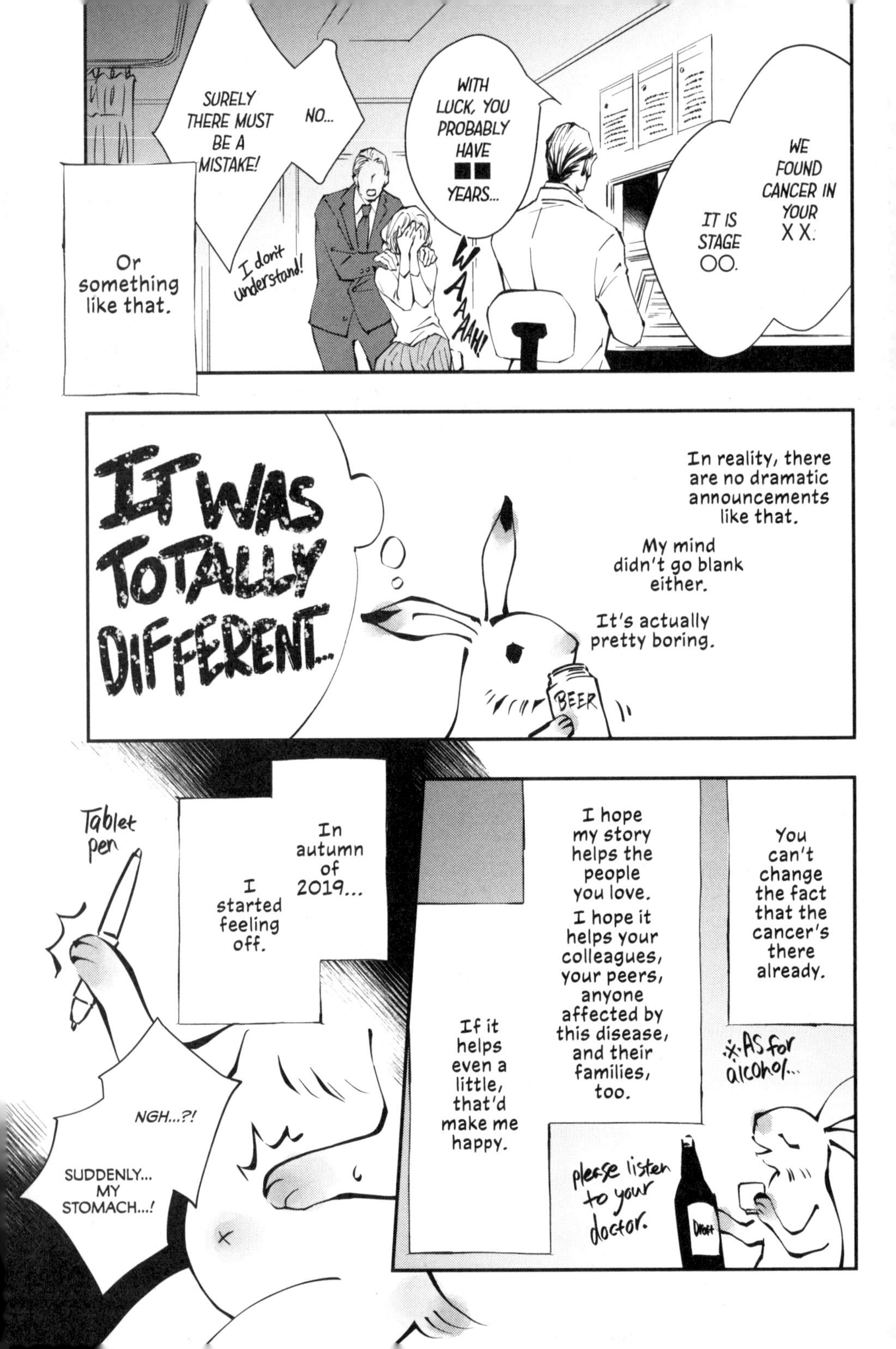
WE FOUND CANCER IN YOUR XX.
IT IS STAGE OO.
WITH LUCK, YOU PROBABLY HAVE [redacted] YEARS...
WAAAAAH!
NO...
SURELY THERE MUST BE A MISTAKE!
I don't understand!
Or something like that.
In reality, there are no dramatic announcements like that.
My mind didn't go blank either.
It's actually pretty boring.
IT WAS TOTALLY DIFFERENT...
BEER
You can't change the fact that the cancer's there already.
※AS for alcohol...
please listen to your doctor.
I hope my story helps the people you love.
I hope it helps your colleagues, your peers, anyone affected by this disease, and their families, too.
If it helps even a little, that'd make me happy.
In autumn of 2019...
I started feeling off.
Tablet pen
NGH...?!
SUDDENLY... MY STOMACH...!

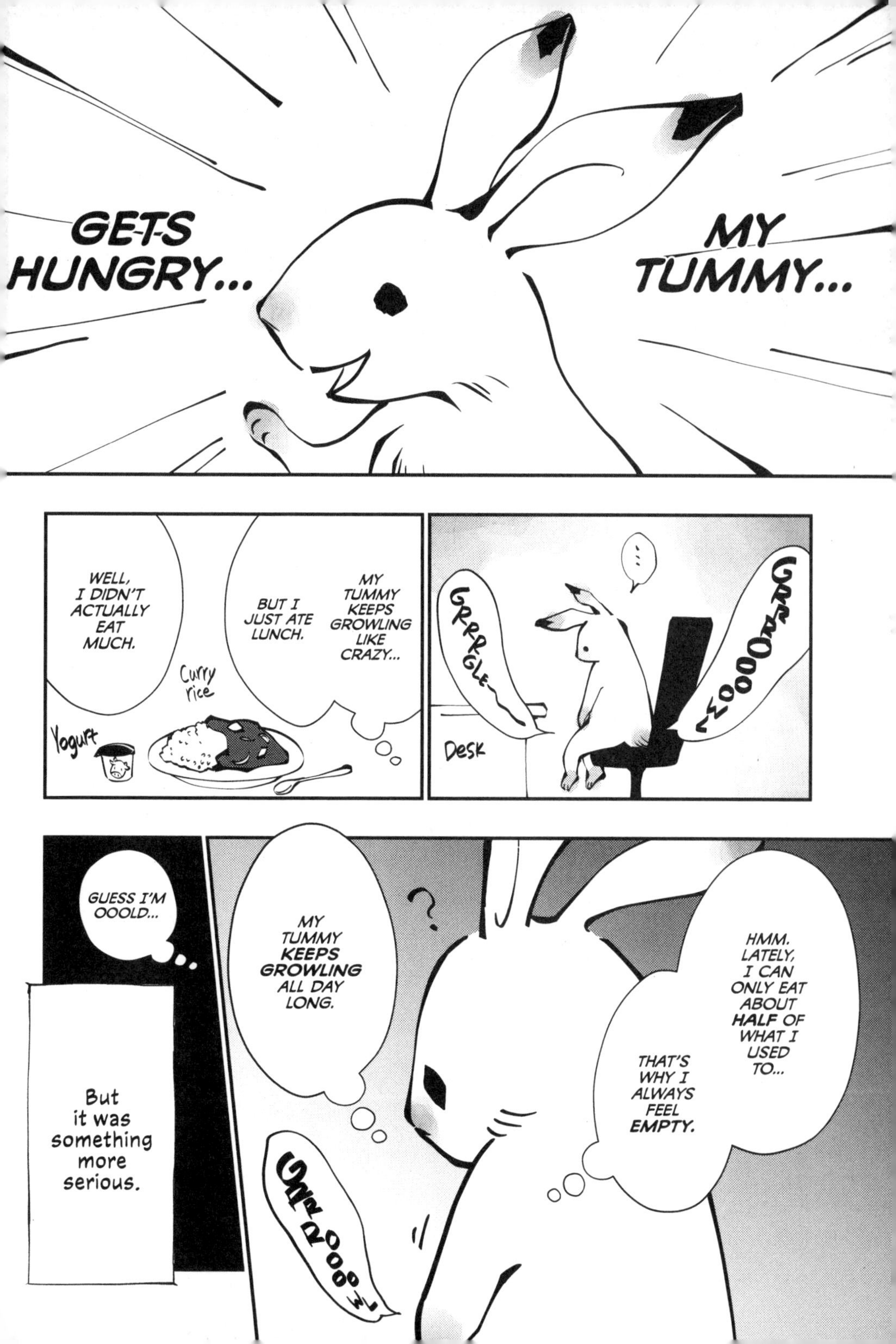
MY TUMMY...
GETS HUNGRY...
GRRROOOO~
...
GRRRGLE~
Desk
MY TUMMY KEEPS GROWLING LIKE CRAZY...
BUT I JUST ATE LUNCH.
WELL, I DIDN'T ACTUALLY EAT MUCH.
Curry rice
Yogurt
HMM. LATELY, I CAN ONLY EAT ABOUT HALF OF WHAT I USED TO...
THAT'S WHY I ALWAYS FEEL EMPTY.
?
MY TUMMY KEEPS GROWLING ALL DAY LONG.
GRRROOOW
GUESS I'M OOOLD...
But it was something more serious.

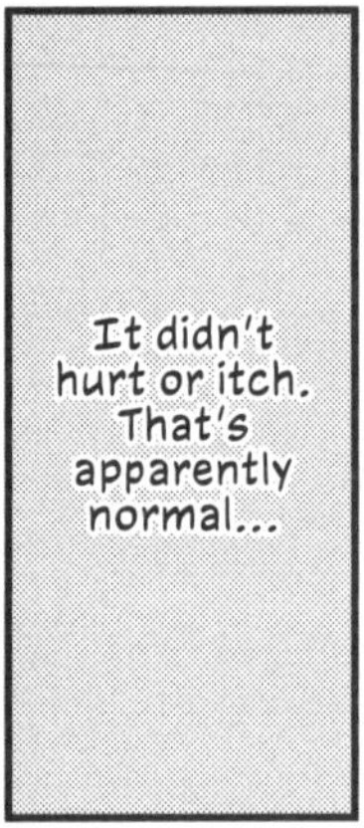
It didn't hurt or itch. That's apparently normal...
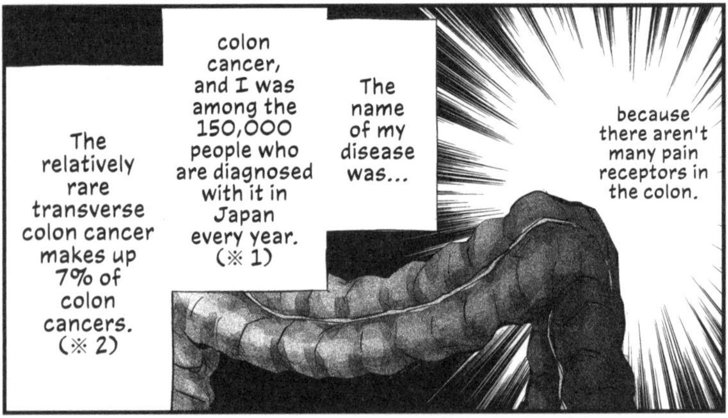
because there aren't many pain receptors in the colon.
The name of my disease was...
colon cancer, and I was among the 150,000 people who are diagnosed with it in Japan every year. (※ 1)
The relatively rare transverse colon cancer makes up 7% of colon cancers. (※ 2)

※ 1 Reference: National Cancer Center Information Service (https://ganjoho.jp/public/cancer/colon/)
※ 2 Reference: Japanese Red Cross Society Ise Red Cross Hospital's official site (http://www.ise.jrc.or.jp/cancer/ca06-06.html)

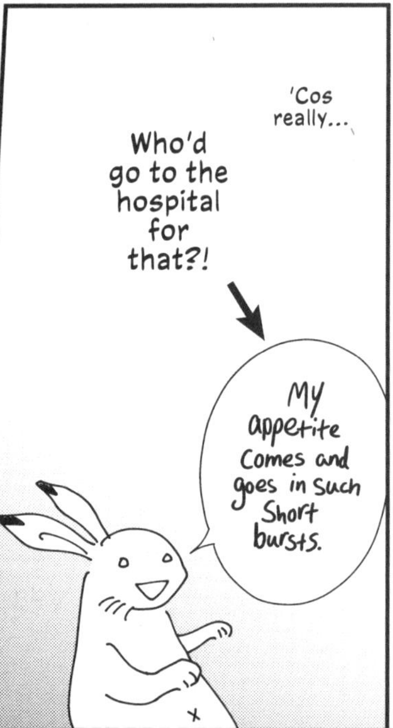
'Cos really...
Who'd go to the hospital for that?!
My appetite comes and goes in such short bursts.
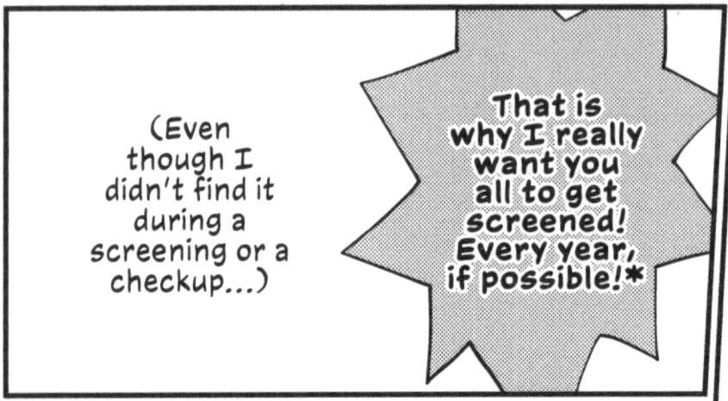
That is why I really want you all to get screened! Every year, if possible!*
(Even though I didn't find it during a screening or a checkup...)

*In the US, screenings start at 45 and are not repeated annually. Three to ten years is typical between tests.

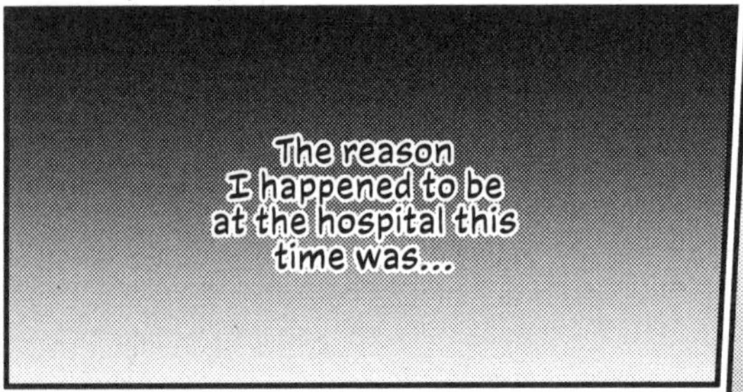
The reason I happened to be at the hospital this time was...

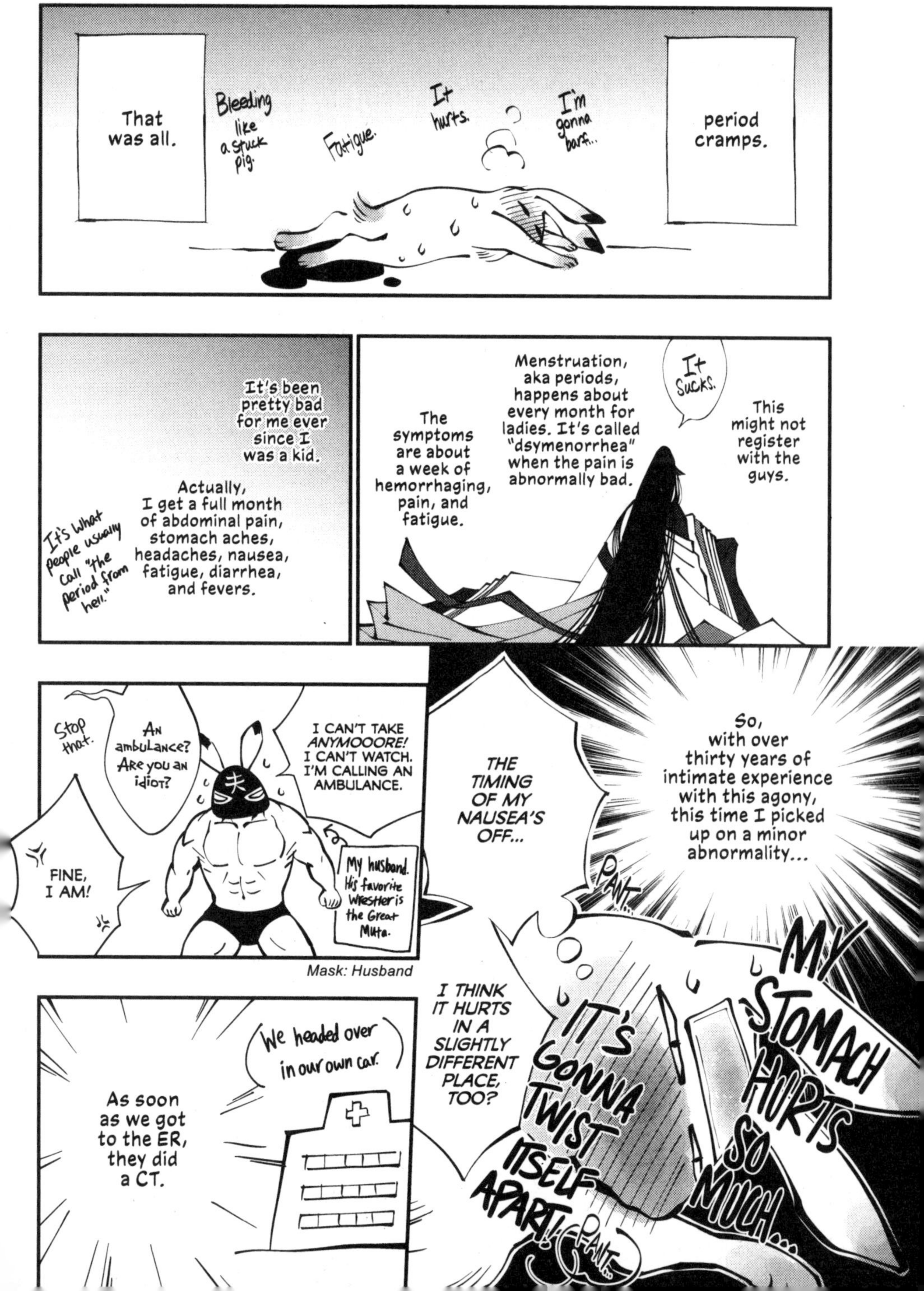

period cramps.
I'm gonna barf...
It hurts.
Fatigue.
Bleeding like a stuck pig.
That was all.
This might not register with the guys.
It sucks.
Menstruation, aka periods, happens about every month for ladies. It's called "dsymenorrhea" when the pain is abnormally bad.
The symptoms are about a week of hemorrhaging, pain, and fatigue.
It's been pretty bad for me ever since I was a kid.
Actually, I get a full month of abdominal pain, stomach aches, headaches, nausea, fatigue, diarrhea, and fevers.
It's what people usually call "the period from hell."
So, with over thirty years of intimate experience with this agony, this time I picked up on a minor abnormality...
THE TIMING OF MY NAUSEA'S OFF...
PANT...
MY STOMACH HURTS SO MUCH...
IT'S GONNA TWIST ITSELF APART!
I THINK IT HURTS IN A SLIGHTLY DIFFERENT PLACE, TOO?
PANT
PANT...
I CAN'T TAKE *ANYMOOORE!* I CAN'T WATCH. I'M CALLING AN AMBULANCE.
An ambulance? Are you an idiot?
Stop that.
My husband. His favorite wrestler is the Great Muta.
FINE, I AM!
Mask: Husband
We headed over in our own car.
As soon as we got to the ER, they did a CT.

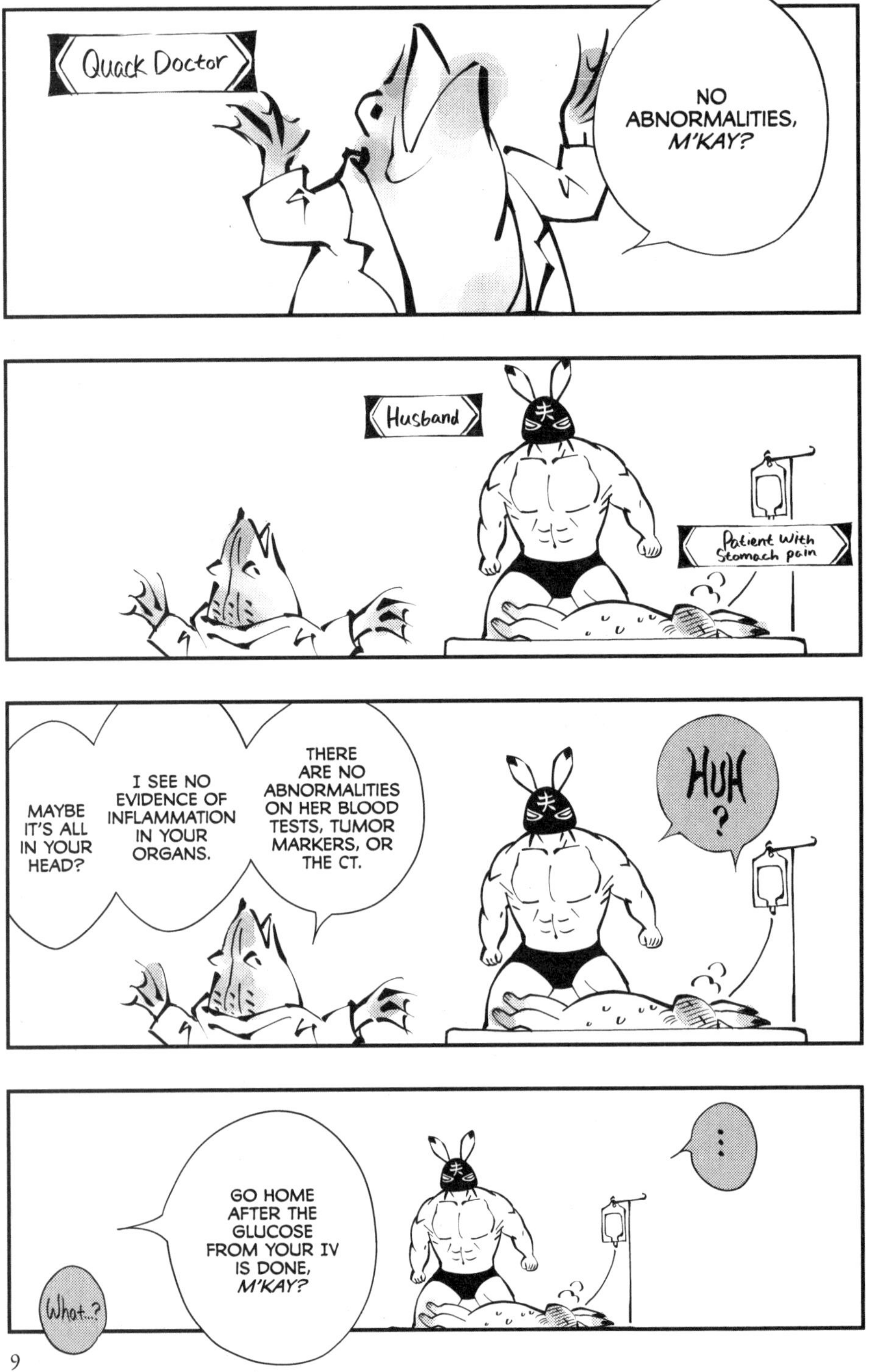
NO ABNORMALITIES, *M'KAY?*
Quack Doctor
Patient With Stomach pain
Husband
HUH ?
THERE ARE NO ABNORMALITIES ON HER BLOOD TESTS, TUMOR MARKERS, OR THE CT.
I SEE NO EVIDENCE OF INFLAMMATION IN YOUR ORGANS.
MAYBE IT'S ALL IN YOUR HEAD?
...
GO HOME AFTER THE GLUCOSE FROM YOUR IV IS DONE, *M'KAY?*
What...?

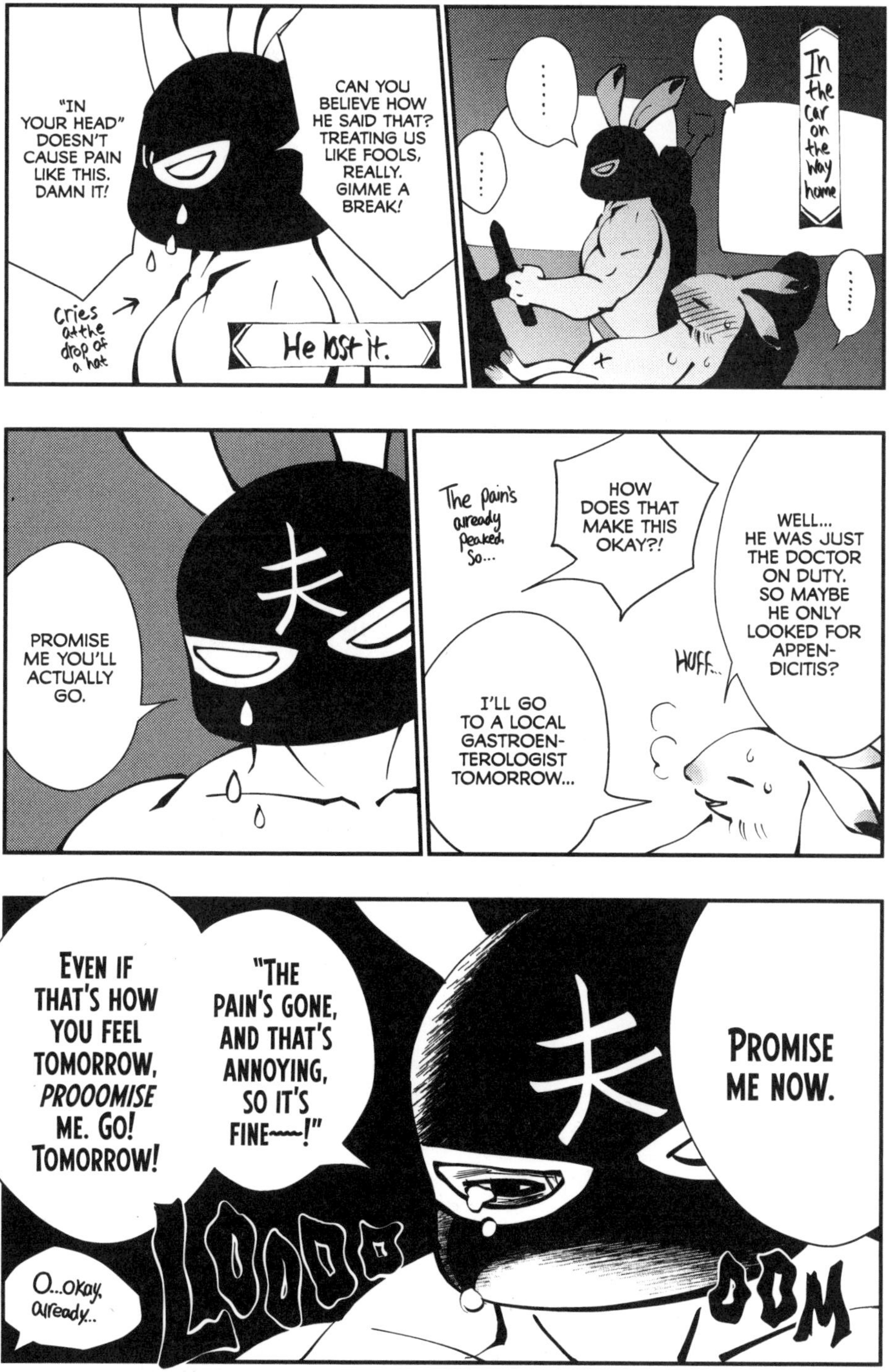
In the car on the way home
......
......
......
......
CAN YOU BELIEVE HOW HE SAID THAT? TREATING US LIKE FOOLS, REALLY. GIMME A BREAK!
"IN YOUR HEAD" DOESN'T CAUSE PAIN LIKE THIS. DAMN IT!
He lost it.
Cries at the drop of a hat
WELL... HE WAS JUST THE DOCTOR ON DUTY. SO MAYBE HE ONLY LOOKED FOR APPEN-DICITIS?
HOW DOES THAT MAKE THIS OKAY?!
The pain's already peaked. So...
HUFF...
I'LL GO TO A LOCAL GASTROEN-TEROLOGIST TOMORROW...
PROMISE ME YOU'LL ACTUALLY GO.
PROMISE ME NOW.
"THE PAIN'S GONE, AND THAT'S ANNOYING, SO IT'S FINE----!"
EVEN IF THAT'S HOW YOU FEEL TOMORROW, *PROOOMISE* ME. GO! TOMORROW!
LOOOO OOM
O...okay, already...

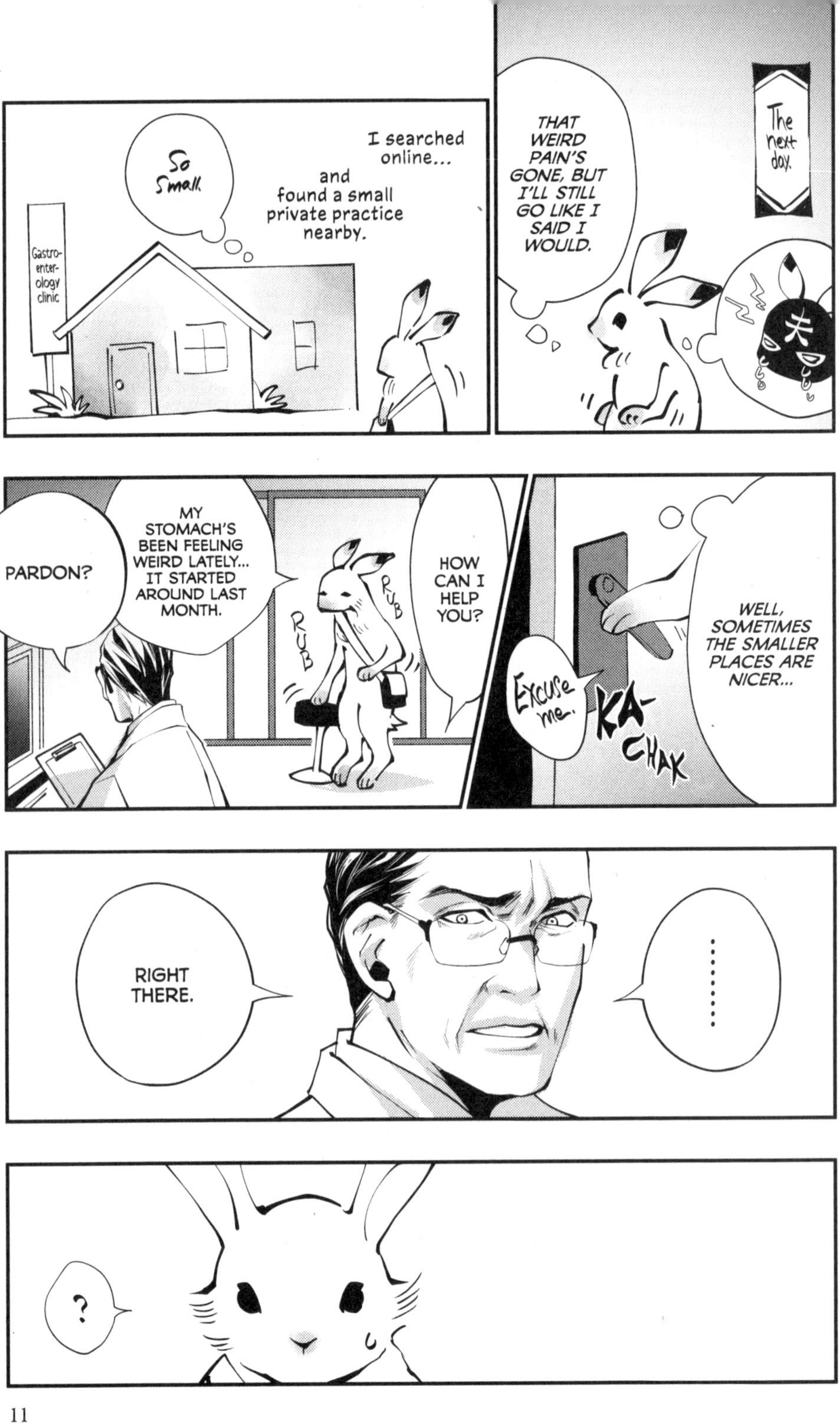
The next day.
THAT WEIRD PAIN'S GONE, BUT I'LL STILL GO LIKE I SAID I WOULD.
I searched online...
and found a small private practice nearby.
So small.
Gastro-enterology clinic
WELL, SOMETIMES THE SMALLER PLACES ARE NICER...
Excuse me.
KA-CHAK
HOW CAN I HELP YOU?
RUB
RUB
MY STOMACH'S BEEN FEELING WEIRD LATELY... IT STARTED AROUND LAST MONTH.
PARDON?
......
RIGHT THERE.
?

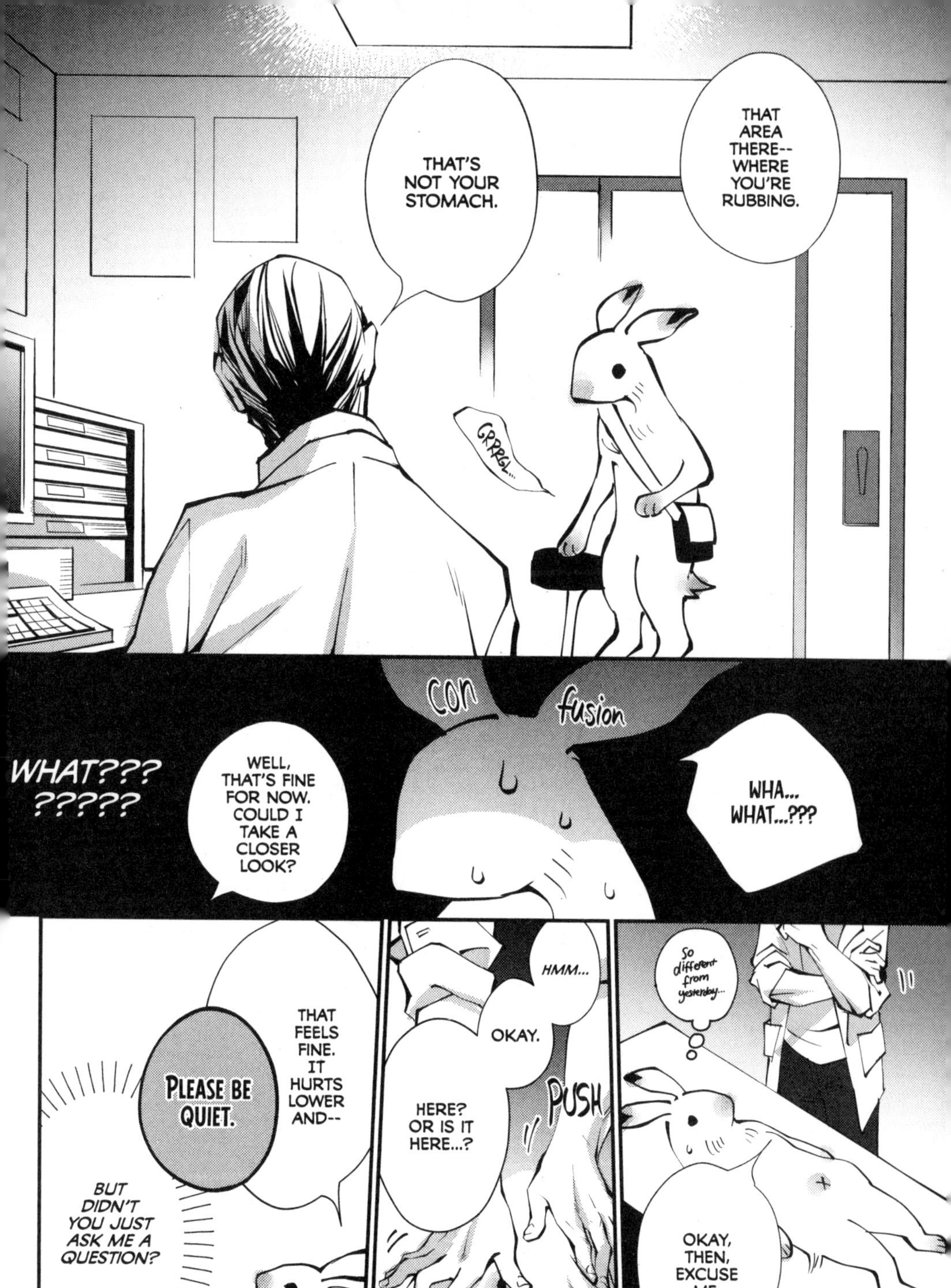
THAT AREA THERE-- WHERE YOU'RE RUBBING.
THAT'S NOT YOUR STOMACH.
GRRRGL...
con fusion
WHA... WHAT...???
WELL, THAT'S FINE FOR NOW. COULD I TAKE A CLOSER LOOK?
WHAT??? ?????
So different from yesterday...
OKAY, THEN, EXCUSE ME.
HMM...
OKAY.
HERE? OR IS IT HERE...?
PUSH
PUSH
THAT FEELS FINE. IT HURTS LOWER AND--
PLEASE BE QUIET.
BUT DIDN'T YOU JUST ASK ME A QUESTION?

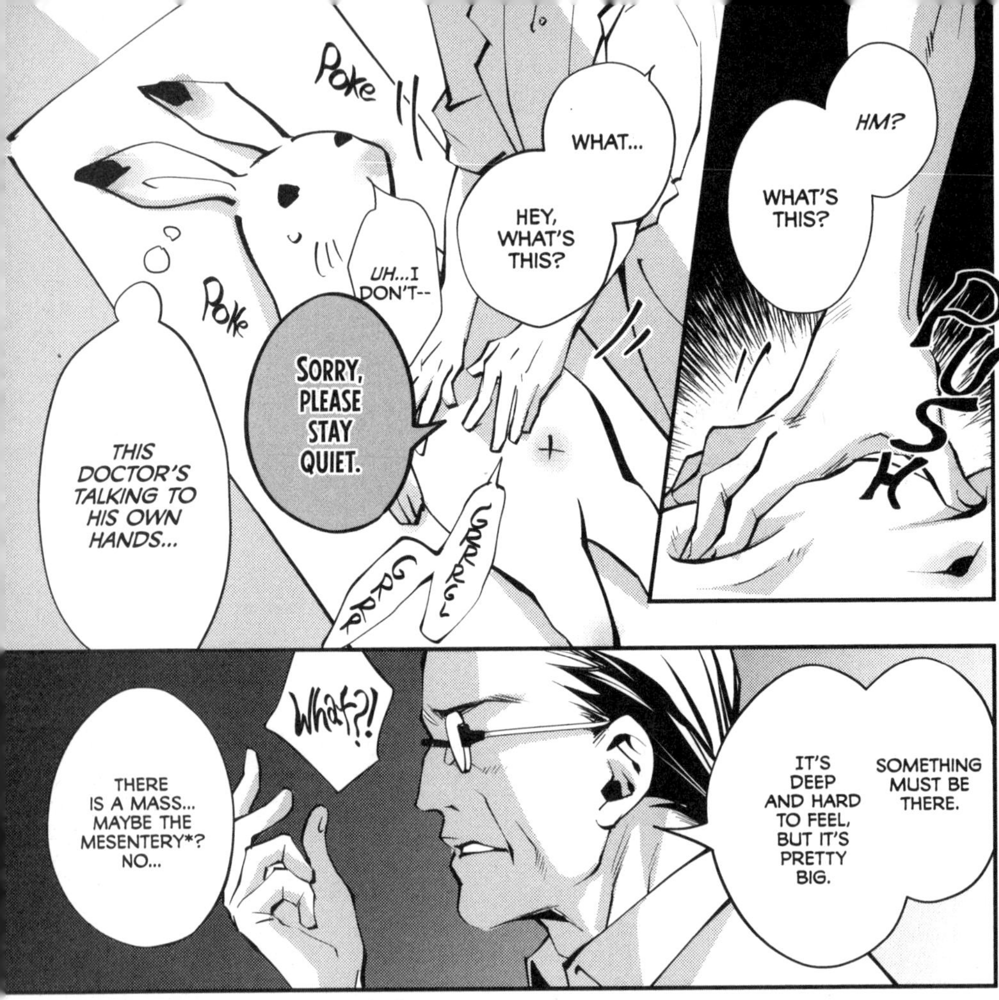
HM?
WHAT'S THIS?
PUSH
WHAT...
HEY, WHAT'S THIS?
Poke
UH...I DON'T--
SORRY, PLEASE STAY QUIET.
Poke
THIS DOCTOR'S TALKING TO HIS OWN HANDS...
GRRR
SOMETHING MUST BE THERE.
IT'S DEEP AND HARD TO FEEL, BUT IT'S PRETTY BIG.
What?!
THERE IS A MASS... MAYBE THE MESENTERY*? NO...

*The membrane holding your organs in place.

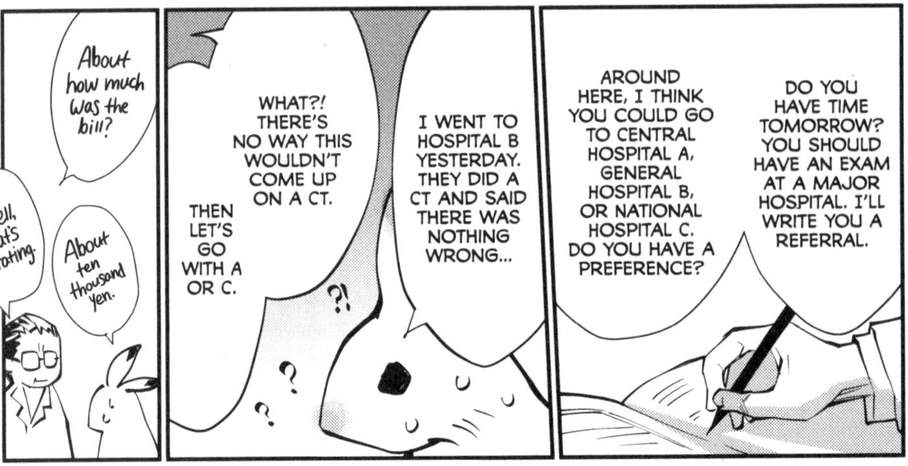
DO YOU HAVE TIME TOMORROW? YOU SHOULD HAVE AN EXAM AT A MAJOR HOSPITAL. I'LL WRITE YOU A REFERRAL.
AROUND HERE, I THINK YOU COULD GO TO CENTRAL HOSPITAL A, GENERAL HOSPITAL B, OR NATIONAL HOSPITAL C. DO YOU HAVE A PREFERENCE?
I WENT TO HOSPITAL B YESTERDAY. THEY DID A CT AND SAID THERE WAS NOTHING WRONG...
WHAT?! THERE'S NO WAY THIS WOULDN'T COME UP ON A CT.
?!
THEN LET'S GO WITH A OR C.
?
?
About how much was the bill?
About ten thousand yen.
Well, that's irritating.

BY THE WAY, MOST OF OUR REFERRALS ARE TO HOSPITAL C, BUT BECAUSE IT'S A NATIONAL FACILITY, IT'S A BIT OLD. THERE ARE A LOT OF GOOD DOCTORS THERE, THOUGH.
UNLIKE MOST LARGE HOSPITALS, A'S COORDINATION BETWEEN THE INTERNAL MEDICINE AND SURGERY DEPARTMENTS IS EXCELLENT. IT'S WELL RUN. IT'S ALSO NEW AND CLOSE BY.
BLAB BLAB
BLAB
SO FAST
WHA... ? TH-THEN, HOSPITAL A...
YES.
BEEP BEEP
OH, HELLO? THIS IS CLINIC P. WHAT IS THE QUICKEST APPOINTMENT I CAN GET? YES, ASAP. TODAY OR TOMORROW, IF POSSIBLE... I KNOW, BUT PLEASE.
I UNDER-STAND. THE BEGINNING OF NEXT WEEK, THEN. YES. THANK YOU.
BEEP
COME HERE TOMORROW.
GRAB
O-OKAY.
WE'LL DO AN ULTRASOUND AND AN UPPER GI ENDOSCOPY.
WE'LL CHECK AS MANY THINGS AS WE CAN BEFORE YOU GO TO HOSPITAL A NEXT WEEK.
SIR!
TOMORROW'S ALREADY FULL! HOW MANY ENDOSCOPIES DO YOU THINK YOU CAN DO?
NURSE
JUST FIT IT IN SOMEWHERE.
I'M TELLING YOU THERE'S NO TIME AT ALL FOR IT.
THEN WE'LL JUST HAVE TO FIGURE IT OUT, WON'T WE? PUT IT IN FOR LUNCH.
WHAAAT...? YOU SURE? DON'T GO AND BLAME ME LATER.
Is this that much of a rush?
To be honest, around this time...

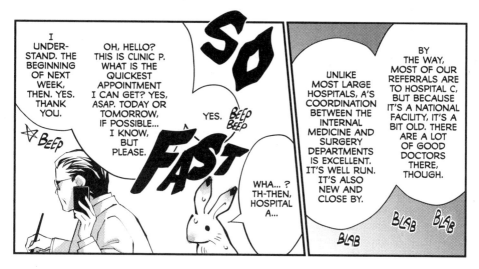

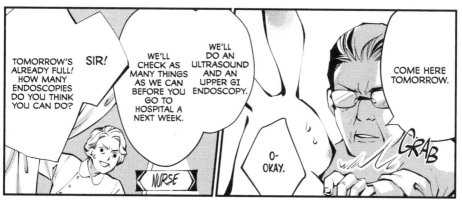

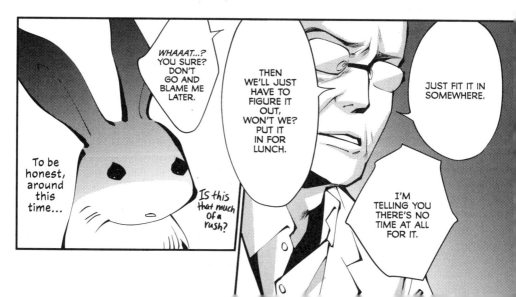

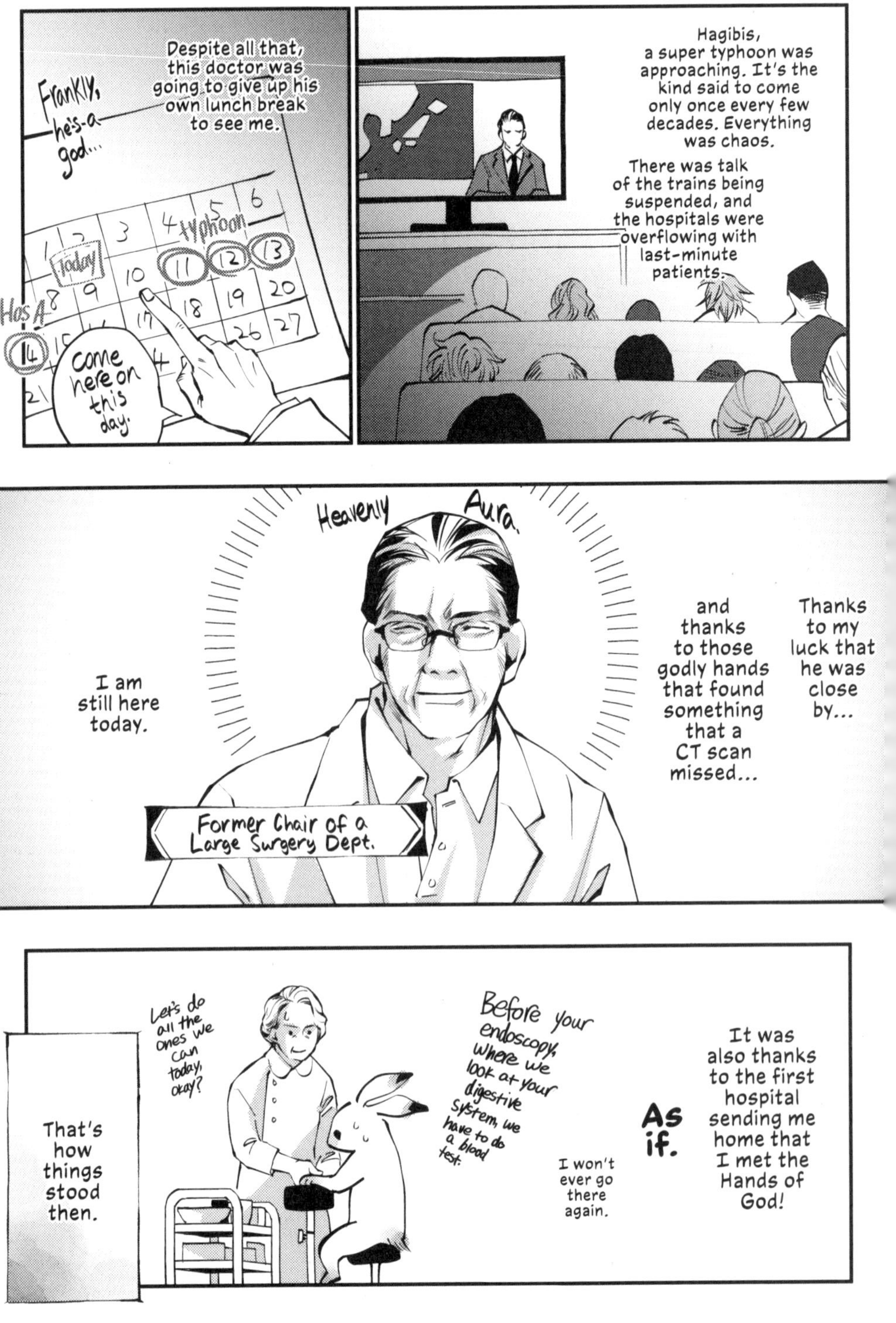
Hagibis, a super typhoon was approaching. It's the kind said to come only once every few decades. Everything was chaos.
There was talk of the trains being suspended, and the hospitals were overflowing with last-minute patients.
Despite all that, this doctor was going to give up his own lunch break to see me.
Frankly, he's-a god...
typhoon
today
Hos A
Come here on this day.
Thanks to my luck that he was close by...
and thanks to those godly hands that found something that a CT scan missed...
Heavenly Aura.
I am still here today.
Former Chair of a Large Surgery Dept.
It was also thanks to the first hospital sending me home that I met the Hands of God!
As if.
I won't ever go there again.
Before your endoscopy, where we look at your digestive system, we have to do a blood test.
Let's do all the ones we can today, okay?
That's how things stood then.

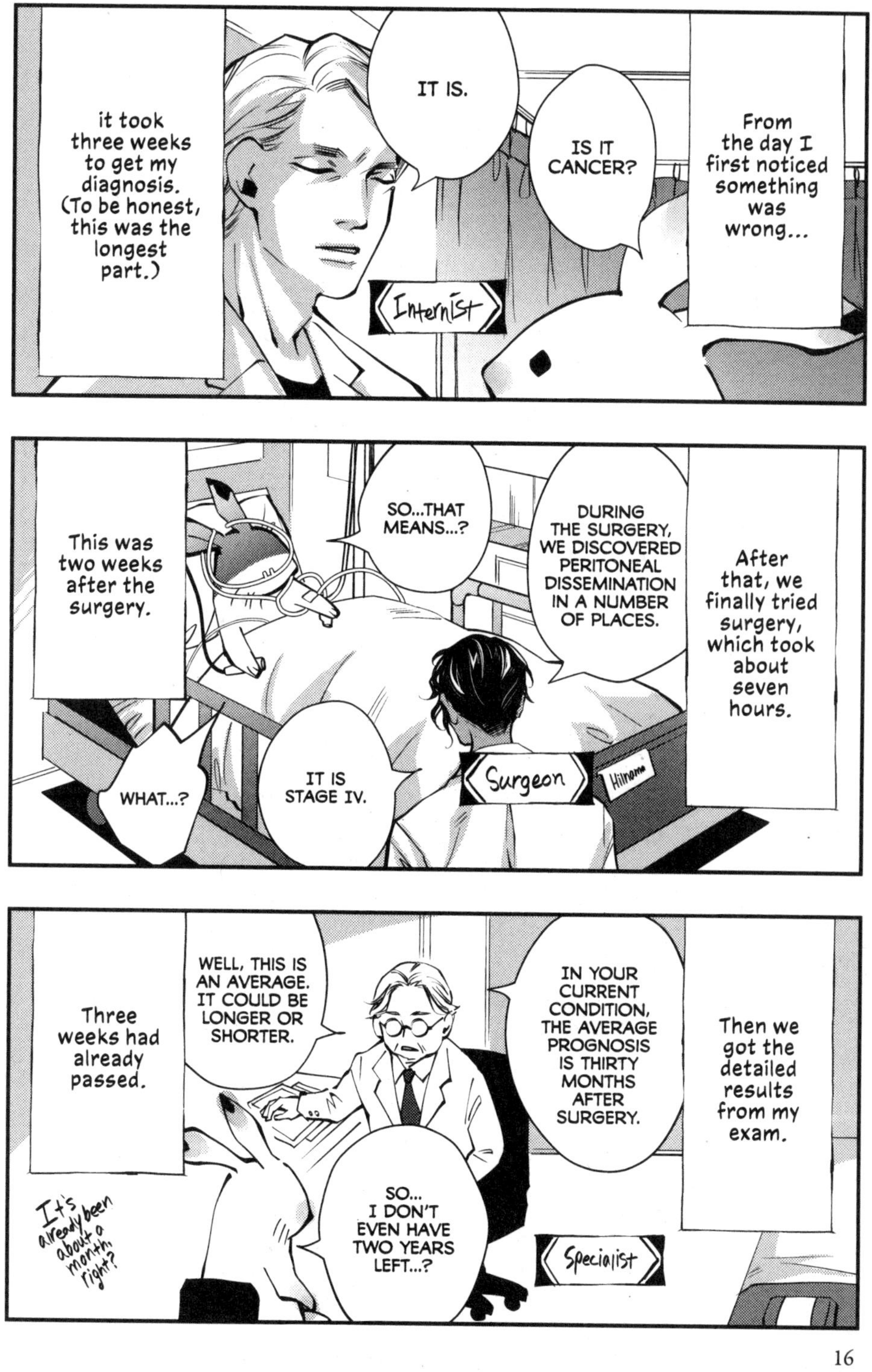
From the day I first noticed something was wrong...
IS IT CANCER?
IT IS.
it took three weeks to get my diagnosis. (To be honest, this was the longest part.)
Internist
After that, we finally tried surgery, which took about seven hours.
DURING THE SURGERY, WE DISCOVERED PERITONEAL DISSEMINATION IN A NUMBER OF PLACES.
SO...THAT MEANS...?
This was two weeks after the surgery.
Surgeon
IT IS STAGE IV.
WHAT...?
Then we got the detailed results from my exam.
IN YOUR CURRENT CONDITION, THE AVERAGE PROGNOSIS IS THIRTY MONTHS AFTER SURGERY.
WELL, THIS IS AN AVERAGE. IT COULD BE LONGER OR SHORTER.
Three weeks had already passed.
Specialist
SO... I DON'T EVEN HAVE TWO YEARS LEFT...?
It's already been about a month, right?

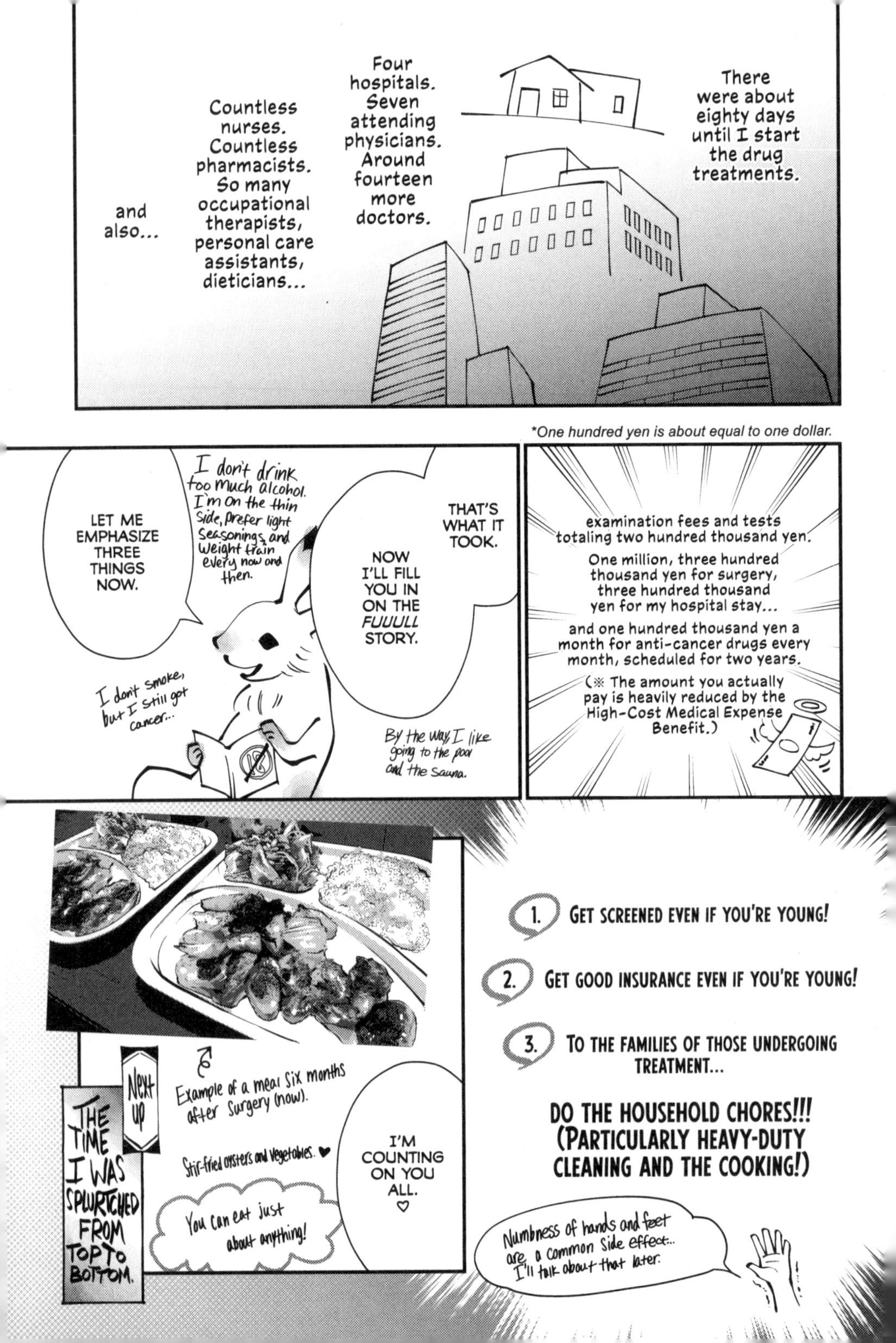
There were about eighty days until I start the drug treatments.
Four hospitals. Seven attending physicians. Around fourteen more doctors.
Countless nurses. Countless pharmacists. So many occupational therapists, personal care assistants, dieticians...
and also...
*One hundred yen is about equal to one dollar.
examination fees and tests totaling two hundred thousand yen.
One million, three hundred thousand yen for surgery, three hundred thousand yen for my hospital stay...
and one hundred thousand yen a month for anti-cancer drugs every month, scheduled for two years.
(※ The amount you actually pay is heavily reduced by the High-Cost Medical Expense Benefit.)
THAT'S WHAT IT TOOK.
NOW I'LL FILL YOU IN ON THE *FUUULL* STORY.
I don't drink too much alcohol. I'm on the thin side, prefer light seasonings, and weight train every now and then.
LET ME EMPHASIZE THREE THINGS NOW.
By the way, I like going to the pool and the sauna.
I don't smoke, but I still got cancer...
1. GET SCREENED EVEN IF YOU'RE YOUNG!
2. GET GOOD INSURANCE EVEN IF YOU'RE YOUNG!
3. TO THE FAMILIES OF THOSE UNDERGOING TREATMENT...
DO THE HOUSEHOLD CHORES!!! (PARTICULARLY HEAVY-DUTY CLEANING AND THE COOKING!)
Numbness of hands and feet are a common side effect... I'll talk about that later.
I'M COUNTING ON YOU ALL. ♡
Example of a meal six months after surgery (now).
Stir-fried oysters and vegetables. ♥
You can eat just about anything!
Next up
THE TIME I WAS SPLURTCHED FROM TOP TO BOTTOM.

Hello. This is the author.
When the first chapter went online, a lot of health-care workers shared it. I'm so grateful for their kind words even though I'm such an amateur about the medical field.

But!!
I'm seriously just a normal person...
To keep on going like this would be kind of irresponsible...so I asked experts to look over my work.

I was unsupervised when I started writing.
Once I was done, I invited two doctors over to review my drafts. Despite the extra work it was for them, they agreed to help me. They checked everything again when all the chapters were going to be made into a book, and I sincerely appreciate their warmth. Their guidance was so helpful.

TO DR. Keiko Kawada and DR. Maki Sakamoto,
thank you So much!

Rest assured, what I chronicled here is credible.
You can read it with confidence. ♡

I'm a Terminal
Cancer
Patient
BUT I'M FINE

I thought I had a Stomachache, but it was terminal cancer. ②

The Time I Was Splurtched from Top to Bottom.

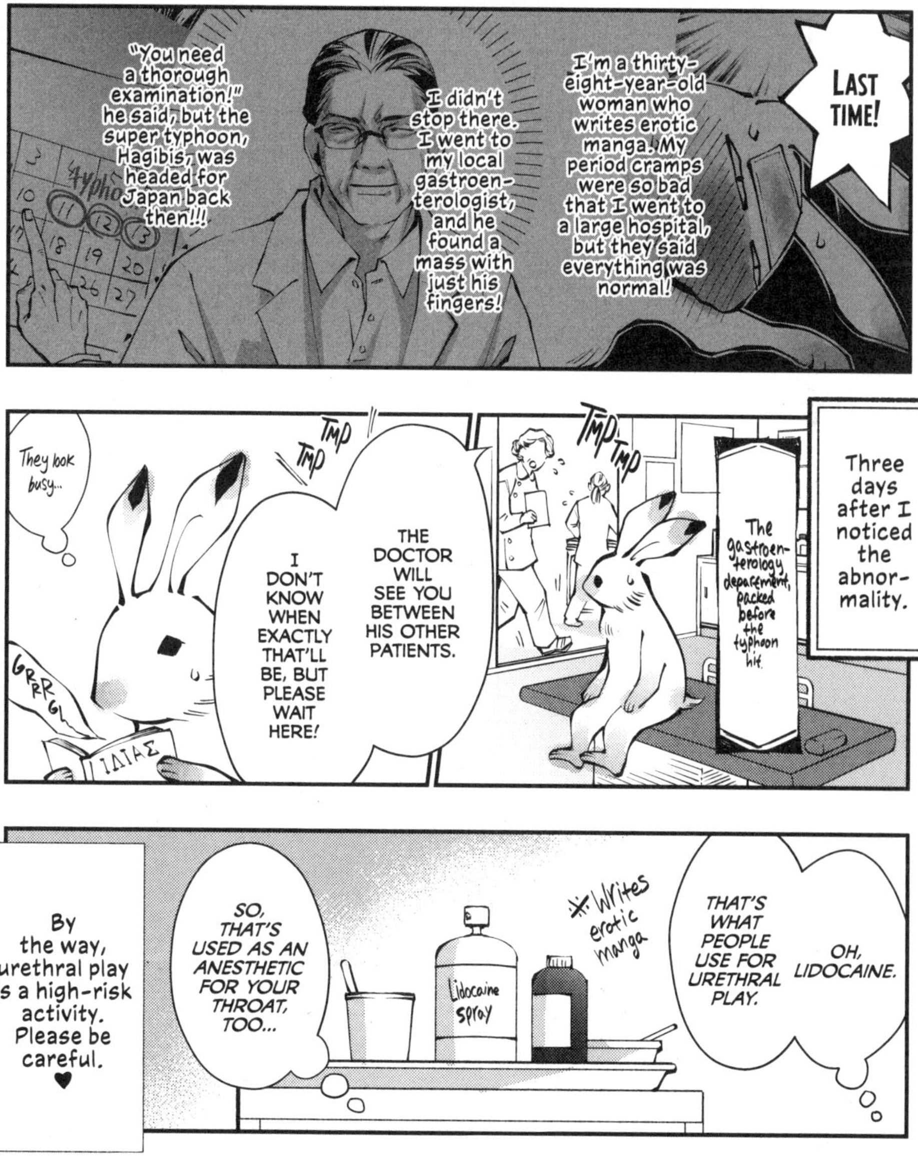
LAST TIME!
I'm a thirty-eight-year-old woman who writes erotic manga. My period cramps were so bad that I went to a large hospital, but they said everything was normal!
I didn't stop there. I went to my local gastroenterologist, and he found a mass with just his fingers!
"You need a thorough examination!" he said, but the super typhoon, Hagibis, was headed for Japan back then!!!
Three days after I noticed the abnormality.
The gastroenterology department, packed before the typhoon hit.
TMP TMP
THE DOCTOR WILL SEE YOU BETWEEN HIS OTHER PATIENTS.
I DON'T KNOW WHEN EXACTLY THAT'LL BE, BUT PLEASE WAIT HERE!
TMP TMP
They look busy...
GRRRGL
OH, LIDOCAINE.
THAT'S WHAT PEOPLE USE FOR URETHRAL PLAY.
※Writes erotic manga
Lidocaine spray
SO, THAT'S USED AS AN ANESTHETIC FOR YOUR THROAT, TOO...
By the way, urethral play is a high-risk activity. Please be careful. ♥

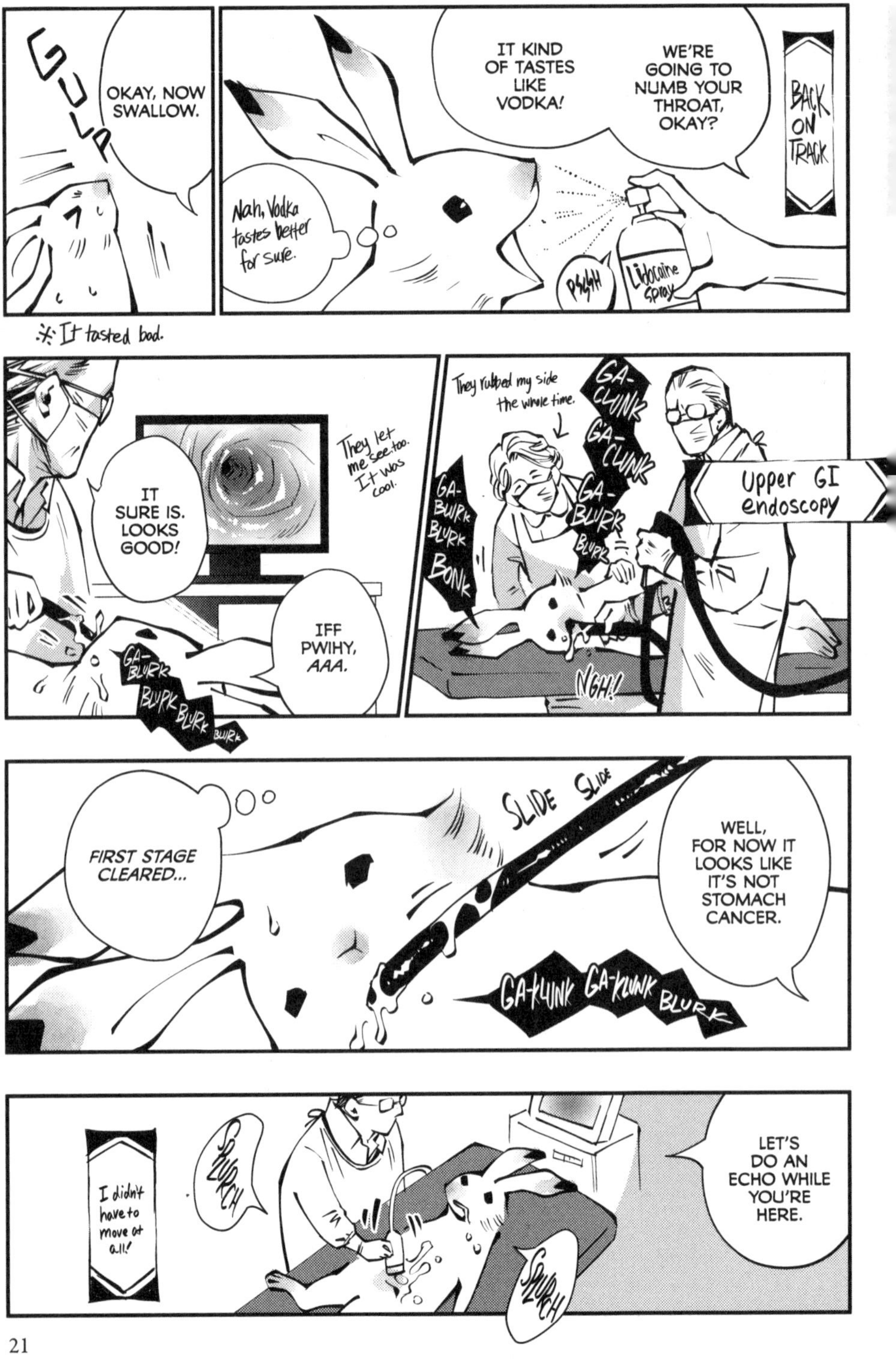
BACK ON TRACK
WE'RE GOING TO NUMB YOUR THROAT, OKAY?
IT KIND OF TASTES LIKE VODKA!
Lidocaine spray
PSSSH
Nah, Vodka tastes better for sure.
OKAY, NOW SWALLOW.
GULP
※It tasted bad.
Upper GI endoscopy
They rubbed my side the whole time.
GA-CLUNK GA-CLUNK
GA-BLURK BLURK
GA-BLURK BLURK BONK
NGH!
They let me see too. It was cool.
IT SURE IS. LOOKS GOOD!
IFF PWIHY, AAA.
GA-BLURK BLURK BLURK BLURK
WELL, FOR NOW IT LOOKS LIKE IT'S NOT STOMACH CANCER.
SLIDE SLIDE
FIRST STAGE CLEARED...
GA-KLUNK GA-KLUNK BLURK
LET'S DO AN ECHO WHILE YOU'RE HERE.
SPLURCH
SPLURCH
I didn't have to move at all!

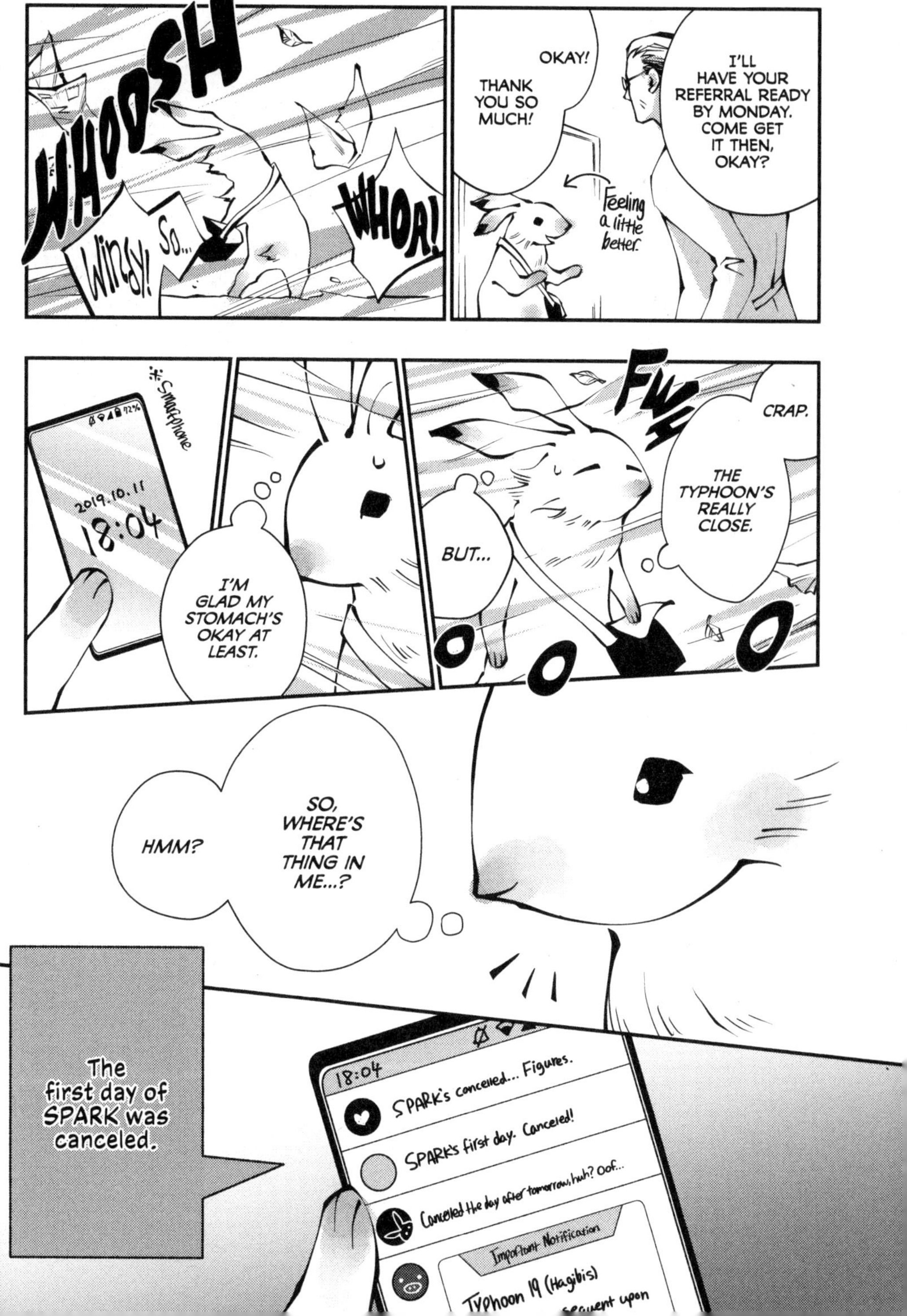
I'LL HAVE YOUR REFERRAL READY BY MONDAY. COME GET IT THEN, OKAY?
OKAY!
THANK YOU SO MUCH!
Feeling a little better.
WHOR!
WHOOSH
So...
Windy!
FWH
CRAP.
THE TYPHOON'S REALLY CLOSE.
BUT...
I'M GLAD MY STOMACH'S OKAY AT LEAST.
※Smartphone
2019.10.11
18:04
SO, WHERE'S THAT THING IN ME...?
HMM?
The first day of SPARK was canceled.
18:04
SPARK's canceled... Figures.
SPARK's first day. Canceled!
Canceled the day after tomorrow, huh? Oof...
Important Notification
Typhoon 19 (Hagibis)

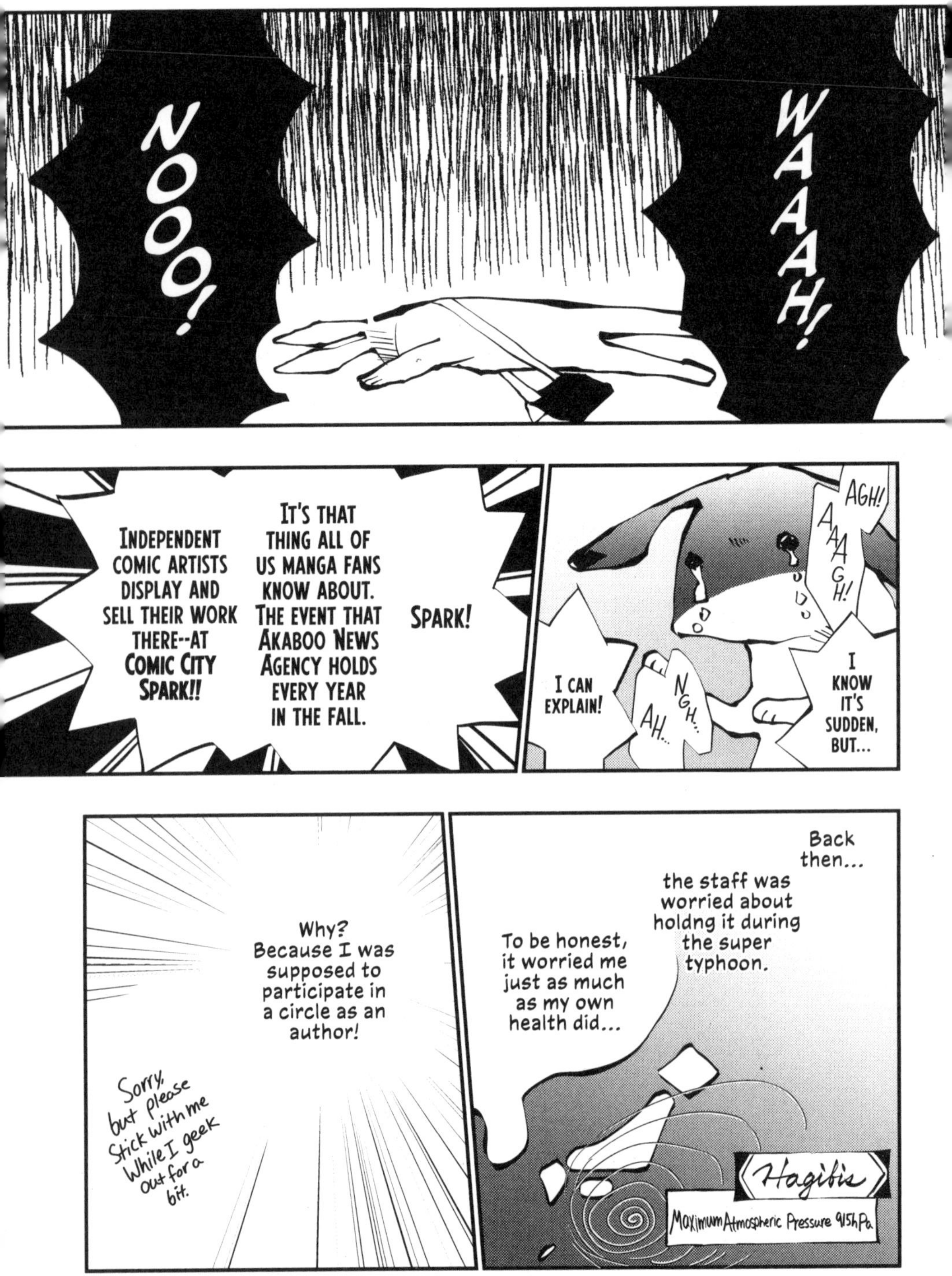
WAAAAH!
NOOOO!
AGH!
AAAAGH!
I KNOW IT'S SUDDEN, BUT...
NGH...
AH...
I CAN EXPLAIN!
SPARK!
IT'S THAT THING ALL OF US MANGA FANS KNOW ABOUT. THE EVENT THAT AKABOO NEWS AGENCY HOLDS EVERY YEAR IN THE FALL.
INDEPENDENT COMIC ARTISTS DISPLAY AND SELL THEIR WORK THERE--AT COMIC CITY SPARK!!
Back then...
the staff was worried about holdng it during the super typhoon.
To be honest, it worried me just as much as my own health did...
Hagibis
Maximum Atmospheric Pressure 915hPa
Why? Because I was supposed to participate in a circle as an author!
Sorry, but please stick with me while I geek out for a bit.

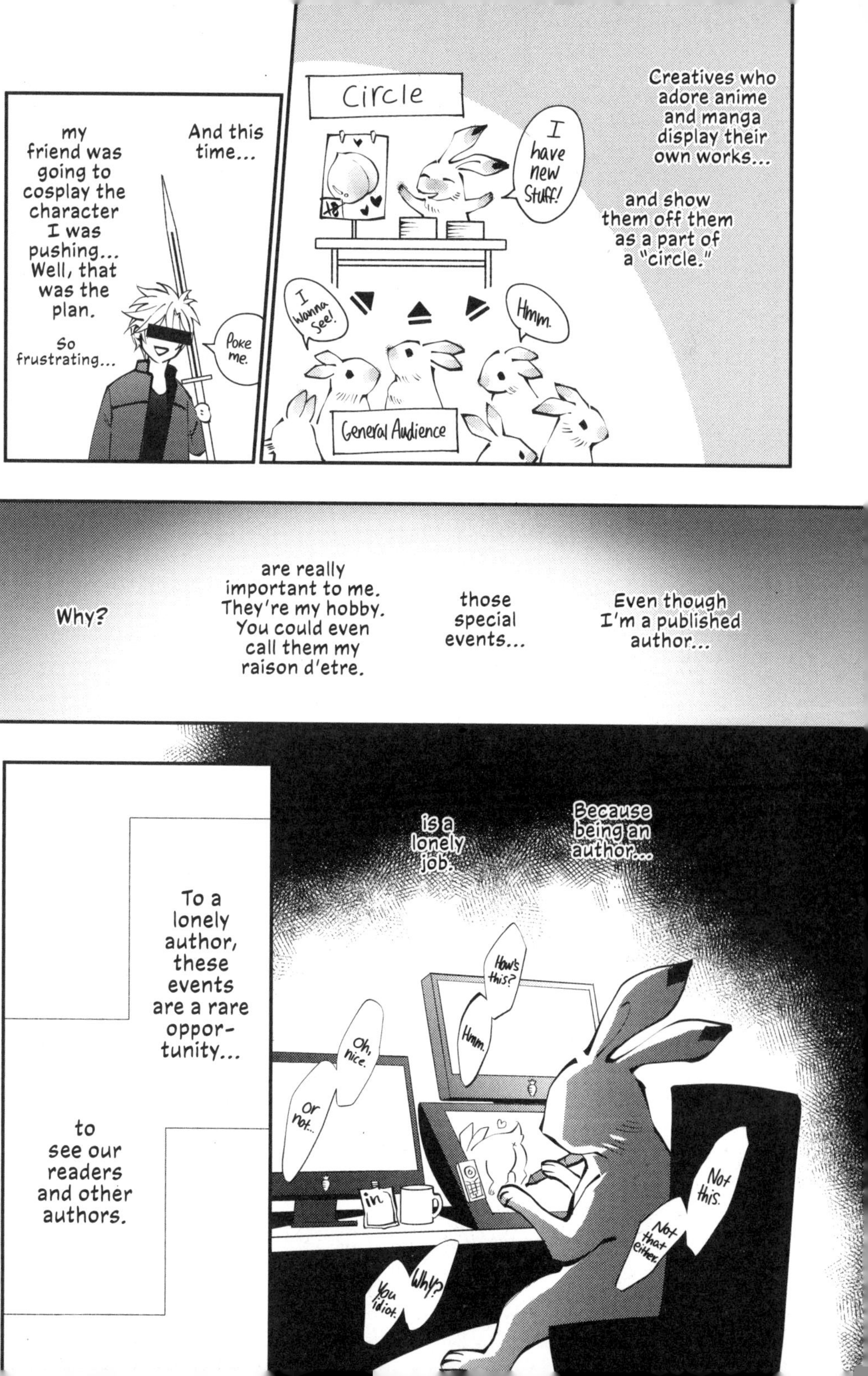
Creatives who adore anime and manga display their own works...
and show them off them as a part of a "circle."
Circle
I have new Stuff!
Hmm.
I Wanna See!
General Audience
And this time...
my friend was going to cosplay the character I was pushing... Well, that was the plan.
Poke me.
So frustrating...
Even though I'm a published author...
those special events...
are really important to me. They're my hobby. You could even call them my raison d'etre.
Why?
Because being an author...
is a lonely job.
How's this?
Hmm.
Oh, nice.
Or not...
Not this.
Not that either.
Why?
You idiot.
in
To a lonely author, these events are a rare opportunity...
to see our readers and other authors.

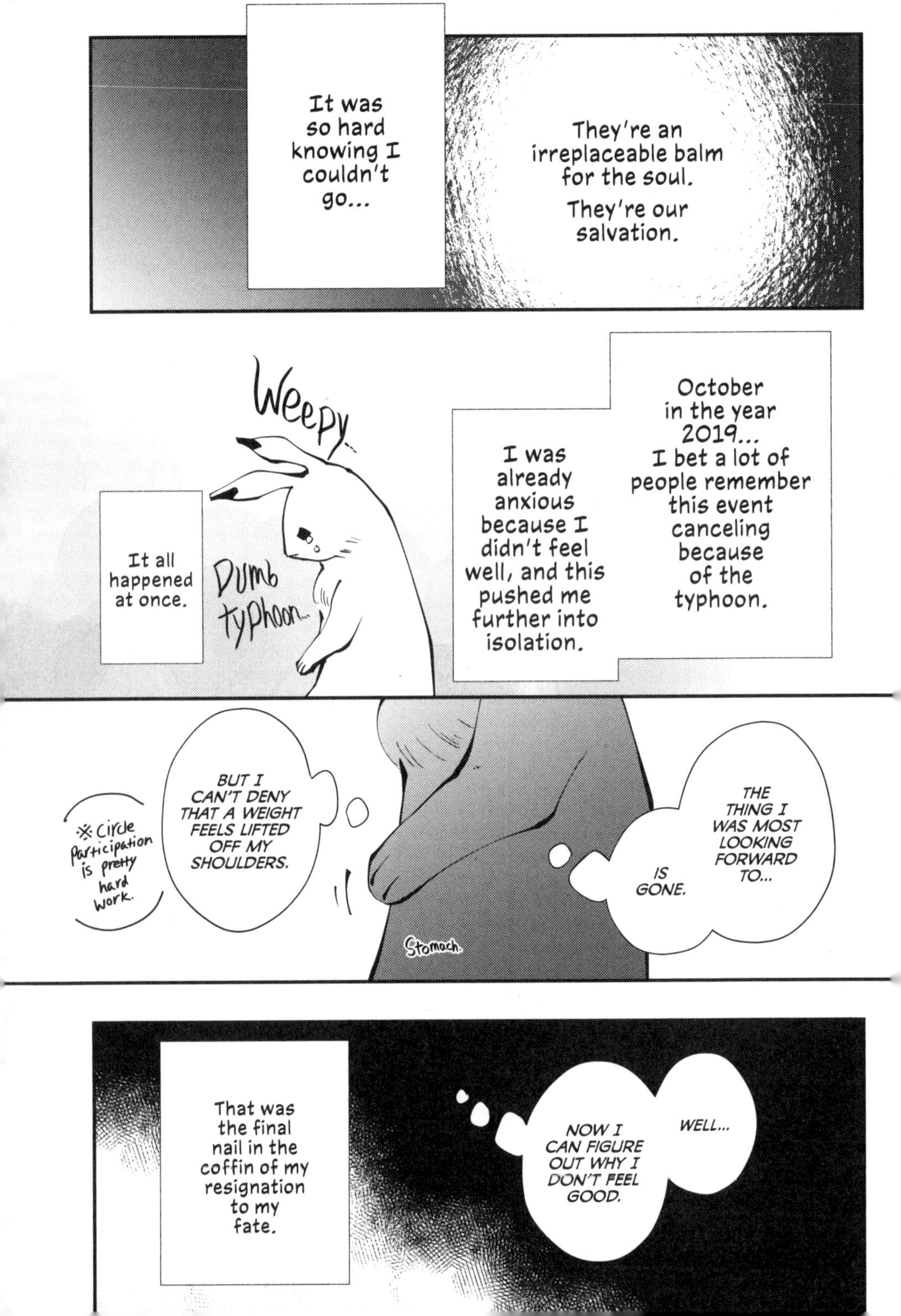
They're an irreplaceable balm for the soul.
They're our salvation.
It was so hard knowing I couldn't go...
October in the year 2019... I bet a lot of people remember this event canceling because of the typhoon.
I was already anxious because I didn't feel well, and this pushed me further into isolation.
Weepy...
Dumb typhoon...
It all happened at once.
THE THING I WAS MOST LOOKING FORWARD TO...
IS GONE.
Stomach.
BUT I CAN'T DENY THAT A WEIGHT FEELS LIFTED OFF MY SHOULDERS.
※Circle participation is pretty hard work.
WELL...
NOW I CAN FIGURE OUT WHY I DON'T FEEL GOOD.
That was the final nail in the coffin of my resignation to my fate.

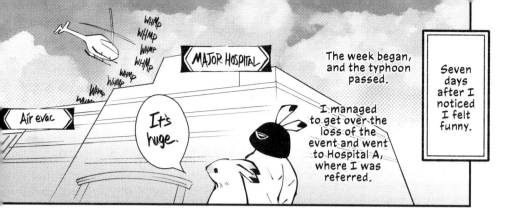

Seven days after I noticed I felt funny.
The week began, and the typhoon passed.
I managed to get over the loss of the event and went to Hospital A, where I was referred.
MAJOR HOSPITAL
WHMP WHMP WHMP WHMP WHMP WHMP WHMP
Air evac
It's huge.
They performed a CT scan right away.
This time it was a contrast CT where they inject a dye to make it easier to see certain things.
Hiinama Female, 38
While waiting for the results, I did a blood test, an EKG, and an FEV test.
BLOW
OKAY, BREATHE DEEPER, PLEASE.
Oh yeah...
This is a test used before surgeries under general anesthesia.
BLOOOOW
IF I GET A BAD RESULT...
WILL THEY SAY THE SURGERY'S OFF BECAUSE MY BODY CAN'T HANDLE IT?
WHAT'S INSIDE ME?
WHAT IS IT?
IS IT A MASS※, A TUMOR※, FAT, OR FOREIGN SUBSTANCE?
We prepared for surgery in the midst of this mystery.
We'll run tests on your stomach and get ready for surgery at the same time!
Doctor from Hospital A

※ Mass: the general term for a mysterious lump or growth. This is often the word used for unidentified things that could be a tumor.
※ Tumor: an abnormal growth. They can be benign or malignant.

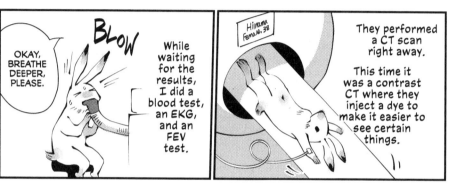

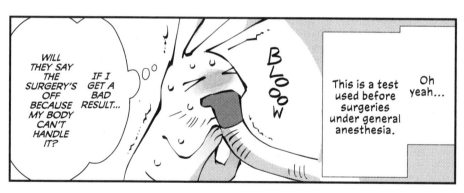

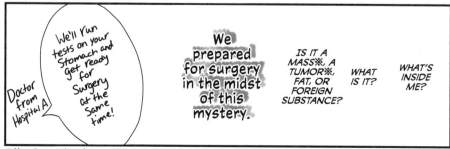

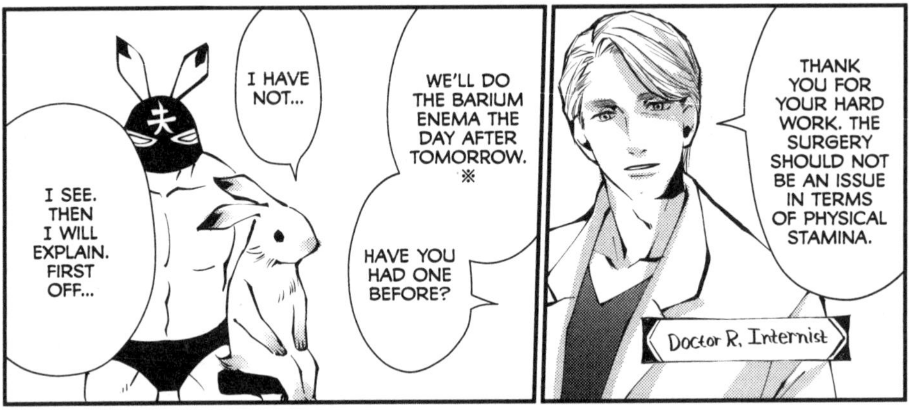
THANK YOU FOR YOUR HARD WORK. THE SURGERY SHOULD NOT BE AN ISSUE IN TERMS OF PHYSICAL STAMINA.
Doctor R, Internist
WE'LL DO THE BARIUM ENEMA THE DAY AFTER TOMORROW. ※
HAVE YOU HAD ONE BEFORE?
I HAVE NOT...
I SEE. THEN I WILL EXPLAIN. FIRST OFF...

※ *This exam uses a lot of radiation, but I told them I have no intention of getting pregnant.*

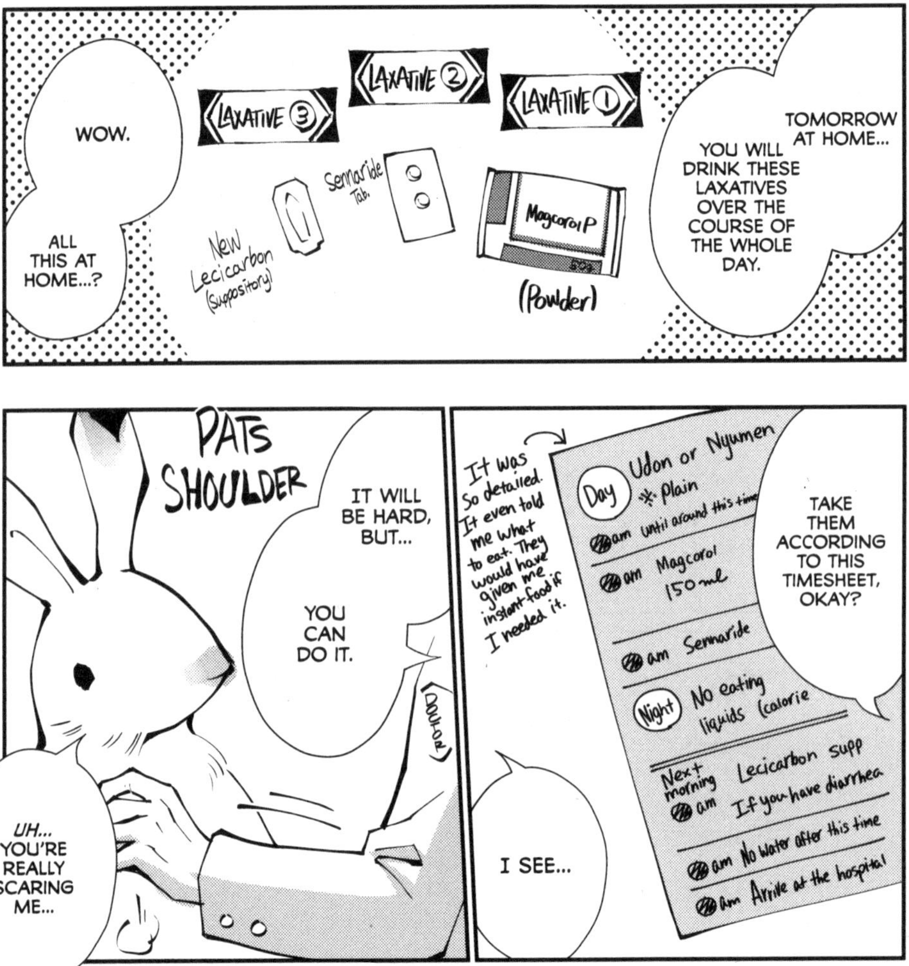
TOMORROW AT HOME...
YOU WILL DRINK THESE LAXATIVES OVER THE COURSE OF THE WHOLE DAY.
LAXATIVE ①
Magcorol P
50g
(Powder)
LAXATIVE ②
Sennaride Tab.
LAXATIVE ③
New Lecicarbon (Suppository)
WOW.
ALL THIS AT HOME...?
TAKE THEM ACCORDING TO THIS TIMESHEET, OKAY?
Day Udon or Nyumen
※ plain
am until around this time
am Magcorol 150 ml
am Sennaride
Night No eating liquids (calorie
Next morning am Lecicarbon supp
If you have diarrhea
am No water after this time
am Arrive at the hospital
It was so detailed. It even told me what to eat. They would have given me instant food if I needed it.
I SEE...
PATS SHOULDER
IT WILL BE HARD, BUT...
YOU CAN DO IT.
(DOCTOR)
UH... YOU'RE REALLY SCARING ME...

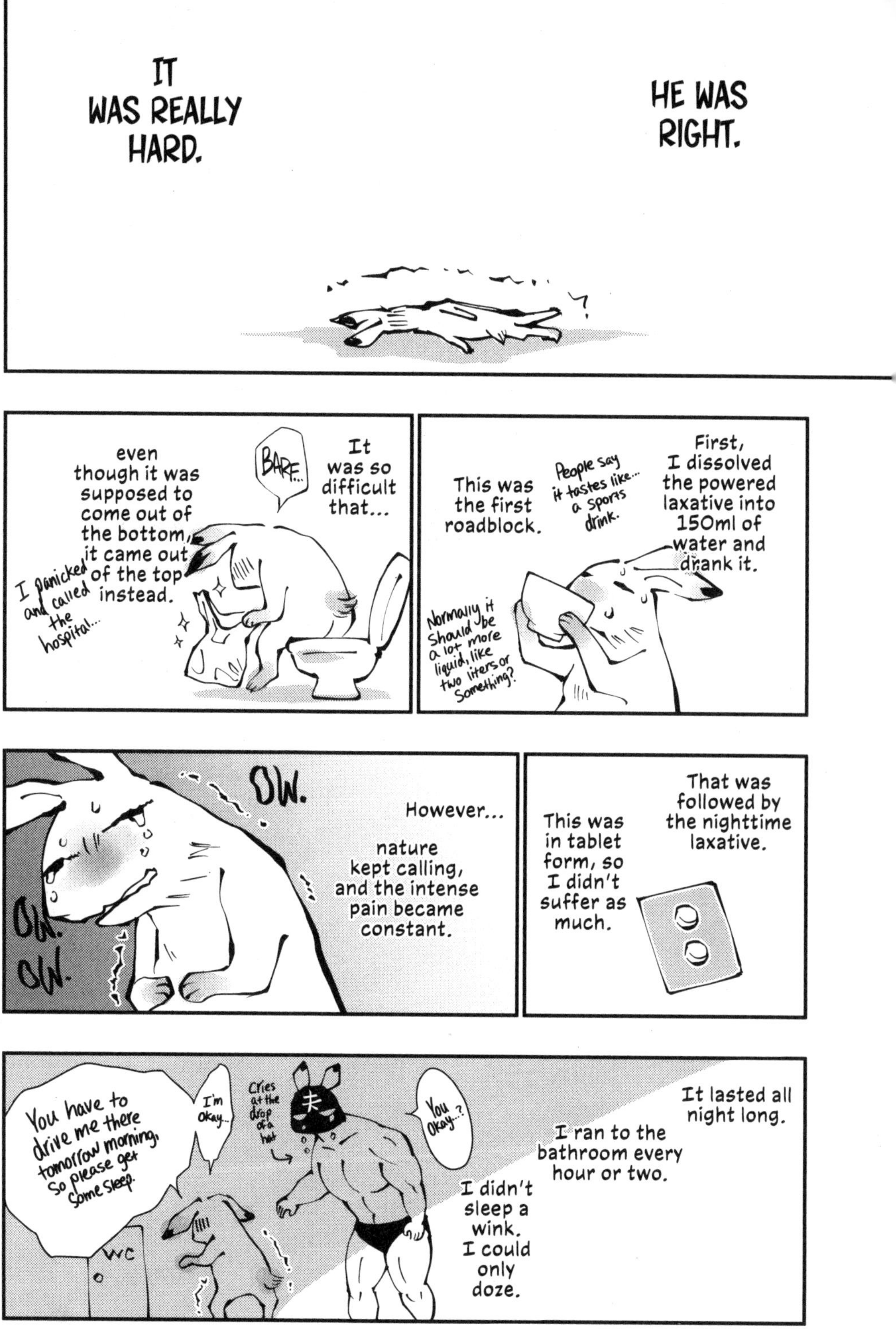
HE WAS RIGHT.
IT WAS REALLY HARD.
First, I dissolved the powered laxative into 150ml of water and drank it.
People say it tastes like... a sports drink.
This was the first roadblock.
Normally it should be a lot more liquid, like two liters or something?
It was so difficult that...
BARF...
even though it was supposed to come out of the bottom, it came out of the top instead.
I panicked and called the hospital...
That was followed by the nighttime laxative.
This was in tablet form, so I didn't suffer as much.
OW.
However...
nature kept calling, and the intense pain became constant.
OW. OW.
It lasted all night long.
I ran to the bathroom every hour or two.
I didn't sleep a wink. I could only doze.
You okay...?
Cries at the drop of a hat
I'm okay...
You have to drive me there tomorrow morning, so please get some sleep.
WC

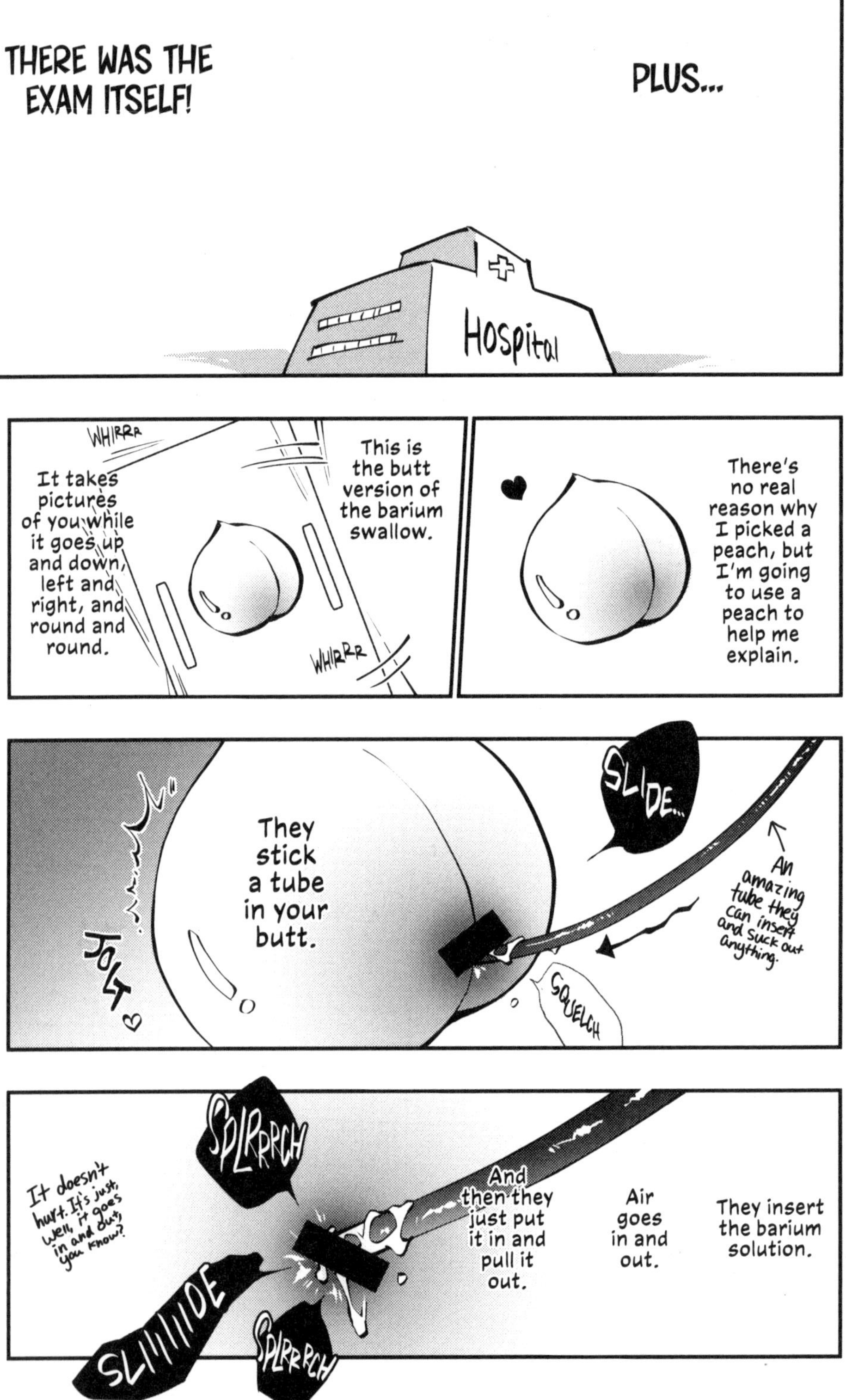
THERE WAS THE EXAM ITSELF!
PLUS...
HOSpital
There's no real reason why I picked a peach, but I'm going to use a peach to help me explain.
This is the butt version of the barium swallow.
WHIRRR
It takes pictures of you while it goes up and down, left and right, and round and round.
WHIRRR
SLIDE...
An amazing tube they can insert and suck out anything.
They stick a tube in your butt.
SQUELCH
JOLT
They insert the barium solution.
Air goes in and out.
And then they just put it in and pull it out.
SPLRRRCH
It doesn't hurt. It's just, well, it goes in and out, you know?
SLIIIIIDE
SPLRRRCH

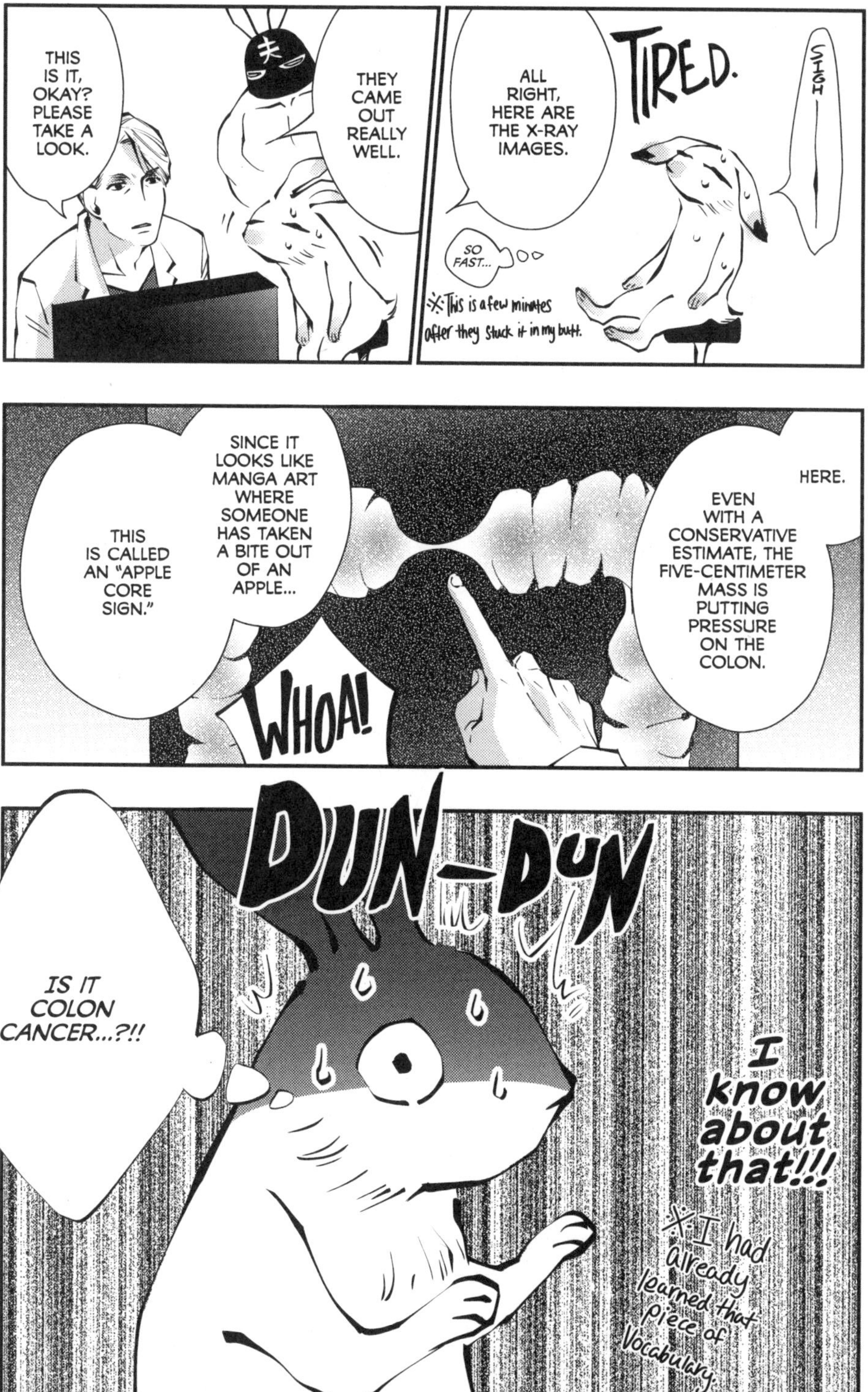
SIGH
TIRED.
ALL RIGHT, HERE ARE THE X-RAY IMAGES.
SO FAST...
※This is a few minutes after they stuck it in my butt.
THEY CAME OUT REALLY WELL.
THIS IS IT, OKAY? PLEASE TAKE A LOOK.
HERE.
EVEN WITH A CONSERVATIVE ESTIMATE, THE FIVE-CENTIMETER MASS IS PUTTING PRESSURE ON THE COLON.
SINCE IT LOOKS LIKE MANGA ART WHERE SOMEONE HAS TAKEN A BITE OUT OF AN APPLE...
THIS IS CALLED AN "APPLE CORE SIGN."
WHOA!
DUN-DUN
I know about that!!!
※I had already learned that piece of Vocabulary.
IS IT COLON CANCER...?!!

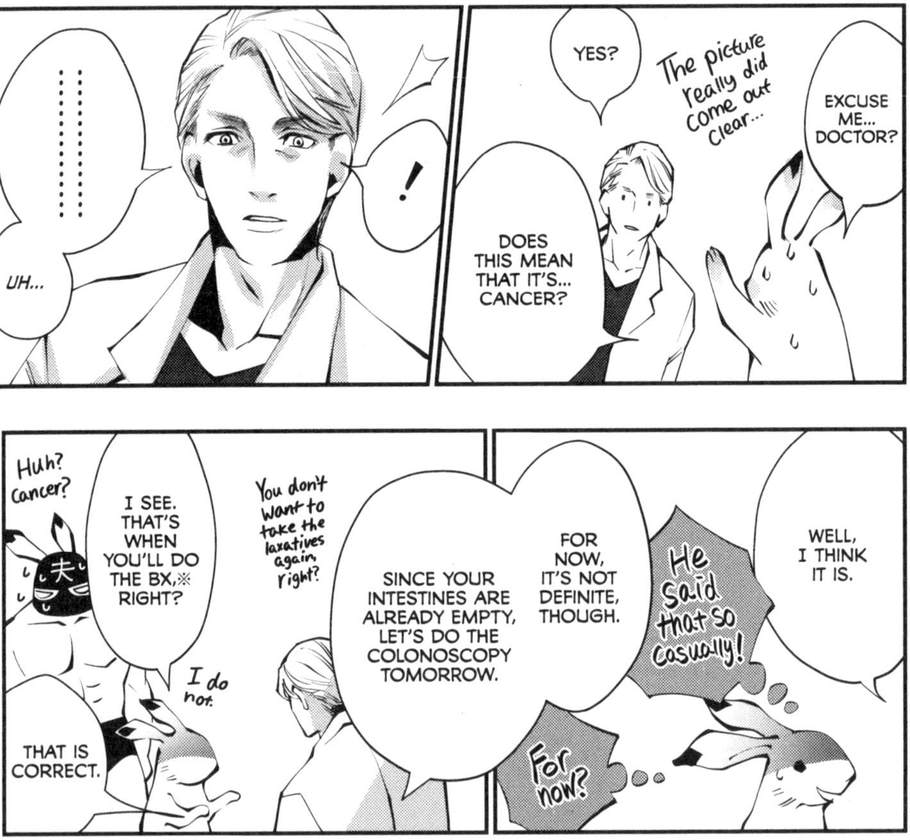
EXCUSE ME... DOCTOR?
YES?
The picture really did come out clear...
DOES THIS MEAN THAT IT'S... CANCER?
!
......
UH...
WELL, I THINK IT IS.
He said that so casually!
FOR NOW, IT'S NOT DEFINITE, THOUGH.
For now?
SINCE YOUR INTESTINES ARE ALREADY EMPTY, LET'S DO THE COLONOSCOPY TOMORROW.
You don't want to take the laxatives again, right?
I SEE. THAT'S WHEN YOU'LL DO THE BX,※ RIGHT?
Huh? cancer?
I do not.
THAT IS CORRECT.

※ bx is an abbreviation for biopsy, in which a portion of the lesion is collected.

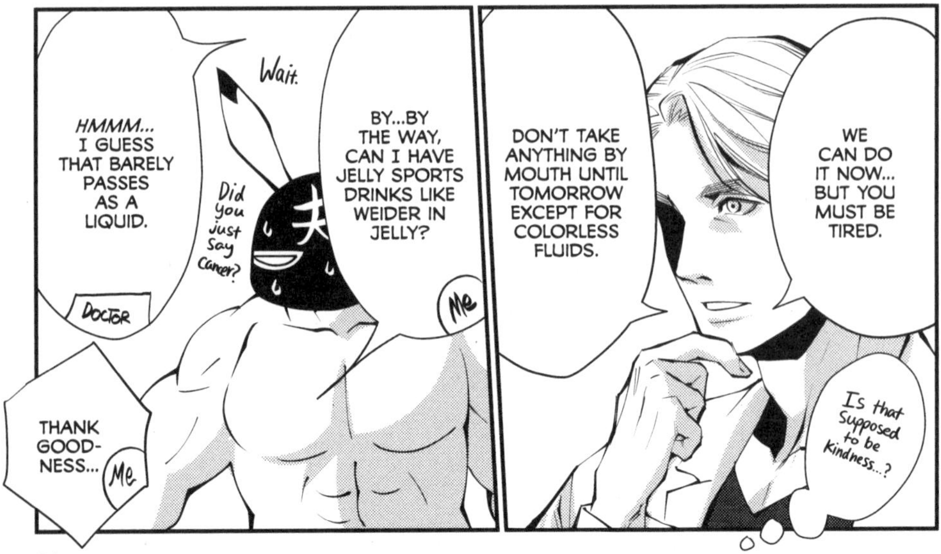
WE CAN DO IT NOW... BUT YOU MUST BE TIRED.
DON'T TAKE ANYTHING BY MOUTH UNTIL TOMORROW EXCEPT FOR COLORLESS FLUIDS.
Is that supposed to be kindness...?
Me
BY...BY THE WAY, CAN I HAVE JELLY SPORTS DRINKS LIKE WEIDER IN JELLY?
Wait.
Did you just say cancer?
HMMM... I GUESS THAT BARELY PASSES AS A LIQUID.
DOCTOR
THANK GOODNESS...
Me.

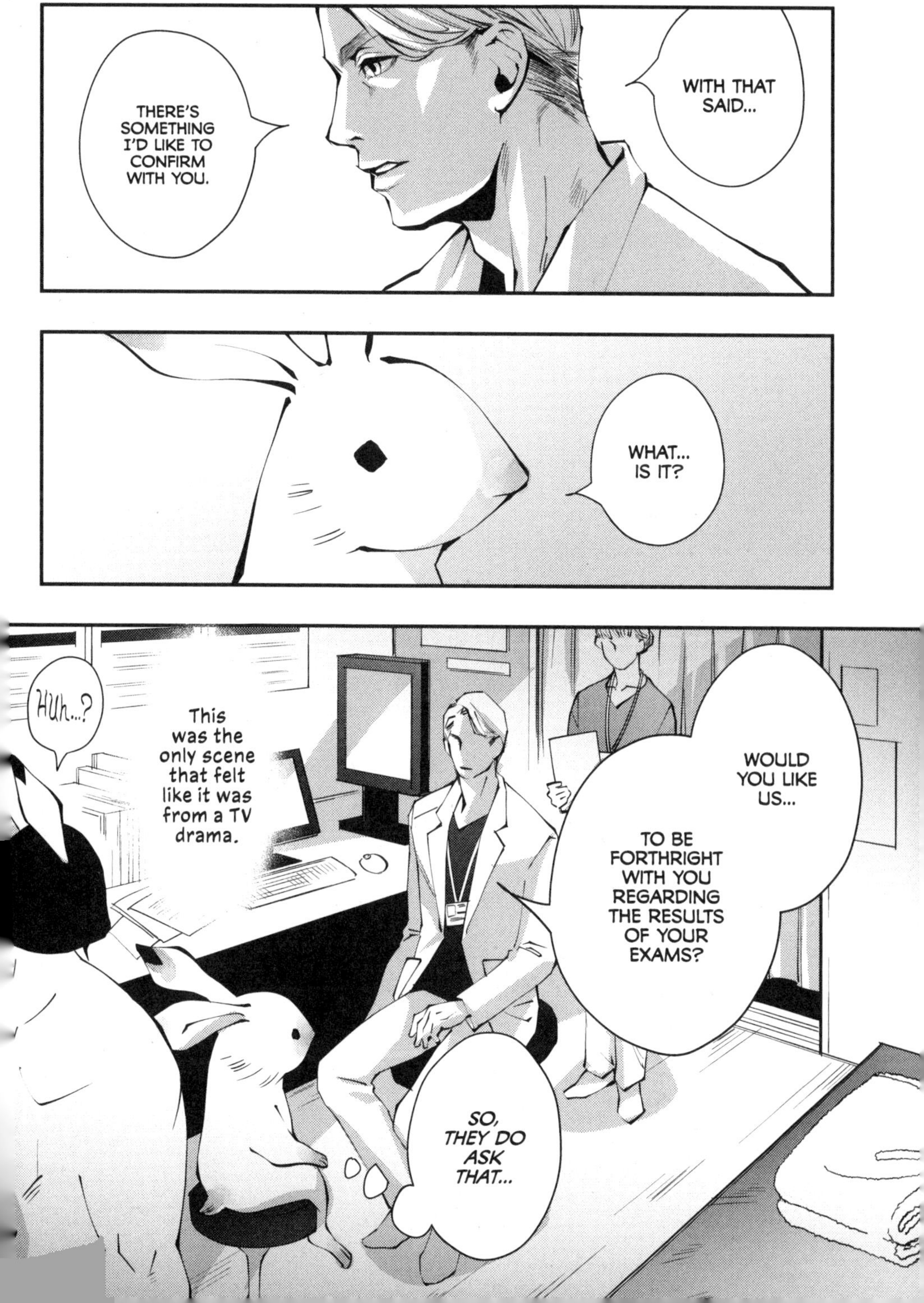
WITH THAT SAID...
THERE'S SOMETHING I'D LIKE TO CONFIRM WITH YOU.
WHAT... IS IT?
WOULD YOU LIKE US...
TO BE FORTHRIGHT WITH YOU REGARDING THE RESULTS OF YOUR EXAMS?
HUh...?
This was the only scene that felt like it was from a TV drama.
SO, THEY DO ASK THAT...

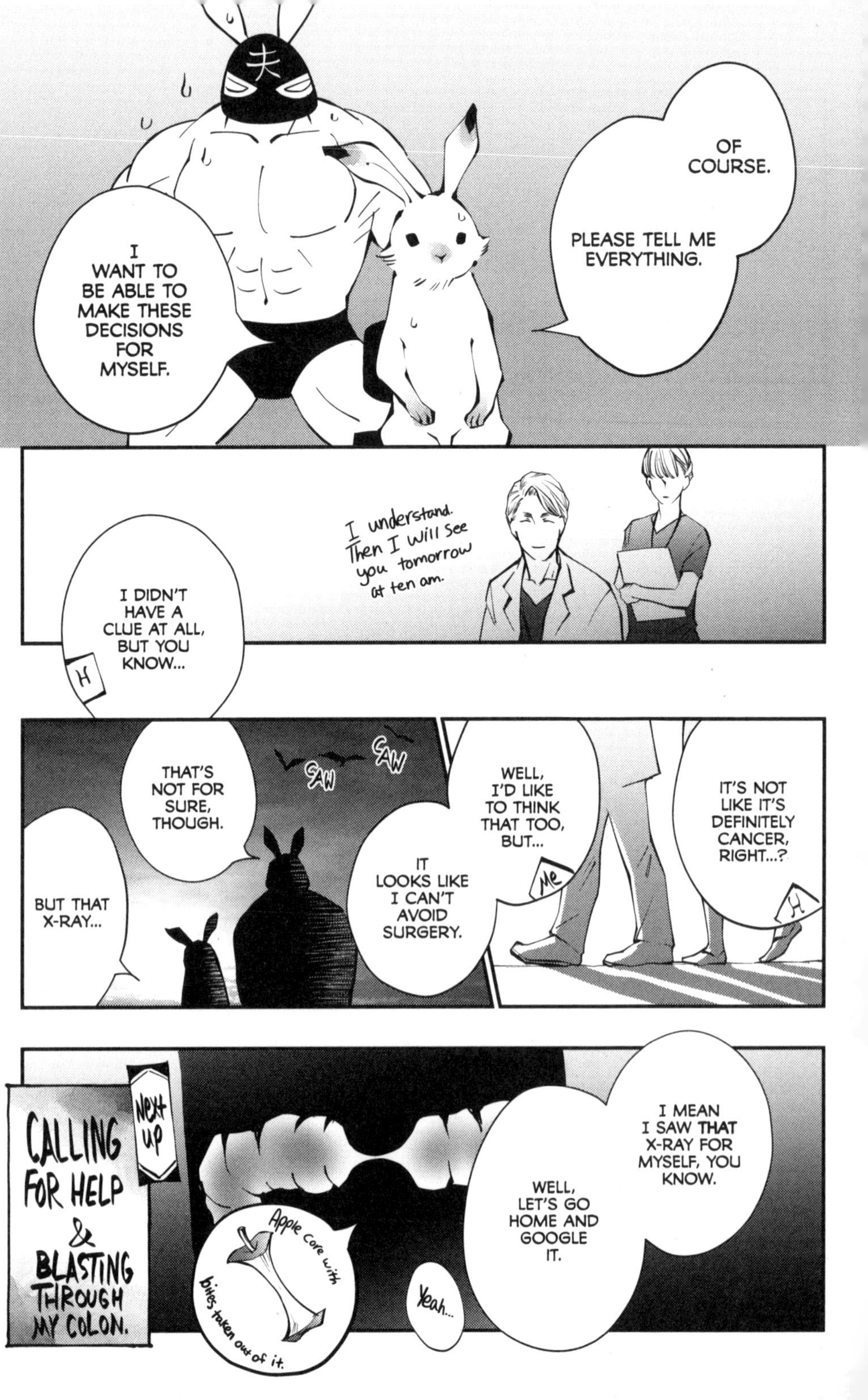

OF COURSE.
PLEASE TELL ME EVERYTHING.
I WANT TO BE ABLE TO MAKE THESE DECISIONS FOR MYSELF.
I understand. Then I will see you tomorrow at ten am.
I DIDN'T HAVE A CLUE AT ALL, BUT YOU KNOW...
H
IT'S NOT LIKE IT'S DEFINITELY CANCER, RIGHT...?
H
WELL, I'D LIKE TO THINK THAT TOO, BUT...
Me
IT LOOKS LIKE I CAN'T AVOID SURGERY.
SAW
SAW
THAT'S NOT FOR SURE, THOUGH.
BUT THAT X-RAY...
I MEAN I SAW THAT X-RAY FOR MYSELF, YOU KNOW.
WELL, LET'S GO HOME AND GOOGLE IT.
Yeah...
Apple core with bites taken out of it.
Next up
CALLING FOR HELP & BLASTING THROUGH MY COLON.

Hi. I'm the author.

Weeell, that was a surprise, wasn't it?
Until I saw the x-ray, I was like...cancer?
Impossible! That was when I was the most anxious.

What's in my *tummyyy?!* What are you?!!!
Who are *youuu?!!!* Kind of like that.

Every day it hurt so bad I thought it had burst...

At least I'd think it did...

I'm a Terminal
Cancer
Patient
// BUT I'M FINE //

I thought I had a Stomachache, but it Was terminal cancer. ③

The time I said I better get help.

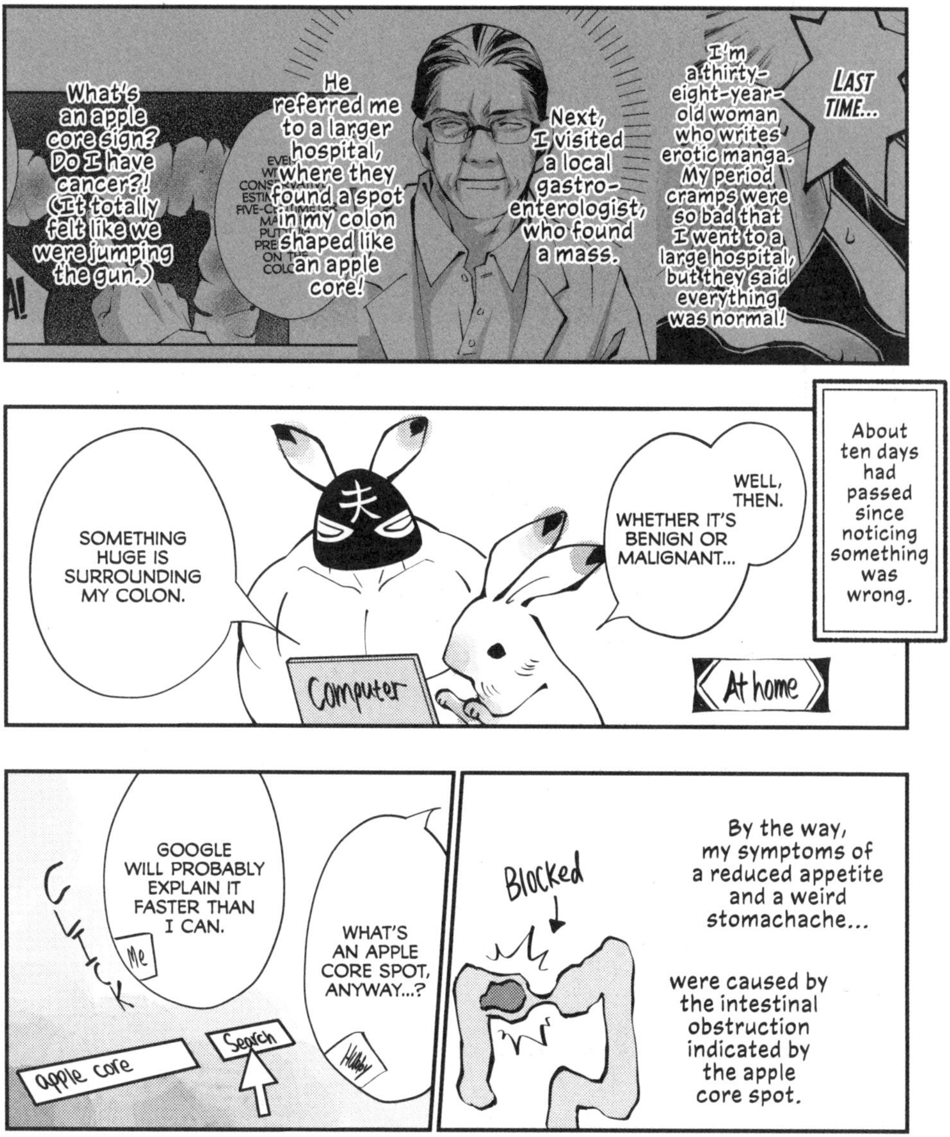
LAST TIME...
I'm a thirty-eight-year-old woman who writes erotic manga. My period cramps were so bad that I went to a large hospital, but they said everything was normal!
Next, I visited a local gastro-enterologist, who found a mass.
He referred me to a larger hospital, where they found a spot in my colon shaped like an apple core!
What's an apple core sign? Do I have cancer?! (It totally felt like we were jumping the gun.)
About ten days had passed since noticing something was wrong.
At home
WELL, THEN. WHETHER IT'S BENIGN OR MALIGNANT...
SOMETHING HUGE IS SURROUNDING MY COLON.
Computer
By the way, my symptoms of a reduced appetite and a weird stomachache...
Blocked
were caused by the intestinal obstruction indicated by the apple core spot.
WHAT'S AN APPLE CORE SPOT, ANYWAY...?
Hubby
GOOGLE WILL PROBABLY EXPLAIN IT FASTER THAN I CAN.
Me
CLICK
Search
apple core

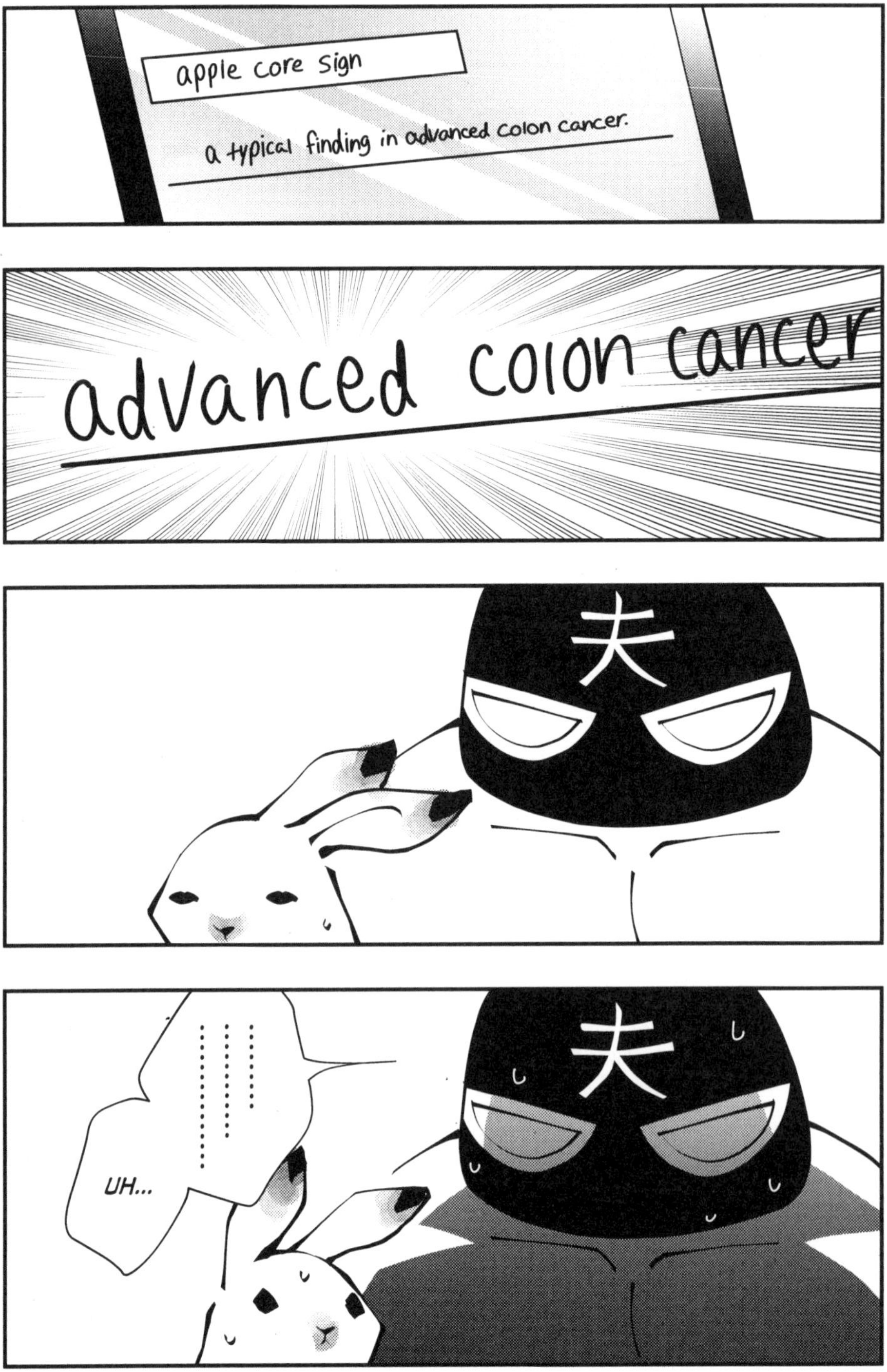
apple core sign
a typical finding in advanced colon cancer.
advanced colon cancer
……
UH...

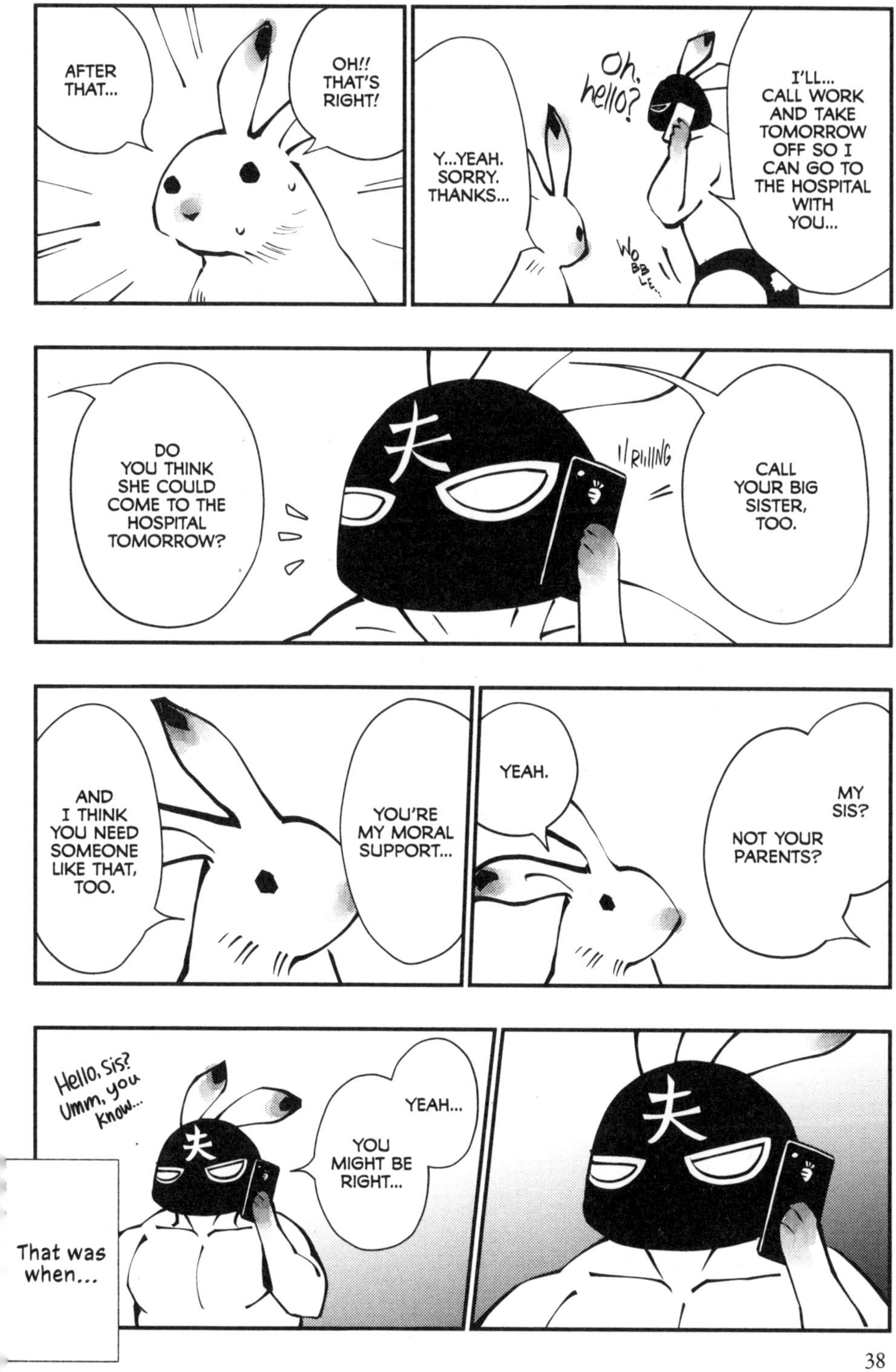
Oh, hello?
I'LL... CALL WORK AND TAKE TOMORROW OFF SO I CAN GO TO THE HOSPITAL WITH YOU...
Y...YEAH. SORRY. THANKS...
WOBBLE...
OH!! THAT'S RIGHT!
AFTER THAT...
CALL YOUR BIG SISTER, TOO.
RIIIING
DO YOU THINK SHE COULD COME TO THE HOSPITAL TOMORROW?
MY SIS? NOT YOUR PARENTS?
YEAH.
YOU'RE MY MORAL SUPPORT...
AND I THINK YOU NEED SOMEONE LIKE THAT, TOO.
YEAH... YOU MIGHT BE RIGHT...
Hello, Sis? Umm, you know...
That was when...

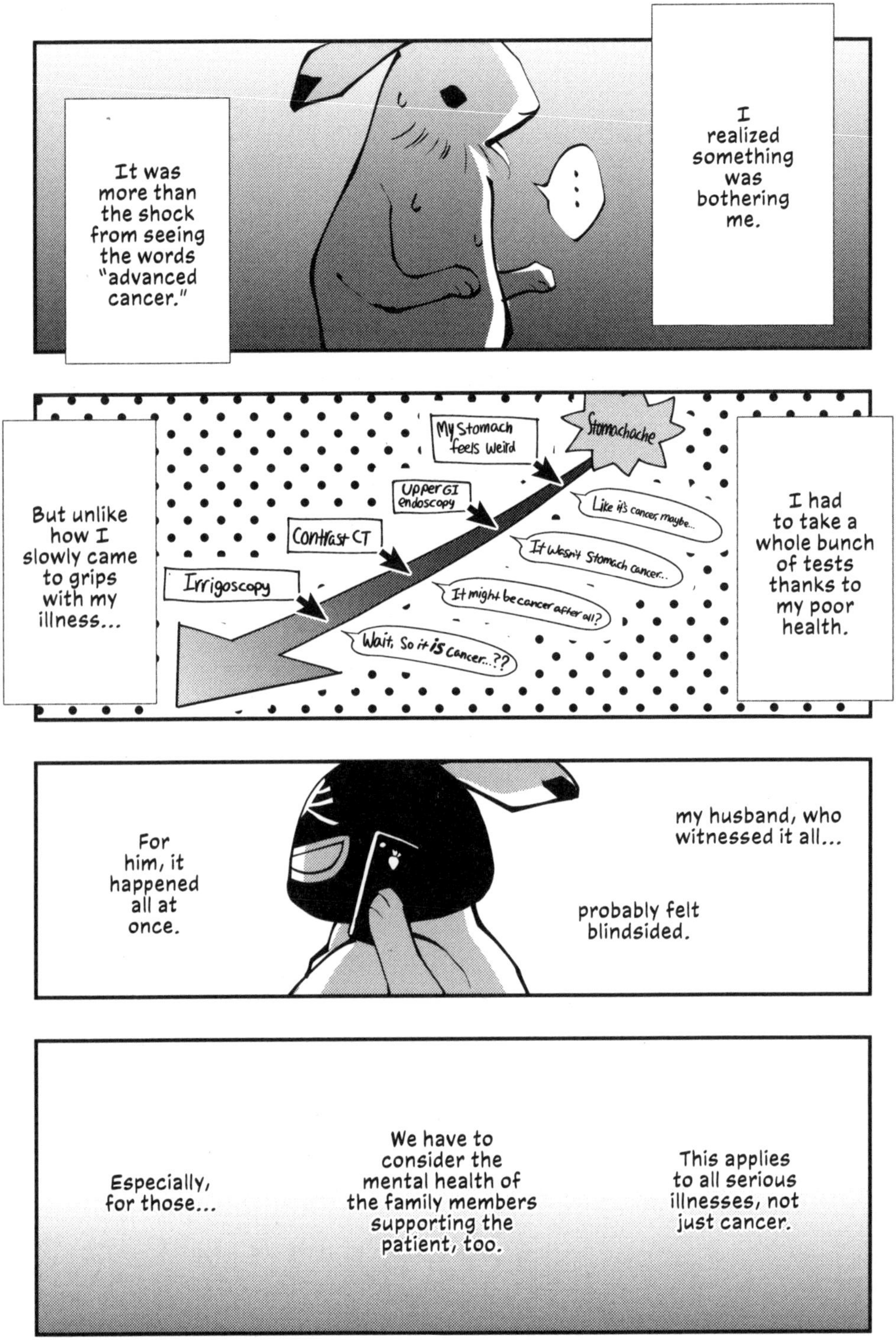
I realized something was bothering me.
...
It was more than the shock from seeing the words "advanced cancer."
I had to take a whole bunch of tests thanks to my poor health.
Stomachache
My Stomach feels weird
Like it's cancer, maybe...
Upper GI endoscopy
It wasn't Stomach cancer...
Contrast CT
It might be cancer after all?
Irrigoscopy
Wait, So it IS cancer...??
But unlike how I slowly came to grips with my illness...
my husband, who witnessed it all...
probably felt blindsided.
For him, it happened all at once.
This applies to all serious illnesses, not just cancer.
We have to consider the mental health of the family members supporting the patient, too.
Especially, for those...

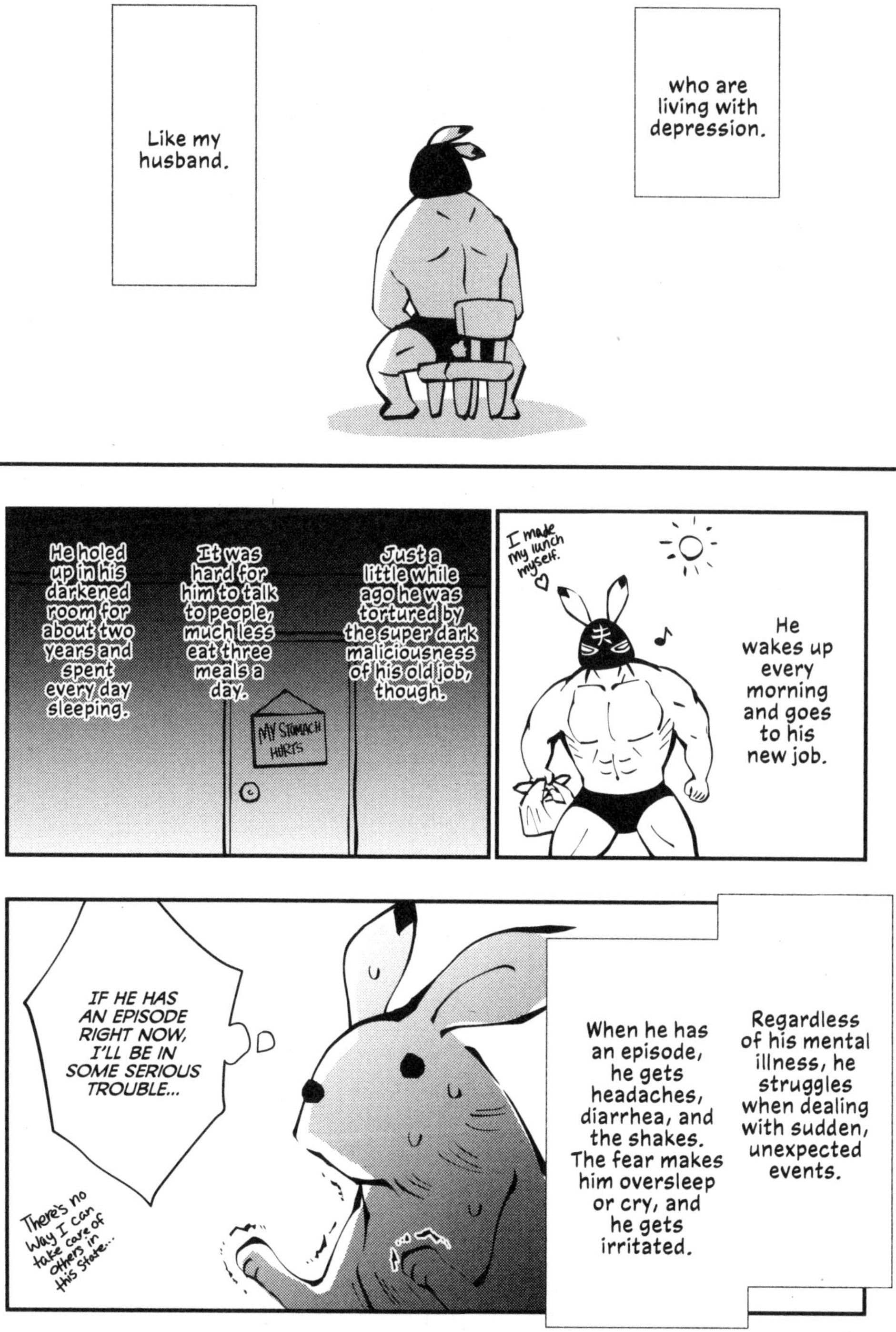
who are living with depression.
Like my husband.
I made my lunch myself. ♡
He wakes up every morning and goes to his new job.
Just a little while ago he was tortured by the super dark maliciousness of his old job, though.
It was hard for him to talk to people, much less eat three meals a day.
He holed up in his darkened room for about two years and spent every day sleeping.
MY STOMACH HURTS
Regardless of his mental illness, he struggles when dealing with sudden, unexpected events.
When he has an episode, he gets headaches, diarrhea, and the shakes. The fear makes him oversleep or cry, and he gets irritated.
IF HE HAS AN EPISODE RIGHT NOW, I'LL BE IN SOME SERIOUS TROUBLE...
There's no way I can take care of others in this state...

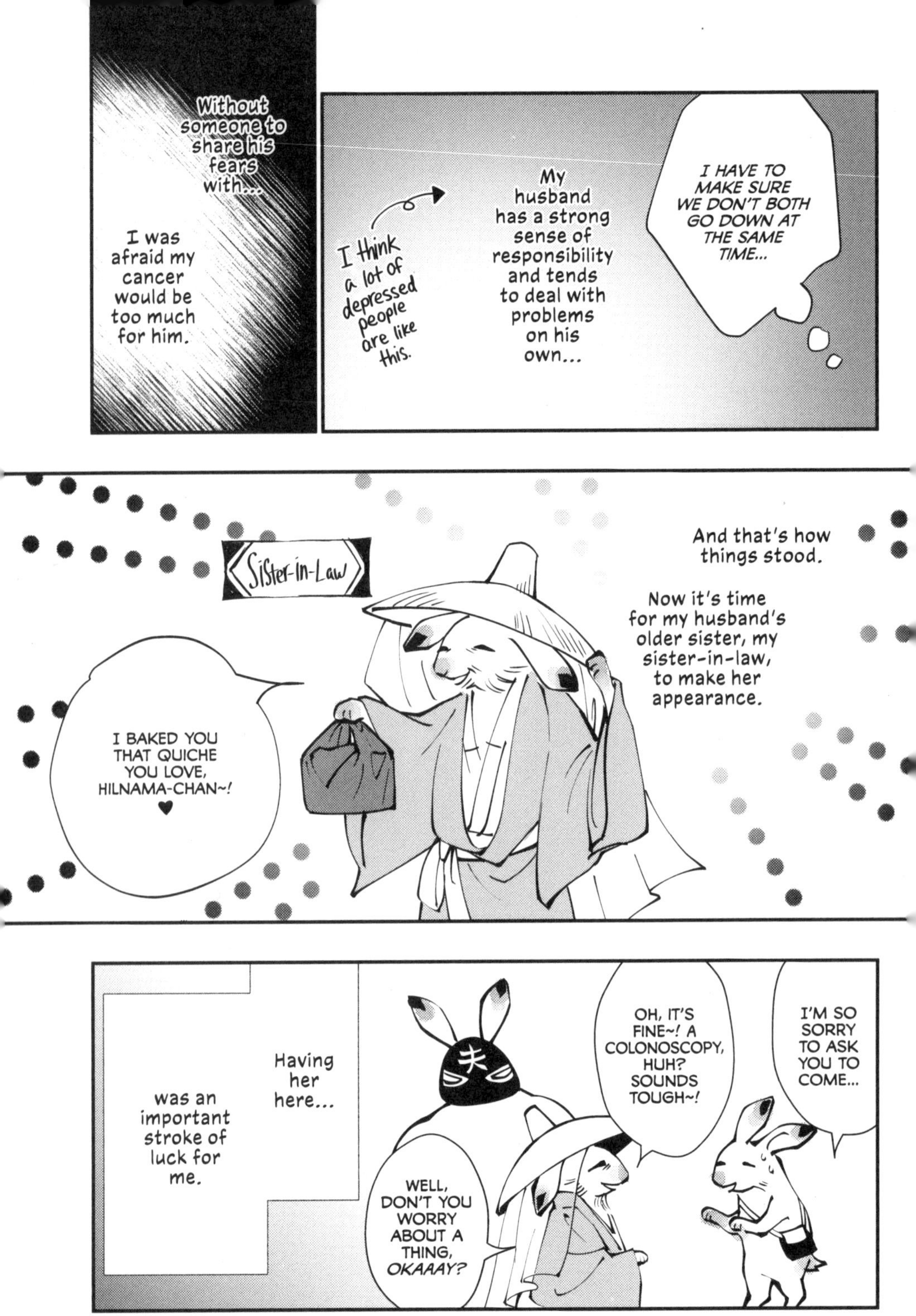
I HAVE TO MAKE SURE WE DON'T BOTH GO DOWN AT THE SAME TIME...
My husband has a strong sense of responsibility and tends to deal with problems on his own...
I think a lot of depressed people are like this.
Without someone to share his fears with...
I was afraid my cancer would be too much for him.
And that's how things stood.
Now it's time for my husband's older sister, my sister-in-law, to make her appearance.
Sister-in-Law
I BAKED YOU THAT QUICHE YOU LOVE, HILNAMA-CHAN~! ♥
I'M SO SORRY TO ASK YOU TO COME...
OH, IT'S FINE~! A COLONOSCOPY, HUH? SOUNDS TOUGH~!
WELL, DON'T YOU WORRY ABOUT A THING, *OKAAAY?*
Having her here...
was an important stroke of luck for me.

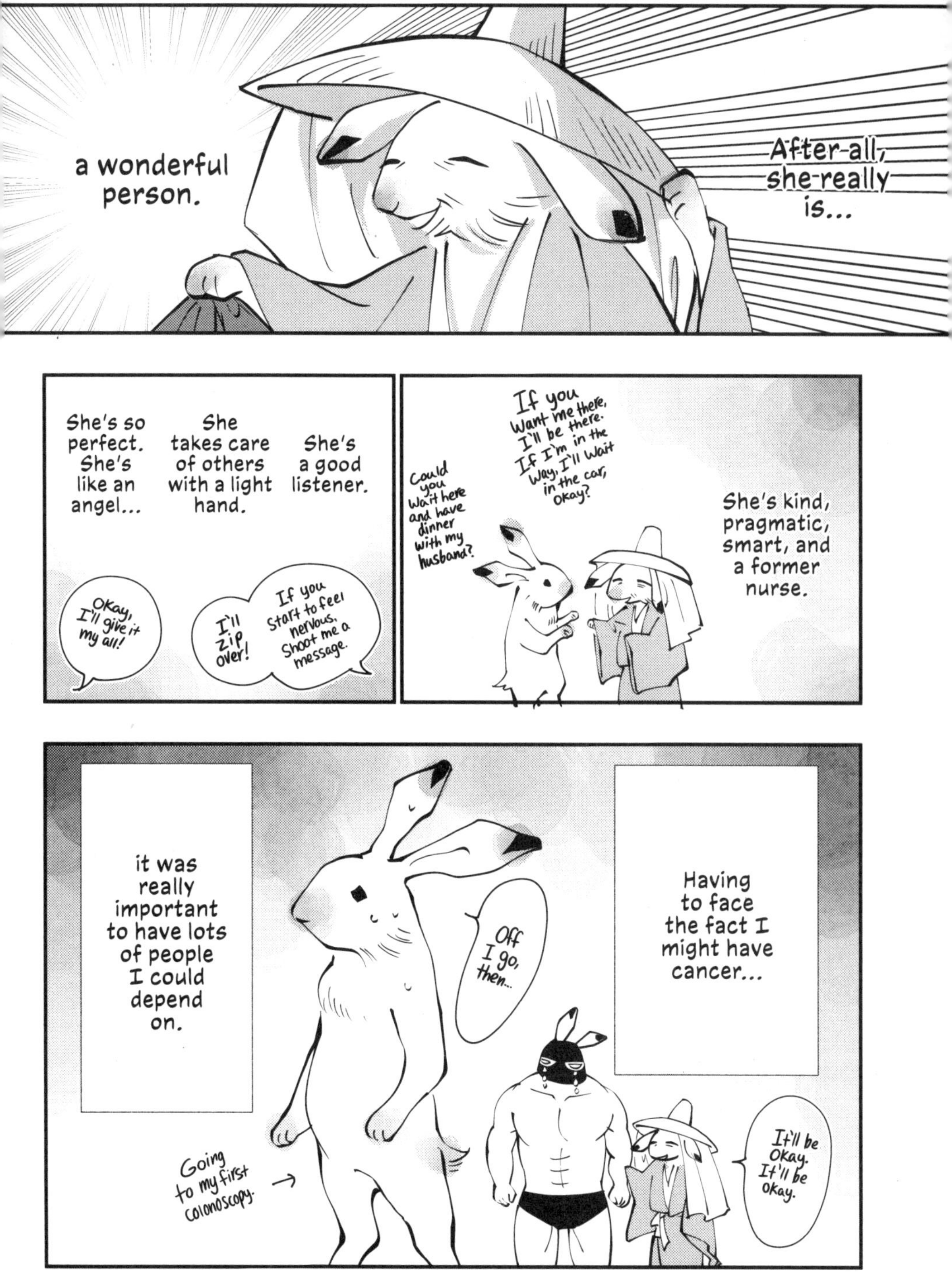

After all, she really is...
a wonderful person.
She's kind, pragmatic, smart, and a former nurse.
If you want me there, I'll be there. If I'm in the way, I'll wait in the car, okay?
Could you wait here and have dinner with my husband?
She's a good listener.
She takes care of others with a light hand.
She's so perfect. She's like an angel...
If you start to feel nervous, shoot me a message.
I'll zip over!
Okay, I'll give it my all!
Having to face the fact I might have cancer...
It'll be okay. It'll be okay.
Off I go, then...
Going to my first colonoscopy.
it was really important to have lots of people I could depend on.

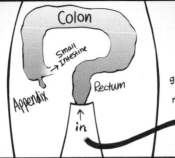

We're finally going to blast through the colon!

Twelve days since noticing the abnormality.
(This introduction has gone on a tangent.)
In short, I got myself ready, gathered my reinforcements, and went to tackle the endoscopy.
Colon
Small Intestine
Rectum
Appendix
in
With this detailed exam, we could finally see full color images and collect cells for the first time to determine whether it was cancer.
This procedure is the rectal version of the upper GI colonoscopy and the details are pretty different.
Wear this, okay?
They look like Chinese potty-training pants.
※ bath towel to cover your butt
During the exam, you wear these paper pants with an open crotch.
They also hand you diapers, but I hear some hospitals don't provide them for you.
Will medium diapers fit you?
I've never worn any, so I don't know.
Adult M
Compared to the upper GI endoscopy, the most different thing about this one was...
the consent form, I think.
Signature
Representative
Attending Physician
UMM... THE CONSENT FORM IS REALLY SERIOUS...
Lots of numbers for incident rates.
THE NUMBERS ARE REALLY LOW...
BUT THERE IS THE RARE POSSIBILITY OF INTESTINAL PERFORATION OR HEMORRHAGE.
You signed the consent forms for the other examinations too, didn't you?
NURSE
TH- THIS IS A PRETTY BIG DEAL, HUH?
The others weren't quite this serious...

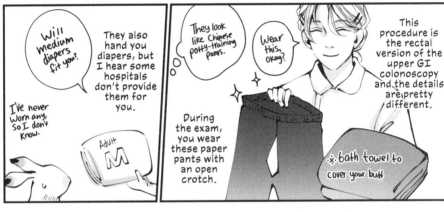

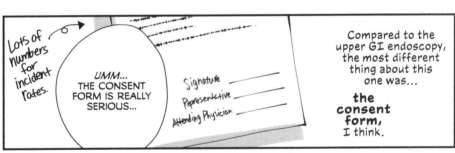

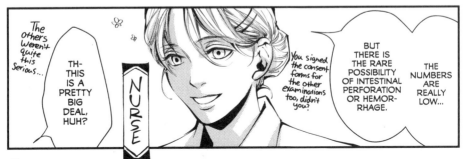

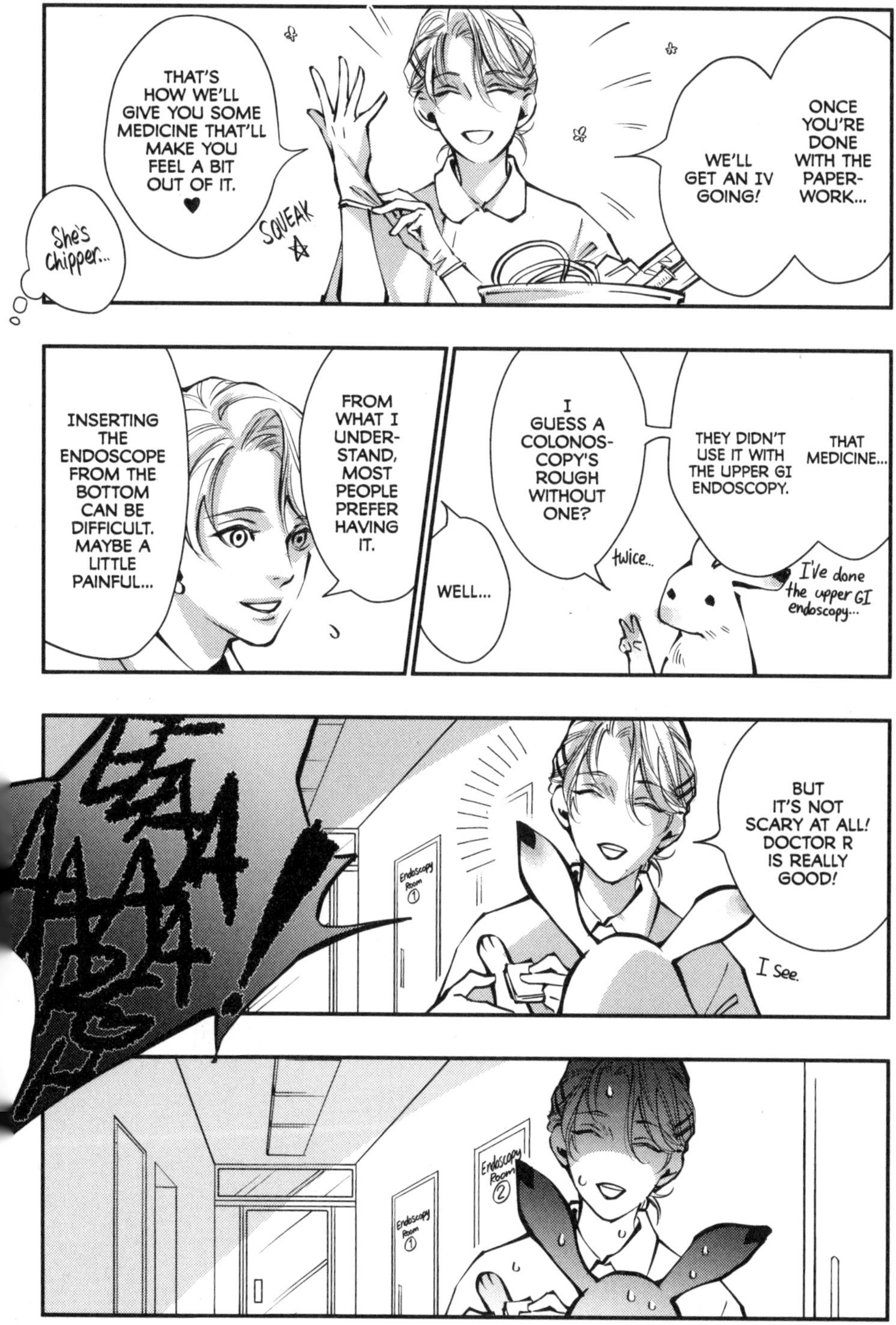
ONCE YOU'RE DONE WITH THE PAPER-WORK...
WE'LL GET AN IV GOING!
THAT'S HOW WE'LL GIVE YOU SOME MEDICINE THAT'LL MAKE YOU FEEL A BIT OUT OF IT. ♥
SQUEAK
She's chipper...
THAT MEDICINE...
THEY DIDN'T USE IT WITH THE UPPER GI ENDOSCOPY.
I've done the upper GI endoscopy...
I GUESS A COLONOS-COPY'S ROUGH WITHOUT ONE?
twice...
WELL...
FROM WHAT I UNDER-STAND, MOST PEOPLE PREFER HAVING IT.
INSERTING THE ENDOSCOPE FROM THE BOTTOM CAN BE DIFFICULT. MAYBE A LITTLE PAINFUL...
BUT IT'S NOT SCARY AT ALL! DOCTOR R IS REALLY GOOD!
Endoscopy Room 1
I see.
Endoscopy Room 2
Endoscopy Room 1

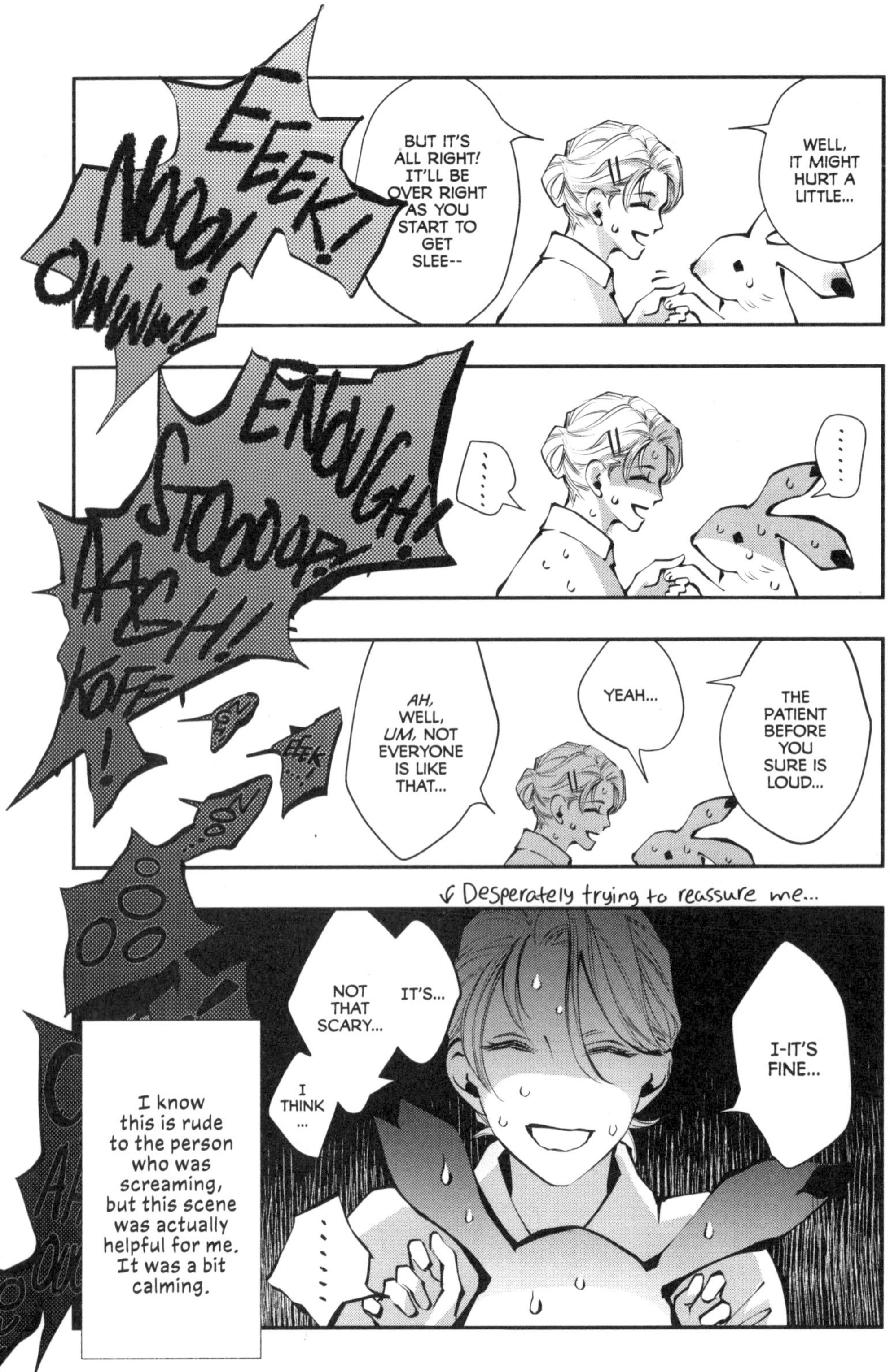
WELL, IT MIGHT HURT A LITTLE...
BUT IT'S ALL RIGHT! IT'LL BE OVER RIGHT AS YOU START TO GET SLEE--
EEEK!!
ENOUGH!!
......
......
THE PATIENT BEFORE YOU SURE IS LOUD...
YEAH...
AH, WELL, UM, NOT EVERYONE IS LIKE THAT...
Desperately trying to reassure me...
I-IT'S FINE...
IT'S... NOT THAT SCARY... I THINK...
......
I know this is rude to the person who was screaming, but this scene was actually helpful for me. It was a bit calming.

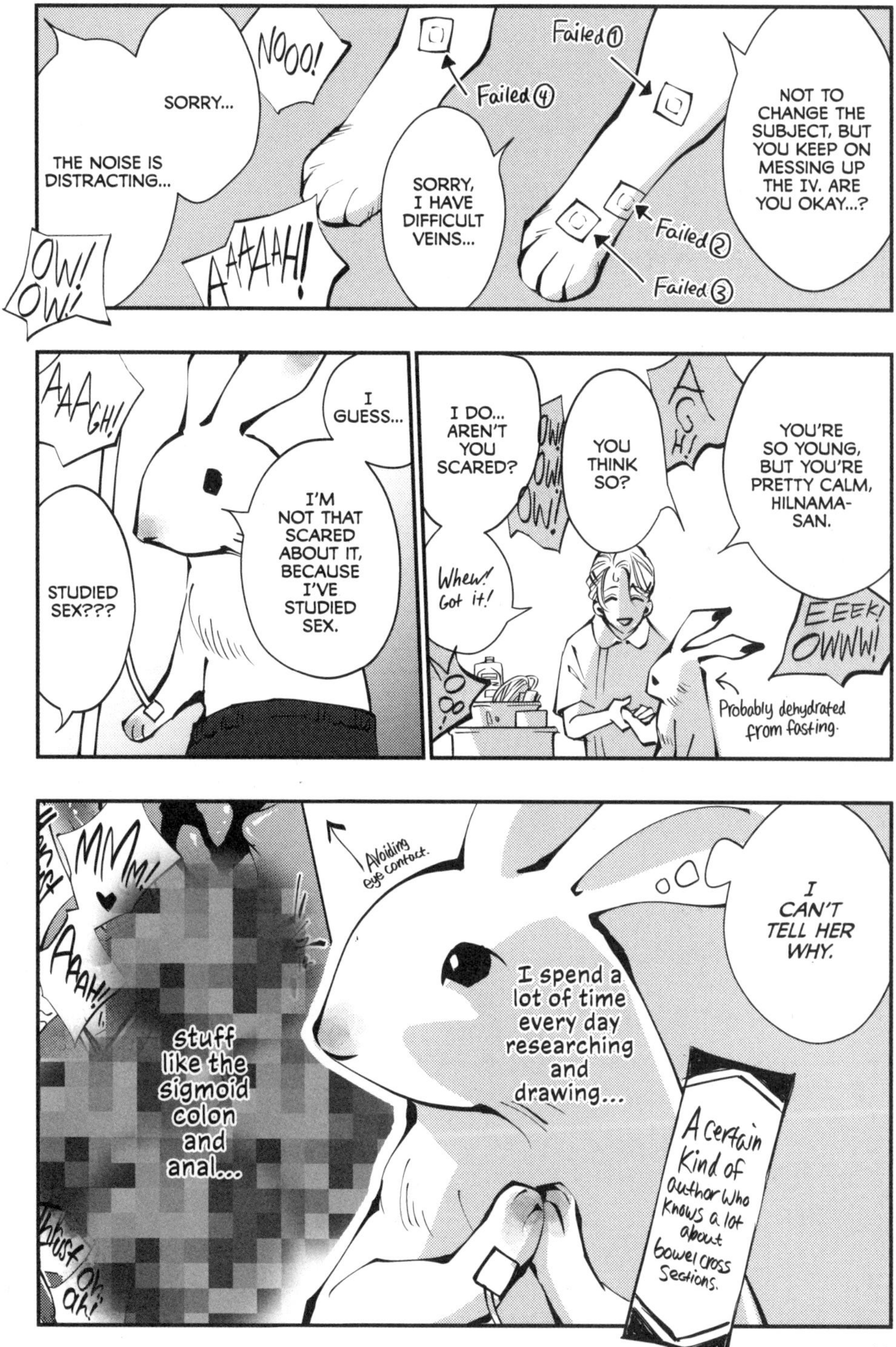
NOT TO CHANGE THE SUBJECT, BUT YOU KEEP ON MESSING UP THE IV. ARE YOU OKAY...?
Failed ①
Failed ②
Failed ③
SORRY, I HAVE DIFFICULT VEINS...
Failed ④
NOOO!
AAAAAH!
SORRY...
THE NOISE IS DISTRACTING...
OW! OW!
YOU'RE SO YOUNG, BUT YOU'RE PRETTY CALM, HILNAMA-SAN.
AGH!
EEEK! OWWW!
YOU THINK SO?
I DO... AREN'T YOU SCARED?
OW! OW! OW!
Whew! Got it!
Probably dehydrated from fasting.
I GUESS...
I'M NOT THAT SCARED ABOUT IT, BECAUSE I'VE STUDIED SEX.
AAAGH!
STUDIED SEX???
I CAN'T TELL HER WHY.
I spend a lot of time every day researching and drawing...
A certain kind of author who knows a lot about bowel cross sections.
Avoiding eye contact.
MMM!
AAAH!
stuff like the sigmoid colon and anal...
Thrust
oh, ah!

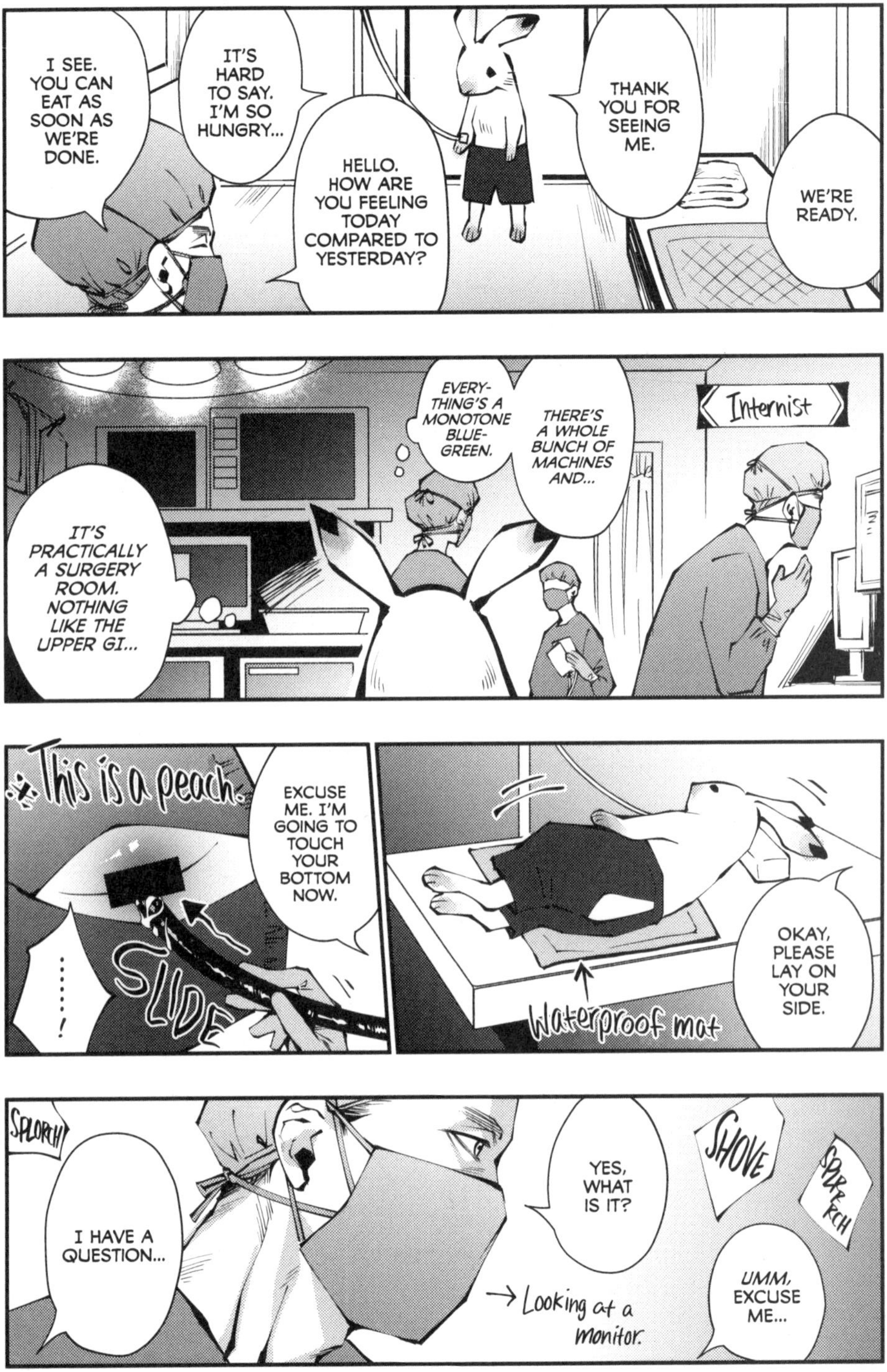
WE'RE READY.
THANK YOU FOR SEEING ME.
HELLO. HOW ARE YOU FEELING TODAY COMPARED TO YESTERDAY?
IT'S HARD TO SAY. I'M SO HUNGRY...
I SEE. YOU CAN EAT AS SOON AS WE'RE DONE.
Internist
THERE'S A WHOLE BUNCH OF MACHINES AND...
EVERYTHING'S A MONOTONE BLUE-GREEN.
IT'S PRACTICALLY A SURGERY ROOM. NOTHING LIKE THE UPPER GI...
OKAY, PLEASE LAY ON YOUR SIDE.
Waterproof mat
This is a peach.
EXCUSE ME. I'M GOING TO TOUCH YOUR BOTTOM NOW.
SLIDE
......!
SPLRRRCH
UMM, EXCUSE ME...
SHOVE
YES, WHAT IS IT?
Looking at a monitor.
I HAVE A QUESTION...
SPLORCH!

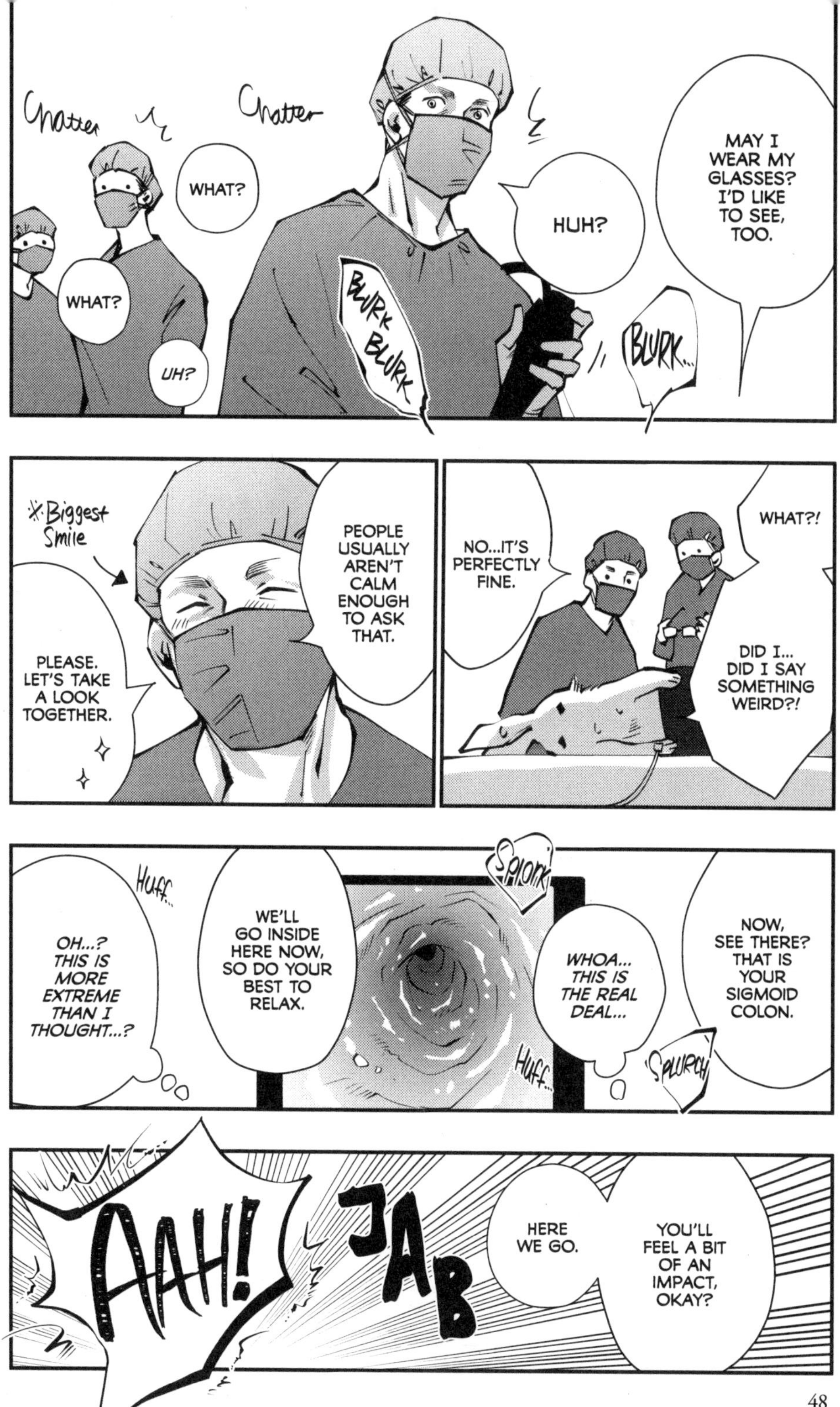

MAY I WEAR MY GLASSES? I'D LIKE TO SEE, TOO.
HUH?
BLURK...
Chatter
BLURK BLURK
WHAT?
Chatter
WHAT?
UH?
WHAT?!
NO...IT'S PERFECTLY FINE.
DID I... DID I SAY SOMETHING WEIRD?!
PEOPLE USUALLY AREN'T CALM ENOUGH TO ASK THAT.
※Biggest Smile
PLEASE. LET'S TAKE A LOOK TOGETHER.
Splork
NOW, SEE THERE? THAT IS YOUR SIGMOID COLON.
SPLURCH
WHOA... THIS IS THE REAL DEAL...
Huff...
WE'LL GO INSIDE HERE NOW, SO DO YOUR BEST TO RELAX.
Huff...
OH...? THIS IS MORE EXTREME THAN I THOUGHT...?
YOU'LL FEEL A BIT OF AN IMPACT, OKAY?
HERE WE GO.
JAB
AAH!

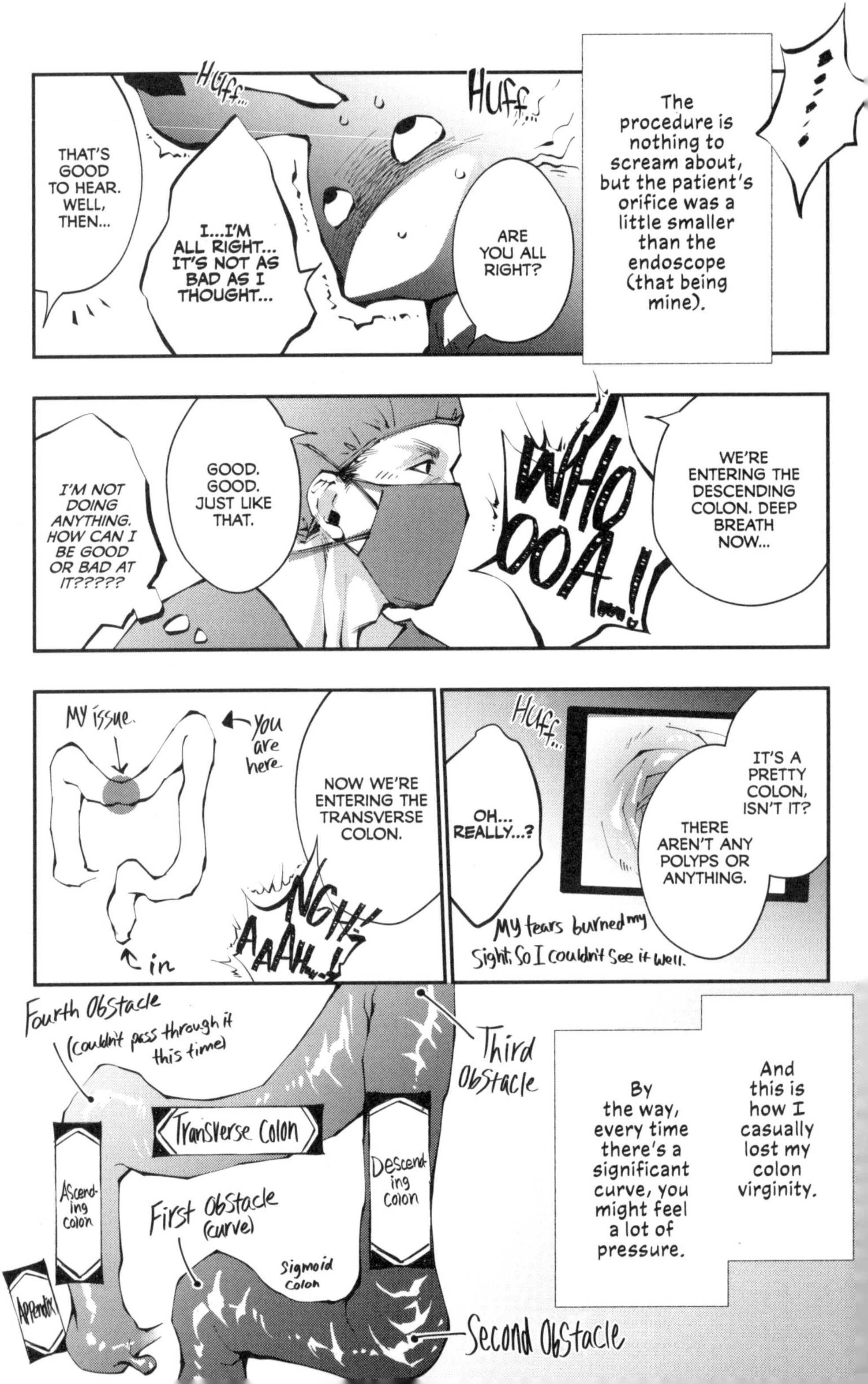
The procedure is nothing to scream about, but the patient's orifice was a little smaller than the endoscope (that being mine).
Huff...
ARE YOU ALL RIGHT?
Huff...
I...I'M ALL RIGHT... IT'S NOT AS BAD AS I THOUGHT...
THAT'S GOOD TO HEAR. WELL, THEN...
WE'RE ENTERING THE DESCENDING COLON. DEEP BREATH NOW...
WHOOOA...!!
GOOD. GOOD. JUST LIKE THAT.
I'M NOT DOING ANYTHING. HOW CAN I BE GOOD OR BAD AT IT?????
Huff...
IT'S A PRETTY COLON, ISN'T IT?
THERE AREN'T ANY POLYPS OR ANYTHING.
OH... REALLY...?
My tears burned my sight, so I couldn't see it well.
NOW WE'RE ENTERING THE TRANSVERSE COLON.
NGH! AAAH...!
you are here
My issue.
in
And this is how I casually lost my colon virginity.
By the way, every time there's a significant curve, you might feel a lot of pressure.
Third Obstacle
Descending Colon
Transverse Colon
Fourth Obstacle (couldn't pass through it this time)
Ascending Colon
First Obstacle (curve)
Sigmoid Colon
Appendix
Second Obstacle

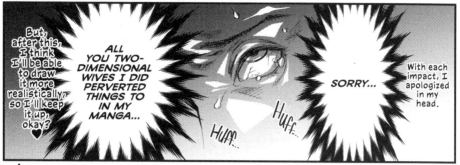

With each impact, I apologized in my head.
SORRY...
Huff...
Huff...
ALL YOU TWO-DIMENSIONAL WIVES I DID PERVERTED THINGS TO IN MY MANGA...
But, after this, I think I'll be able to draw it more realistically, so I'll keep it up, okay? ♥
Didn't learn a thing (ha ha)
HILNAMA-SAN.
Oh. Yes?
WE'VE REACHED THE ISSUE.
CAN YOU SEE IT?
There I saw...
Huff...
Glasses
Huff...
a pink fluffy thing unlike what I'd imagined.
I calmly thought, "Looks yummy, like the organ meats at the yakiniku restaurants."
※Cancer cells
BIOPSY COMPLETED.
I CAN'T GO ANY FARTHER, SO I'M GOING TO TAKE IT OUT, OKAY?
SPLRRRCH BLURK BLURK
HUFF...
SPLRRRCH BLURK
BY THE WAY, HILNAMA-SAN...

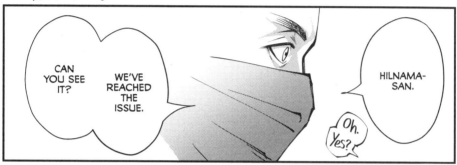

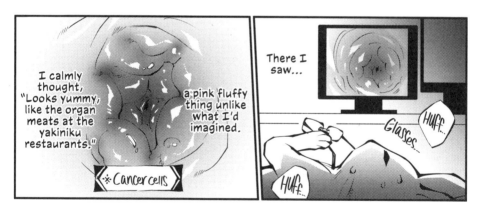

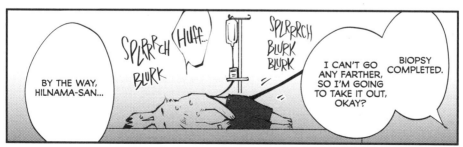

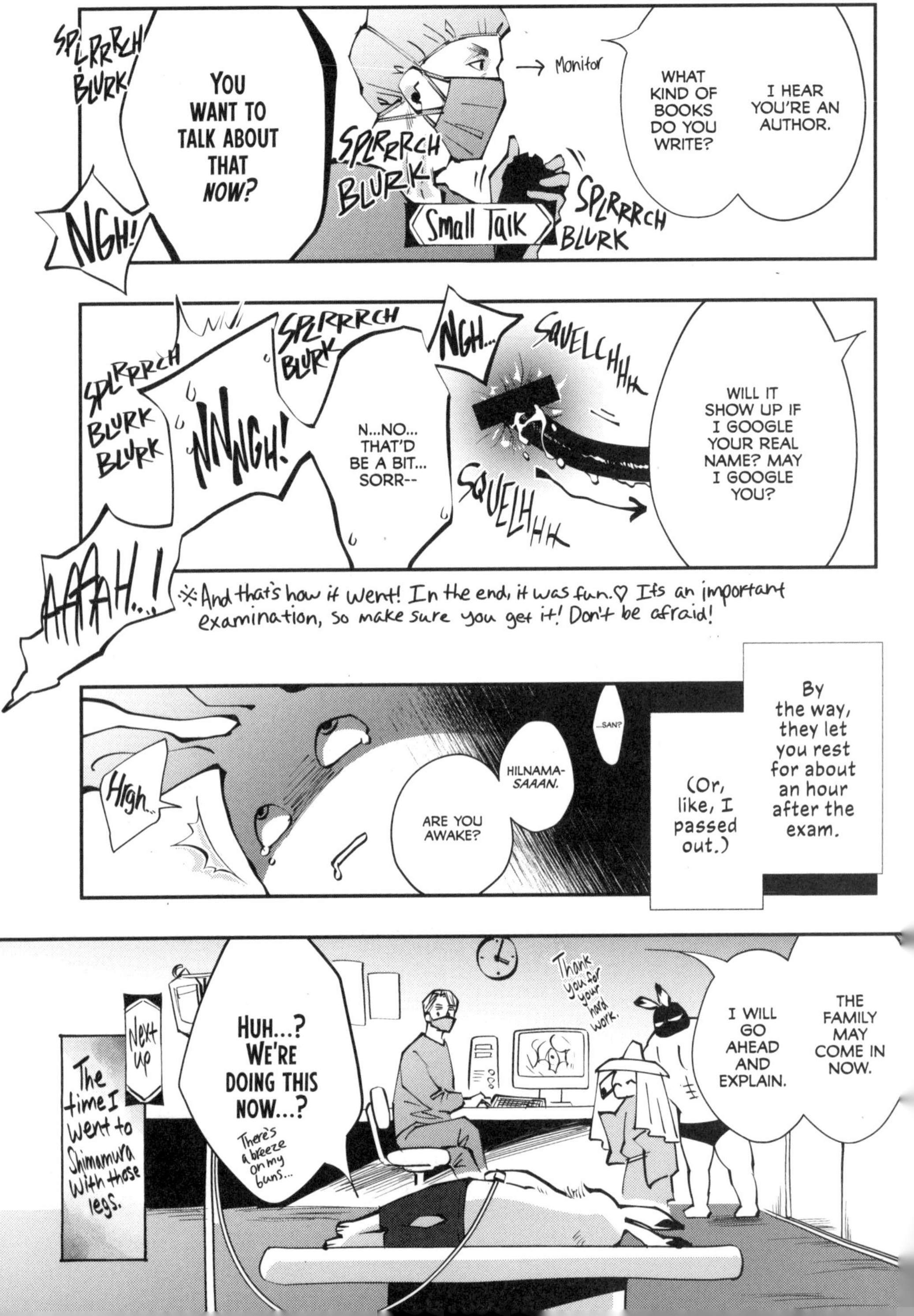
I HEAR YOU'RE AN AUTHOR.
WHAT KIND OF BOOKS DO YOU WRITE?
→ Monitor
SPLRRRCH BLURK
Small Talk
SPLRRRCH BLURK
SPLRRRCH BLURK
YOU WANT TO TALK ABOUT THAT NOW?
NGH!
WILL IT SHOW UP IF I GOOGLE YOUR REAL NAME? MAY I GOOGLE YOU?
SQUELCHHHH
SQUELHHHH
NGH...
N...NO... THAT'D BE A BIT... SORR--
SPLRRRCH BLURK
NNNGH!
SPLRRRCH BLURK BLURK BLURK
AAAH...!
※And that's how it went! In the end, it was fun.♡ It's an important examination, so make sure you get it! Don't be afraid!
By the way, they let you rest for about an hour after the exam.
(Or, like, I passed out.)
...SAN?
HILNAMA-SAAAN.
ARE YOU AWAKE?
Hrgh...
THE FAMILY MAY COME IN NOW.
I WILL GO AHEAD AND EXPLAIN.
Thank you for your hard work.
HUH...? WE'RE DOING THIS NOW...?
There's a breeze on my buns...
Next up
The time I went to Shimamura with those legs.

Weeell, I love all of you. That was the time I had a colonoscopy. I read a really wide range of responses after this went online. Some people said it didn't hurt at all! Others said it hurt so badly! Some people experienced complications. Other people thought it was the most fun they've ever had...! *(Ha ha.)*

Well, the difficulties of the exam probably run the gamut depending on a person's health and situation. You shouldn't laugh at other people's pain. (Sorry...)

By the way, I wrote this in the afterword, too, but during my first colonoscopy, I did say "yelp" and stuff, but the second time (a year after my surgery) it was completely healthy and I thought about Chkmeruli, a Georgian chicken and garlic sauce dish.
— It's because my colon got shorter. *Wooow!*

I'm a Terminal
Cancer
Patient
// BUT I'M FINE \\

I thought I had a Stomachache, but it was terminal cancer. ④
The time I went to Shimamura with those legs.

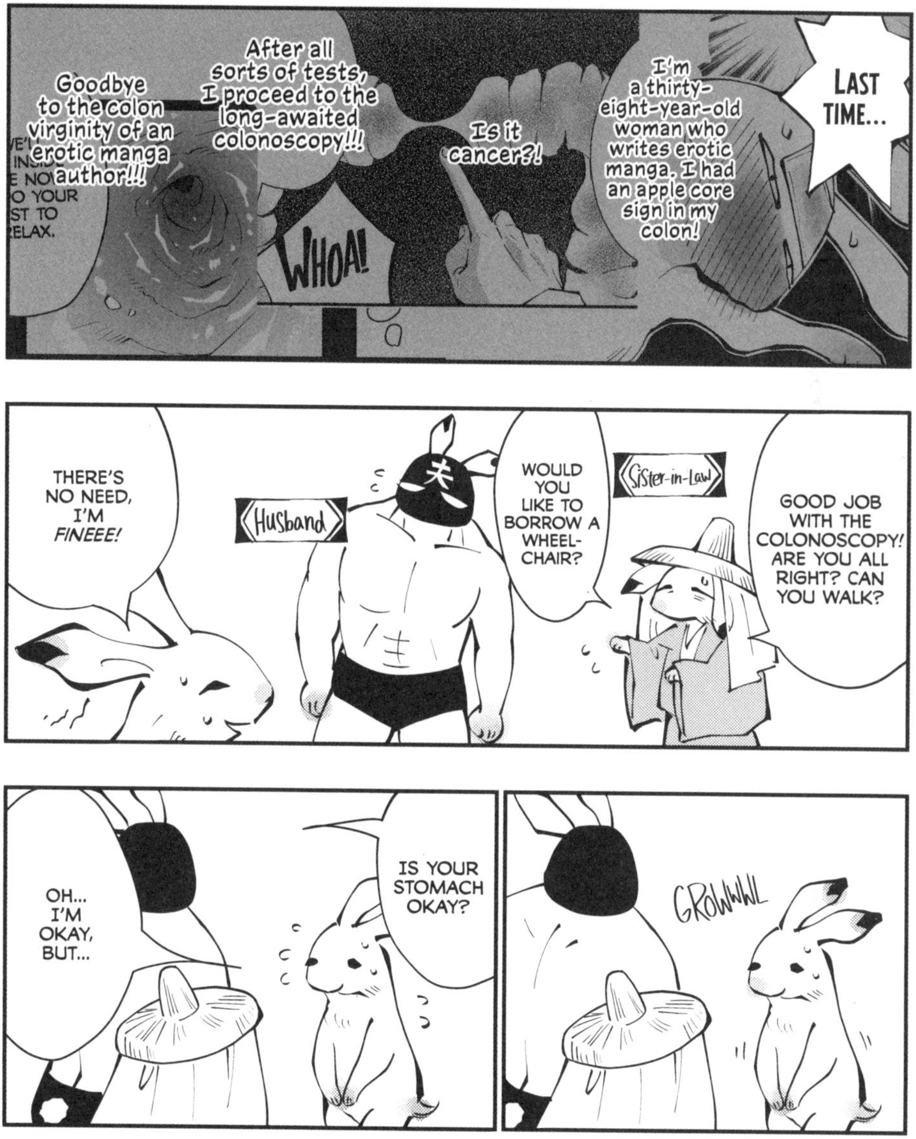

LAST TIME...
I'm a thirty-eight-year-old woman who writes erotic manga. I had an apple core sign in my colon!
Is it cancer?!
WHOA!
After all sorts of tests, I proceed to the long-awaited colonoscopy!!!
Goodbye to the colon virginity of an erotic manga author!!!
GOOD JOB WITH THE COLONOSCOPY! ARE YOU ALL RIGHT? CAN YOU WALK?
Sister-in-Law
WOULD YOU LIKE TO BORROW A WHEEL-CHAIR?
Husband
THERE'S NO NEED, I'M *FINEEE!*
GROWWWL
IS YOUR STOMACH OKAY?
OH... I'M OKAY, BUT...

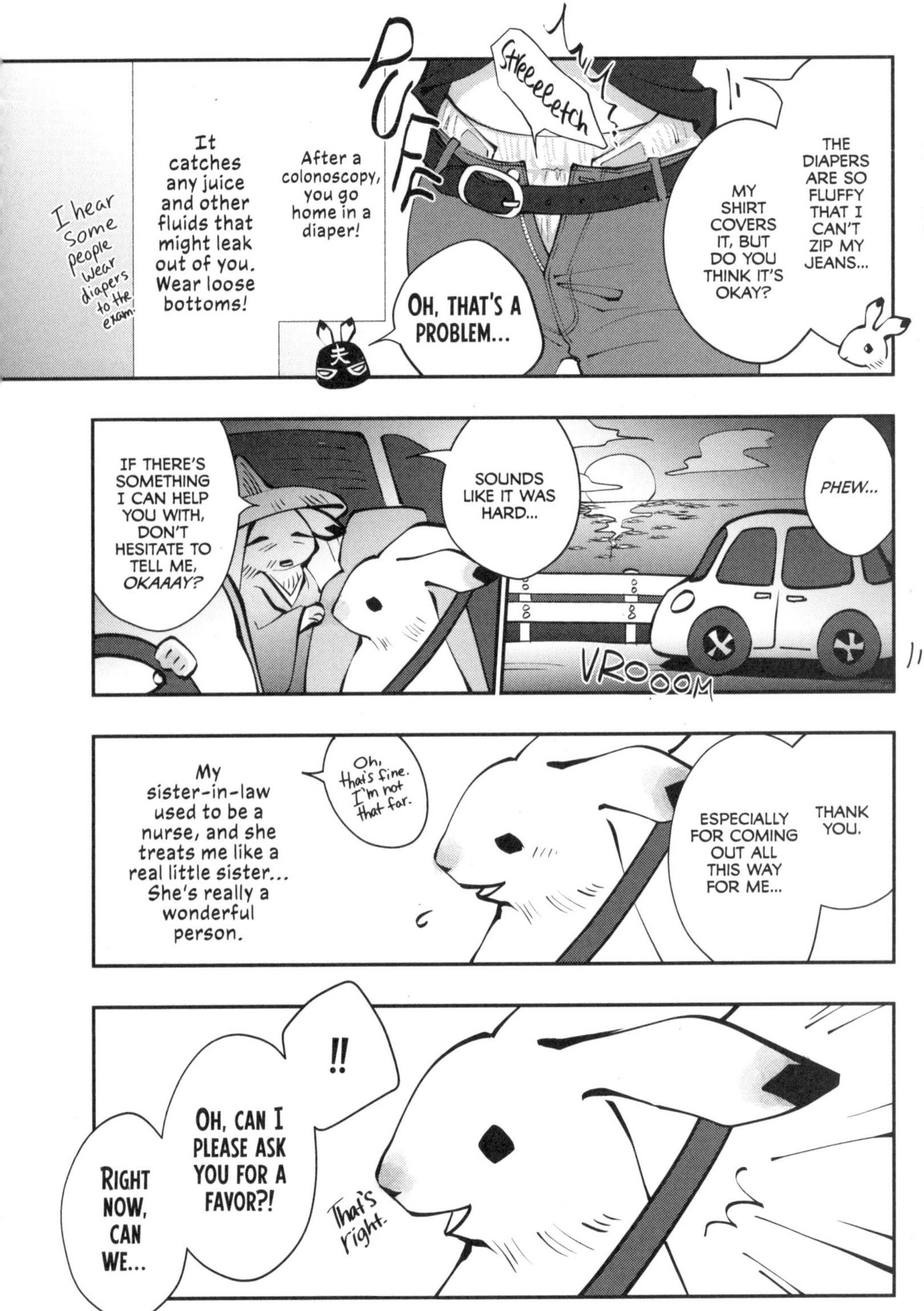
PUFF
Streeeetch
THE DIAPERS ARE SO FLUFFY THAT I CAN'T ZIP MY JEANS...
MY SHIRT COVERS IT, BUT DO YOU THINK IT'S OKAY?
OH, THAT'S A PROBLEM...
After a colonoscopy, you go home in a diaper!
It catches any juice and other fluids that might leak out of you. Wear loose bottoms!
I hear some people wear diapers to the exam.
PHEW...
VROOOOM
SOUNDS LIKE IT WAS HARD...
IF THERE'S SOMETHING I CAN HELP YOU WITH, DON'T HESITATE TO TELL ME, *OKAAAY?*
THANK YOU.
ESPECIALLY FOR COMING OUT ALL THIS WAY FOR ME...
Oh, that's fine. I'm not that far.
My sister-in-law used to be a nurse, and she treats me like a real little sister... She's really a wonderful person.
!!
That's right.
OH, CAN I PLEASE ASK YOU FOR A FAVOR?!
RIGHT NOW, CAN WE...

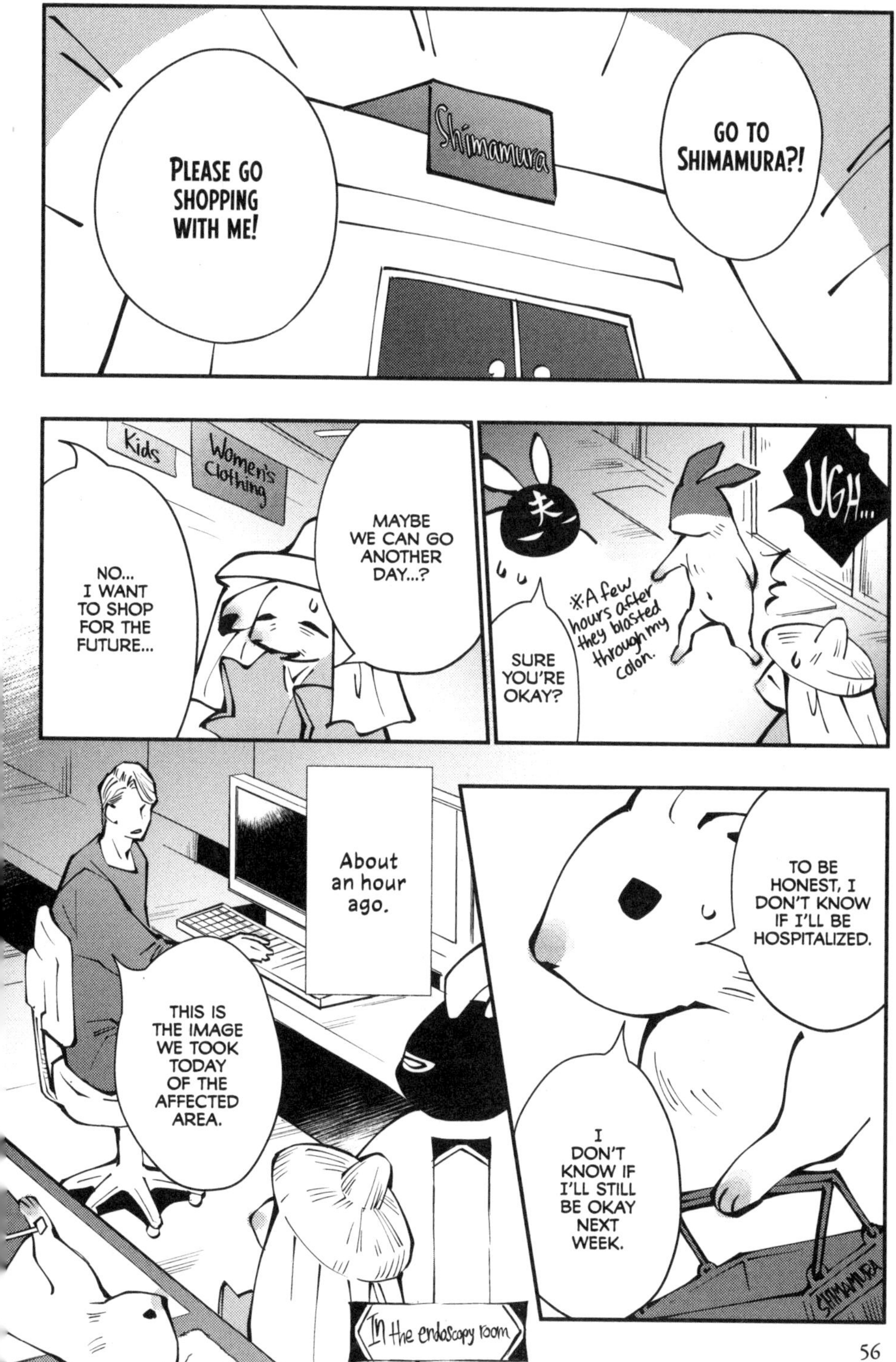
Shimamura
GO TO SHIMAMURA?!
PLEASE GO SHOPPING WITH ME!
UGH...
※A few hours after they blasted through my colon.
SURE YOU'RE OKAY?
Kids
Women's Clothing
MAYBE WE CAN GO ANOTHER DAY...?
NO... I WANT TO SHOP FOR THE FUTURE...
TO BE HONEST, I DON'T KNOW IF I'LL BE HOSPITALIZED.
I DON'T KNOW IF I'LL STILL BE OKAY NEXT WEEK.
SHIMAMURA
About an hour ago.
THIS IS THE IMAGE WE TOOK TODAY OF THE AFFECTED AREA.
In the endoscopy room

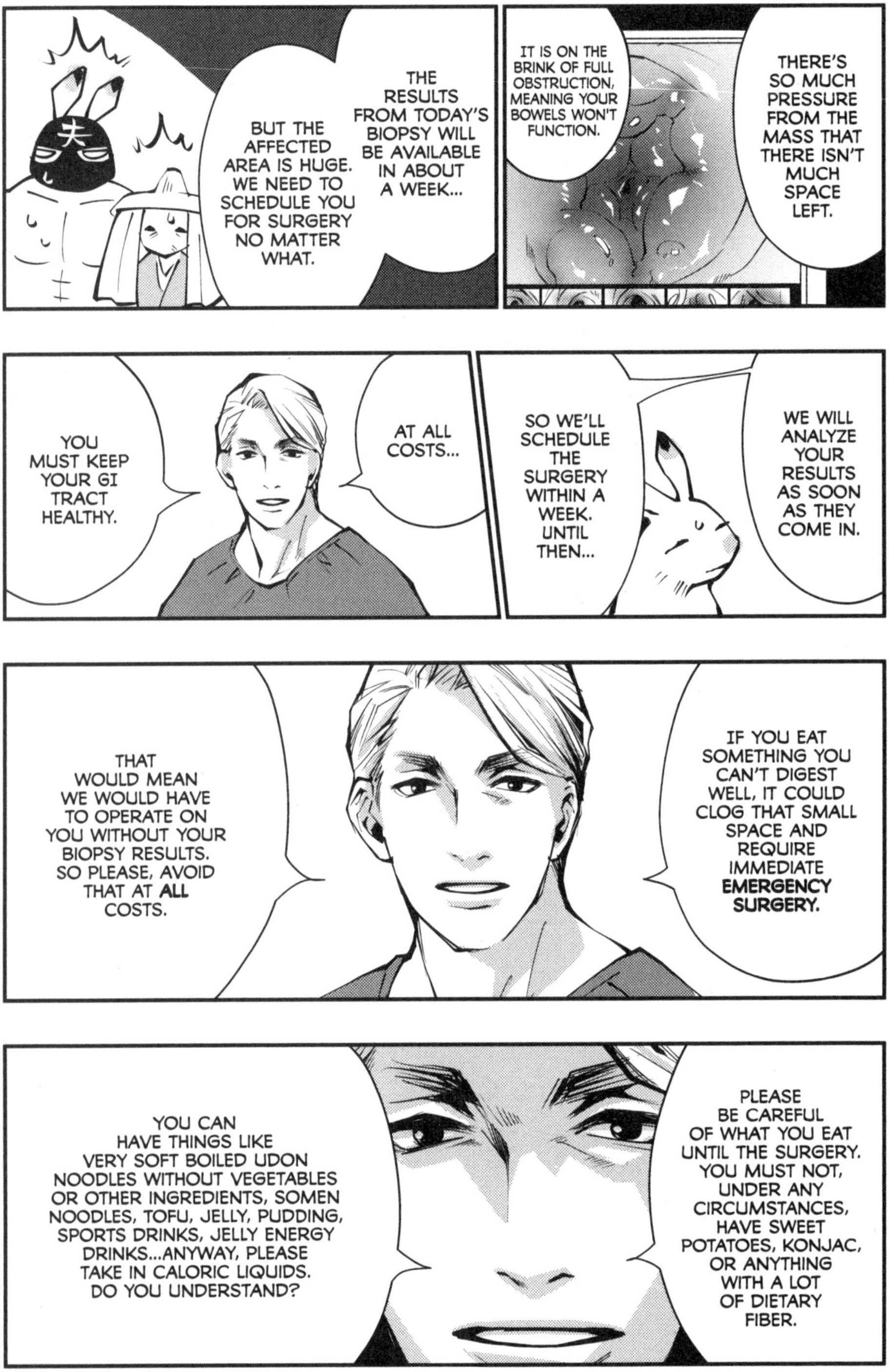
THERE'S SO MUCH PRESSURE FROM THE MASS THAT THERE ISN'T MUCH SPACE LEFT.
IT IS ON THE BRINK OF FULL OBSTRUCTION, MEANING YOUR BOWELS WON'T FUNCTION.
THE RESULTS FROM TODAY'S BIOPSY WILL BE AVAILABLE IN ABOUT A WEEK...
BUT THE AFFECTED AREA IS HUGE. WE NEED TO SCHEDULE YOU FOR SURGERY NO MATTER WHAT.
夫
WE WILL ANALYZE YOUR RESULTS AS SOON AS THEY COME IN.
SO WE'LL SCHEDULE THE SURGERY WITHIN A WEEK. UNTIL THEN...
AT ALL COSTS...
YOU MUST KEEP YOUR GI TRACT HEALTHY.
IF YOU EAT SOMETHING YOU CAN'T DIGEST WELL, IT COULD CLOG THAT SMALL SPACE AND REQUIRE IMMEDIATE **EMERGENCY SURGERY.**
THAT WOULD MEAN WE WOULD HAVE TO OPERATE ON YOU WITHOUT YOUR BIOPSY RESULTS. SO PLEASE, AVOID THAT AT **ALL** COSTS.
PLEASE BE CAREFUL OF WHAT YOU EAT UNTIL THE SURGERY. YOU MUST NOT, UNDER ANY CIRCUMSTANCES, HAVE SWEET POTATOES, KONJAC, OR ANYTHING WITH A LOT OF DIETARY FIBER.
YOU CAN HAVE THINGS LIKE VERY SOFT BOILED UDON NOODLES WITHOUT VEGETABLES OR OTHER INGREDIENTS, SOMEN NOODLES, TOFU, JELLY, PUDDING, SPORTS DRINKS, JELLY ENERGY DRINKS...ANYWAY, PLEASE TAKE IN CALORIC LIQUIDS. DO YOU UNDERSTAND?

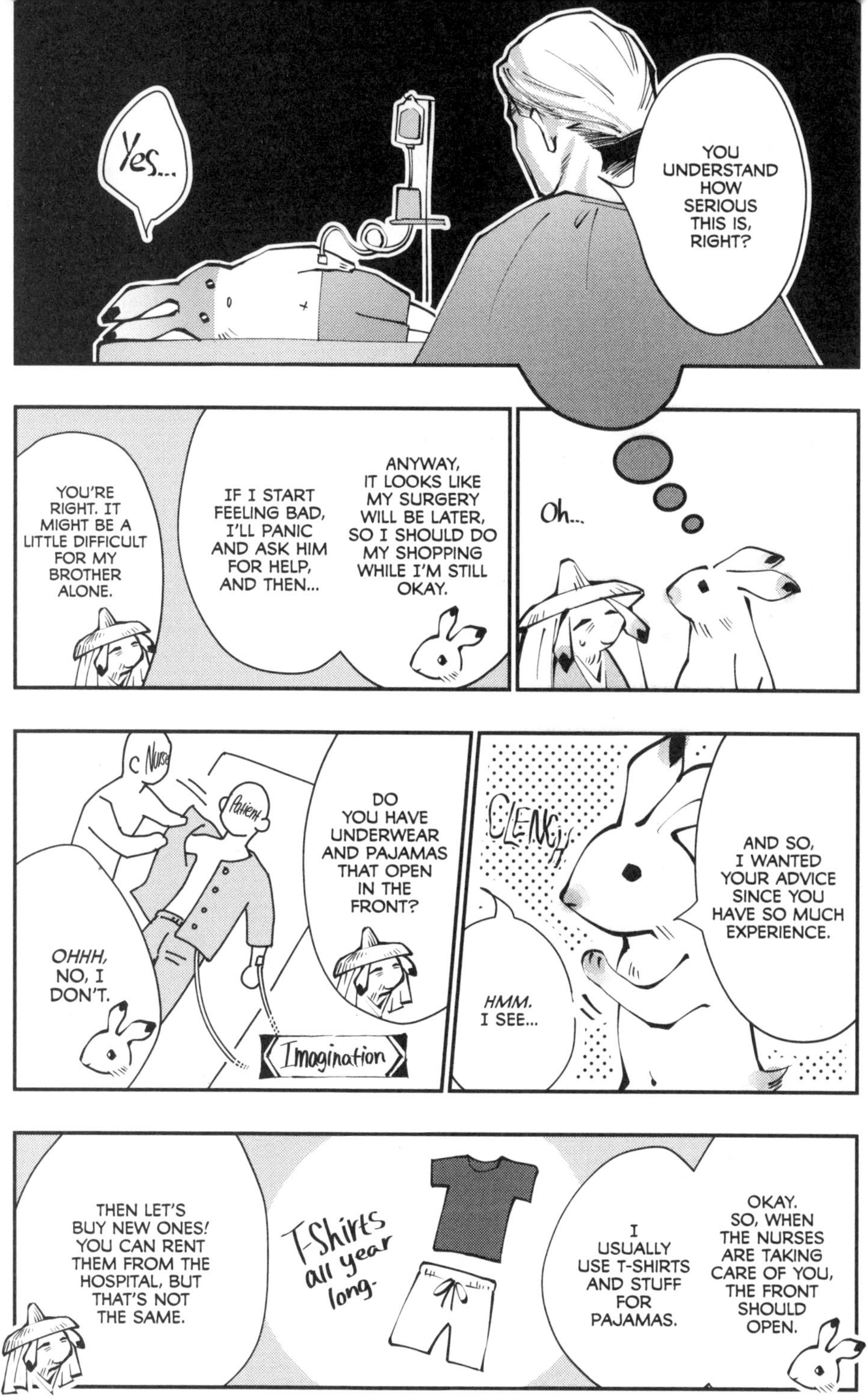
YOU UNDERSTAND HOW SERIOUS THIS IS, RIGHT?
Yes...
Oh...
ANYWAY, IT LOOKS LIKE MY SURGERY WILL BE LATER, SO I SHOULD DO MY SHOPPING WHILE I'M STILL OKAY.
IF I START FEELING BAD, I'LL PANIC AND ASK HIM FOR HELP, AND THEN...
YOU'RE RIGHT. IT MIGHT BE A LITTLE DIFFICULT FOR MY BROTHER ALONE.
AND SO, I WANTED YOUR ADVICE SINCE YOU HAVE SO MUCH EXPERIENCE.
CLENCH
HMM. I SEE...
DO YOU HAVE UNDERWEAR AND PAJAMAS THAT OPEN IN THE FRONT?
Nurse
Patient
OHHH, NO, I DON'T.
Imagination
OKAY. SO, WHEN THE NURSES ARE TAKING CARE OF YOU, THE FRONT SHOULD OPEN.
I USUALLY USE T-SHIRTS AND STUFF FOR PAJAMAS.
T-Shirts all year long.
THEN LET'S BUY NEW ONES! YOU CAN RENT THEM FROM THE HOSPITAL, BUT THAT'S NOT THE SAME.

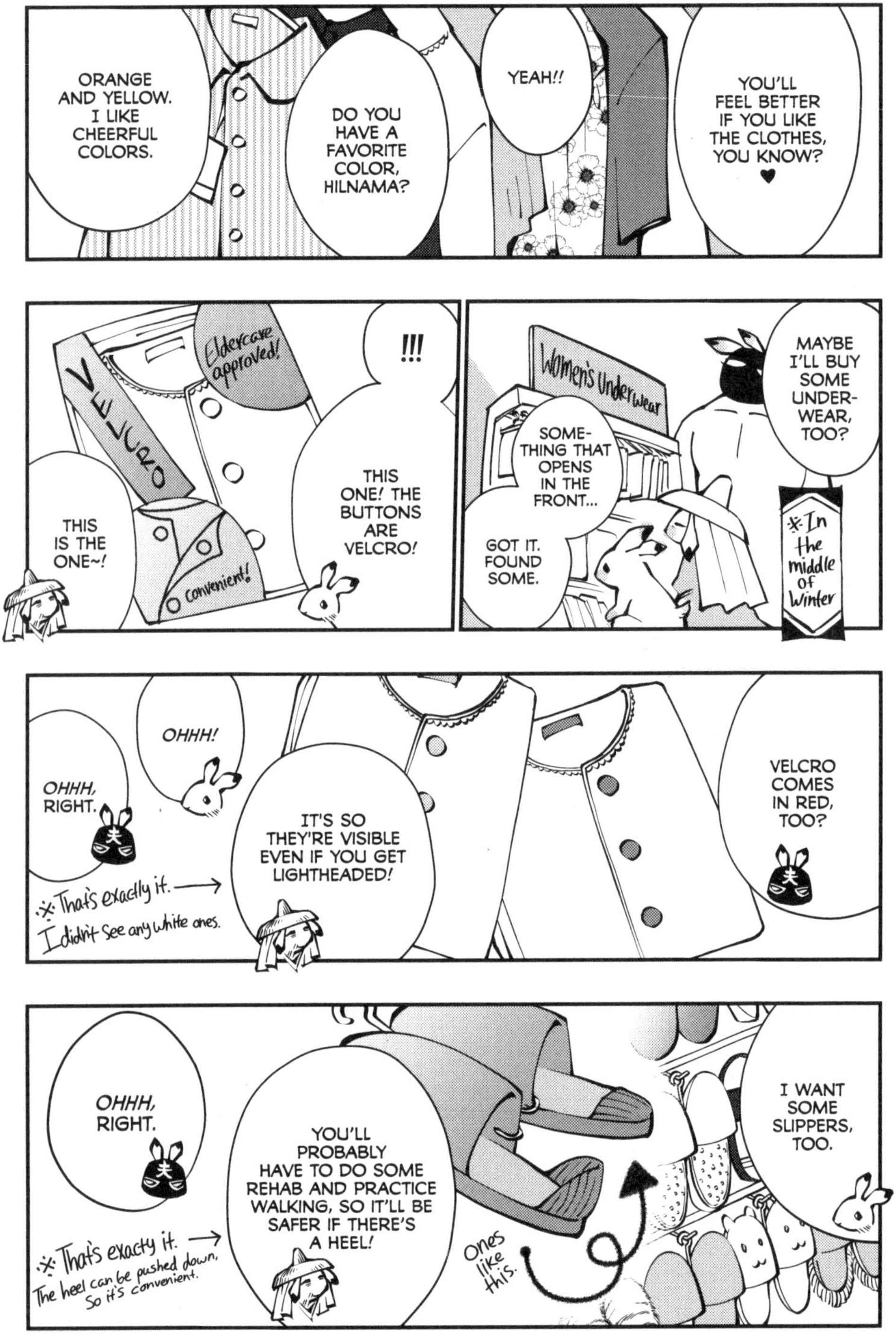
YOU'LL FEEL BETTER IF YOU LIKE THE CLOTHES, YOU KNOW? ♥
YEAH!!
DO YOU HAVE A FAVORITE COLOR, HILNAMA?
ORANGE AND YELLOW. I LIKE CHEERFUL COLORS.
MAYBE I'LL BUY SOME UNDER-WEAR, TOO?
※In the middle of Winter
Women's Underwear
SOME-THING THAT OPENS IN THE FRONT...
GOT IT. FOUND SOME.
!!!
Eldercare approved!
VELCRO
THIS ONE! THE BUTTONS ARE VELCRO!
convenient!
THIS IS THE ONE~!
VELCRO COMES IN RED, TOO?
IT'S SO THEY'RE VISIBLE EVEN IF YOU GET LIGHTHEADED!
OHHH!
OHHH, RIGHT.
※That's exactly it. →
I didn't see any white ones.
I WANT SOME SLIPPERS, TOO.
Ones like this.
YOU'LL PROBABLY HAVE TO DO SOME REHAB AND PRACTICE WALKING, SO IT'LL BE SAFER IF THERE'S A HEEL!
OHHH, RIGHT.
※That's exacty it. →
The heel can be pushed down, so it's convenient.

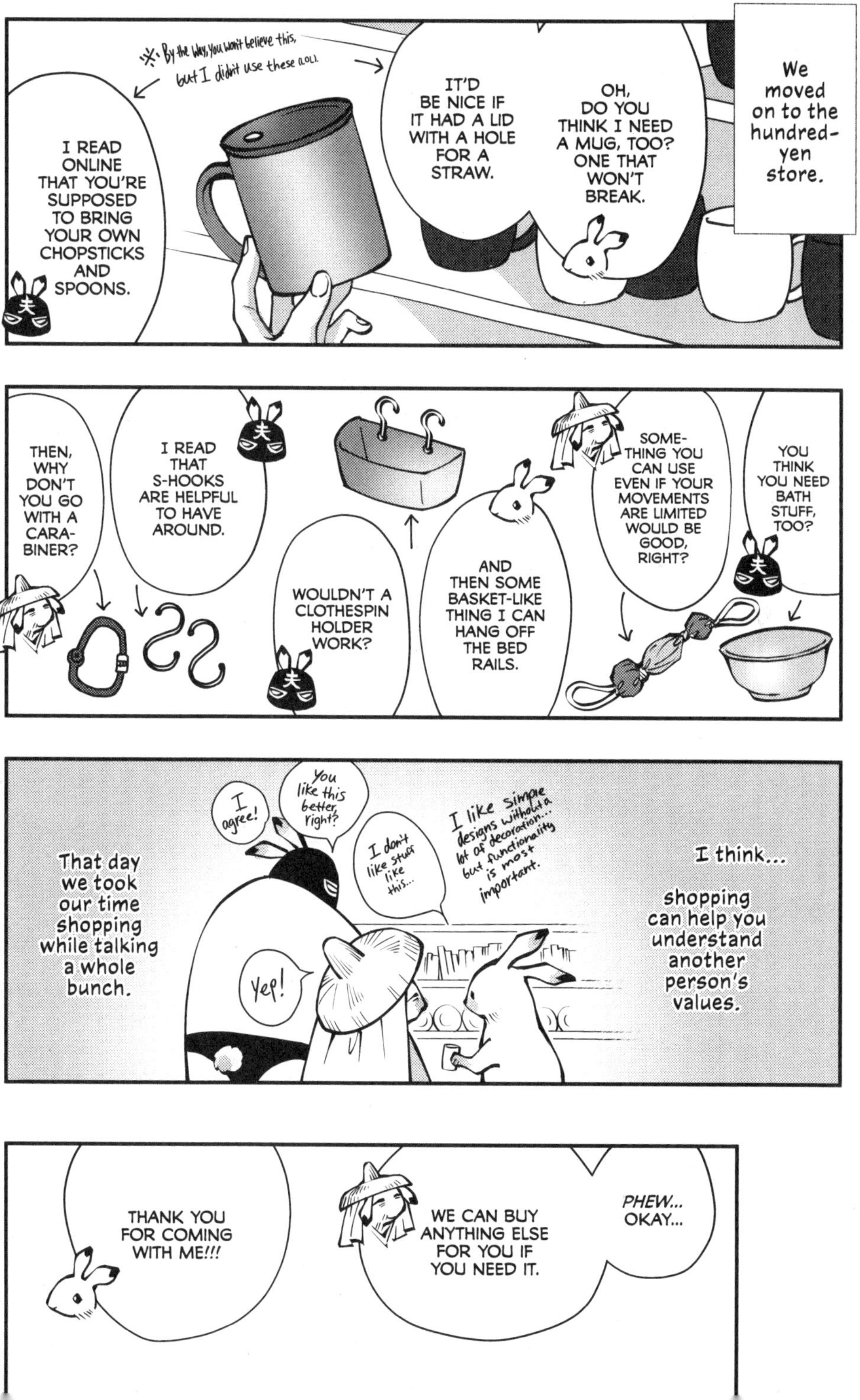
We moved on to the hundred-yen store.
OH, DO YOU THINK I NEED A MUG, TOO? ONE THAT WON'T BREAK.
IT'D BE NICE IF IT HAD A LID WITH A HOLE FOR A STRAW.
※ By the way, you won't believe this, but I didn't use these (LOL).
I READ ONLINE THAT YOU'RE SUPPOSED TO BRING YOUR OWN CHOPSTICKS AND SPOONS.
YOU THINK YOU NEED BATH STUFF, TOO?
SOME-THING YOU CAN USE EVEN IF YOUR MOVEMENTS ARE LIMITED WOULD BE GOOD, RIGHT?
AND THEN SOME BASKET-LIKE THING I CAN HANG OFF THE BED RAILS.
WOULDN'T A CLOTHESPIN HOLDER WORK?
I READ THAT S-HOOKS ARE HELPFUL TO HAVE AROUND.
THEN, WHY DON'T YOU GO WITH A CARA-BINER?
I think... shopping can help you understand another person's values.
I like simple designs without a lot of decoration... but functionality is most important.
I don't like stuff like this...
You like this better, right?
I agree!
Yep!
That day we took our time shopping while talking a whole bunch.
PHEW... OKAY...
WE CAN BUY ANYTHING ELSE FOR YOU IF YOU NEED IT.
THANK YOU FOR COMING WITH ME!!!

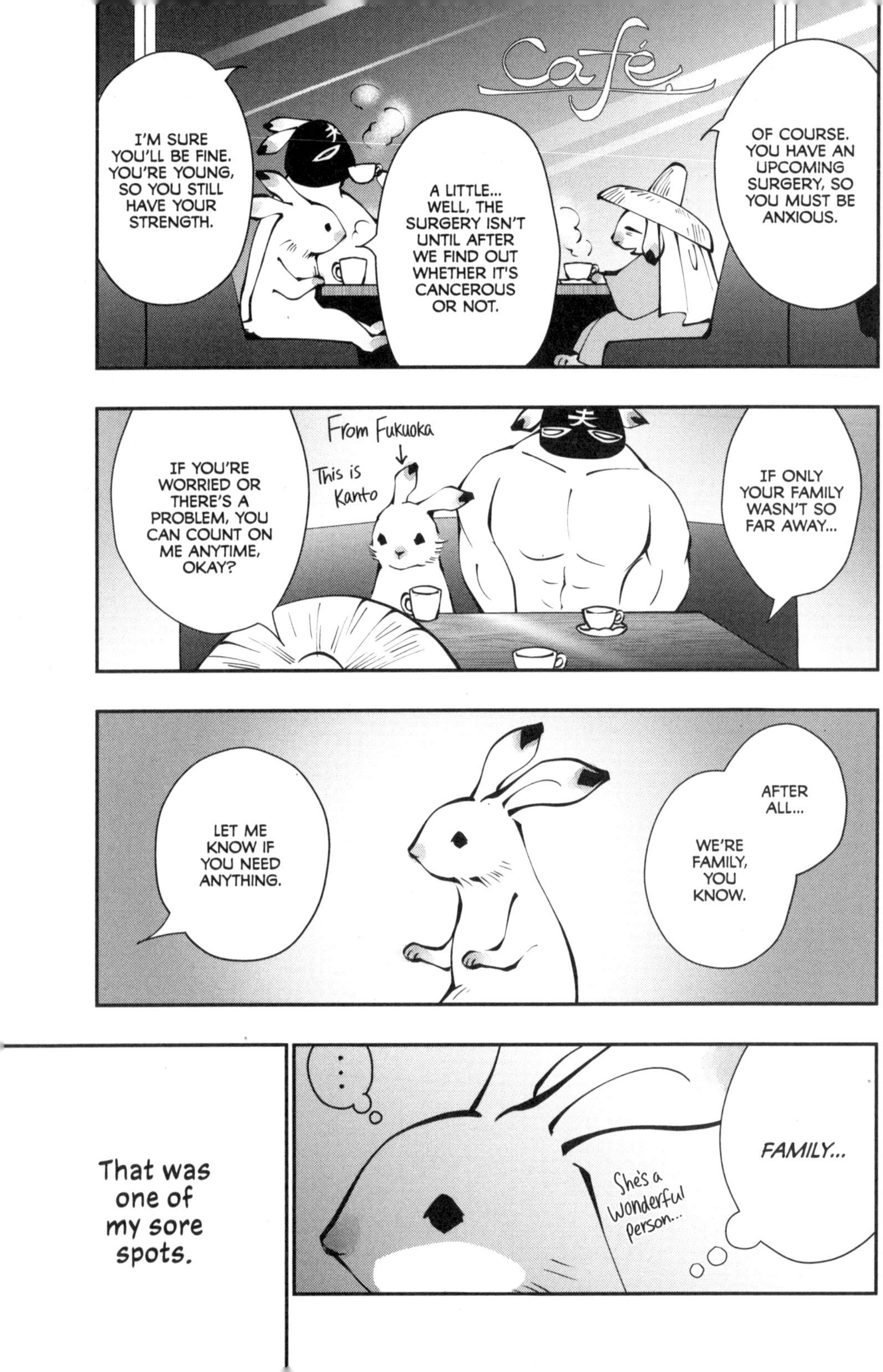
Café
OF COURSE. YOU HAVE AN UPCOMING SURGERY, SO YOU MUST BE ANXIOUS.
A LITTLE... WELL, THE SURGERY ISN'T UNTIL AFTER WE FIND OUT WHETHER IT'S CANCEROUS OR NOT.
I'M SURE YOU'LL BE FINE. YOU'RE YOUNG, SO YOU STILL HAVE YOUR STRENGTH.
IF ONLY YOUR FAMILY WASN'T SO FAR AWAY...
From Fukuoka
This is Kanto
IF YOU'RE WORRIED OR THERE'S A PROBLEM, YOU CAN COUNT ON ME ANYTIME, OKAY?
AFTER ALL...
WE'RE FAMILY, YOU KNOW.
LET ME KNOW IF YOU NEED ANYTHING.
FAMILY...
She's a wonderful person...
...
That was one of my sore spots.

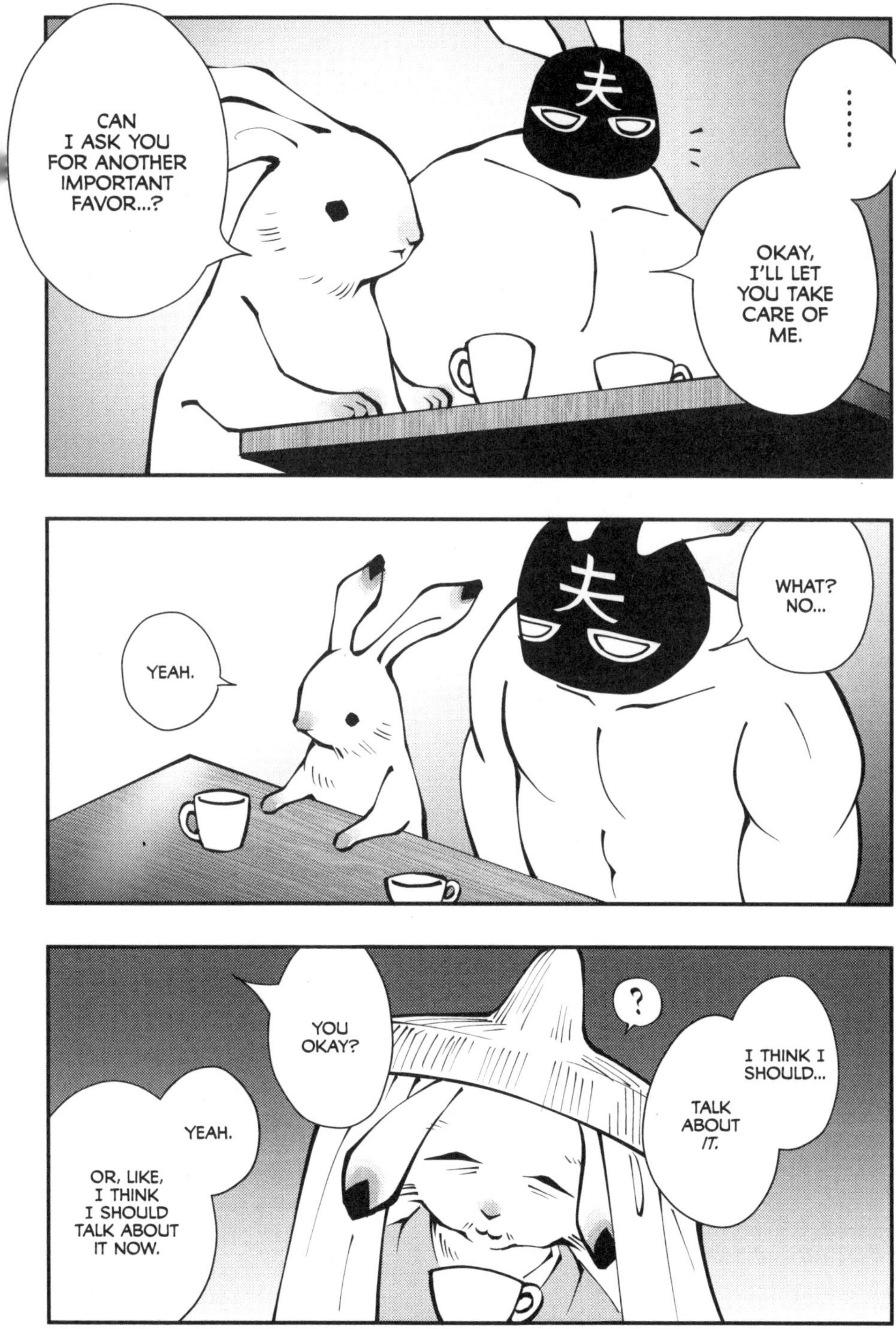
……
CAN I ASK YOU FOR ANOTHER IMPORTANT FAVOR...?
OKAY, I'LL LET YOU TAKE CARE OF ME.
WHAT? NO...
YEAH.
?
I THINK I SHOULD...
TALK ABOUT *IT.*
YOU OKAY?
YEAH.
OR, LIKE, I THINK I SHOULD TALK ABOUT IT NOW.

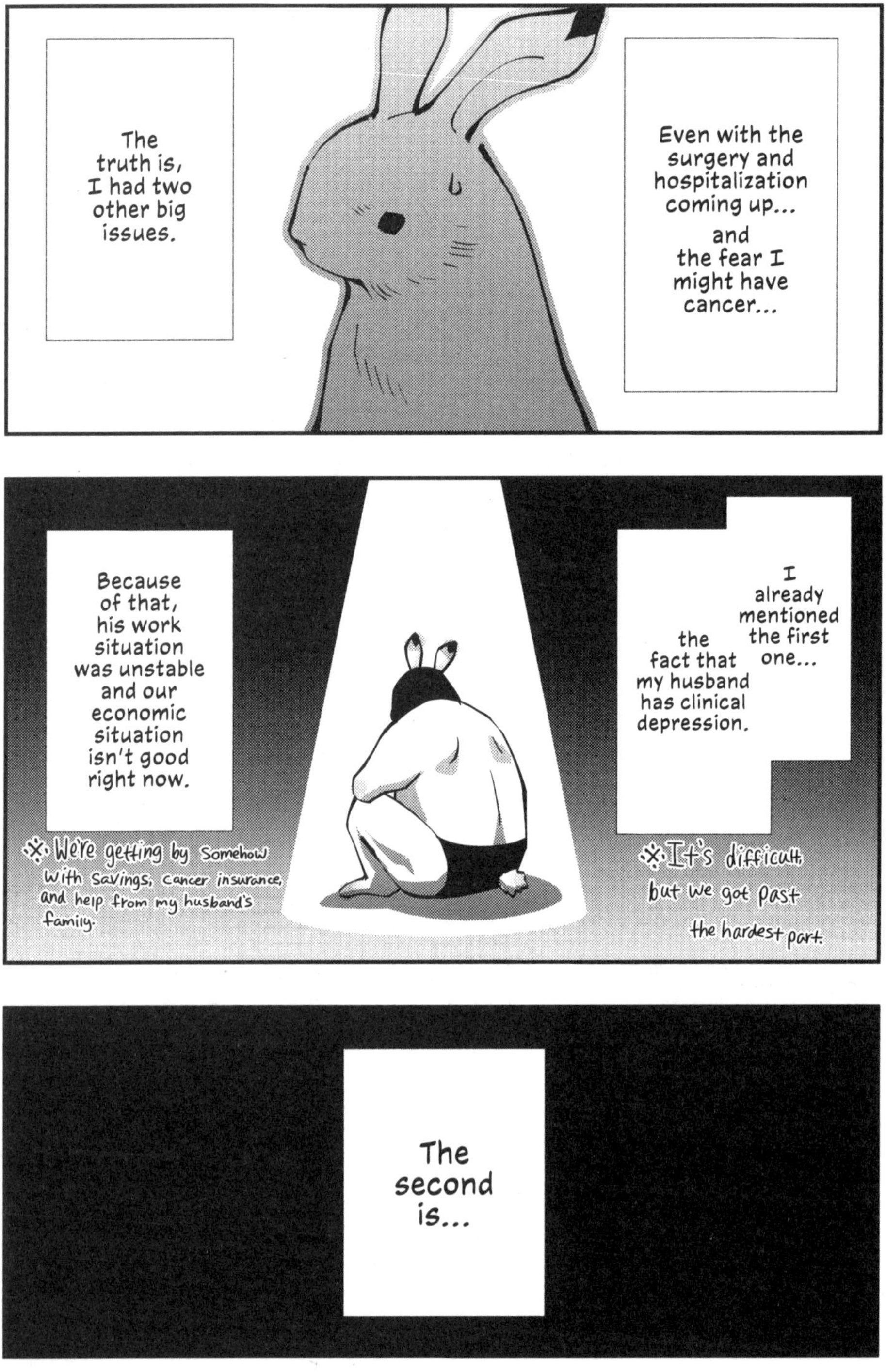
Even with the surgery and hospitalization coming up... and the fear I might have cancer...
The truth is, I had two other big issues.
I already mentioned the first one...
the fact that my husband has clinical depression.
※It's difficult but we got past the hardest part.
Because of that, his work situation was unstable and our economic situation isn't good right now.
※We're getting by somehow with savings, cancer insurance, and help from my husband's family.
The second is...

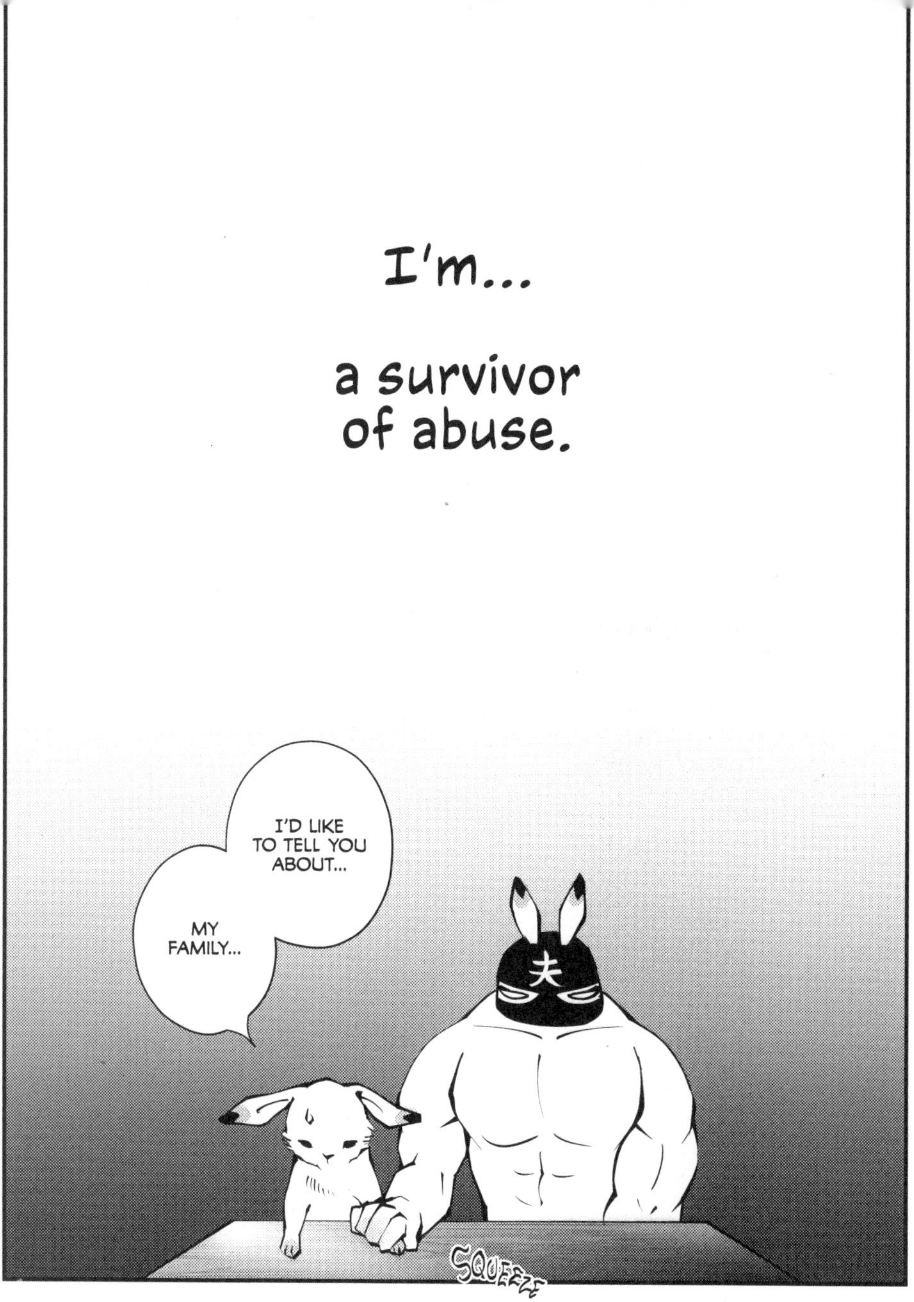
I'm...
a survivor of abuse.
I'D LIKE TO TELL YOU ABOUT...
MY FAMILY...
SQUEEZE

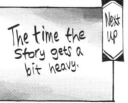

Next up

The time the story gets a bit heavy.

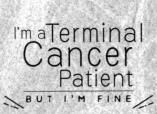

I'm a Terminal
Cancer
Patient
BUT I'M FINE

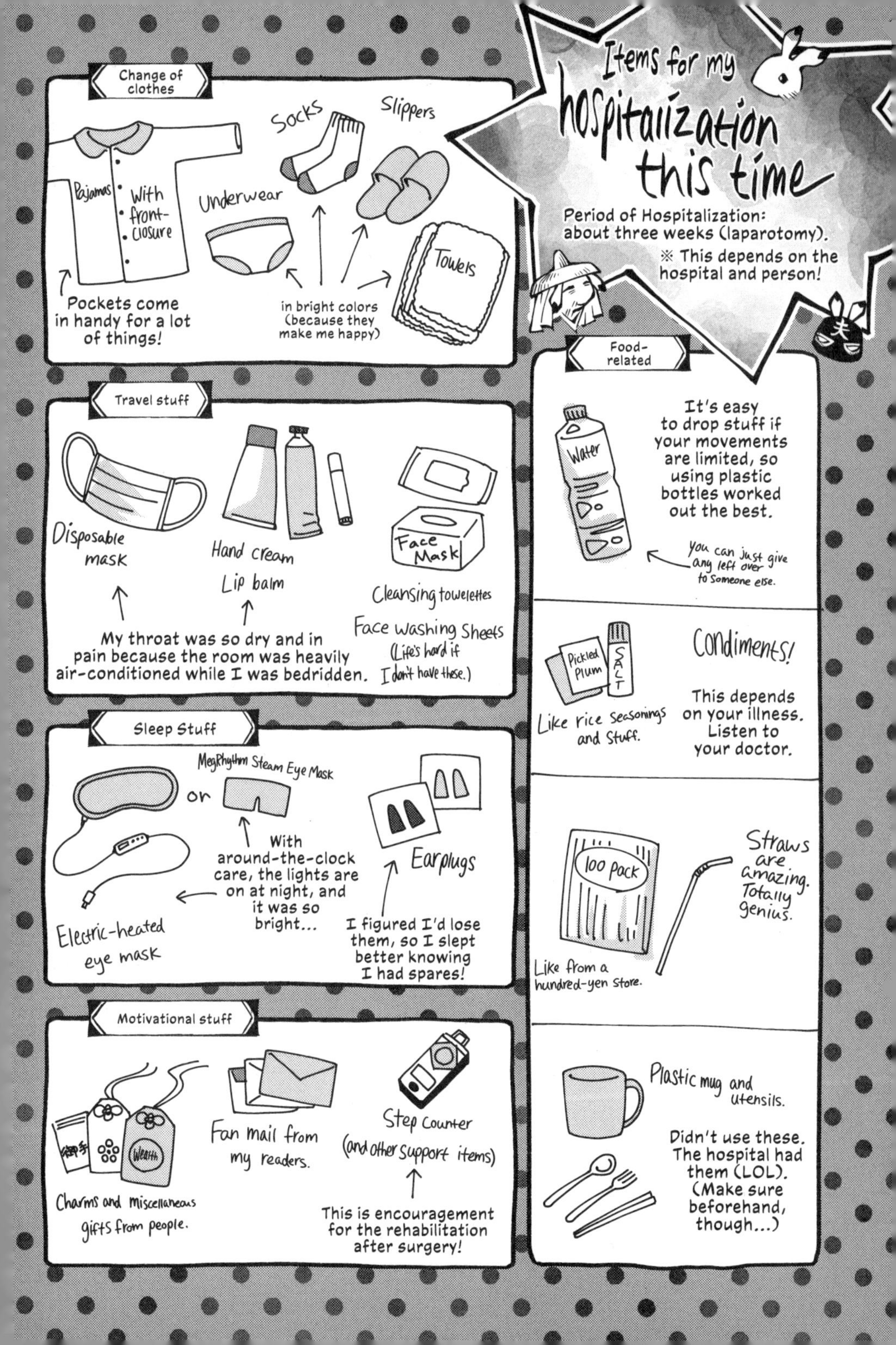

Items for my hospitalization this time
Period of Hospitalization: about three weeks (laparotomy).
※ This depends on the hospital and person!
Food-related
Water
It's easy to drop stuff if your movements are limited, so using plastic bottles worked out the best.
You can just give any left over to someone else.
Condiments!
Pickled Plum
SALT
Like rice seasonings and stuff.
This depends on your illness. Listen to your doctor.
100 pack
Straws are amazing. Totally genius.
Like from a hundred-yen store.
Plastic mug and utensils.
Didn't use these. The hospital had them (LOL). (Make sure beforehand, though...)
Change of clothes
Pajamas
With front-closure
Pockets come in handy for a lot of things!
Socks
Slippers
Underwear
Towels
in bright colors (because they make me happy)
Travel stuff
Disposable mask
Hand cream
Lip balm
My throat was so dry and in pain because the room was heavily air-conditioned while I was bedridden.
Face Mask
Cleansing towelettes
Face washing sheets
(Life's hard if I don't have these.)
Sleep Stuff
MegRhythm Steam Eye Mask
or
With around-the-clock care, the lights are on at night, and it was so bright...
Electric-heated eye mask
Earplugs
I figured I'd lose them, so I slept better knowing I had spares!
Motivational stuff
Wealth
Charms and miscellaneous gifts from people.
Fan mail from my readers.
Step Counter
(and other support items)
This is encouragement for the rehabilitation after surgery!

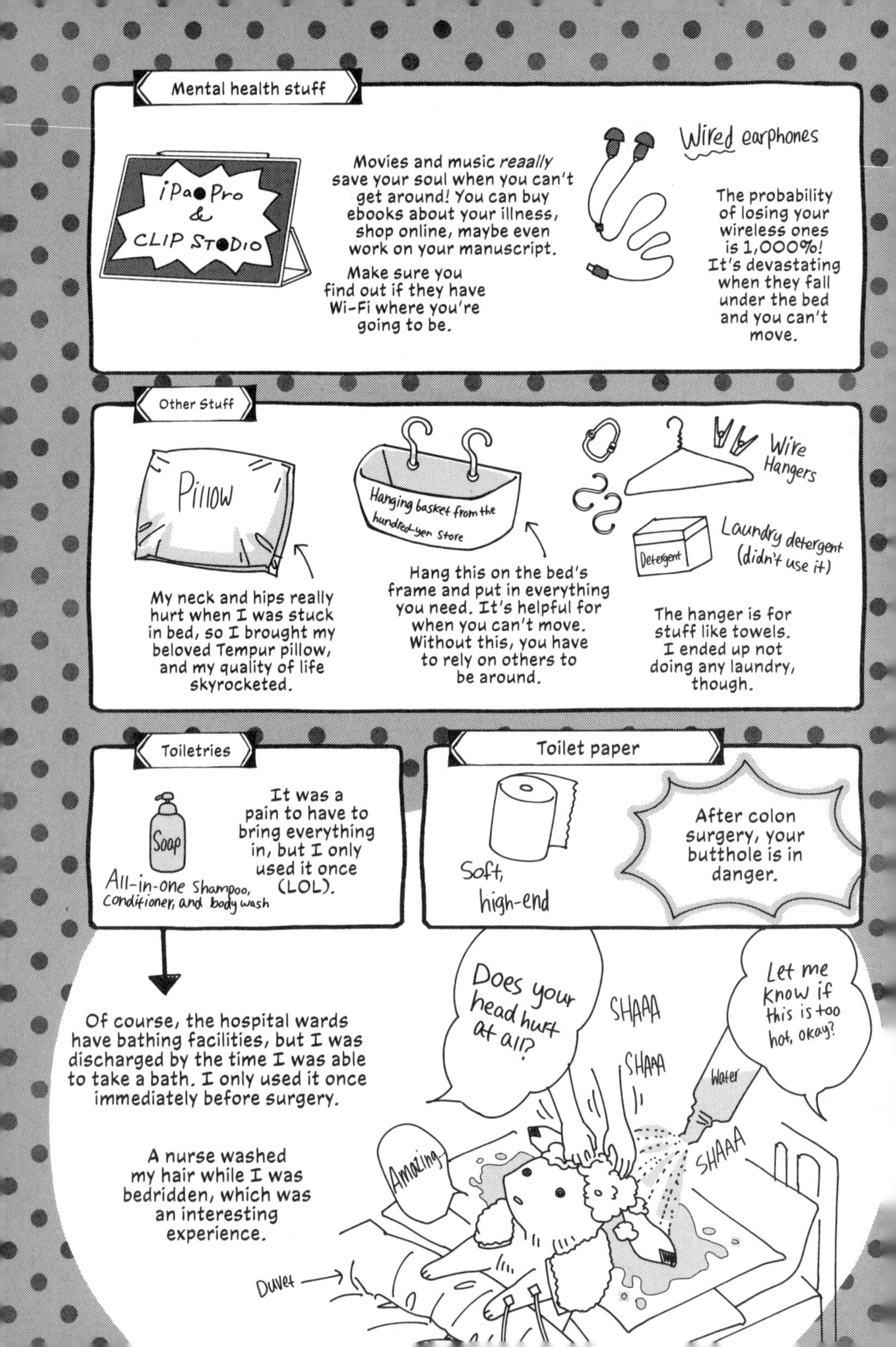

Mental health stuff
Wired earphones
The probability of losing your wireless ones is 1,000%! It's devastating when they fall under the bed and you can't move.
Movies and music reaally save your soul when you can't get around! You can buy ebooks about your illness, shop online, maybe even work on your manuscript.
Make sure you find out if they have Wi-Fi where you're going to be.
iPa● Pro & CLIP ST●DIO
Other Stuff
Wire Hangers
Laundry detergent (didn't use it)
Detergent
The hanger is for stuff like towels. I ended up not doing any laundry, though.
Hanging basket from the hundred-yen store
Hang this on the bed's frame and put in everything you need. It's helpful for when you can't move. Without this, you have to rely on others to be around.
Pillow
My neck and hips really hurt when I was stuck in bed, so I brought my beloved Tempur pillow, and my quality of life skyrocketed.
Toilet paper
After colon surgery, your butthole is in danger.
Soft, high-end
Toiletries
It was a pain to have to bring everything in, but I only used it once (LOL).
Soap
All-in-one shampoo, conditioner, and body wash
Let me know if this is too hot, okay?
Water
SHAAA
SHAAA
SHAAA
Does your head hurt at all?
Amazing...
Of course, the hospital wards have bathing facilities, but I was discharged by the time I was able to take a bath. I only used it once immediately before surgery.
A nurse washed my hair while I was bedridden, which was an interesting experience.
Duvet

I thought I had a Stomachache, but it Was terminal cancer. 5
The time the Story gets a bit heavy.

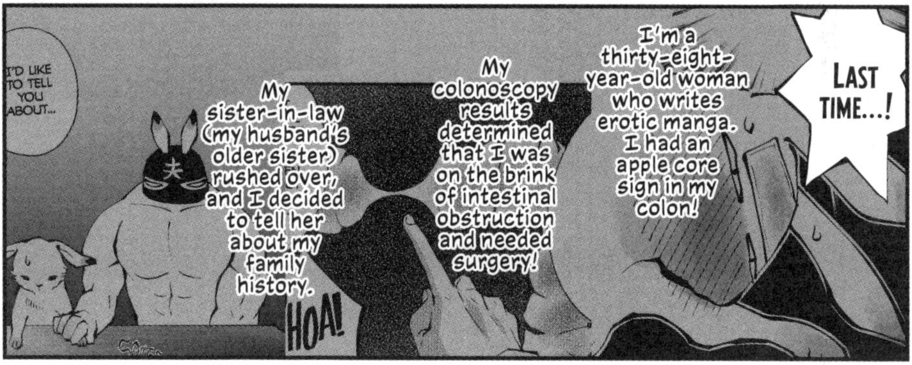
LAST TIME...!
I'm a thirty-eight-year-old woman who writes erotic manga. I had an apple core sign in my colon!
My colonoscopy results determined that I was on the brink of intestinal obstruction and needed surgery!
HOA!
My sister-in-law (my husband's older sister) rushed over, and I decided to tell her about my family history.
I'D LIKE TO TELL YOU ABOUT...

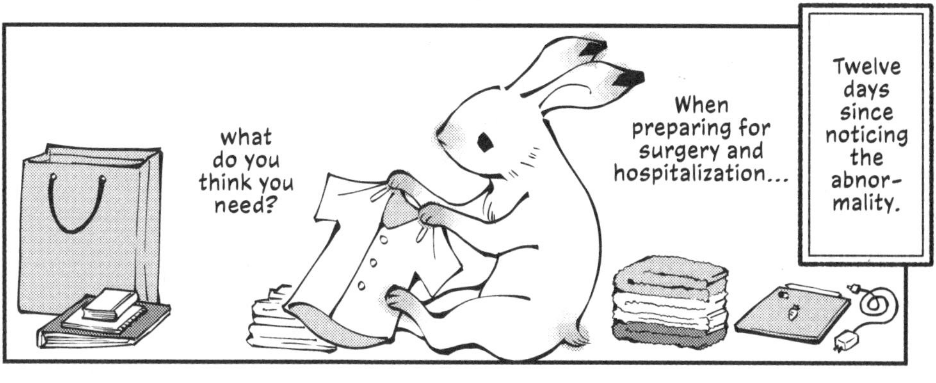
Twelve days since noticing the abnormality.
When preparing for surgery and hospitalization...
what do you think you need?

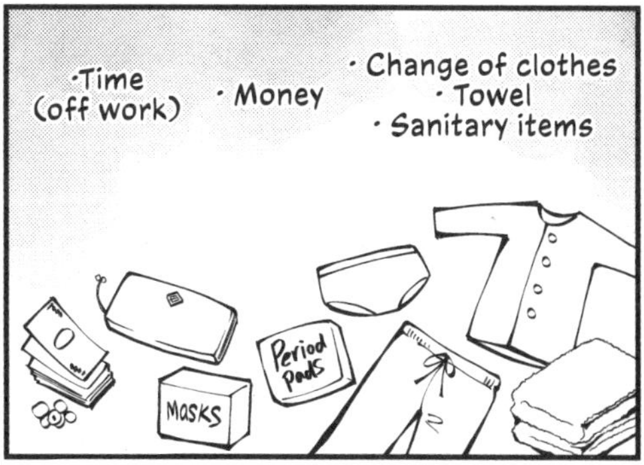
· Change of clothes
· Towel
· Sanitary items
· Money
·Time (off work)
Period Pads
Masks

There's one more thing even more important.

Depending on the person, it could be the most difficult to prepare.

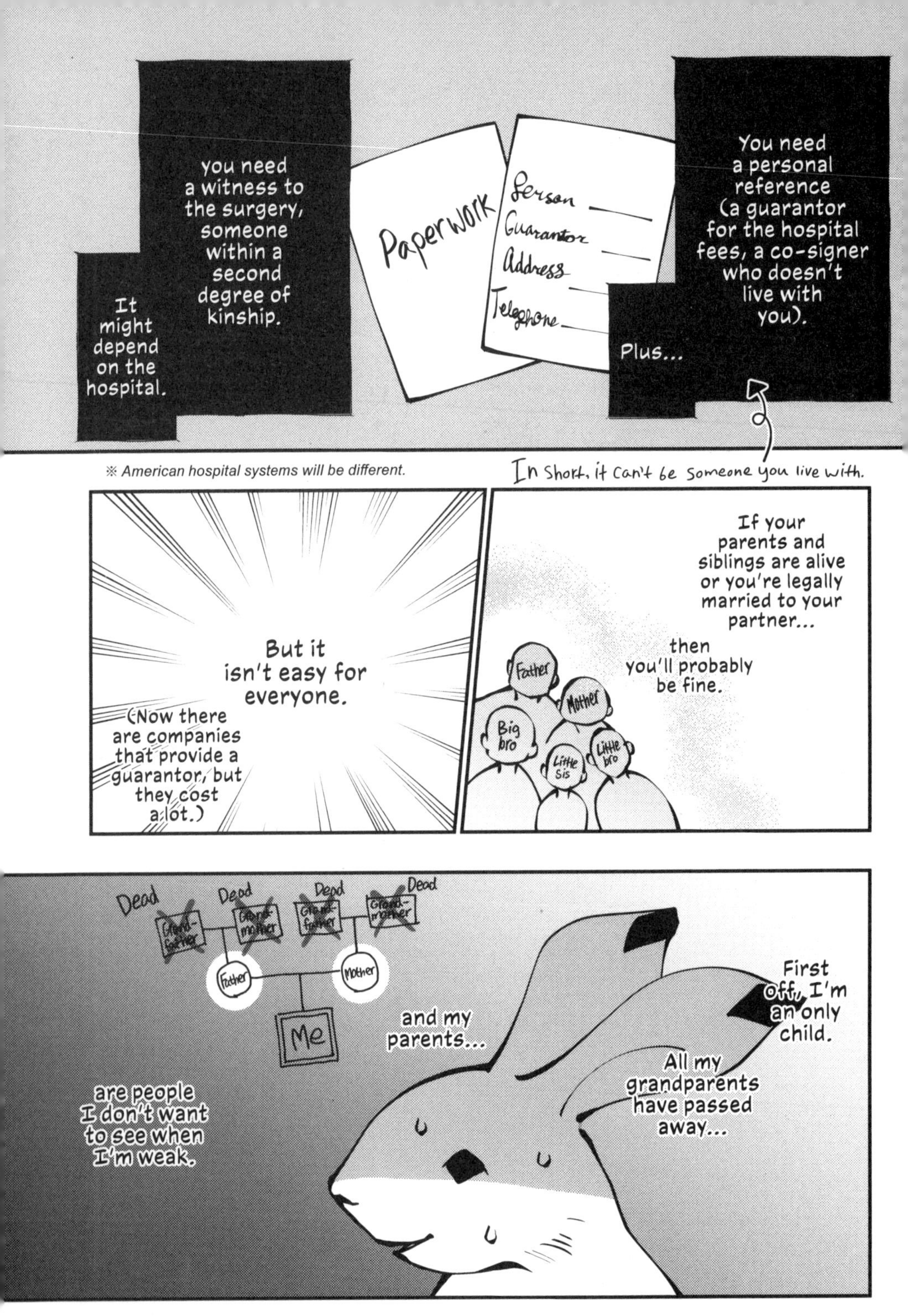
You need a personal reference (a guarantor for the hospital fees, a co-signer who doesn't live with you).
Plus...
Paperwork
Person
Guarantor
Address
Telephone
you need a witness to the surgery, someone within a second degree of kinship.
It might depend on the hospital.
In short, it can't be someone you live with.
※ American hospital systems will be different.
If your parents and siblings are alive or you're legally married to your partner...
then you'll probably be fine.
Father
Mother
Big bro
Little bro
Little sis
But it isn't easy for everyone.
(Now there are companies that provide a guarantor, but they cost a lot.)
First off, I'm an only child.
All my grandparents have passed away...
Dead
Dead
Dead
Dead
Grand-father
Grand-mother
Grand-father
Grand-mother
Father
Mother
Me
and my parents...
are people I don't want to see when I'm weak.

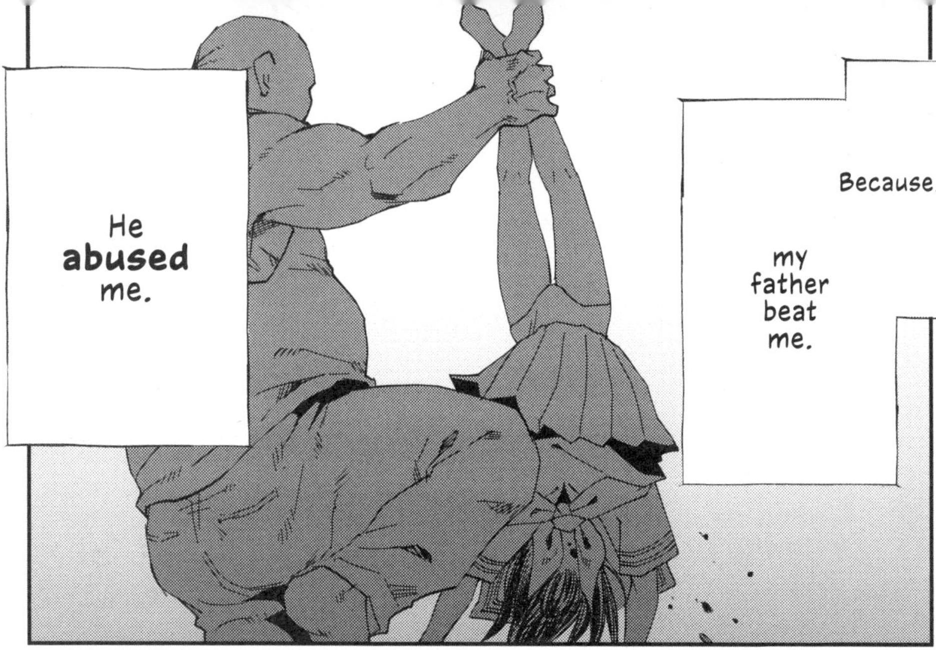
Because...
my father beat me.
He abused me.

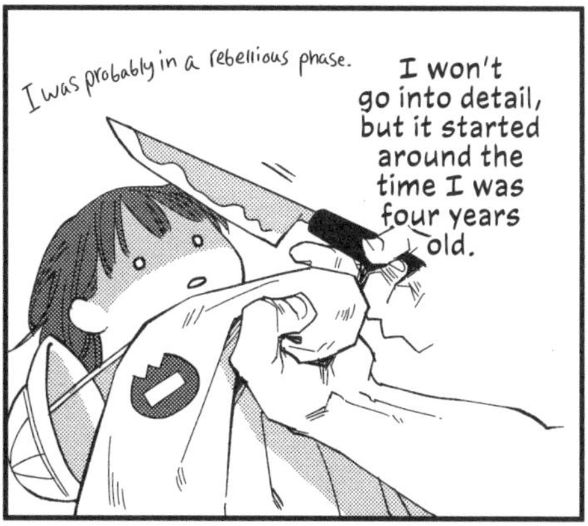
I won't go into detail, but it started around the time I was four years old.
I was probably in a rebellious phase.

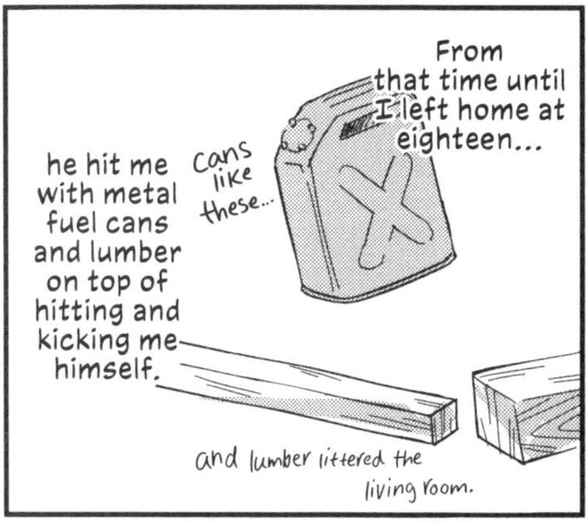
From that time until I left home at eighteen...
he hit me with metal fuel cans and lumber on top of hitting and kicking me himself.
Cans like these...
and lumber littered the living room.

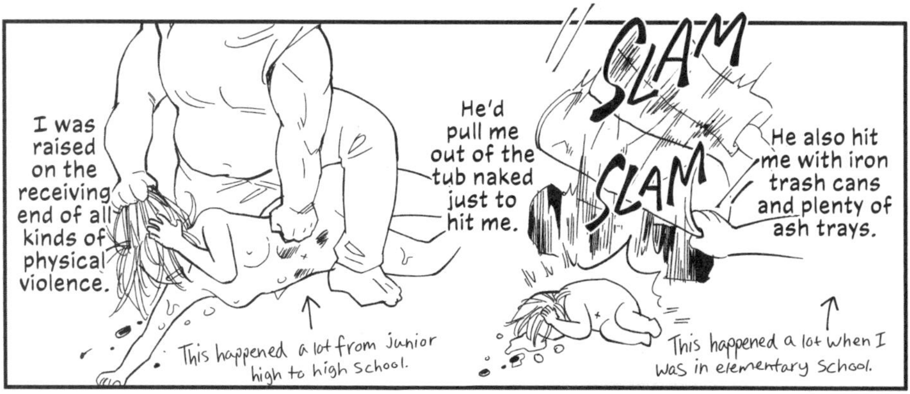
SLAM
SLAM
He also hit me with iron trash cans and plenty of ash trays.
This happened a lot when I was in elementary school.
He'd pull me out of the tub naked just to hit me.
I was raised on the receiving end of all kinds of physical violence.
This happened a lot from junior high to high school.

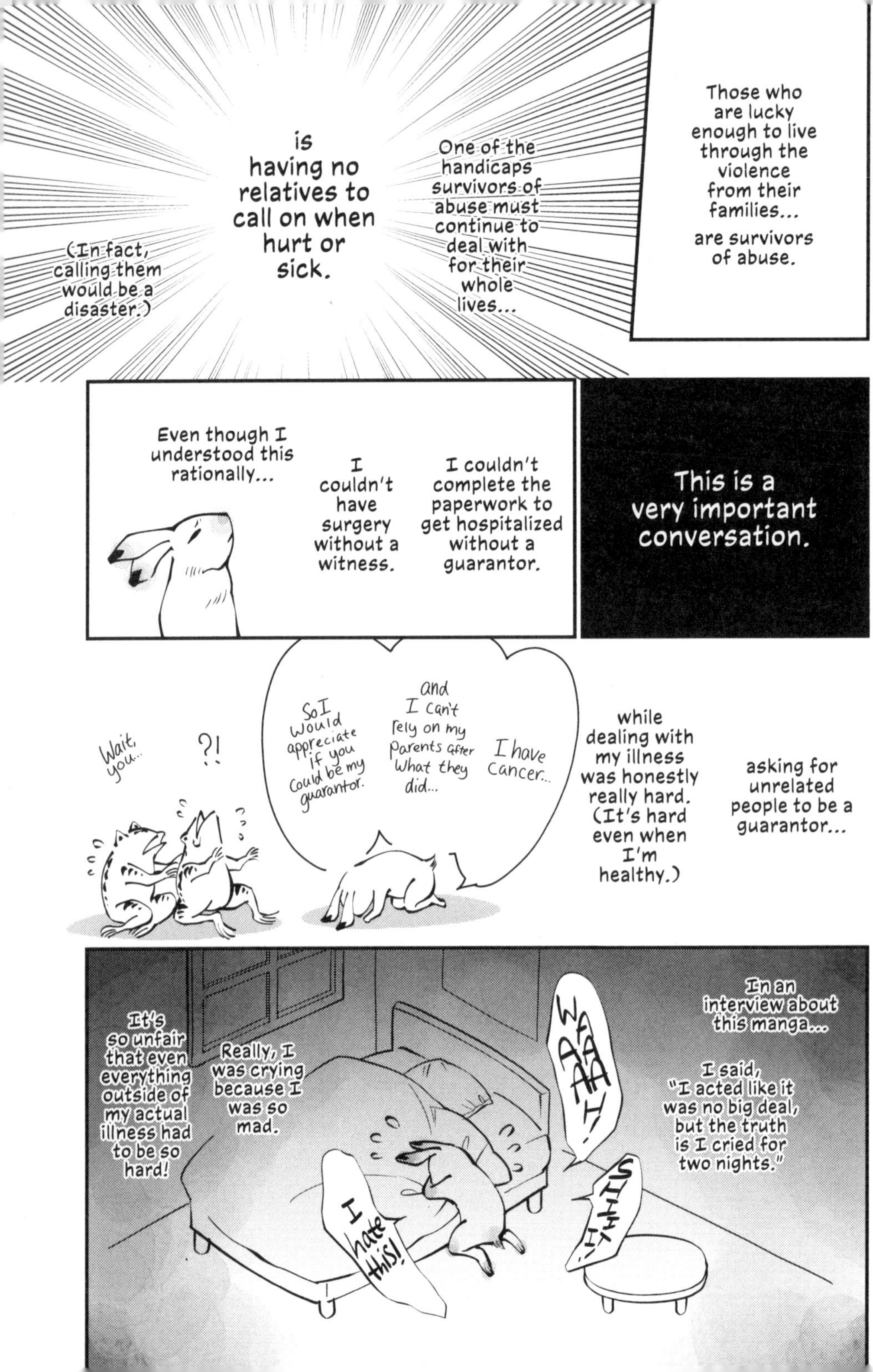
Those who are lucky enough to live through the violence from their families...
are survivors of abuse.
One of the handicaps survivors of abuse must continue to deal with for their whole lives...
is having no relatives to call on when hurt or sick.
(In fact, calling them would be a disaster.)
This is a very important conversation.
I couldn't complete the paperwork to get hospitalized without a guarantor.
I couldn't have surgery without a witness.
Even though I understood this rationally...
asking for unrelated people to be a guarantor...
while dealing with my illness was honestly really hard. (It's hard even when I'm healthy.)
I have cancer...
and I can't rely on my parents after what they did...
So I would appreciate if you could be my guarantor.
?!
Wait, you...
In an interview about this manga...
I said, "I acted like it was no big deal, but the truth is I cried for two nights."
I hate this!
Really, I was crying because I was so mad.
It's so unfair that even everything outside of my actual illness had to be so hard!

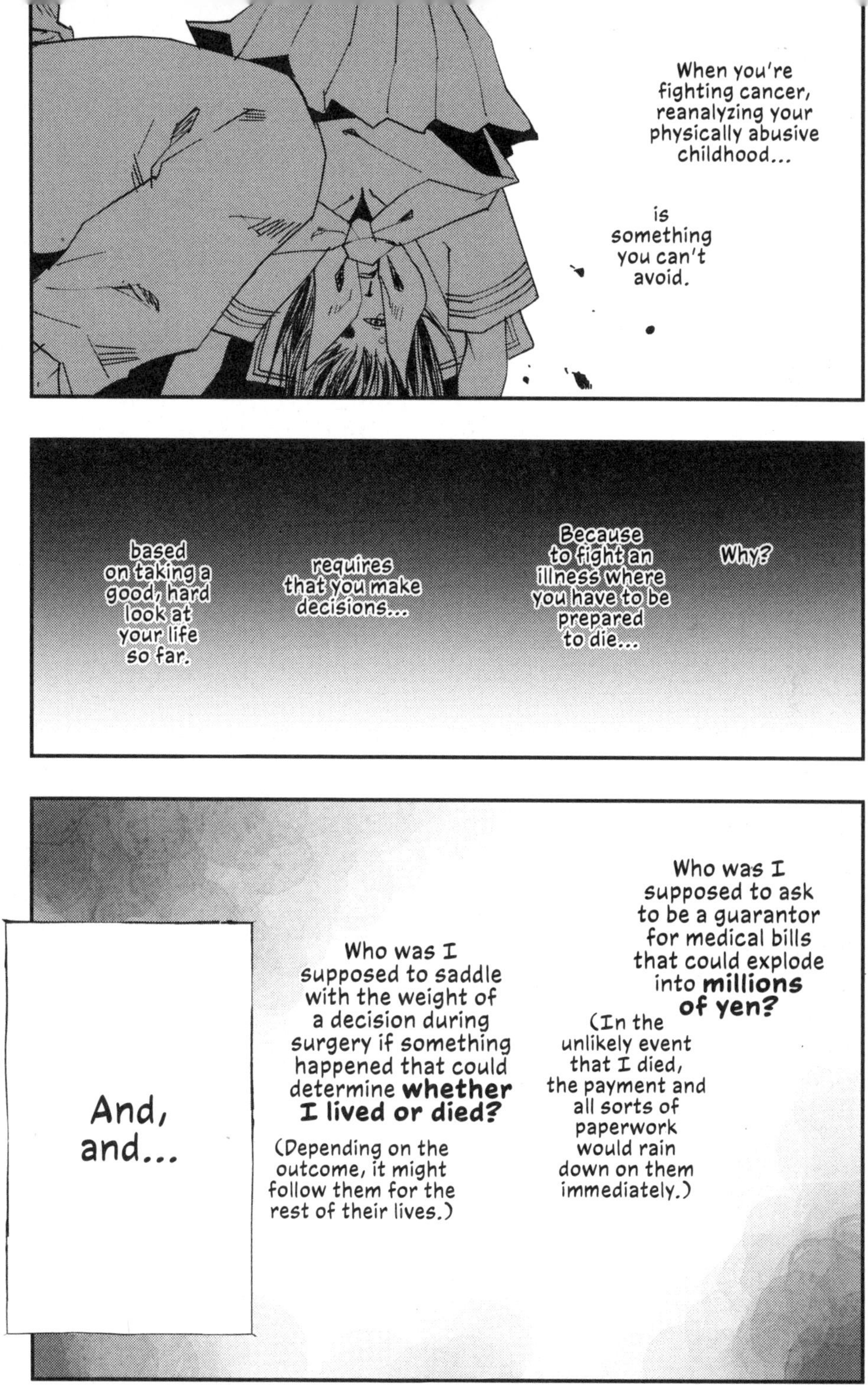
When you're fighting cancer, reanalyzing your physically abusive childhood...
is something you can't avoid.
Why?
Because to fight an illness where you have to be prepared to die...
requires that you make decisions...
based on taking a good, hard look at your life so far.
Who was I supposed to ask to be a guarantor for medical bills that could explode into **millions of yen?**
(In the unlikely event that I died, the payment and all sorts of paperwork would rain down on them immediately.)
Who was I supposed to saddle with the weight of a decision during surgery if something happened that could determine **whether I lived or died?**
(Depending on the outcome, it might follow them for the rest of their lives.)
And, and...

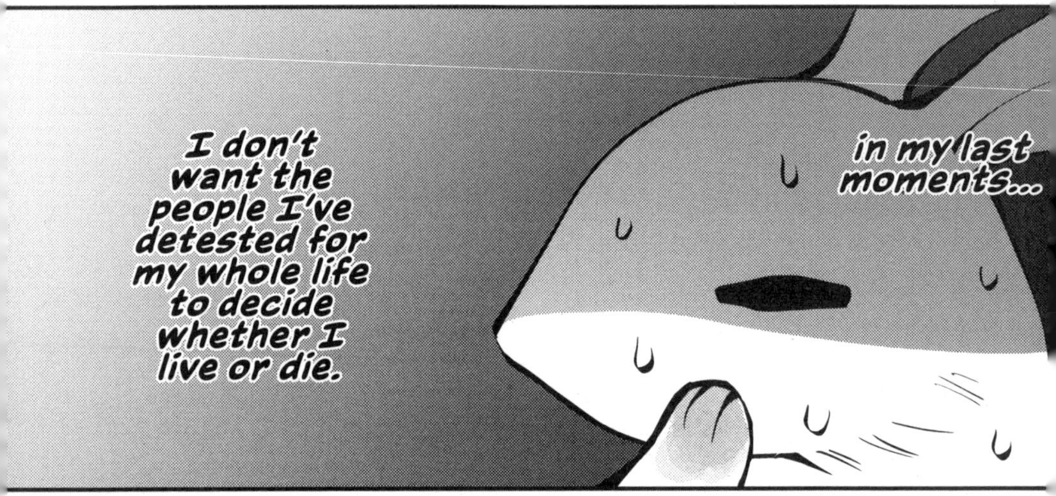
in my last moments...
I don't want the people I've detested for my whole life to decide whether I live or die.

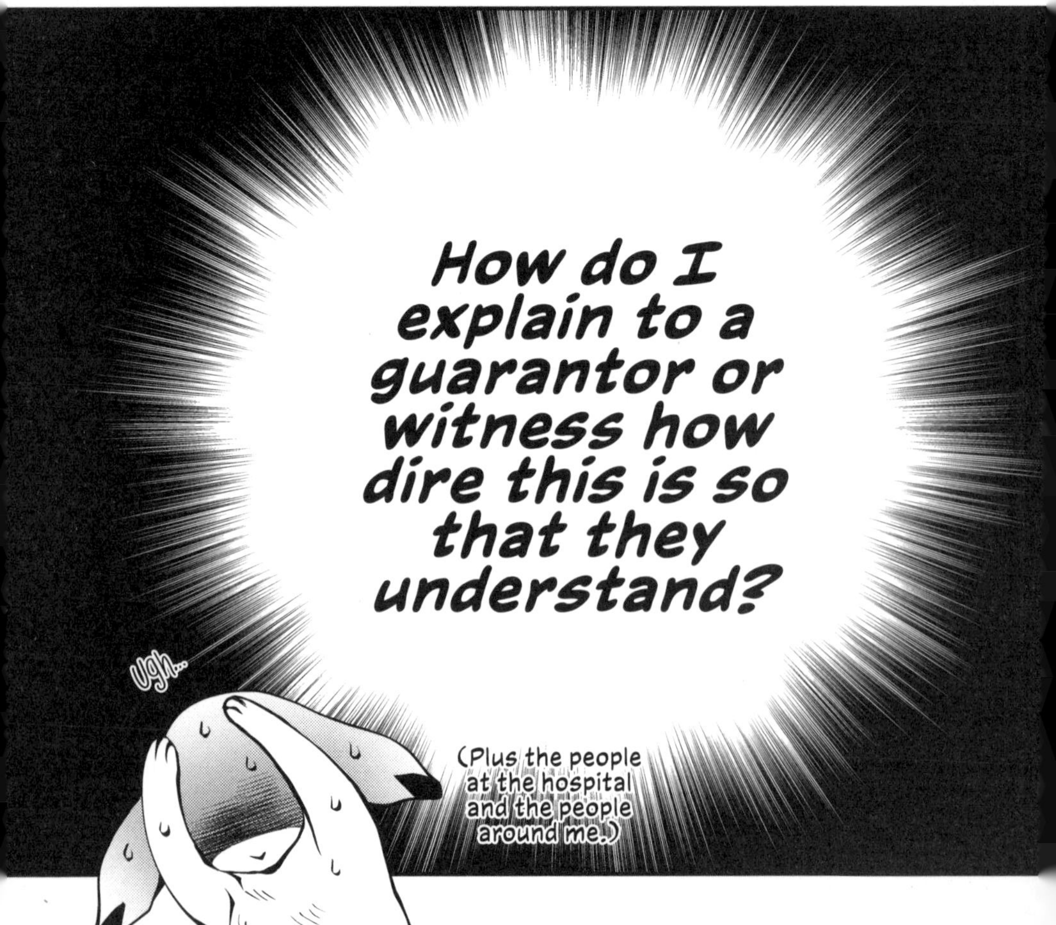
How do I explain to a guarantor or witness how dire this is so that they understand?
Ugh...
(Plus the people at the hospital and the people around me.)

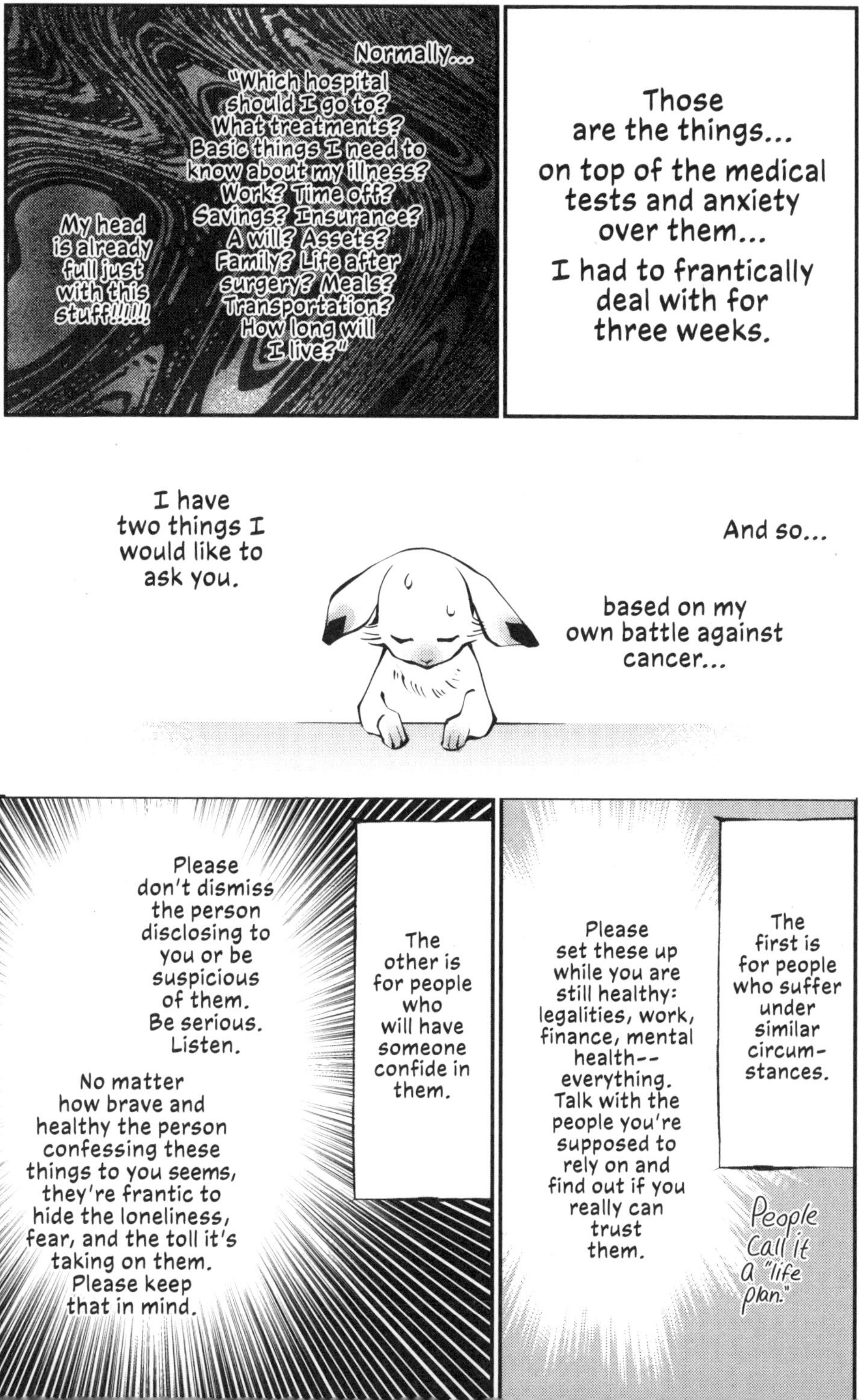
Those are the things...
on top of the medical tests and anxiety over them...
I had to frantically deal with for three weeks.
Normally...
"Which hospital should I go to? What treatments? Basic things I need to know about my illness? Work? Time off? Savings? Insurance? A will? Assets? Family? Life after surgery? Meals? Transportation? How long will I live?"
My head is already full just with this stuff!!!!!!
And so...
based on my own battle against cancer...
I have two things I would like to ask you.
The first is for people who suffer under similar circum-stances.
Please set these up while you are still healthy: legalities, work, finance, mental health--everything. Talk with the people you're supposed to rely on and find out if you really can trust them.
People call it a "life plan."
The other is for people who will have someone confide in them.
Please don't dismiss the person disclosing to you or be suspicious of them. Be serious. Listen.
No matter how brave and healthy the person confessing these things to you seems, they're frantic to hide the loneliness, fear, and the toll it's taking on them. Please keep that in mind.

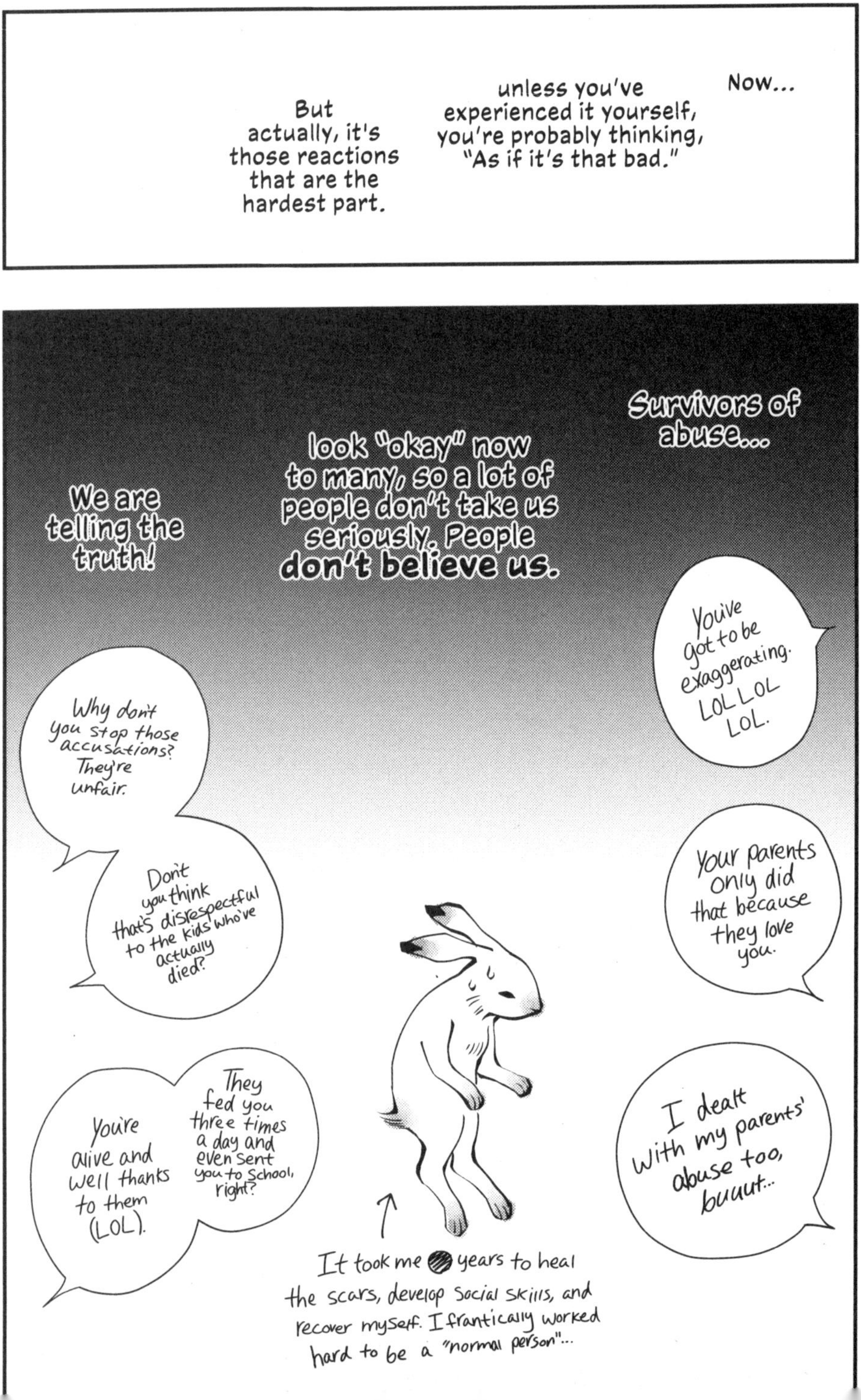

Now...
unless you've experienced it yourself, you're probably thinking, "As if it's that bad."
But actually, it's those reactions that are the hardest part.
Survivors of abuse...
look "okay" now to many, so a lot of people don't take us seriously. People don't believe us.
We are telling the truth!
You've got to be exaggerating. LOL LOL LOL.
Why don't you stop those accusations? They're unfair.
Don't you think that's disrespectful to the kids who've actually died?
Your parents only did that because they love you.
I dealt with my parents' abuse too, buuut...
They fed you three times a day and even sent you to school, right?
You're alive and well thanks to them (LOL).
It took me [redacted] years to heal the scars, develop social skills, and recover myself. I frantically worked hard to be a "normal person"...

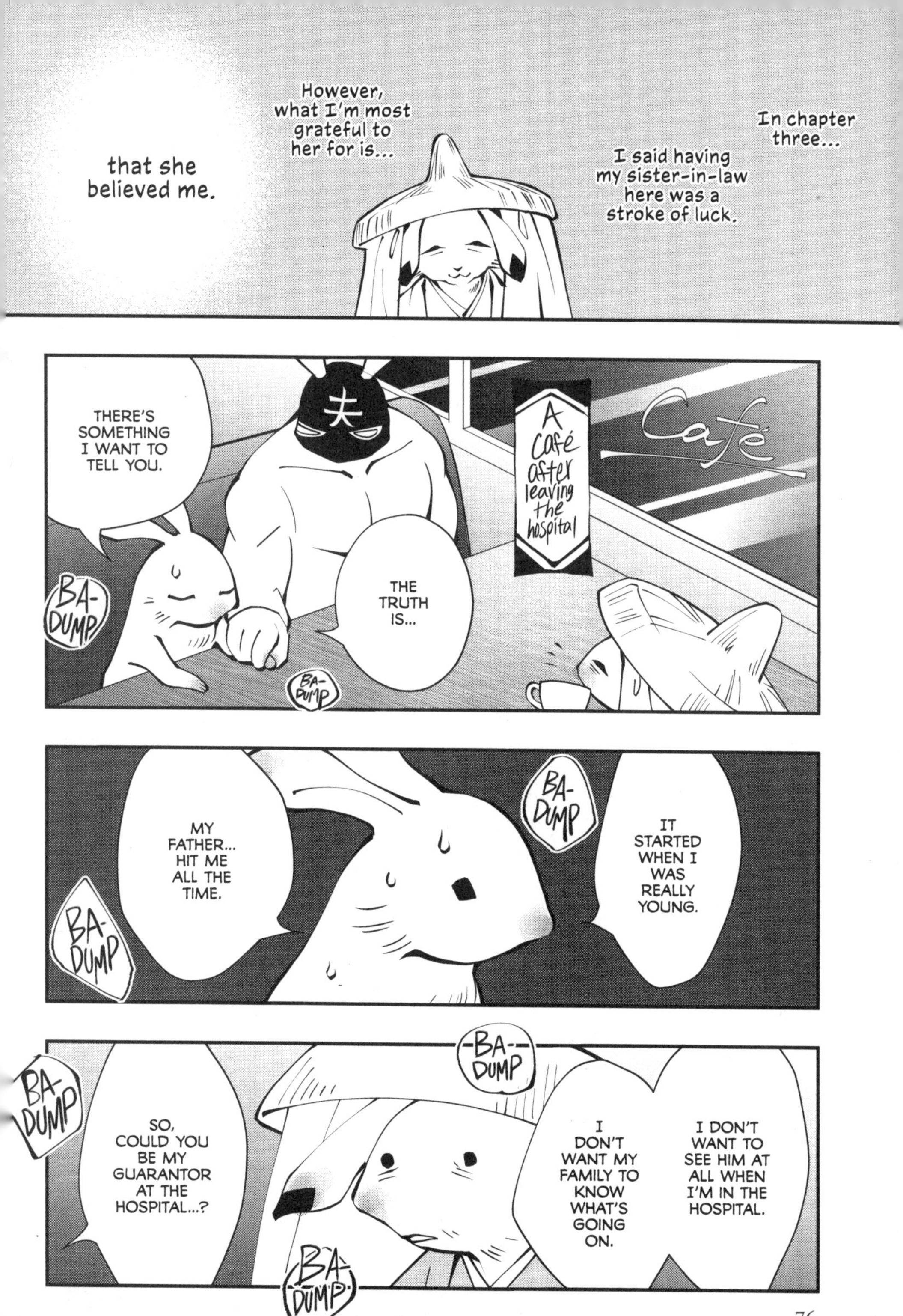

In chapter three...
I said having my sister-in-law here was a stroke of luck.
However, what I'm most grateful to her for is...
that she believed me.
Café
A café after leaving the hospital
THERE'S SOMETHING I WANT TO TELL YOU.
THE TRUTH IS...
BA-DUMP
BA-DUMP
BA-DUMP
IT STARTED WHEN I WAS REALLY YOUNG.
MY FATHER... HIT ME ALL THE TIME.
BA-DUMP
BA-DUMP
I DON'T WANT TO SEE HIM AT ALL WHEN I'M IN THE HOSPITAL.
I DON'T WANT MY FAMILY TO KNOW WHAT'S GOING ON.
SO, COULD YOU BE MY GUARANTOR AT THE HOSPITAL...?
BA-DUMP
BA-DUMP

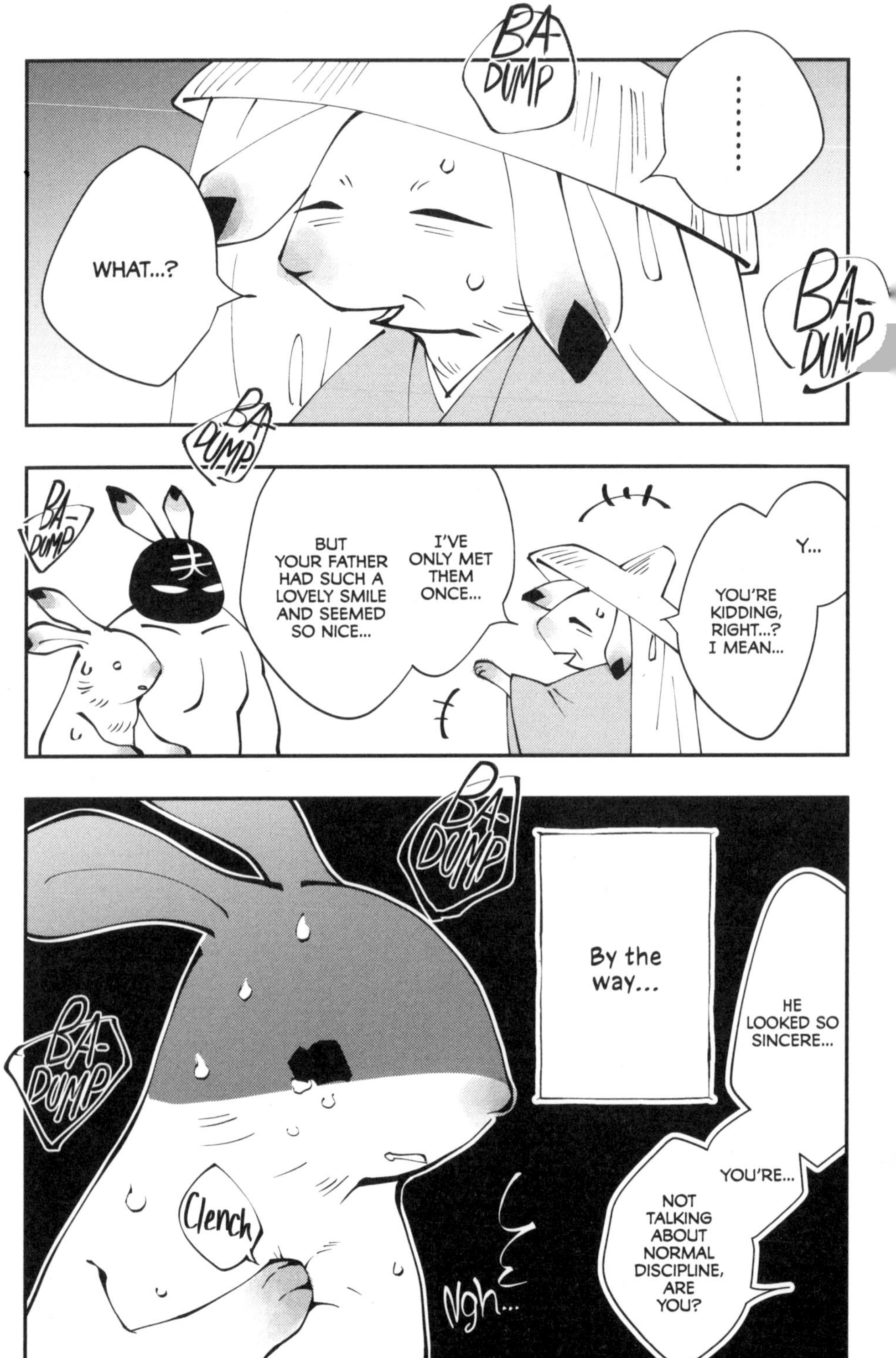
BA-DUMP
......
BA-DUMP
WHAT...?
BA-DUMP
Y... YOU'RE KIDDING, RIGHT...? I MEAN...
I'VE ONLY MET THEM ONCE...
BUT YOUR FATHER HAD SUCH A LOVELY SMILE AND SEEMED SO NICE...
BA-DUMP
BA-DUMP
By the way...
HE LOOKED SO SINCERE...
YOU'RE...
NOT TALKING ABOUT NORMAL DISCIPLINE, ARE YOU?
Ngh...
Clench
BA-DUMP

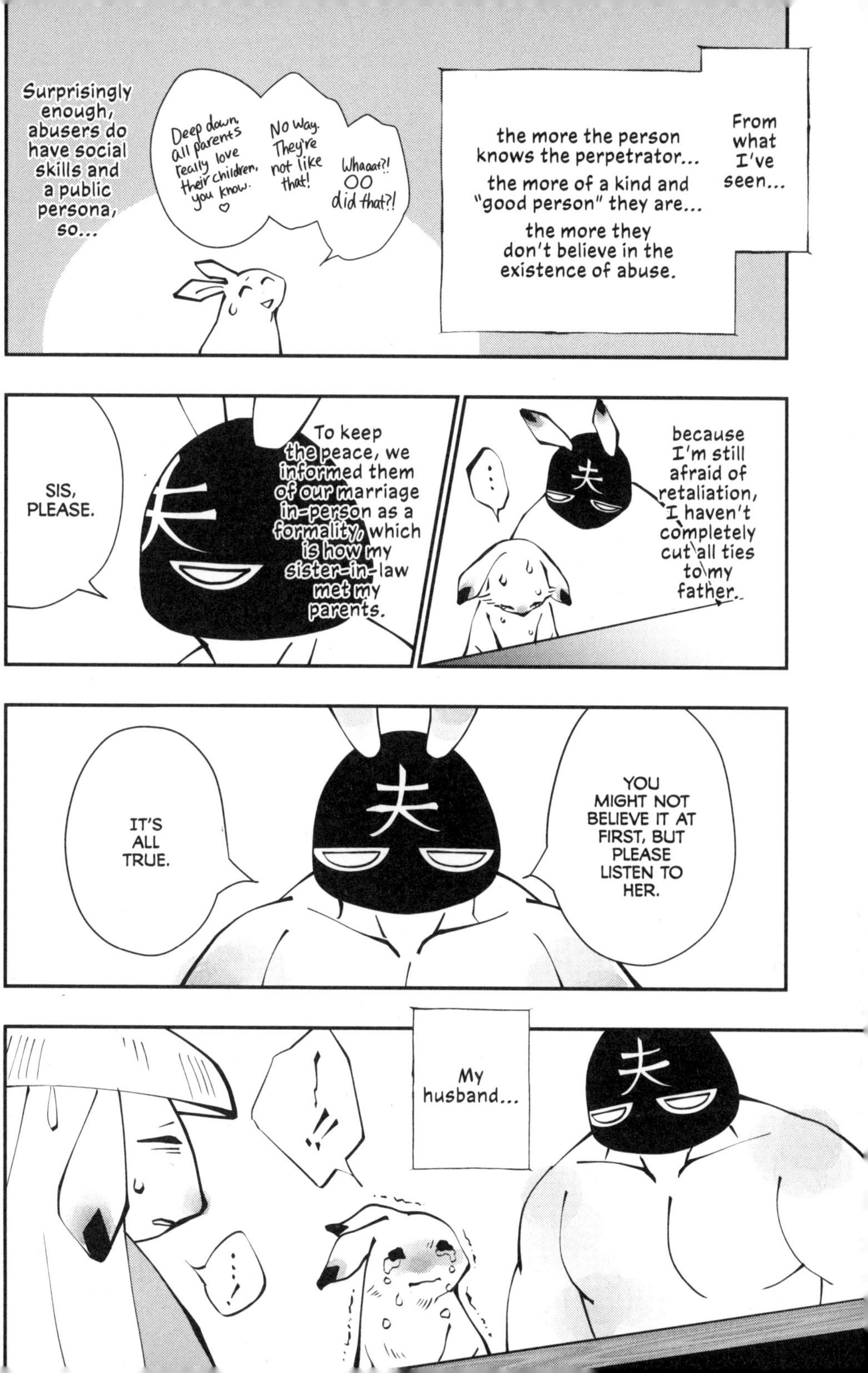
From what I've seen...
the more the person knows the perpetrator... the more of a kind and "good person" they are... the more they don't believe in the existence of abuse.
Whaaat?! OO did that?!
No Way. They're not like that!
Deep down, all parents really love their children, you know. ♡
Surprisingly enough, abusers do have social skills and a public persona, so...
because I'm still afraid of retaliation, I haven't completely cut all ties to my father.
...
To keep the peace, we informed them of our marriage in-person as a formality, which is how my sister-in-law met my parents.
SIS, PLEASE.
YOU MIGHT NOT BELIEVE IT AT FIRST, BUT PLEASE LISTEN TO HER.
IT'S ALL TRUE.
My husband...
!!
...!

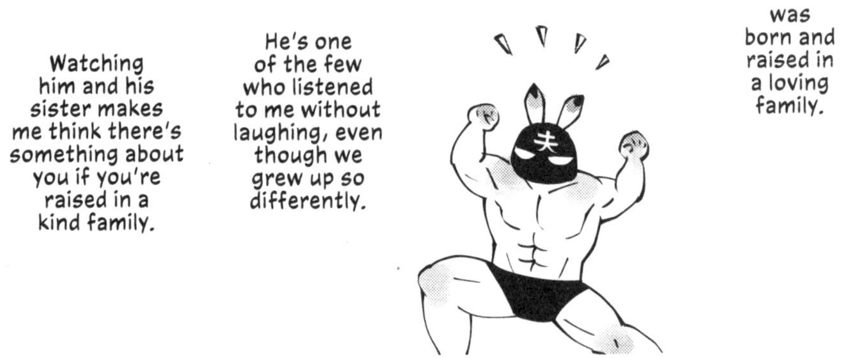
was born and raised in a loving family.
He's one of the few who listened to me without laughing, even though we grew up so differently.
Watching him and his sister makes me think there's something about you if you're raised in a kind family.
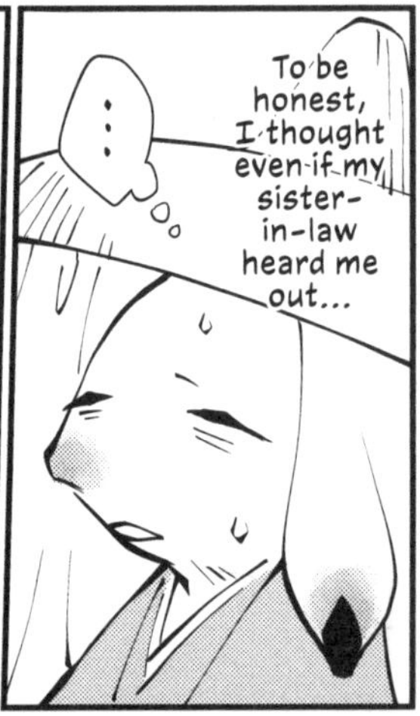
To be honest, I thought even if my sister-in-law heard me out...
...
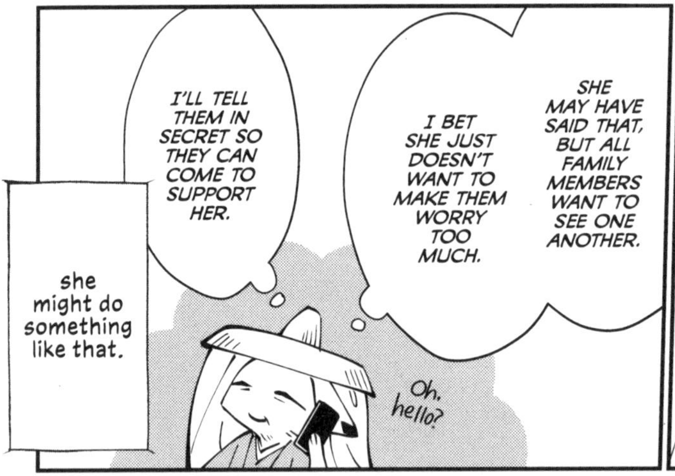
SHE MAY HAVE SAID THAT, BUT ALL FAMILY MEMBERS WANT TO SEE ONE ANOTHER.
I BET SHE JUST DOESN'T WANT TO MAKE THEM WORRY TOO MUCH.
I'LL TELL THEM IN SECRET SO THEY CAN COME TO SUPPORT HER.
she might do something like that.
Oh, hello?
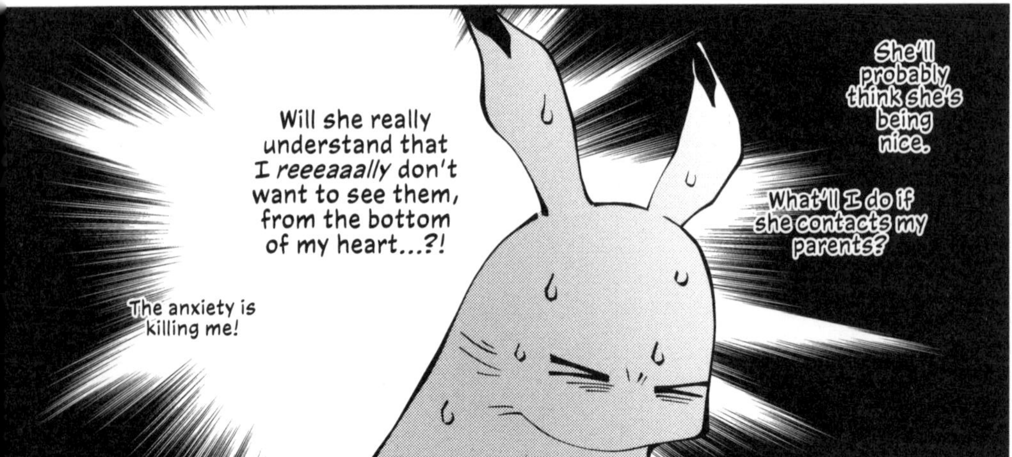
She'll probably think she's being nice.
What'll I do if she contacts my parents?
Will she really understand that I *reeeaaally* don't want to see them, from the bottom of my heart...?!
The anxiety is killing me!

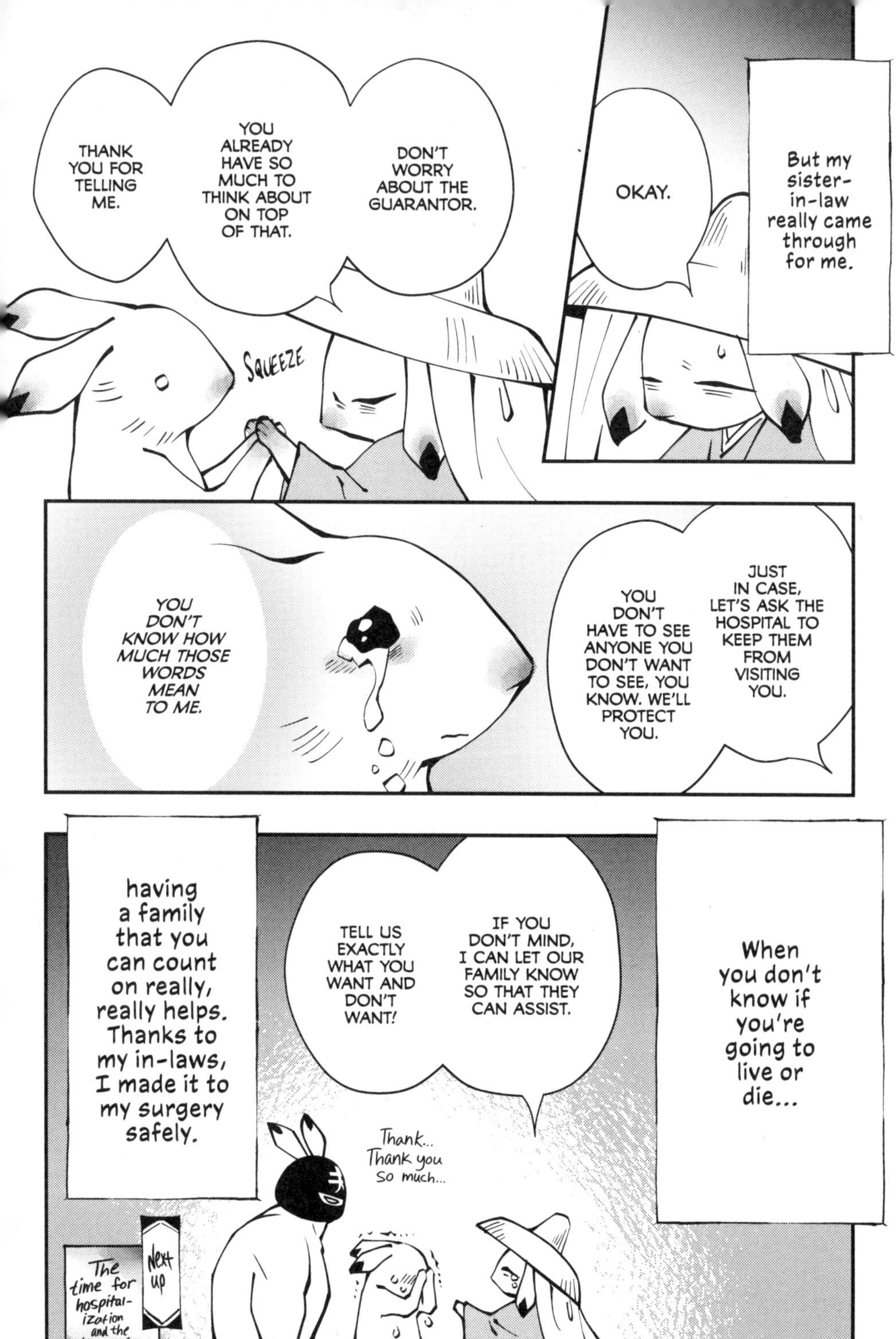
But my sister-in-law really came through for me.
OKAY.
DON'T WORRY ABOUT THE GUARANTOR.
YOU ALREADY HAVE SO MUCH TO THINK ABOUT ON TOP OF THAT.
THANK YOU FOR TELLING ME.
SQUEEZE
JUST IN CASE, LET'S ASK THE HOSPITAL TO KEEP THEM FROM VISITING YOU.
YOU DON'T HAVE TO SEE ANYONE YOU DON'T WANT TO SEE, YOU KNOW. WE'LL PROTECT YOU.
YOU DON'T KNOW HOW MUCH THOSE WORDS MEAN TO ME.
When you don't know if you're going to live or die...
IF YOU DON'T MIND, I CAN LET OUR FAMILY KNOW SO THAT THEY CAN ASSIST.
TELL US EXACTLY WHAT YOU WANT AND DON'T WANT!
having a family that you can count on really, really helps. Thanks to my in-laws, I made it to my surgery safely.
Thank... Thank you so much...
Next up
The time for hospitalization and the diagnosis.

I'm a Terminal
Cancer
Patient
BUT I'M FINE

I thought I had a stomachache, but it was terminal cancer. ⑥
The time for hospitalization and the diagnosis.

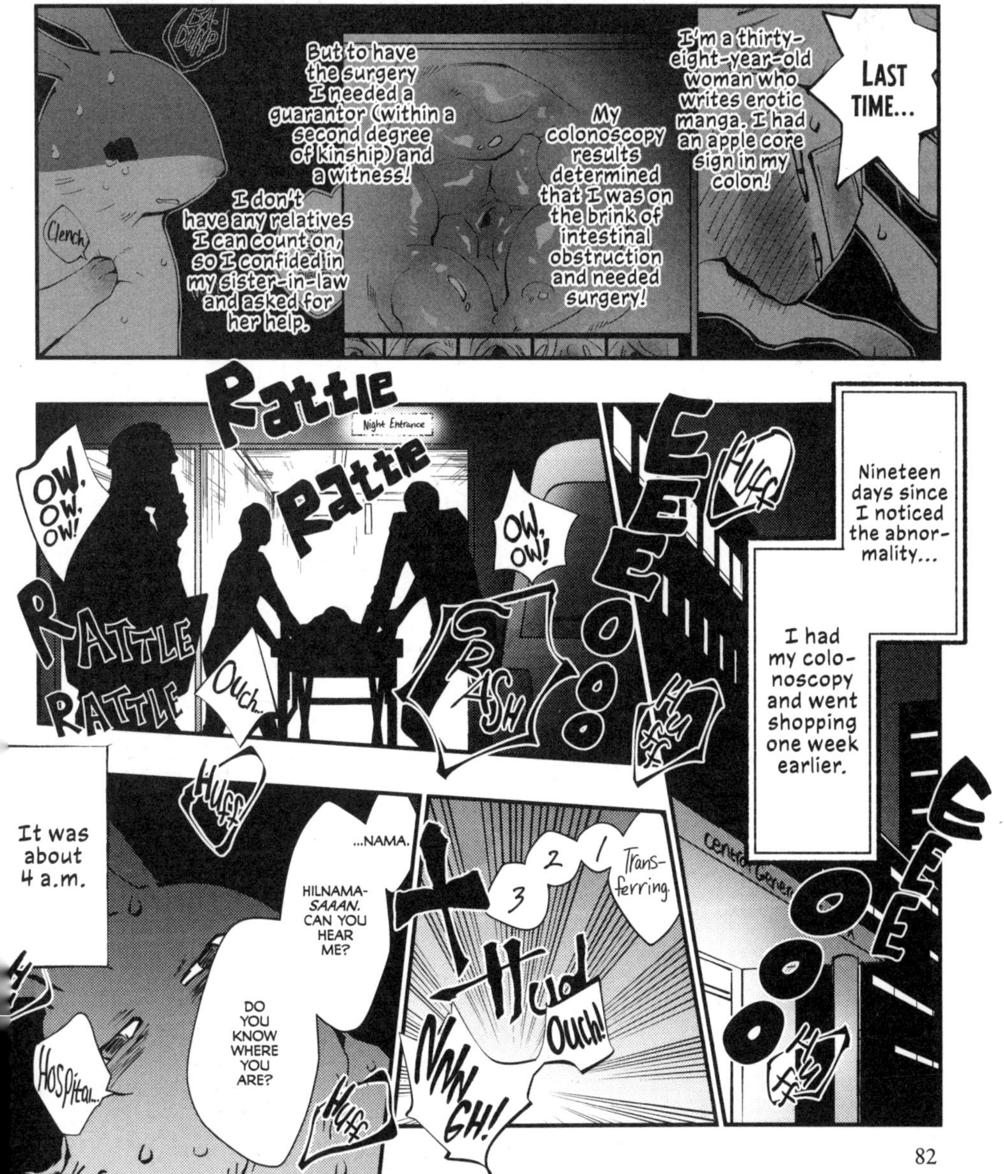

LAST TIME...
I'm a thirty-eight-year-old woman who writes erotic manga. I had an apple core sign in my colon!
My colonoscopy results determined that I was on the brink of intestinal obstruction and needed surgery!
But to have the surgery I needed a guarantor (within a second degree of kinship) and a witness!
I don't have any relatives I can count on, so I confided in my sister-in-law and asked for her help.
BA-DUMP
Clench
Nineteen days since I noticed the abnormality...
I had my colonoscopy and went shopping one week earlier.
EEEOOO
Huff
Huff
Rattle Rattle
Night Entrance
OW, OW!
CRASH
OW, OW, OW!
RATTLE RATTLE
Ouch...
EEEOOO
Huff
1 2 3
Transferring.
Ouch!
NNNGH!
...NAMA.
HILNAMA-SAAAN. CAN YOU HEAR ME?
DO YOU KNOW WHERE YOU ARE?
Huff
Huff
Hospital...
It was about 4 a.m.

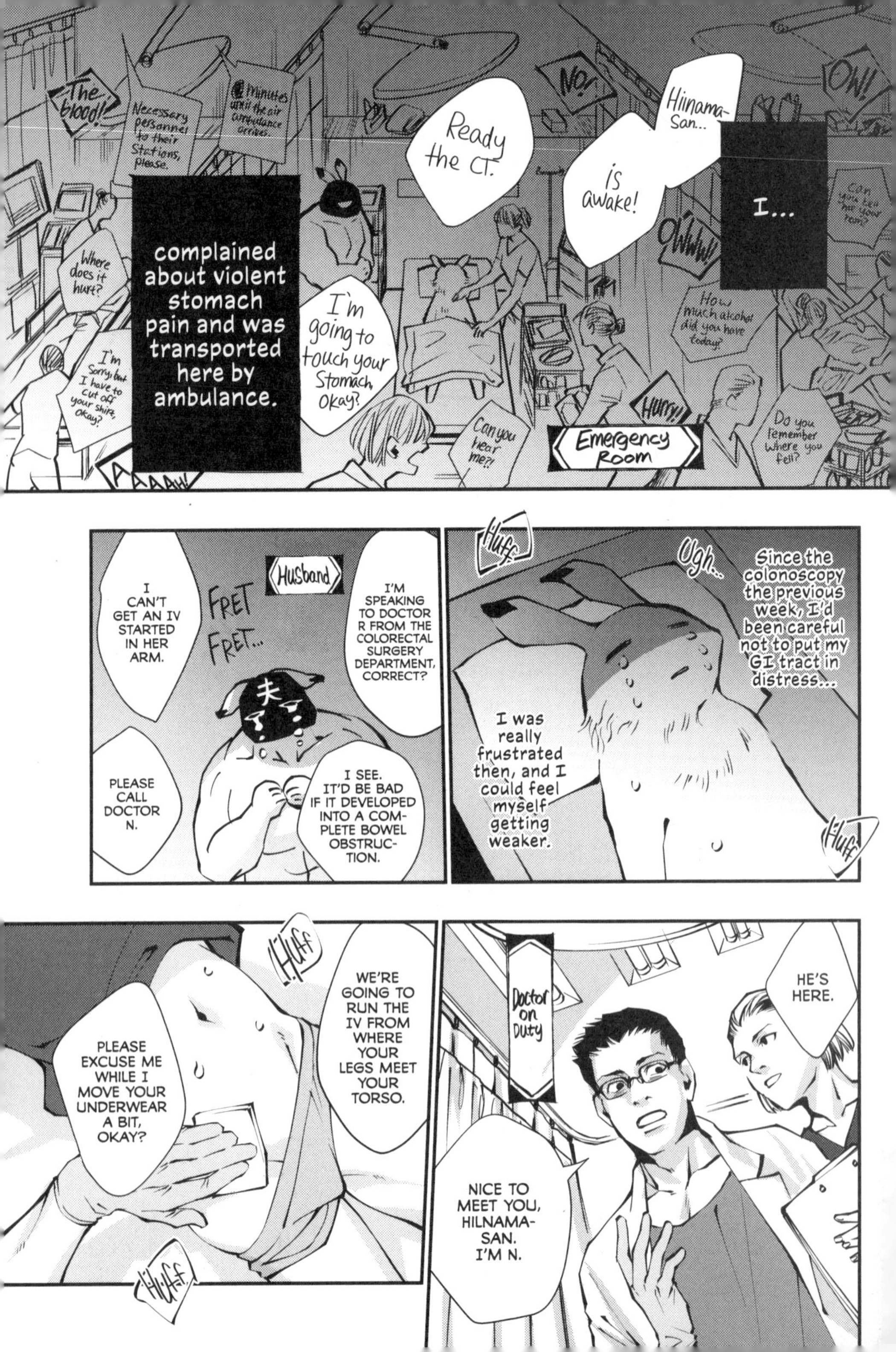
OW!
Hiinama-San...
is awake!
I...
Can you tell me your name?
Ready the CT.
NO!
OWWW!
How much alcohol did you have today?
Do you remember where you fell?
HURRY!
Emergency Room
Can you hear me?!
I'm going to touch your Stomach, Okay?
Minutes until the air ambulance arrives.
complained about violent stomach pain and was transported here by ambulance.
Necessary personnel to their Stations, please.
The blood!
Where does it hurt?
I'm Sorry, but I have to cut off your Shirt, okay?
AAAAH!
Huff
Ugh...
Since the colonoscopy the previous week, I'd been careful not to put my GI tract in distress...
I was really frustrated then, and I could feel myself getting weaker.
Huff
Husband
I'M SPEAKING TO DOCTOR R FROM THE COLORECTAL SURGERY DEPARTMENT, CORRECT?
I CAN'T GET AN IV STARTED IN HER ARM.
FRET FRET...
夫
I SEE. IT'D BE BAD IF IT DEVELOPED INTO A COMPLETE BOWEL OBSTRUCTION.
PLEASE CALL DOCTOR N.
HE'S HERE.
Doctor on Duty
NICE TO MEET YOU, HILNAMA-SAN. I'M N.
Huff
WE'RE GOING TO RUN THE IV FROM WHERE YOUR LEGS MEET YOUR TORSO.
PLEASE EXCUSE ME WHILE I MOVE YOUR UNDERWEAR A BIT, OKAY?
Huff

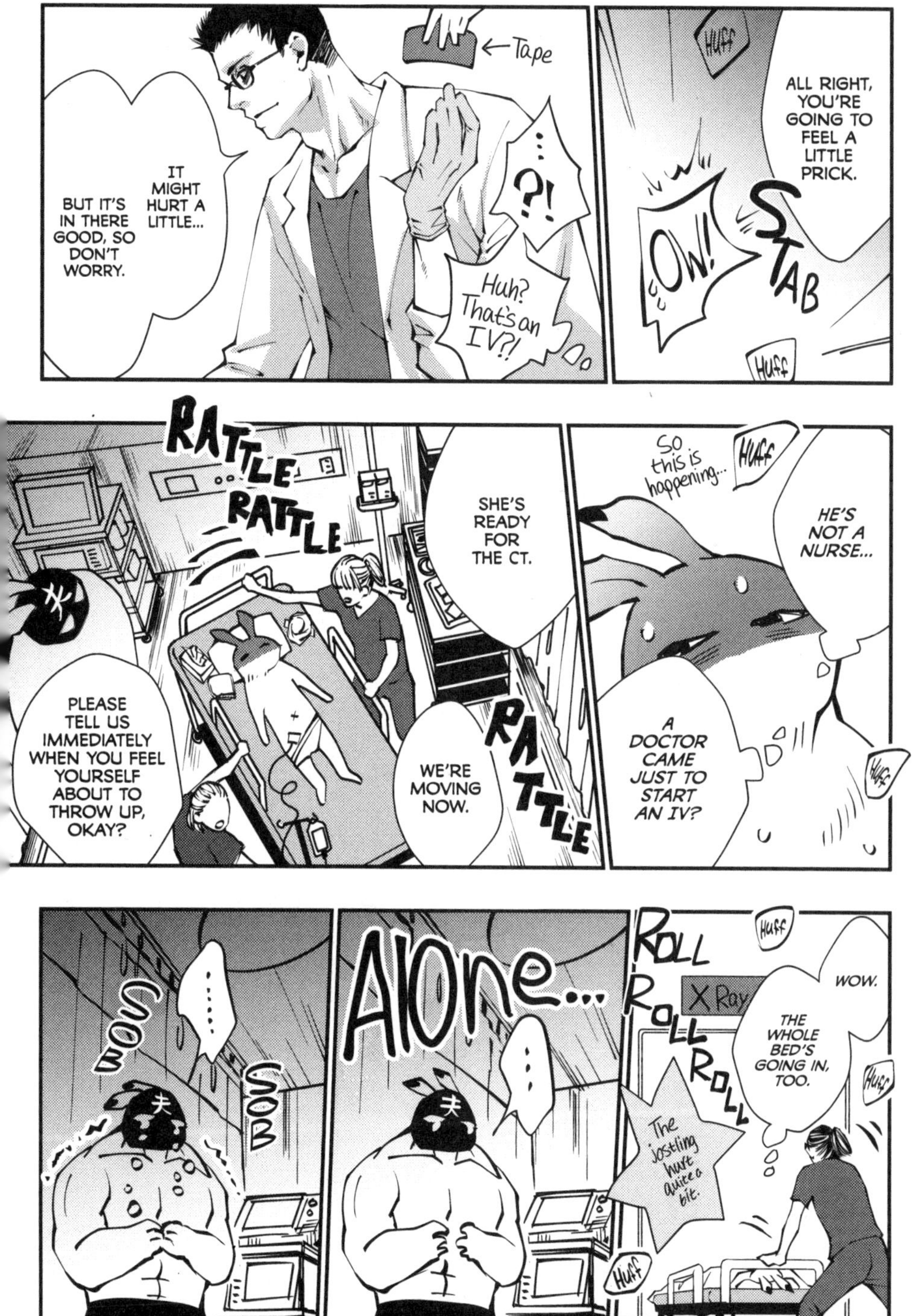
Huff
ALL RIGHT, YOU'RE GOING TO FEEL A LITTLE PRICK.
STAB
OW!
Huff
← Tape
...?!
Huh? That's an IV?!
IT MIGHT HURT A LITTLE...
BUT IT'S IN THERE GOOD, SO DON'T WORRY.
Huff
So this is happening...
HE'S NOT A NURSE...
A DOCTOR CAME JUST TO START AN IV?
Huff
RATTLE RATTLE
SHE'S READY FOR THE CT.
RATTLE
WE'RE MOVING NOW.
PLEASE TELL US IMMEDIATELY WHEN YOU FEEL YOURSELF ABOUT TO THROW UP, OKAY?
Huff
WOW.
THE WHOLE BED'S GOING IN, TOO.
ROLL ROLL ROLL
X Ray
Huff
The jostling hurt quite a bit.
Huff
Alone...
...
......
SOB
SOB

They wheel the bed in, just like a drive-through. Amazing!

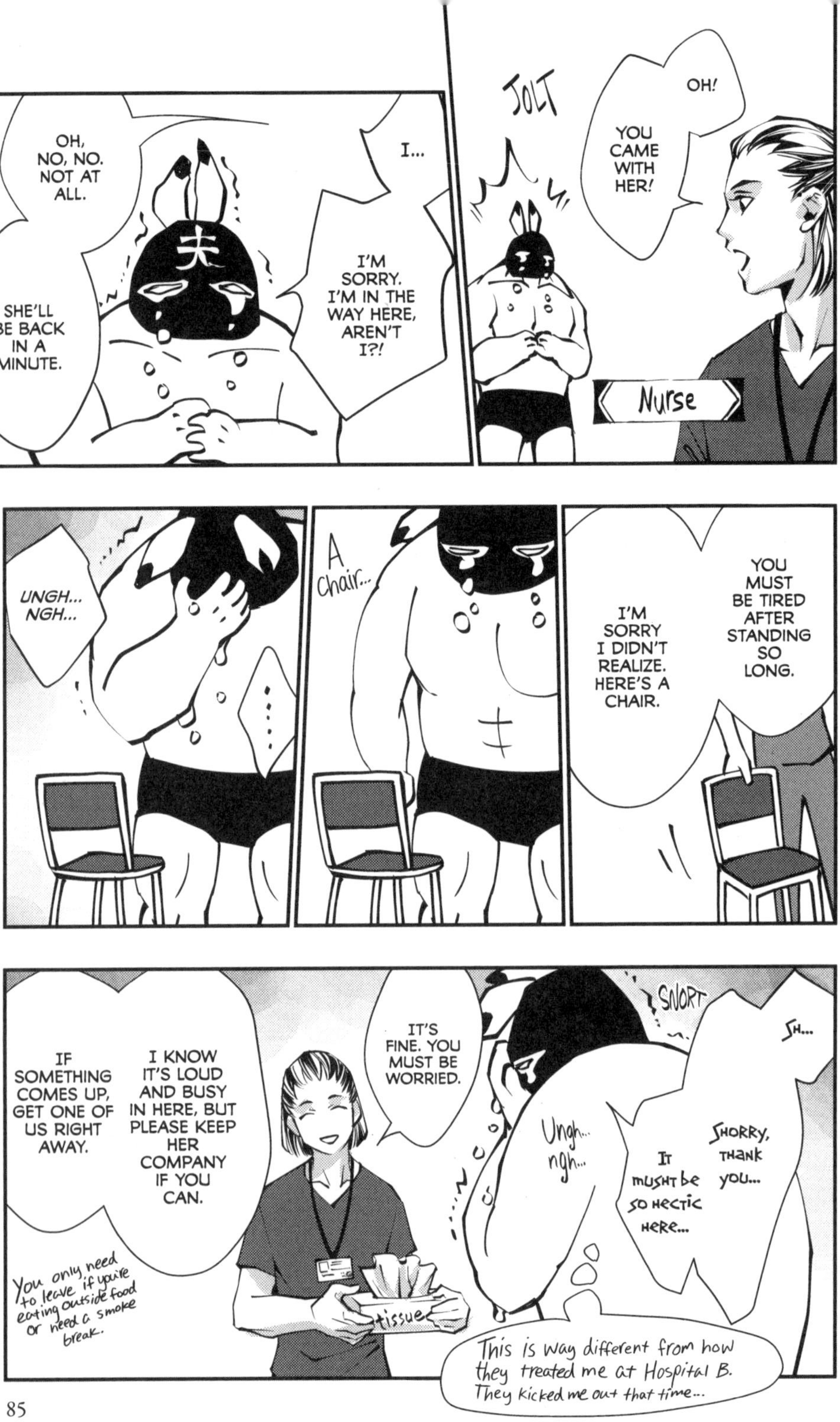
JOLT
OH!
YOU CAME WITH HER!
Nurse
I...
I'M SORRY. I'M IN THE WAY HERE, AREN'T I?!
OH, NO, NO. NOT AT ALL.
SHE'LL BE BACK IN A MINUTE.
YOU MUST BE TIRED AFTER STANDING SO LONG.
I'M SORRY I DIDN'T REALIZE. HERE'S A CHAIR.
A chair...
UNGH... NGH...
SNORT
Sh...
Shorry, thank you...
It musht be so hectic here...
Ungh... ngh...
IT'S FINE. YOU MUST BE WORRIED.
I KNOW IT'S LOUD AND BUSY IN HERE, BUT PLEASE KEEP HER COMPANY IF YOU CAN.
IF SOMETHING COMES UP, GET ONE OF US RIGHT AWAY.
You only need to leave if you're eating outside food or need a smoke break.
tissue
This is way different from how they treated me at Hospital B. They kicked me out that time...

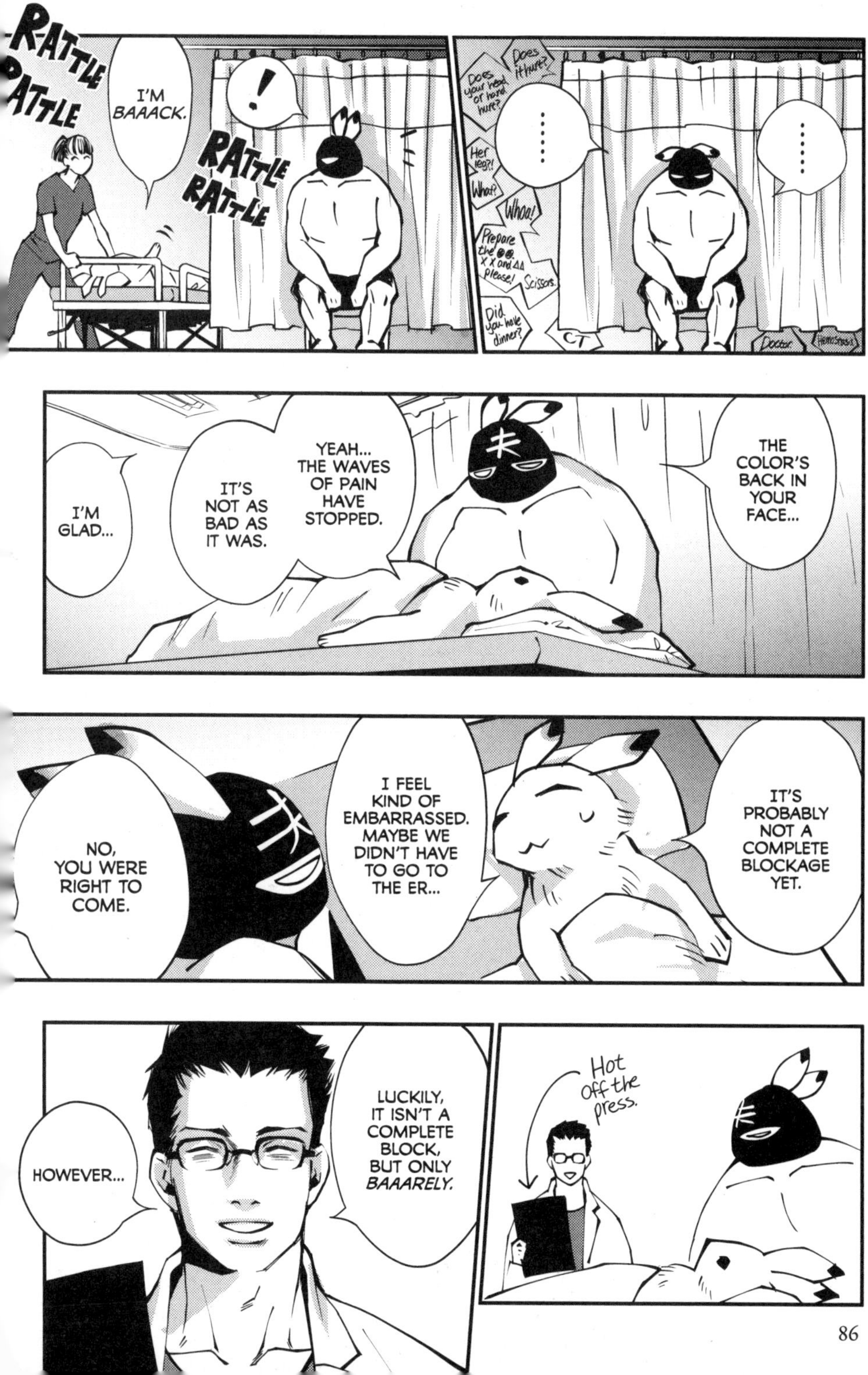
……
……
Does it hurt?
Does your head or hand hurt?
Her leg?!
What?
Whoa!
Prepare the ◎◎, ×× and ΔΔ please!
Scissors.
Did you have dinner?
CT
Doctor.
Hemostasis
!
RATTLE RATTLE
I'M *BAAACK.*
RATTLE RATTLE
THE COLOR'S BACK IN YOUR FACE...
YEAH... THE WAVES OF PAIN HAVE STOPPED.
IT'S NOT AS BAD AS IT WAS.
I'M GLAD...
IT'S PROBABLY NOT A COMPLETE BLOCKAGE YET.
I FEEL KIND OF EMBARRASSED. MAYBE WE DIDN'T HAVE TO GO TO THE ER...
NO, YOU WERE RIGHT TO COME.
Hot off the press.
LUCKILY, IT ISN'T A COMPLETE BLOCK, BUT ONLY *BAAARELY.*
HOWEVER...

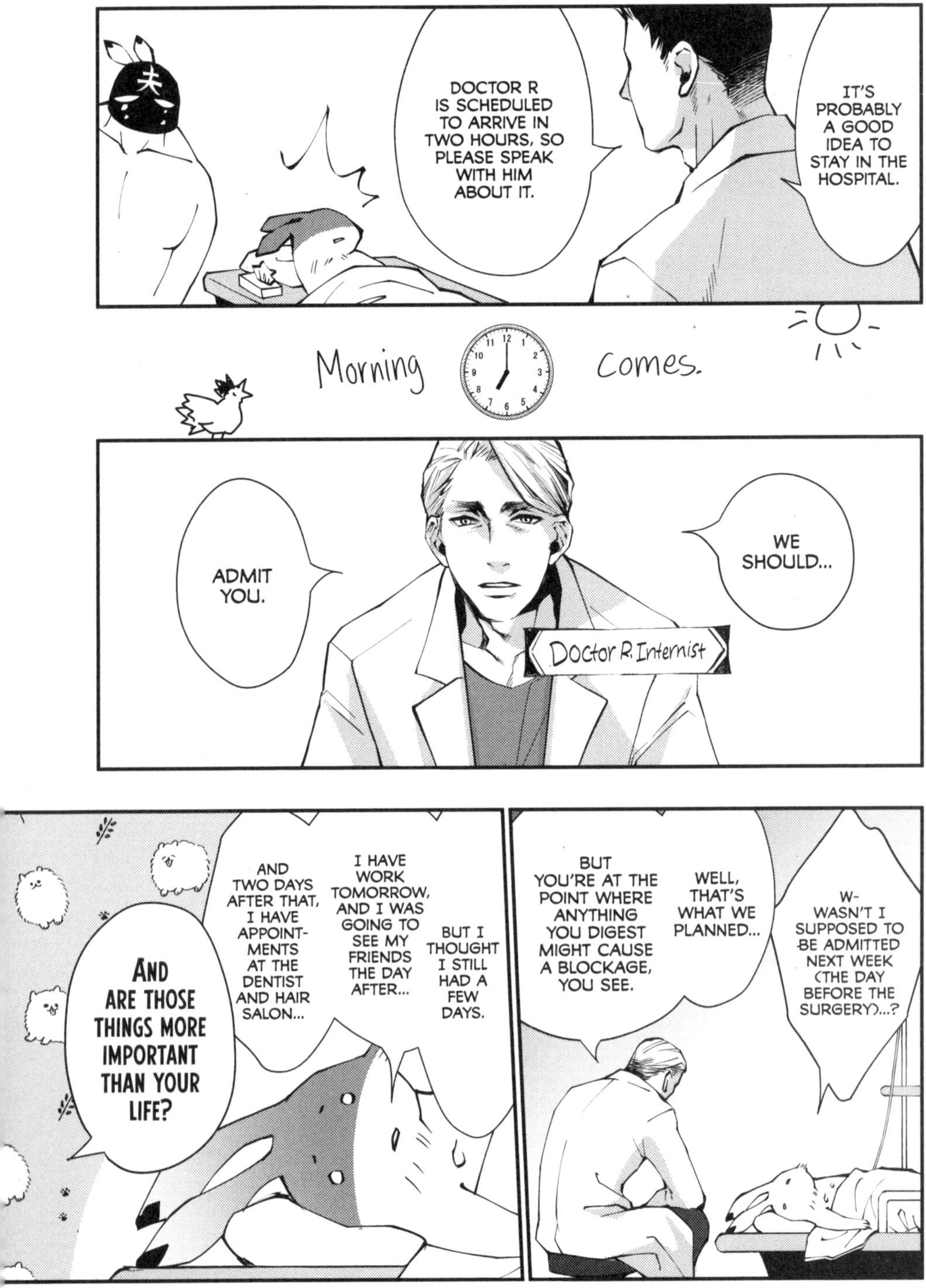
IT'S PROBABLY A GOOD IDEA TO STAY IN THE HOSPITAL.
DOCTOR R IS SCHEDULED TO ARRIVE IN TWO HOURS, SO PLEASE SPEAK WITH HIM ABOUT IT.
Morning comes.
WE SHOULD...
ADMIT YOU.
Doctor R. Internist
W-WASN'T I SUPPOSED TO BE ADMITTED NEXT WEEK (THE DAY BEFORE THE SURGERY)...?
WELL, THAT'S WHAT WE PLANNED...
BUT YOU'RE AT THE POINT WHERE ANYTHING YOU DIGEST MIGHT CAUSE A BLOCKAGE, YOU SEE.
BUT I THOUGHT I STILL HAD A FEW DAYS.
I HAVE WORK TOMORROW, AND I WAS GOING TO SEE MY FRIENDS THE DAY AFTER...
AND TWO DAYS AFTER THAT, I HAVE APPOINTMENTS AT THE DENTIST AND HAIR SALON...
AND ARE THOSE THINGS MORE IMPORTANT THAN YOUR LIFE?

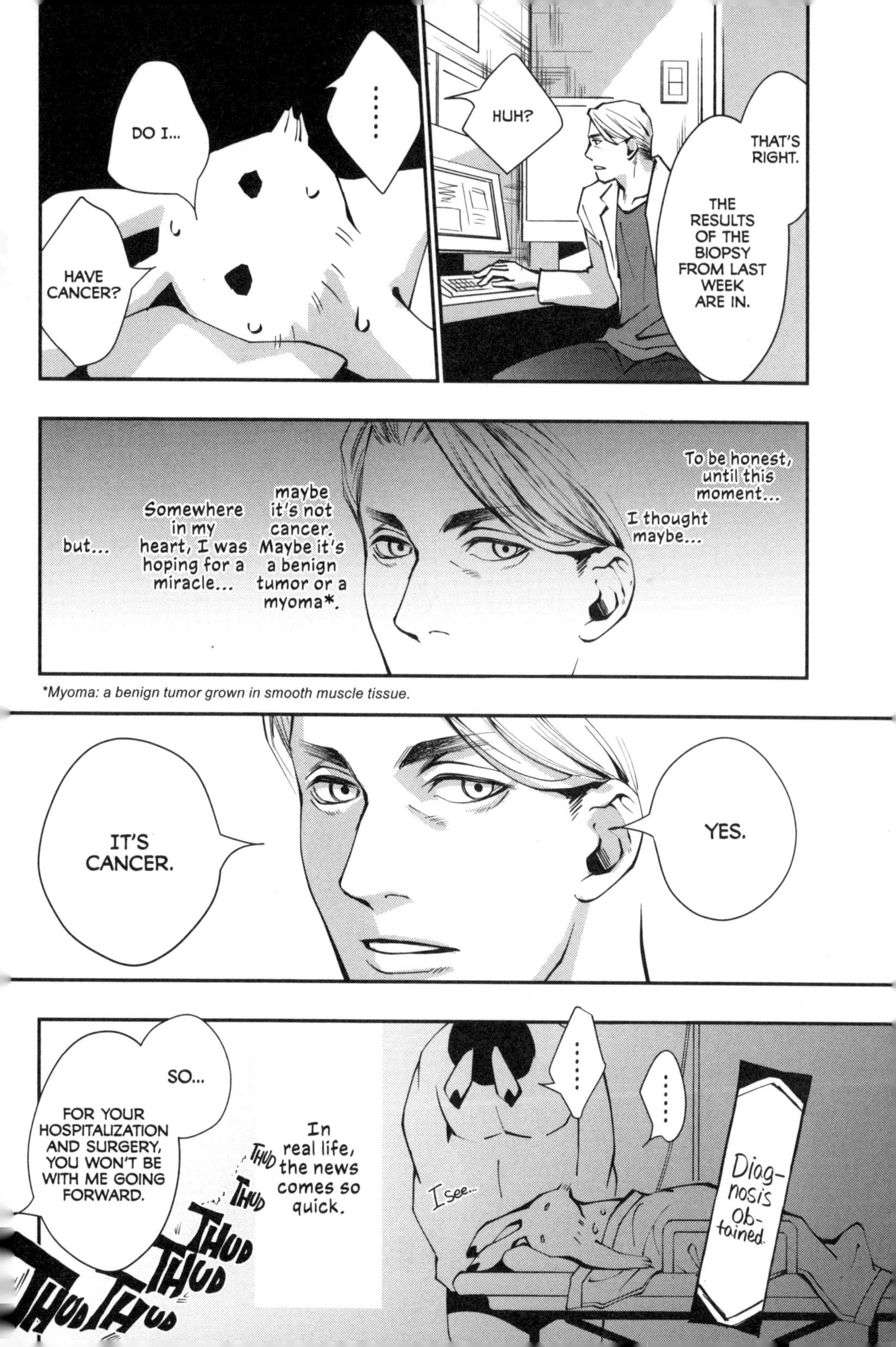
THAT'S RIGHT.
THE RESULTS OF THE BIOPSY FROM LAST WEEK ARE IN.
HUH?
......
DO I...
HAVE CANCER?
To be honest, until this moment...
I thought maybe...
maybe it's not cancer. Maybe it's a benign tumor or a myoma*.
Somewhere in my heart, I was hoping for a miracle...
but...
YES.
IT'S CANCER.
Diag-nosis Ob-tained.
......
......
I see...
In real life, the news comes so quick.
SO...
FOR YOUR HOSPITALIZATION AND SURGERY, YOU WON'T BE WITH ME GOING FORWARD.
THUD THUD THUD THUD THUD THUD

*Myoma: a benign tumor grown in smooth muscle tissue.

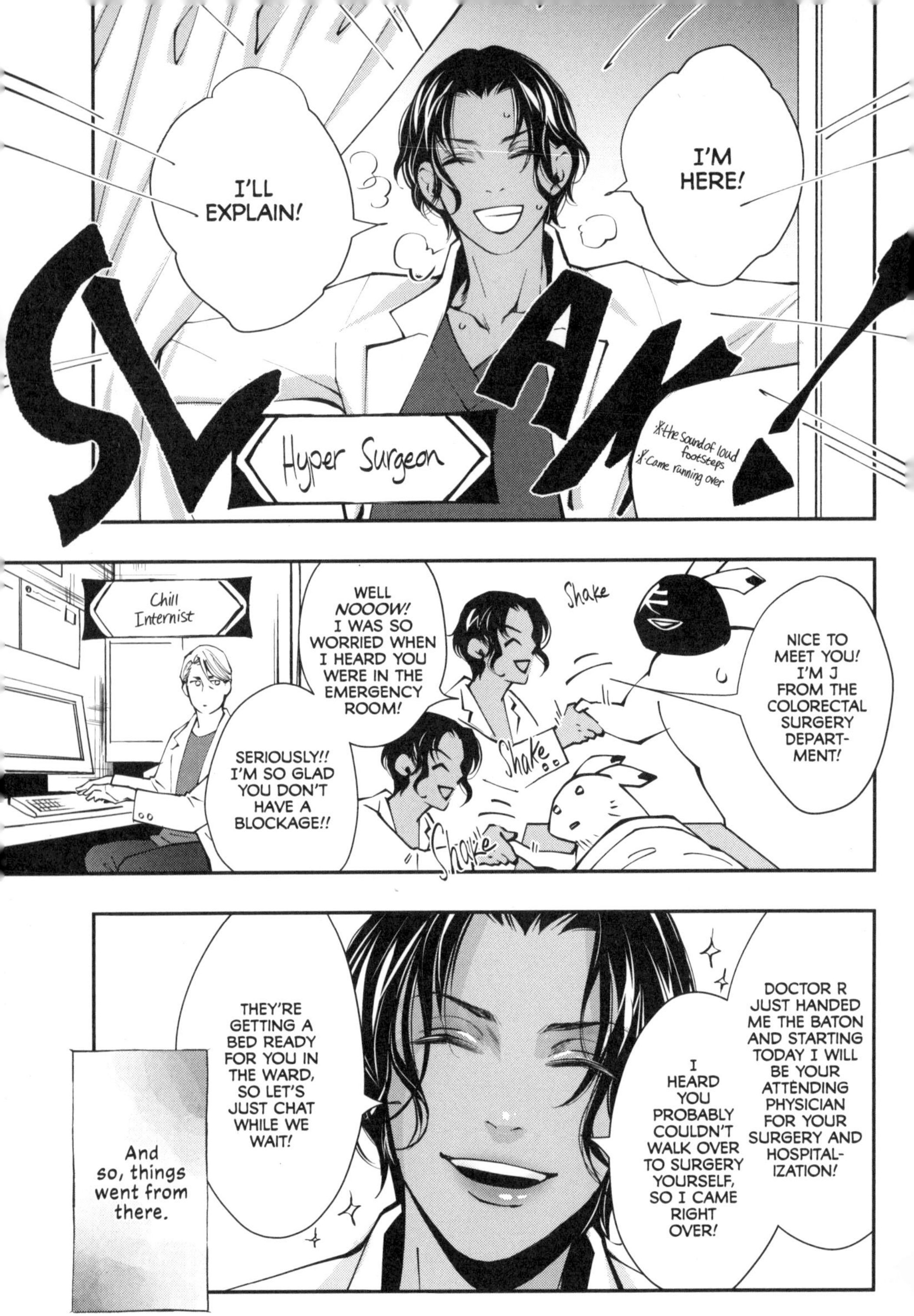
I'M HERE!
I'LL EXPLAIN!
SLAM!
※the sound of loud footsteps
※Came running over
Hyper Surgeon
NICE TO MEET YOU! I'M J FROM THE COLORECTAL SURGERY DEPART-MENT!
Shake
WELL NOOOW! I WAS SO WORRIED WHEN I HEARD YOU WERE IN THE EMERGENCY ROOM!
Shake
Shake
SERIOUSLY!! I'M SO GLAD YOU DON'T HAVE A BLOCKAGE!!
Chill Internist
DOCTOR R JUST HANDED ME THE BATON AND STARTING TODAY I WILL BE YOUR ATTENDING PHYSICIAN FOR YOUR SURGERY AND HOSPITAL-IZATION!
I HEARD YOU PROBABLY COULDN'T WALK OVER TO SURGERY YOURSELF, SO I CAME RIGHT OVER!
THEY'RE GETTING A BED READY FOR YOU IN THE WARD, SO LET'S JUST CHAT WHILE WE WAIT!
And so, things went from there.

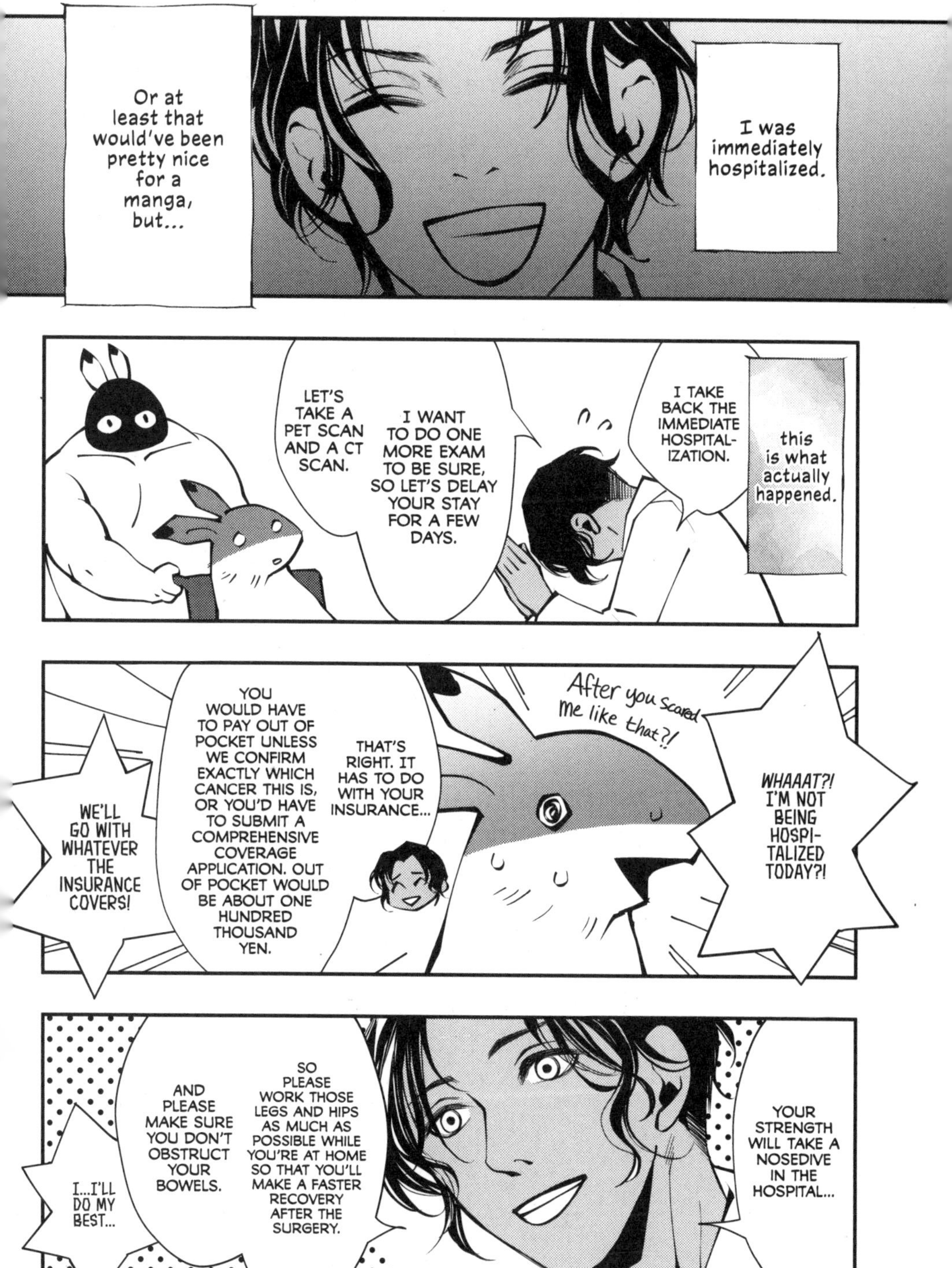
I was immediately hospitalized.
Or at least that would've been pretty nice for a manga, but...
this is what actually happened.
I TAKE BACK THE IMMEDIATE HOSPITAL-IZATION.
I WANT TO DO ONE MORE EXAM TO BE SURE, SO LET'S DELAY YOUR STAY FOR A FEW DAYS.
LET'S TAKE A PET SCAN AND A CT SCAN.
WHAAAT?! I'M NOT BEING HOSPI-TALIZED TODAY?!
After you scared me like that?!
THAT'S RIGHT. IT HAS TO DO WITH YOUR INSURANCE...
YOU WOULD HAVE TO PAY OUT OF POCKET UNLESS WE CONFIRM EXACTLY WHICH CANCER THIS IS, OR YOU'D HAVE TO SUBMIT A COMPREHENSIVE COVERAGE APPLICATION. OUT OF POCKET WOULD BE ABOUT ONE HUNDRED THOUSAND YEN.
WE'LL GO WITH WHATEVER THE INSURANCE COVERS!
YOUR STRENGTH WILL TAKE A NOSEDIVE IN THE HOSPITAL...
SO PLEASE WORK THOSE LEGS AND HIPS AS MUCH AS POSSIBLE WHILE YOU'RE AT HOME SO THAT YOU'LL MAKE A FASTER RECOVERY AFTER THE SURGERY.
AND PLEASE MAKE SURE YOU DON'T OBSTRUCT YOUR BOWELS.
I...I'LL DO MY BEST...

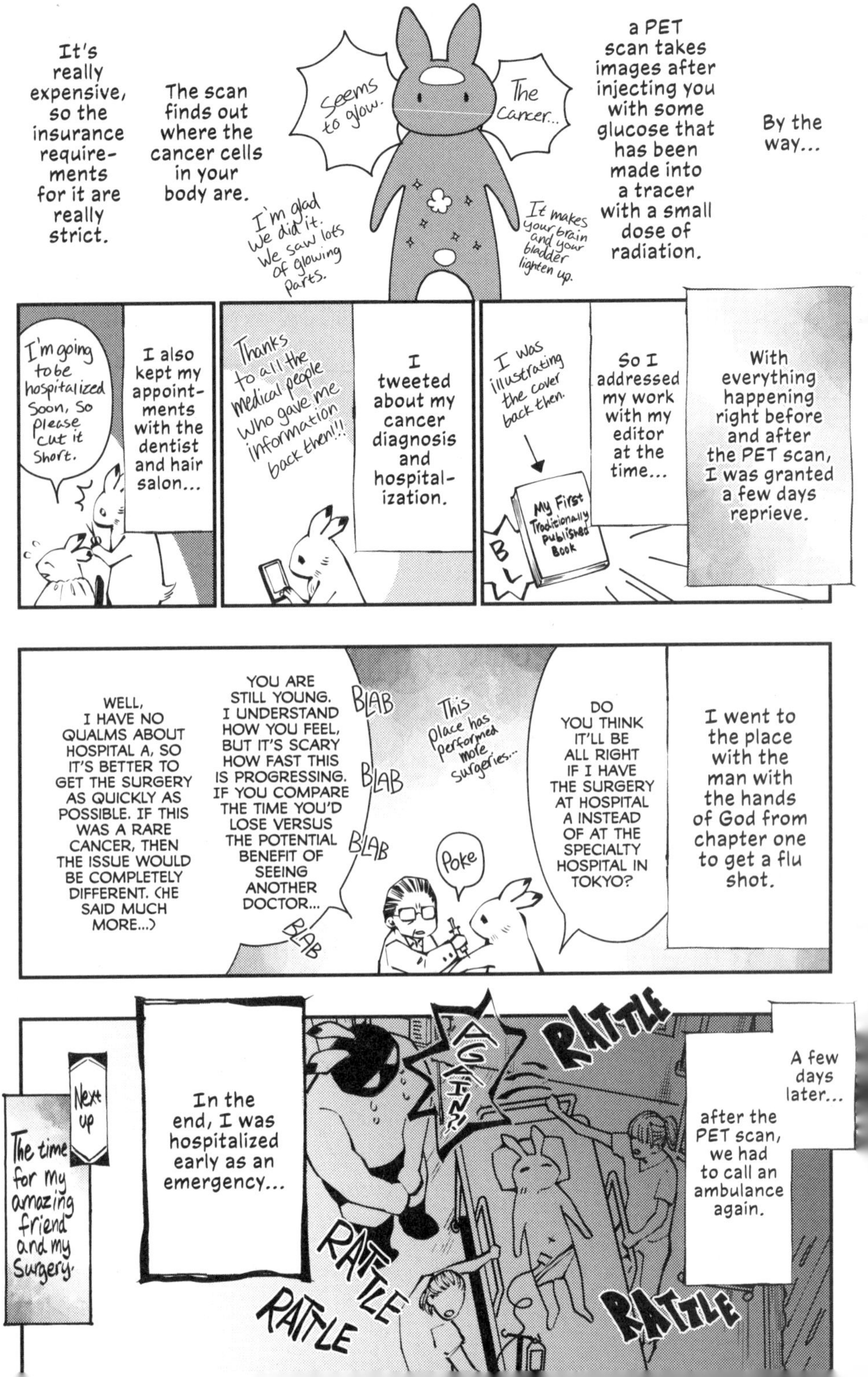

By the way...
a PET scan takes images after injecting you with some glucose that has been made into a tracer with a small dose of radiation.
The Cancer...
Seems to glow.
It makes your brain and your bladder lighten up.
I'm glad we did it. We saw lots of glowing parts.
The scan finds out where the cancer cells in your body are.
It's really expensive, so the insurance require-ments for it are really strict.
With everything happening right before and after the PET scan, I was granted a few days reprieve.
So I addressed my work with my editor at the time...
I was illustrating the cover back then.
My First Traditionally Published Book
BL
I tweeted about my cancer diagnosis and hospital-ization.
Thanks to all the medical people who gave me information back then!!!
I also kept my appoint-ments with the dentist and hair salon...
I'm going to be hospitalized soon, so please cut it short.
I went to the place with the man with the hands of God from chapter one to get a flu shot.
DO YOU THINK IT'LL BE ALL RIGHT IF I HAVE THE SURGERY AT HOSPITAL A INSTEAD OF AT THE SPECIALTY HOSPITAL IN TOKYO?
This place has performed more surgeries...
Poke
YOU ARE STILL YOUNG. I UNDERSTAND HOW YOU FEEL, BUT IT'S SCARY HOW FAST THIS IS PROGRESSING. IF YOU COMPARE THE TIME YOU'D LOSE VERSUS THE POTENTIAL BENEFIT OF SEEING ANOTHER DOCTOR...
BLAB
BLAB
BLAB
BLAB
WELL, I HAVE NO QUALMS ABOUT HOSPITAL A, SO IT'S BETTER TO GET THE SURGERY AS QUICKLY AS POSSIBLE. IF THIS WAS A RARE CANCER, THEN THE ISSUE WOULD BE COMPLETELY DIFFERENT. (HE SAID MUCH MORE...)
A few days later...
after the PET scan, we had to call an ambulance again.
RATTLE
AGAHN?!
RATTLE
In the end, I was hospitalized early as an emergency...
RATTLE
RATTLE
Next up
The time for my amazing friend and my surgery.

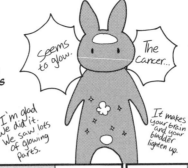

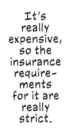

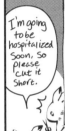

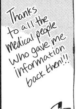

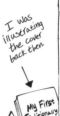

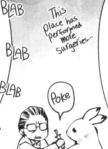

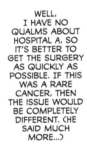

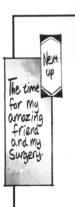

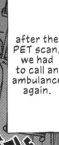

I was so busy back then...
The pain in my abdomen was off the charts.
I left it out of the manga, but I pretty much
had some kind of exam every day, and they'd say,
"Get admitted," and then they'd say, "Get admitted
next week," and then, "No, you should do it today,"
and...I had no clue what was going on.

I was completely out of it while in the ambulance,
so I don't remember *aaanything*...but I wanted to
show that tension, so I got a lot of advice from the
doctors looking over the chapter for the ER part.

Oh, the part where my husband was offered a chair
and cried? I wasn't there for that, but he remembered
it clearly. To think that someone would take the time to
care for him in the midst of that busy, battlefield-like
area...it warms my heart. I can't thank all the
people at the hospital enough.

I'm a Terminal Cancer Patient

BUT I'M FINE

I thought I had a Stomachache, but it Was terminal cancer. 7

The time for my amazing friend and my surgery.

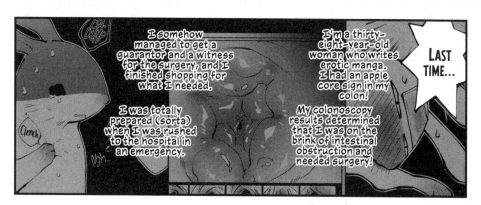

LAST TIME...
I'm a thirty-eight-year-old woman who writes erotic manga. I had an apple core sign in my colon!
My colonoscopy results determined that I was on the brink of intestinal obstruction and needed surgery!
I somehow managed to get a guarantor and a witness for the surgery, and I finished shopping for what I needed.
I was totally prepared (sorta) when I was rushed to the hospital in an emergency.
Clench
Ngh...
One week after the cancer diag-nosis...
and about thirty days after I noticed some-thing off.
......
Hiinama
My life at the hospital had finally begun.
There were just five days until the surgery.
I was near a total shutdown of my GI tract...
and my anxiety ballooned over the days of nonstop abdominal pain and nausea.
Water
My meals back then.
Enteral Nutrition
laxative
Huff...
In the midst of it all, the thing that comforted me the most was...
Huff...

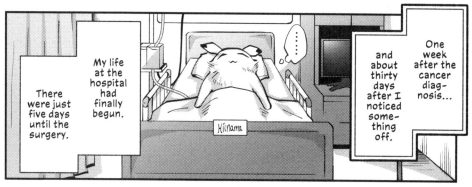

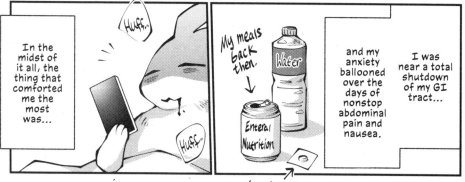

※ I make sure that I ask my attending physician about any information I receive from anyone before trying it out.

Organizing my stuff

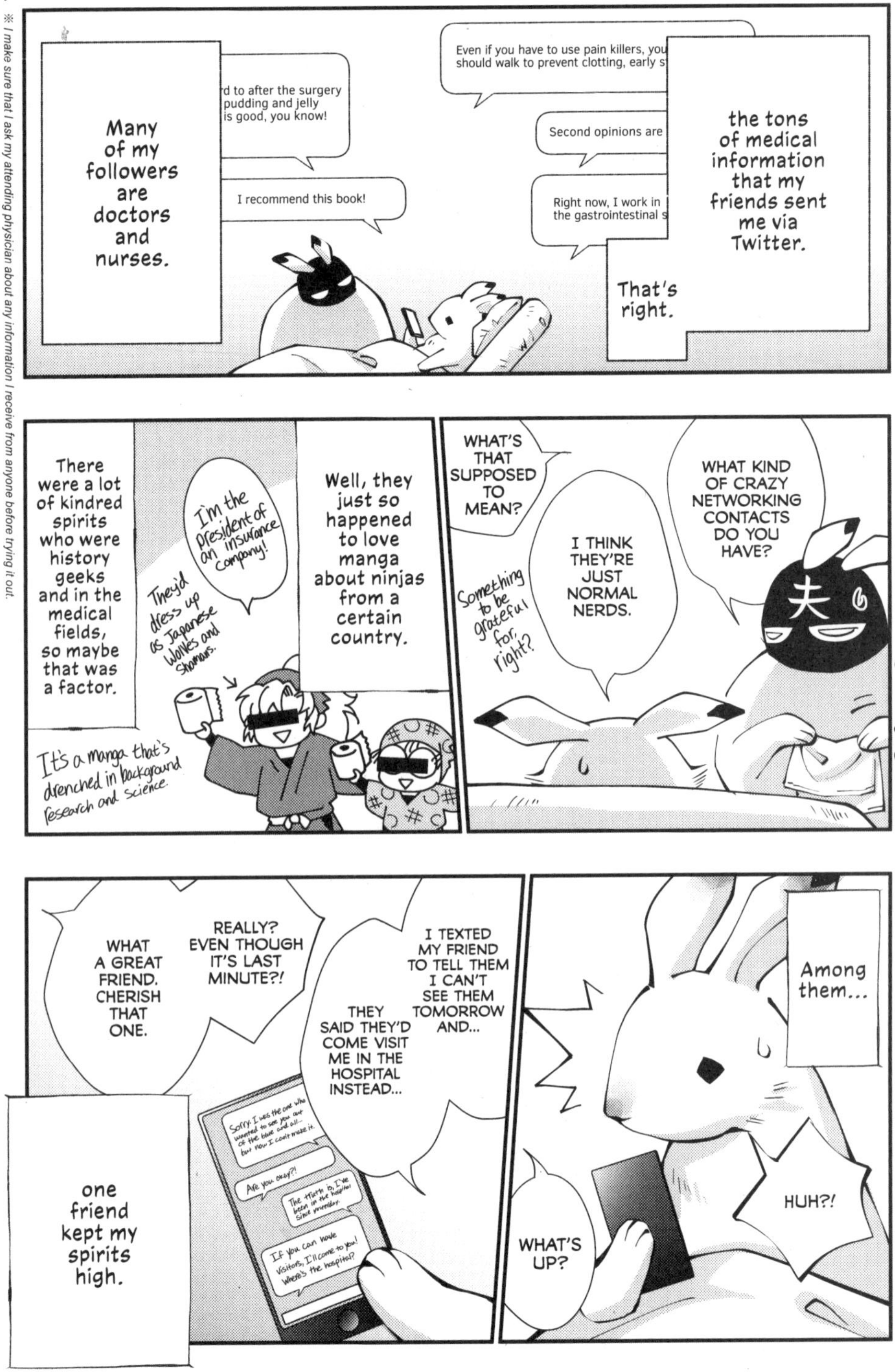

the tons of medical information that my friends sent me via Twitter.
That's right.
Even if you have to use pain killers, you should walk to prevent clotting, early s
Second opinions are
Right now, I work in the gastrointestinal s
rd to after the surgery pudding and jelly is good, you know!
I recommend this book!
Many of my followers are doctors and nurses.
WHAT KIND OF CRAZY NETWORKING CONTACTS DO YOU HAVE?
WHAT'S THAT SUPPOSED TO MEAN?
I THINK THEY'RE JUST NORMAL NERDS.
Something to be grateful for, right?
Well, they just so happened to love manga about ninjas from a certain country.
I'm the president of an insurance company!
There were a lot of kindred spirits who were history geeks and in the medical fields, so maybe that was a factor.
They'd dress up as Japanese Wolves and Shamans.
It's a manga that's drenched in background research and science.
Among them...
HUH?!
WHAT'S UP?
I TEXTED MY FRIEND TO TELL THEM I CAN'T SEE THEM TOMORROW AND...
THEY SAID THEY'D COME VISIT ME IN THE HOSPITAL INSTEAD...
REALLY? EVEN THOUGH IT'S LAST MINUTE?!
WHAT A GREAT FRIEND. CHERISH THAT ONE.
Sorry. I was the one who wanted to see you out of the blue and all... but now I can't make it.
Are you okay?!
The truth is, I've been in the hospital since yesterday.
If you can have visitors, I'll come to you! Where's the hospital?
one friend kept my spirits high.

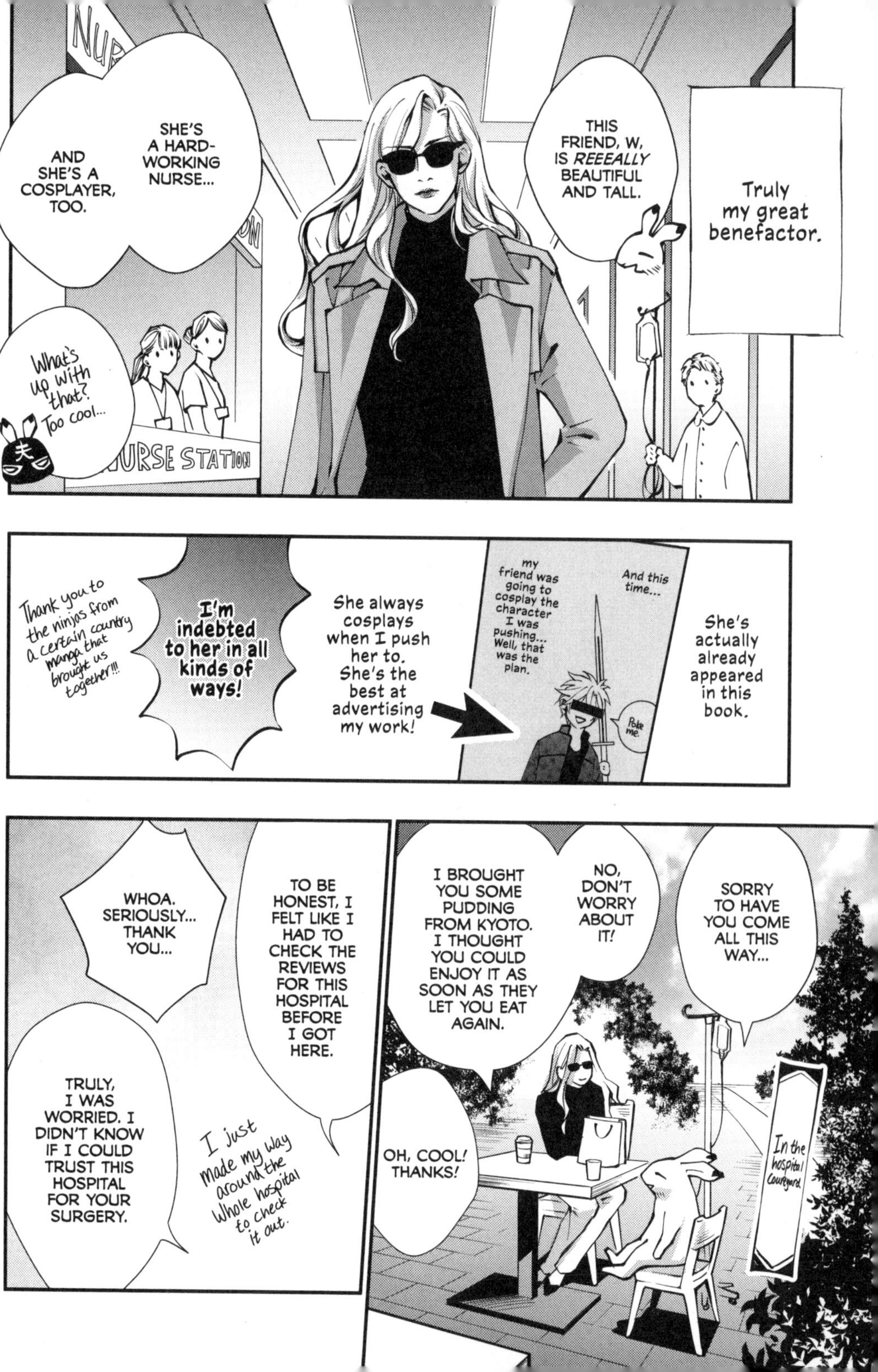
Truly my great benefactor.
THIS FRIEND, W, IS REEEALLY BEAUTIFUL AND TALL.
SHE'S A HARD-WORKING NURSE...
AND SHE'S A COSPLAYER, TOO.
What's up with that? Too cool...
NURSE STATION
She's actually already appeared in this book.
And this time... my friend was going to cosplay the character I was pushing... Well, that was the plan.
Poke me.
She always cosplays when I push her to. She's the best at advertising my work!
I'm indebted to her in all kinds of ways!
Thank you to the ninjas from a certain country manga that brought us together!!!
In the hospital courtyard.
SORRY TO HAVE YOU COME ALL THIS WAY...
NO, DON'T WORRY ABOUT IT!
I BROUGHT YOU SOME PUDDING FROM KYOTO. I THOUGHT YOU COULD ENJOY IT AS SOON AS THEY LET YOU EAT AGAIN.
OH, COOL! THANKS!
TO BE HONEST, I FELT LIKE I HAD TO CHECK THE REVIEWS FOR THIS HOSPITAL BEFORE I GOT HERE.
WHOA. SERIOUSLY... THANK YOU...
I just made my way around the whole hospital to check it out.
TRULY, I WAS WORRIED. I DIDN'T KNOW IF I COULD TRUST THIS HOSPITAL FOR YOUR SURGERY.

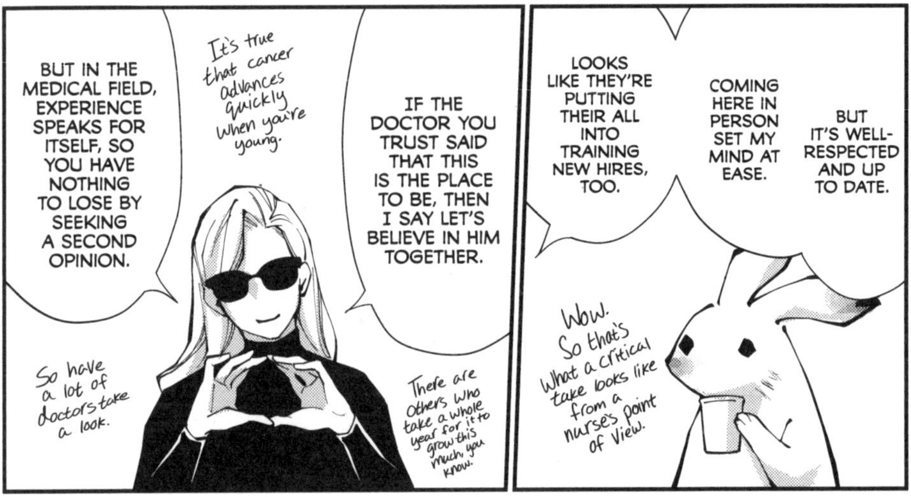
BUT IT'S WELL-RESPECTED AND UP TO DATE.
COMING HERE IN PERSON SET MY MIND AT EASE.
LOOKS LIKE THEY'RE PUTTING THEIR ALL INTO TRAINING NEW HIRES, TOO.
Wow. So that's what a critical take looks like from a nurse's point of view.
IF THE DOCTOR YOU TRUST SAID THAT THIS IS THE PLACE TO BE, THEN I SAY LET'S BELIEVE IN HIM TOGETHER.
It's true that cancer advances quickly when you're young.
BUT IN THE MEDICAL FIELD, EXPERIENCE SPEAKS FOR ITSELF, SO YOU HAVE NOTHING TO LOSE BY SEEKING A SECOND OPINION.
There are others who take a whole year for it to grow this much, you know.
So have a lot of doctors take a look.

※ *Many people will visit multiple doctors to get varied opinions for a diagnosis.*

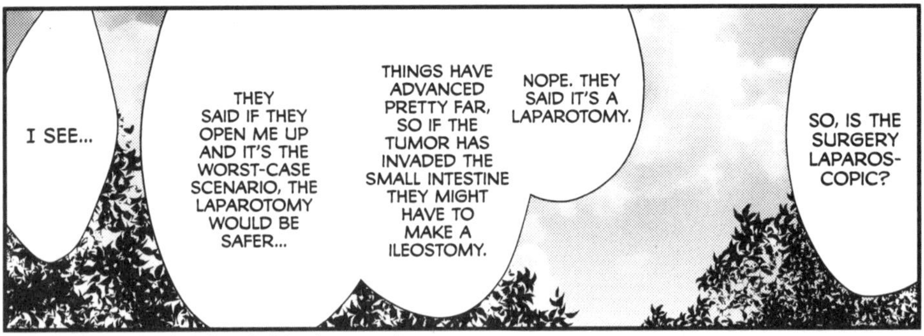
SO, IS THE SURGERY LAPAROS-COPIC?
NOPE. THEY SAID IT'S A LAPAROTOMY.
THINGS HAVE ADVANCED PRETTY FAR, SO IF THE TUMOR HAS INVADED THE SMALL INTESTINE THEY MIGHT HAVE TO MAKE A ILEOSTOMY.
THEY SAID IF THEY OPEN ME UP AND IT'S THE WORST-CASE SCENARIO, THE LAPAROTOMY WOULD BE SAFER...
I SEE...

**A laparotomy uses a single large incision; laparoscopic surgery involves small (<1cm) incisions and long narrow instruments.*

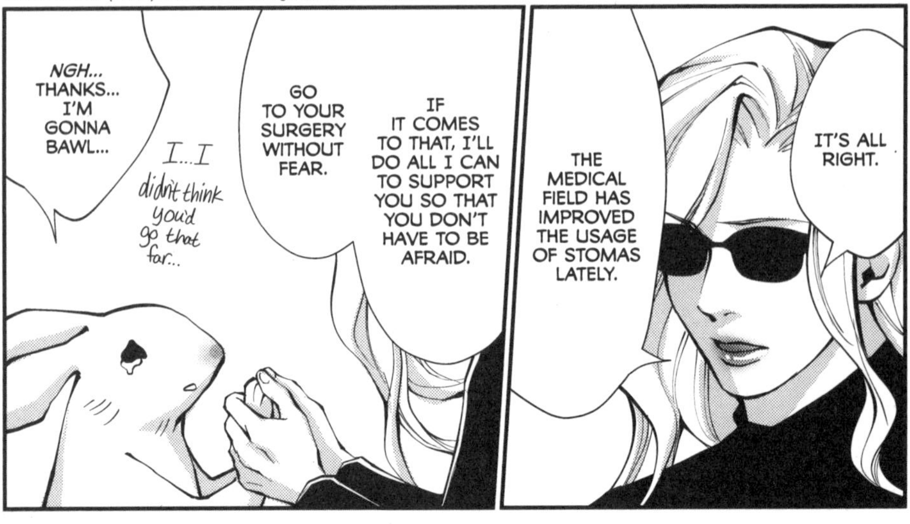
IT'S ALL RIGHT.
THE MEDICAL FIELD HAS IMPROVED THE USAGE OF STOMAS LATELY.
IF IT COMES TO THAT, I'LL DO ALL I CAN TO SUPPORT YOU SO THAT YOU DON'T HAVE TO BE AFRAID.
GO TO YOUR SURGERY WITHOUT FEAR.
I...I didn't think you'd go that far...
NGH... THANKS... I'M GONNA BAWL...

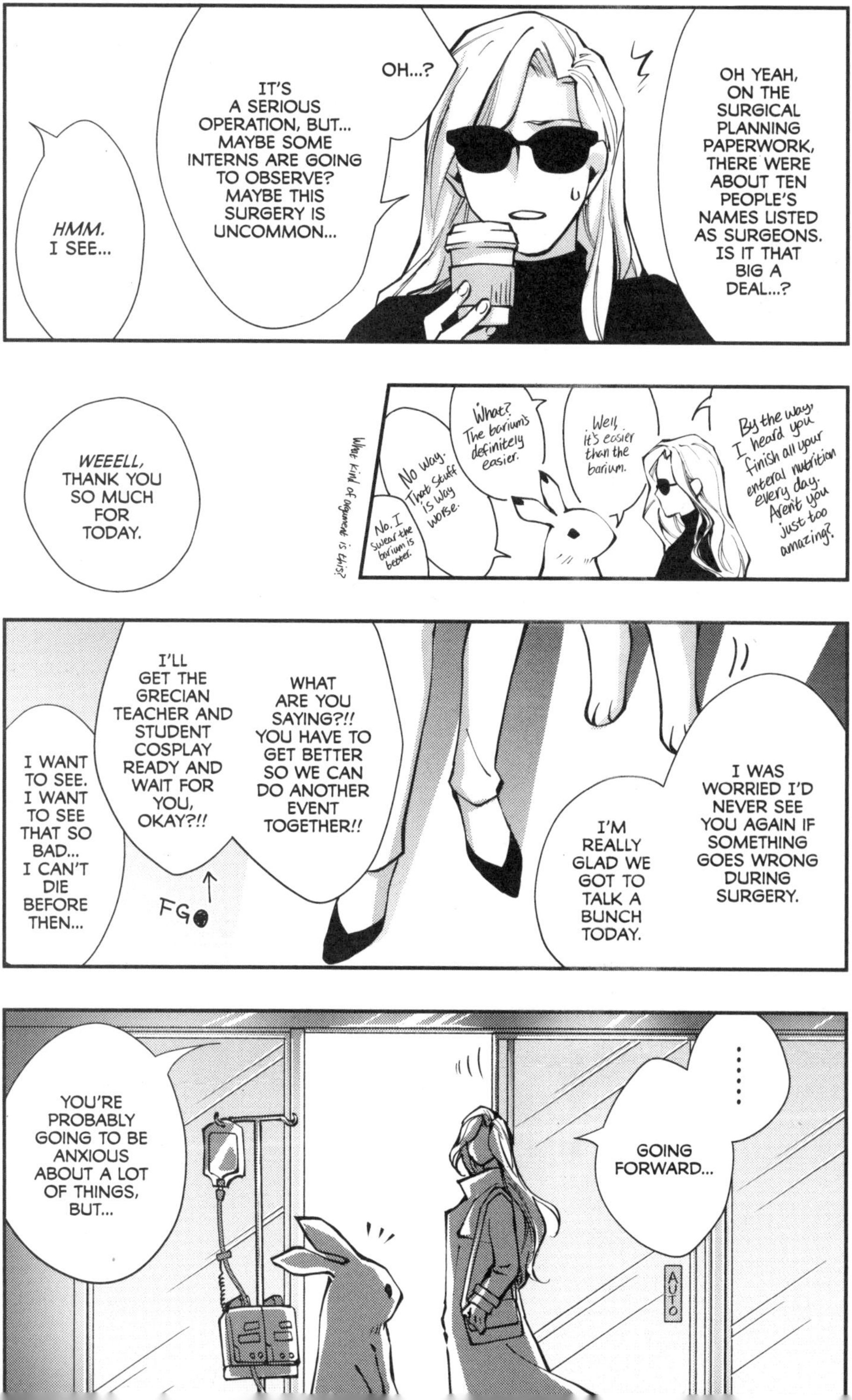

OH YEAH, ON THE SURGICAL PLANNING PAPERWORK, THERE WERE ABOUT TEN PEOPLE'S NAMES LISTED AS SURGEONS. IS IT THAT BIG A DEAL...?
OH...?
IT'S A SERIOUS OPERATION, BUT... MAYBE SOME INTERNS ARE GOING TO OBSERVE? MAYBE THIS SURGERY IS UNCOMMON...
HMM. I SEE...
By the way, I heard you finish all your enteral nutrition every day. Aren't you just too amazing?
Well, it's easier than the barium.
What? The barium's definitely easier.
No way. That stuff is way worse.
No. I swear the barium is better.
What kind of argument is this?
WEEELL, THANK YOU SO MUCH FOR TODAY.
I WAS WORRIED I'D NEVER SEE YOU AGAIN IF SOMETHING GOES WRONG DURING SURGERY.
I'M REALLY GLAD WE GOT TO TALK A BUNCH TODAY.
WHAT ARE YOU SAYING?!! YOU HAVE TO GET BETTER SO WE CAN DO ANOTHER EVENT TOGETHER!!
I'LL GET THE GRECIAN TEACHER AND STUDENT COSPLAY READY AND WAIT FOR YOU, OKAY?!!
FG
I WANT TO SEE. I WANT TO SEE THAT SO BAD... I CAN'T DIE BEFORE THEN...
......
GOING FORWARD...
YOU'RE PROBABLY GOING TO BE ANXIOUS ABOUT A LOT OF THINGS, BUT...
AUTO

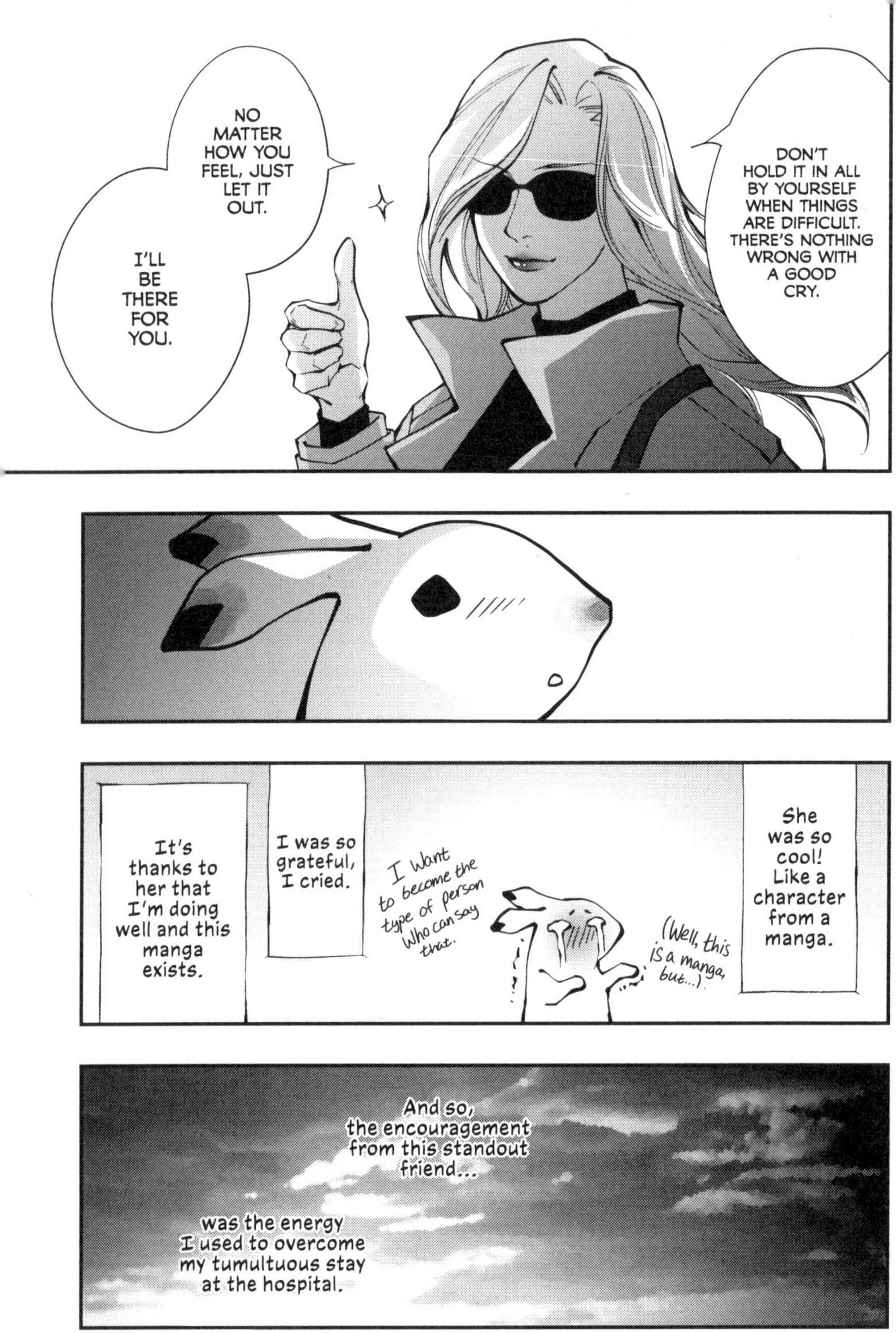
DON'T HOLD IT IN ALL BY YOURSELF WHEN THINGS ARE DIFFICULT. THERE'S NOTHING WRONG WITH A GOOD CRY.
NO MATTER HOW YOU FEEL, JUST LET IT OUT.
I'LL BE THERE FOR YOU.
She was so cool! Like a character from a manga.
(Well, this is a manga, but...)
I want to become the type of person who can say that.
I was so grateful, I cried.
It's thanks to her that I'm doing well and this manga exists.
And so, the encouragement from this standout friend...
was the energy I used to overcome my tumultuous stay at the hospital.

It begins! THE WAVE OF EXPLANATIONS!

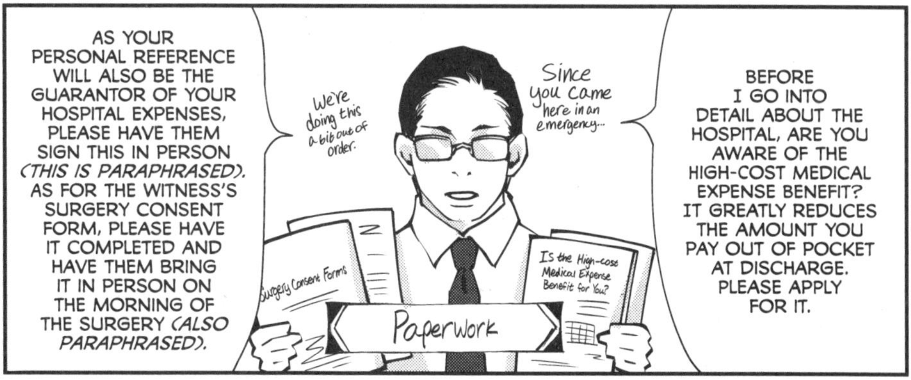

BEFORE I GO INTO DETAIL ABOUT THE HOSPITAL, ARE YOU AWARE OF THE HIGH-COST MEDICAL EXPENSE BENEFIT? IT GREATLY REDUCES THE AMOUNT YOU PAY OUT OF POCKET AT DISCHARGE. PLEASE APPLY FOR IT.
Since you came here in an emergency...
We're doing this a bit out of order.
AS YOUR PERSONAL REFERENCE WILL ALSO BE THE GUARANTOR OF YOUR HOSPITAL EXPENSES, PLEASE HAVE THEM SIGN THIS IN PERSON *(THIS IS PARAPHRASED)*. AS FOR THE WITNESS'S SURGERY CONSENT FORM, PLEASE HAVE IT COMPLETED AND HAVE THEM BRING IT IN PERSON ON THE MORNING OF THE SURGERY *(ALSO PARAPHRASED)*.
Is the High-cost Medical Expense Benefit for You?
Surgery Consent Forms
Paperwork

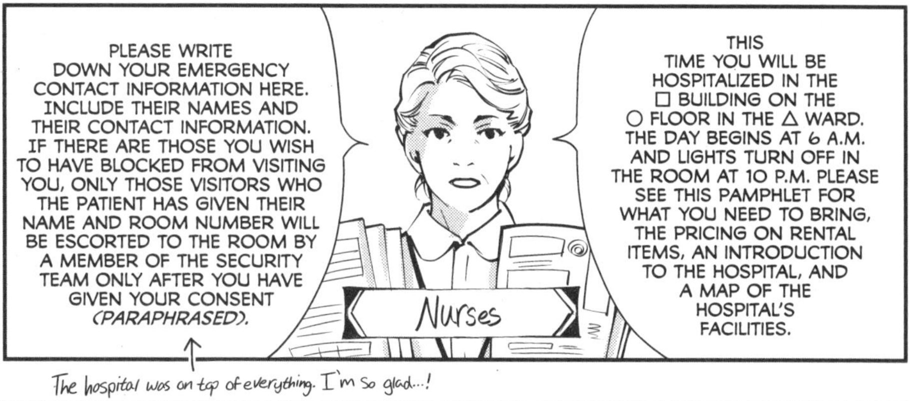

THIS TIME YOU WILL BE HOSPITALIZED IN THE □ BUILDING ON THE ○ FLOOR IN THE △ WARD. THE DAY BEGINS AT 6 A.M. AND LIGHTS TURN OFF IN THE ROOM AT 10 P.M. PLEASE SEE THIS PAMPHLET FOR WHAT YOU NEED TO BRING, THE PRICING ON RENTAL ITEMS, AN INTRODUCTION TO THE HOSPITAL, AND A MAP OF THE HOSPITAL'S FACILITIES.
PLEASE WRITE DOWN YOUR EMERGENCY CONTACT INFORMATION HERE. INCLUDE THEIR NAMES AND THEIR CONTACT INFORMATION. IF THERE ARE THOSE YOU WISH TO HAVE BLOCKED FROM VISITING YOU, ONLY THOSE VISITORS WHO THE PATIENT HAS GIVEN THEIR NAME AND ROOM NUMBER WILL BE ESCORTED TO THE ROOM BY A MEMBER OF THE SECURITY TEAM ONLY AFTER YOU HAVE GIVEN YOUR CONSENT *(PARAPHRASED)*.
Nurses
The hospital was on top of everything. I'm so glad...!

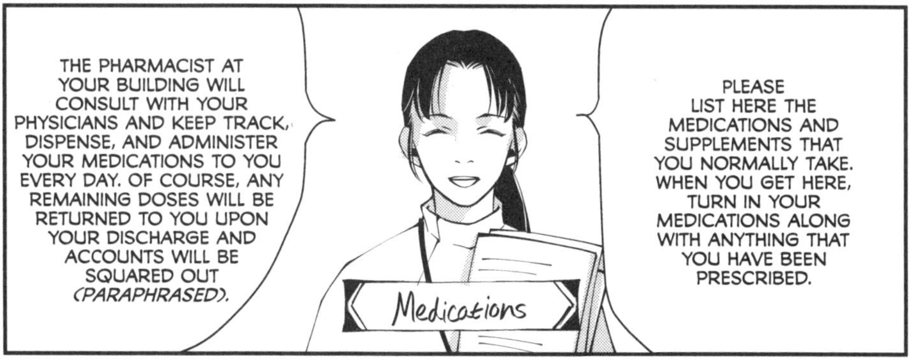

PLEASE LIST HERE THE MEDICATIONS AND SUPPLEMENTS THAT YOU NORMALLY TAKE. WHEN YOU GET HERE, TURN IN YOUR MEDICATIONS ALONG WITH ANYTHING THAT YOU HAVE BEEN PRESCRIBED.
THE PHARMACIST AT YOUR BUILDING WILL CONSULT WITH YOUR PHYSICIANS AND KEEP TRACK, DISPENSE, AND ADMINISTER YOUR MEDICATIONS TO YOU EVERY DAY. OF COURSE, ANY REMAINING DOSES WILL BE RETURNED TO YOU UPON YOUR DISCHARGE AND ACCOUNTS WILL BE SQUARED OUT *(PARAPHRASED)*.
Medications

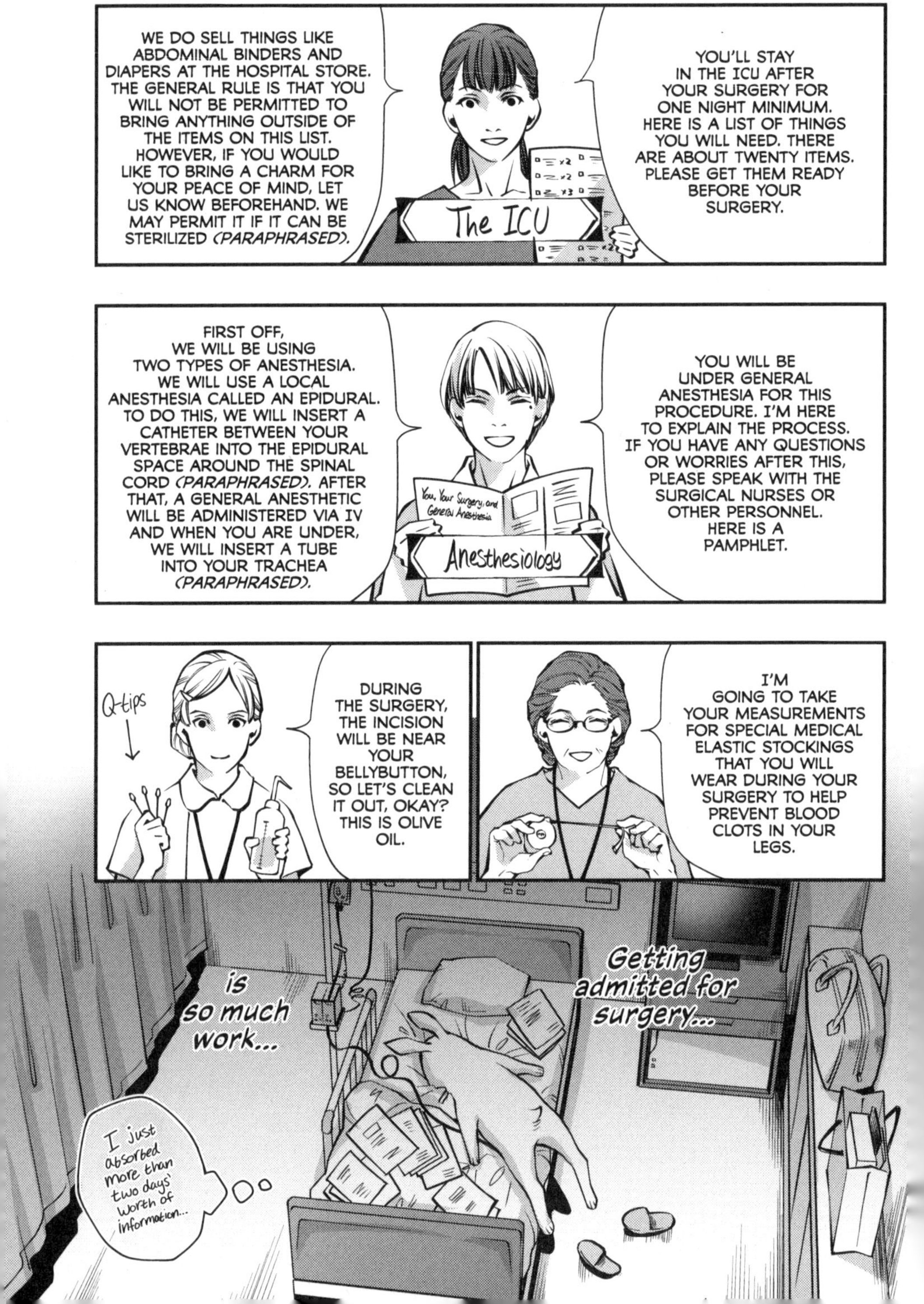
YOU'LL STAY IN THE ICU AFTER YOUR SURGERY FOR ONE NIGHT MINIMUM. HERE IS A LIST OF THINGS YOU WILL NEED. THERE ARE ABOUT TWENTY ITEMS. PLEASE GET THEM READY BEFORE YOUR SURGERY.
WE DO SELL THINGS LIKE ABDOMINAL BINDERS AND DIAPERS AT THE HOSPITAL STORE. THE GENERAL RULE IS THAT YOU WILL NOT BE PERMITTED TO BRING ANYTHING OUTSIDE OF THE ITEMS ON THIS LIST. HOWEVER, IF YOU WOULD LIKE TO BRING A CHARM FOR YOUR PEACE OF MIND, LET US KNOW BEFOREHAND. WE MAY PERMIT IT IF IT CAN BE STERILIZED *(PARAPHRASED)*.
The ICU
YOU WILL BE UNDER GENERAL ANESTHESIA FOR THIS PROCEDURE. I'M HERE TO EXPLAIN THE PROCESS. IF YOU HAVE ANY QUESTIONS OR WORRIES AFTER THIS, PLEASE SPEAK WITH THE SURGICAL NURSES OR OTHER PERSONNEL. HERE IS A PAMPHLET.
FIRST OFF, WE WILL BE USING TWO TYPES OF ANESTHESIA. WE WILL USE A LOCAL ANESTHESIA CALLED AN EPIDURAL. TO DO THIS, WE WILL INSERT A CATHETER BETWEEN YOUR VERTEBRAE INTO THE EPIDURAL SPACE AROUND THE SPINAL CORD *(PARAPHRASED)*. AFTER THAT, A GENERAL ANESTHETIC WILL BE ADMINISTERED VIA IV AND WHEN YOU ARE UNDER, WE WILL INSERT A TUBE INTO YOUR TRACHEA *(PARAPHRASED)*.
You, Your Surgery, and General Anesthesia
Anesthesiology
I'M GOING TO TAKE YOUR MEASUREMENTS FOR SPECIAL MEDICAL ELASTIC STOCKINGS THAT YOU WILL WEAR DURING YOUR SURGERY TO HELP PREVENT BLOOD CLOTS IN YOUR LEGS.
DURING THE SURGERY, THE INCISION WILL BE NEAR YOUR BELLYBUTTON, SO LET'S CLEAN IT OUT, OKAY? THIS IS OLIVE OIL.
Q-tips
Getting admitted for surgery...
is so much work...
I just absorbed more than two days' worth of information...

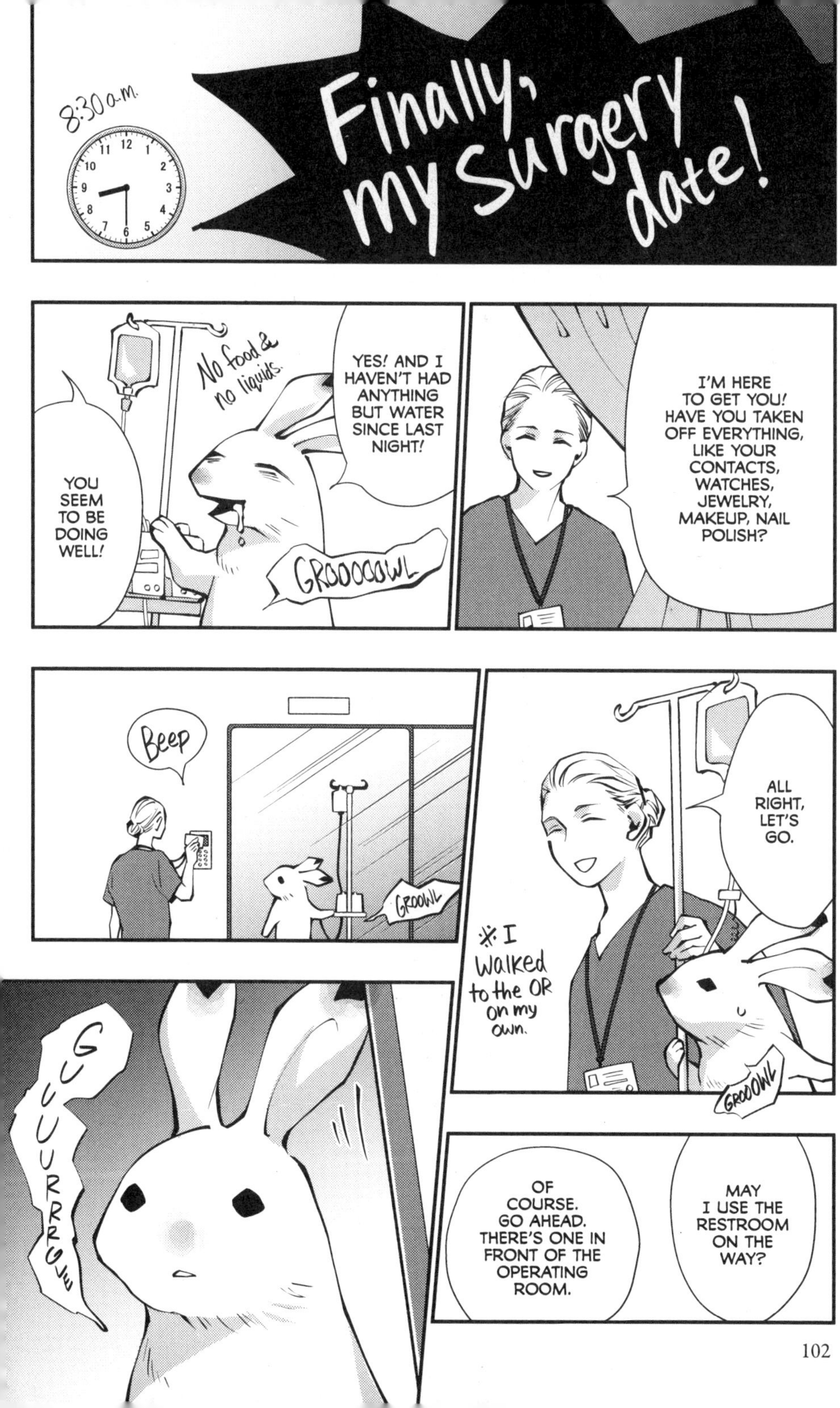
Finally, my surgery date!
8:30 a.m.
I'M HERE TO GET YOU! HAVE YOU TAKEN OFF EVERYTHING, LIKE YOUR CONTACTS, WATCHES, JEWELRY, MAKEUP, NAIL POLISH?
YES! AND I HAVEN'T HAD ANYTHING BUT WATER SINCE LAST NIGHT!
No food & no liquids.
YOU SEEM TO BE DOING WELL!
GROOOOOWL
ALL RIGHT, LET'S GO.
※I walked to the OR on my own.
GROOOWL
Beep
GROOWL
MAY I USE THE RESTROOM ON THE WAY?
OF COURSE. GO AHEAD. THERE'S ONE IN FRONT OF THE OPERATING ROOM.
GUUUURRRGLE

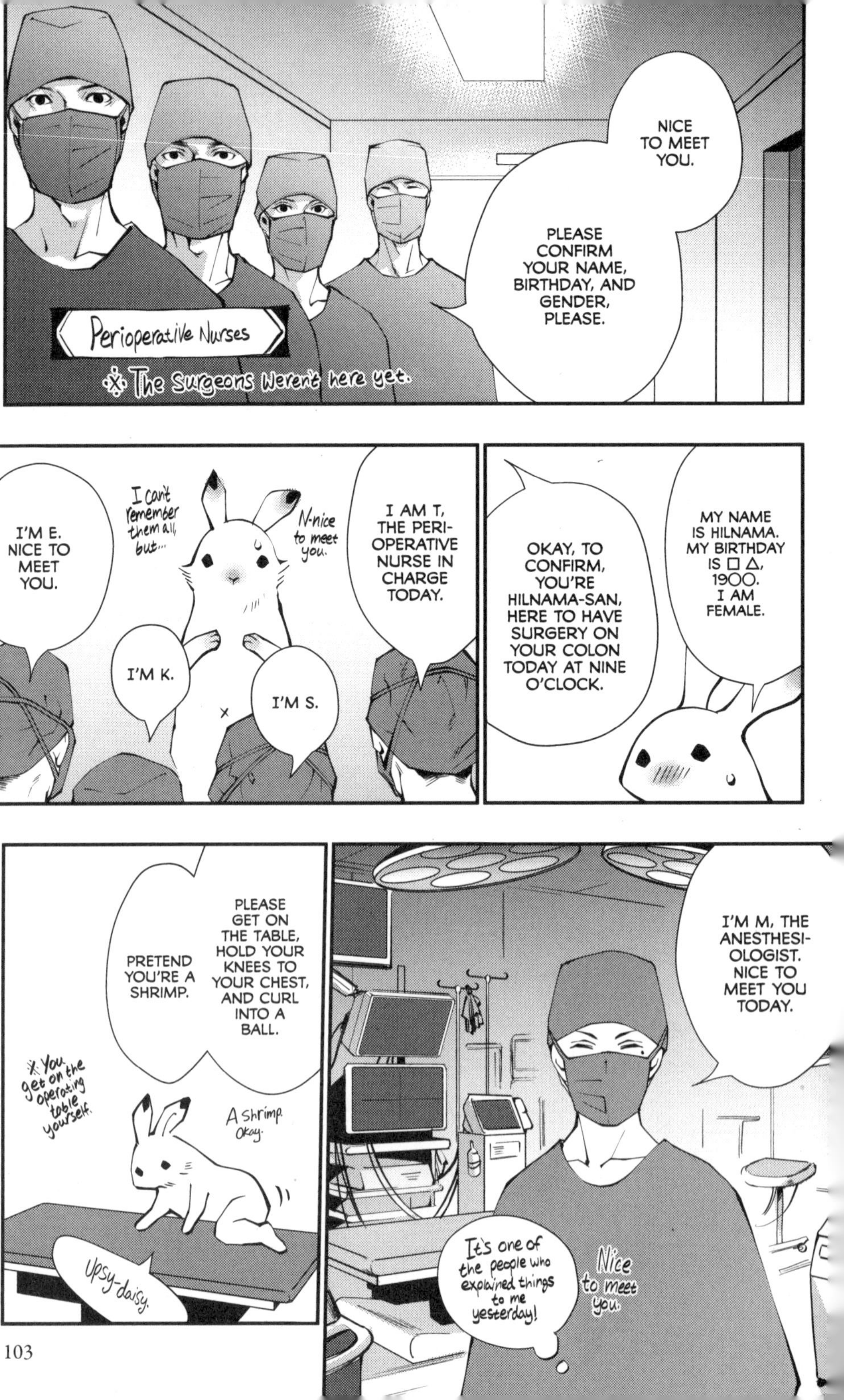
NICE TO MEET YOU.
PLEASE CONFIRM YOUR NAME, BIRTHDAY, AND GENDER, PLEASE.
Perioperative Nurses
※The Surgeons weren't here yet.
MY NAME IS HILNAMA. MY BIRTHDAY IS □ △, 19○○. I AM FEMALE.
OKAY, TO CONFIRM, YOU'RE HILNAMA-SAN, HERE TO HAVE SURGERY ON YOUR COLON TODAY AT NINE O'CLOCK.
I AM T, THE PERI-OPERATIVE NURSE IN CHARGE TODAY.
N-nice to meet you.
I'M S.
I can't remember them all, but...
I'M K.
I'M E. NICE TO MEET YOU.
I'M M, THE ANESTHESI-OLOGIST. NICE TO MEET YOU TODAY.
Nice to meet you.
It's one of the people who explained things to me yesterday!
PLEASE GET ON THE TABLE, HOLD YOUR KNEES TO YOUR CHEST, AND CURL INTO A BALL.
PRETEND YOU'RE A SHRIMP.
A shrimp. Okay.
※You get on the operating table yourself.
Upsy-daisy.

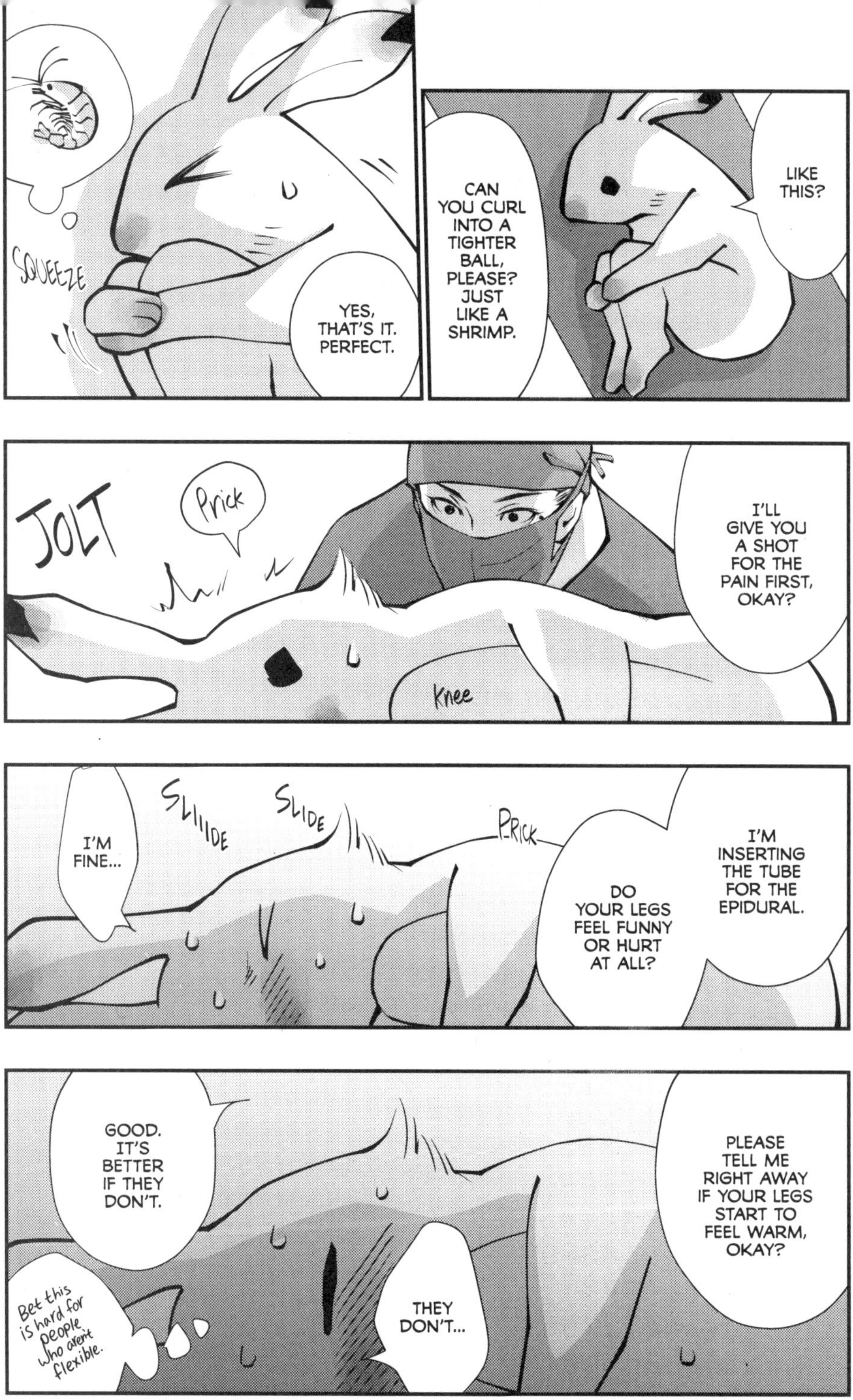
CAN YOU CURL INTO A TIGHTER BALL, PLEASE? JUST LIKE A SHRIMP.
LIKE THIS?
YES, THAT'S IT. PERFECT.
SQUEEZE
I'LL GIVE YOU A SHOT FOR THE PAIN FIRST, OKAY?
Prick
JOLT
Knee
I'M INSERTING THE TUBE FOR THE EPIDURAL.
DO YOUR LEGS FEEL FUNNY OR HURT AT ALL?
PRICK
SLIDE
SLIIIDE
I'M FINE...
PLEASE TELL ME RIGHT AWAY IF YOUR LEGS START TO FEEL WARM, OKAY?
THEY DON'T...
GOOD. IT'S BETTER IF THEY DON'T.
Bet this is hard for people who aren't flexible.

IT'S IN.
PLEASE MOVE SLOWLY WHILE LOOKING STRAIGHT UP UNTIL YOU ARE FLAT ON YOUR BACK.
※You have to move yourself onto your back.
THIS IS A NARROW TABLE.
OPERATING TABLES ARE REALLY WARM, AREN'T THEY?
MY WHOLE BODY'S SLOWLY GETTING WARM AND COZY...
OH, THAT'S NORMAL. DON'T WORRY.
Okay
ALL RIGHT...
I'M PUTTING AN OXYGEN MASK ON YOU.
PLOP
Shooo-tok—...
YOUR IV...
HAS ANESTHESIA FLOWING NOW.
YOU'LL START TO FEEL SLEEPY.
SHOOO—
GROAN......
SHOOO—

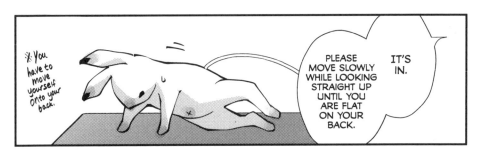

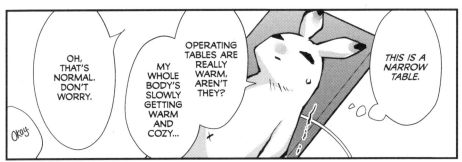

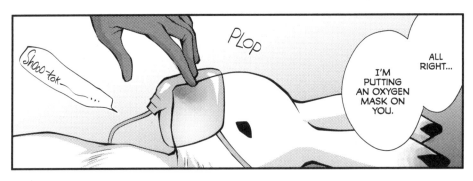

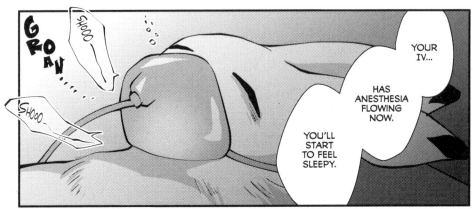

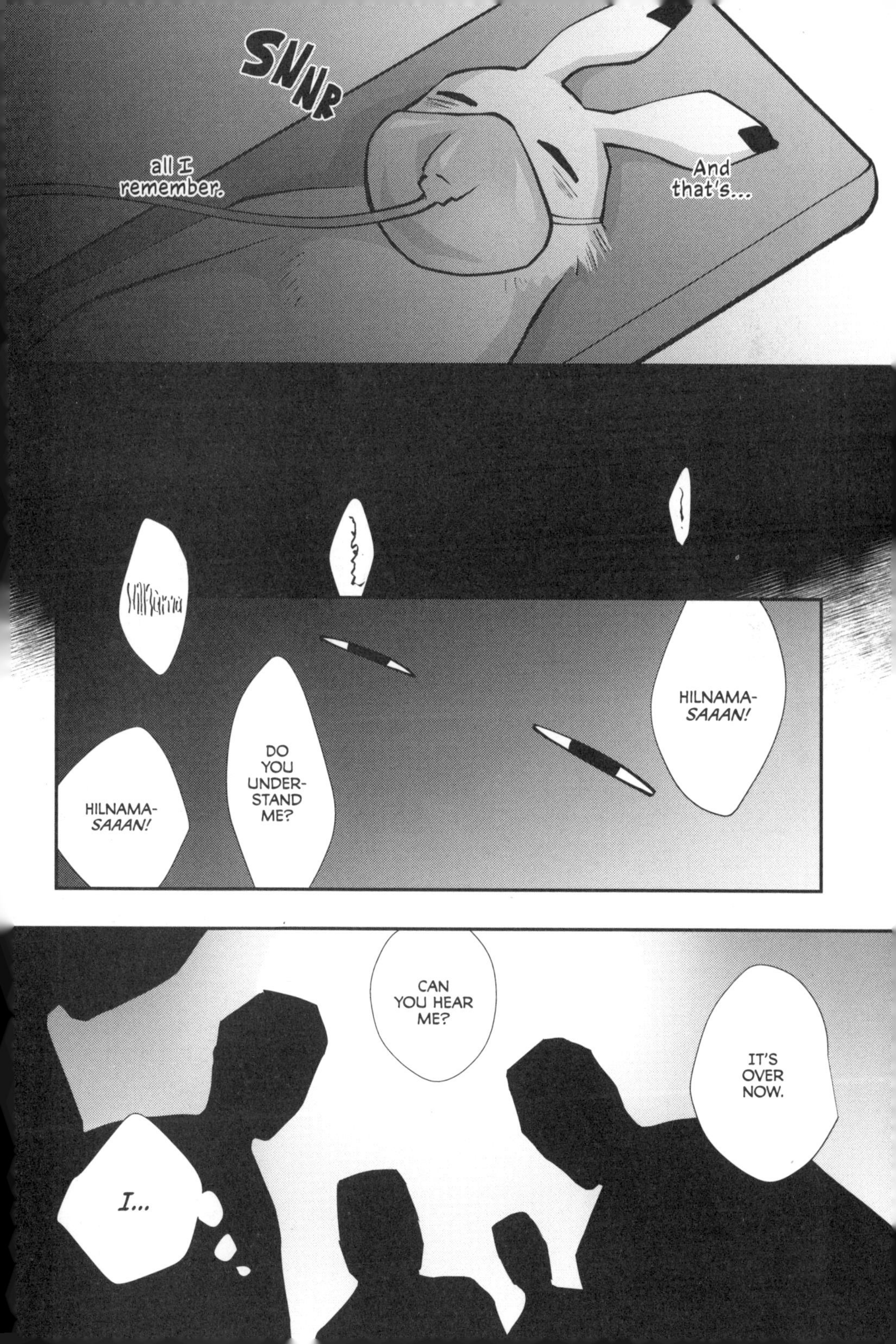

SNNR
And that's...
all I remember.
HILNAMA-SAAAN!
DO YOU UNDER-STAND ME?
HILNAMA-SAAAN!
IT'S OVER NOW.
CAN YOU HEAR ME?
I...

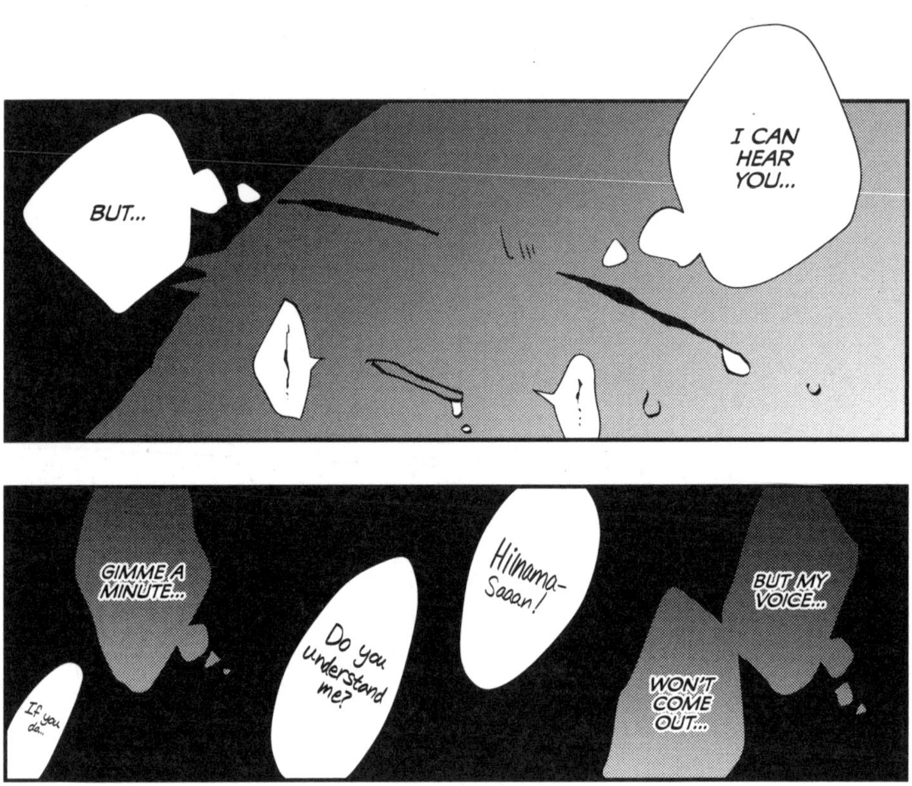
I CAN HEAR YOU...
BUT...
BUT MY VOICE...
WON'T COME OUT...
Himama-Saaan!
Do you understand me?
GIMME A MINUTE...
If you da...

※. Your trachea's intubated during surgery, so you might find it hard to speak afterward.

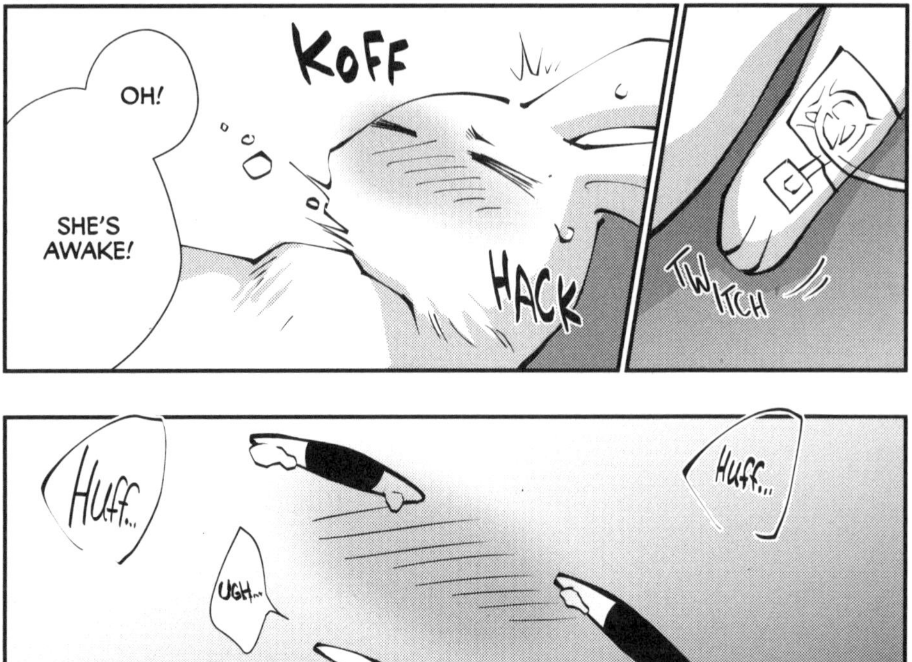
TWITCH
KOFF
HACK
OH!
SHE'S AWAKE!
Huff...
Huff...
UGH...

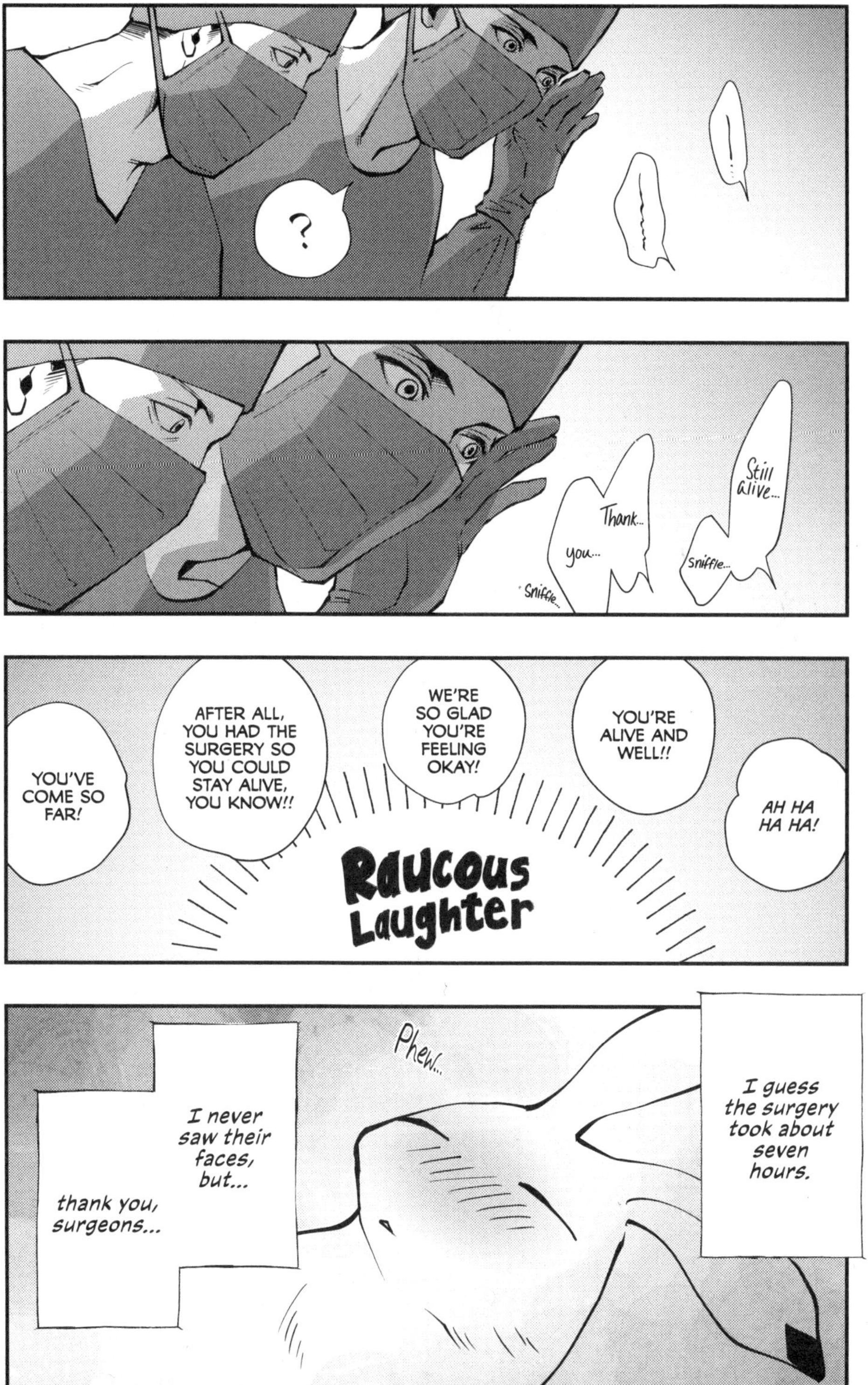
!
?
Still alive...
sniffle...
Thank... you...
Sniffle...
AH HA HA HA!
YOU'RE ALIVE AND WELL!!
WE'RE SO GLAD YOU'RE FEELING OKAY!
AFTER ALL, YOU HAD THE SURGERY SO YOU COULD STAY ALIVE, YOU KNOW!!
YOU'VE COME SO FAR!
Raucous Laughter
I guess the surgery took about seven hours.
Phew...
I never saw their faces, but...
thank you, surgeons...

Thank...
......
※My head was still fuzzy plus I didn't have my glasses...
I don't remember the room or machines at all.
《ICU》
WHEEZE
Huff
THIS PAIN IS...
SO BAD!
WHEEZE
SHOOO-TOK
Huff
WHEEZE
Huff
NO, NO, NO, NO!
WHEEZE
THIS HURTS TOO MUCH, RIGHT?!
SHOOO-TOK
Huff

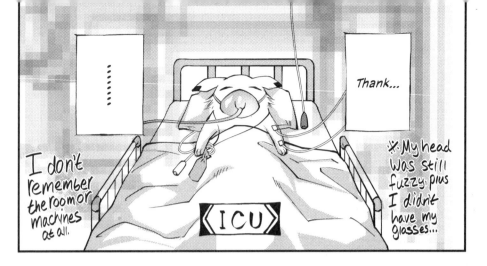

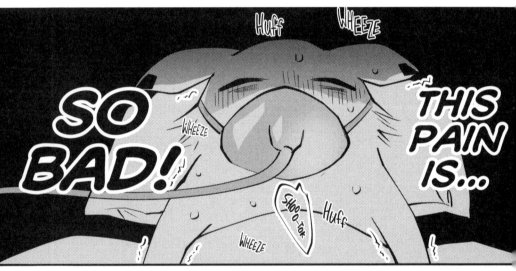

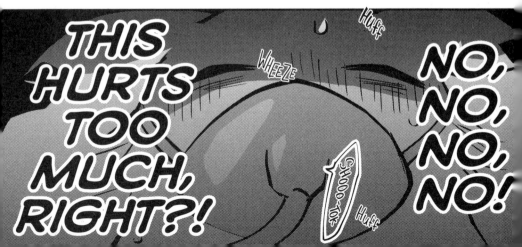

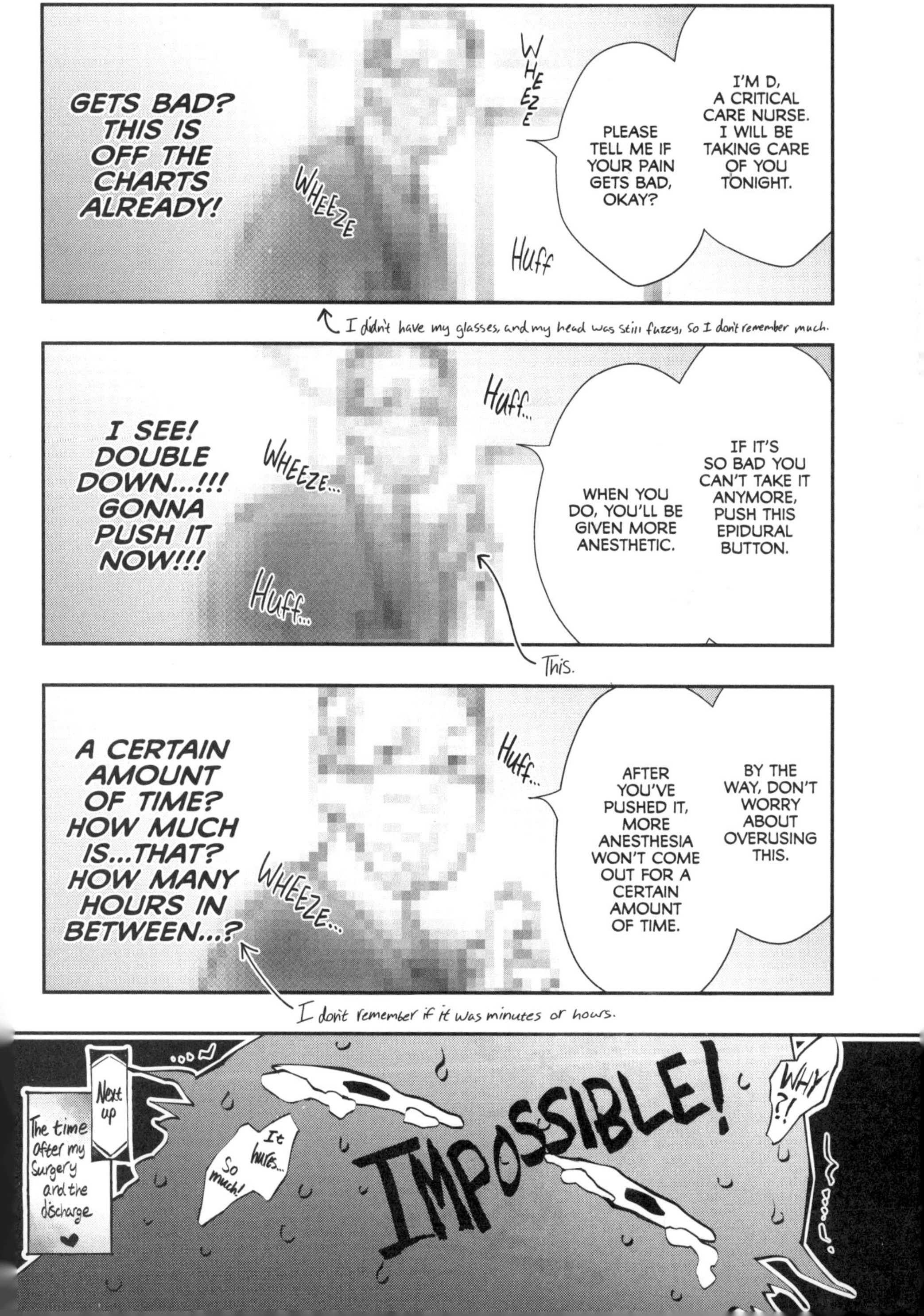
I'M D, A CRITICAL CARE NURSE. I WILL BE TAKING CARE OF YOU TONIGHT.
PLEASE TELL ME IF YOUR PAIN GETS BAD, OKAY?
WHEEZE
Huff
WHEEZE
GETS BAD? THIS IS OFF THE CHARTS ALREADY!
I didn't have my glasses, and my head was still fuzzy, so I don't remember much.
IF IT'S SO BAD YOU CAN'T TAKE IT ANYMORE, PUSH THIS EPIDURAL BUTTON.
WHEN YOU DO, YOU'LL BE GIVEN MORE ANESTHETIC.
Huff...
This.
WHEEZE...
Huff...
I SEE! DOUBLE DOWN...!!! GONNA PUSH IT NOW!!!
BY THE WAY, DON'T WORRY ABOUT OVERUSING THIS.
AFTER YOU'VE PUSHED IT, MORE ANESTHESIA WON'T COME OUT FOR A CERTAIN AMOUNT OF TIME.
Huff...
WHEEZE...
A CERTAIN AMOUNT OF TIME? HOW MUCH IS...THAT? HOW MANY HOURS IN BETWEEN...?
I don't remember if it was minutes or hours.
WHY?!
IMPOSSIBLE!
It hurts...
So much!
Next up
The time after my surgery and the discharge ♥

I'm a Terminal
Cancer
Patient
=≈ BUT I'M FINE ≈=

I thought I had a Stomachache, but it Was terminal cancer. ⑧ The time after my surgery and the discharge.

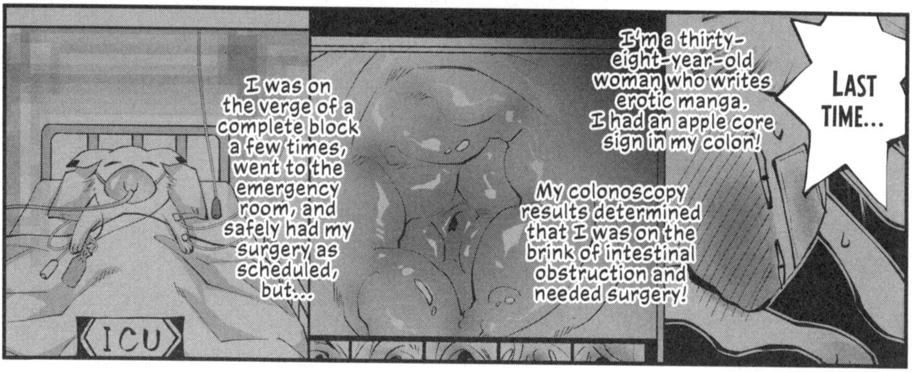
LAST TIME...
I'm a thirty-eight-year-old woman who writes erotic manga. I had an apple core sign in my colon!
My colonoscopy results determined that I was on the brink of intestinal obstruction and needed surgery!
I was on the verge of a complete block a few times, went to the emergency room, and safely had my surgery as scheduled, but...
ICU

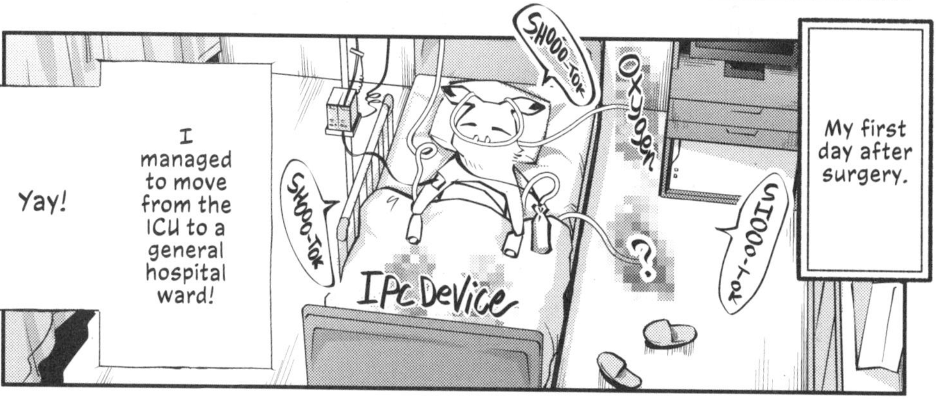
My first day after surgery.
SHOOO-TOK
Oxygen
SHOOO-TOK
?
SHOOO-TOK
IPC Device
I managed to move from the ICU to a general hospital ward!
Yay!

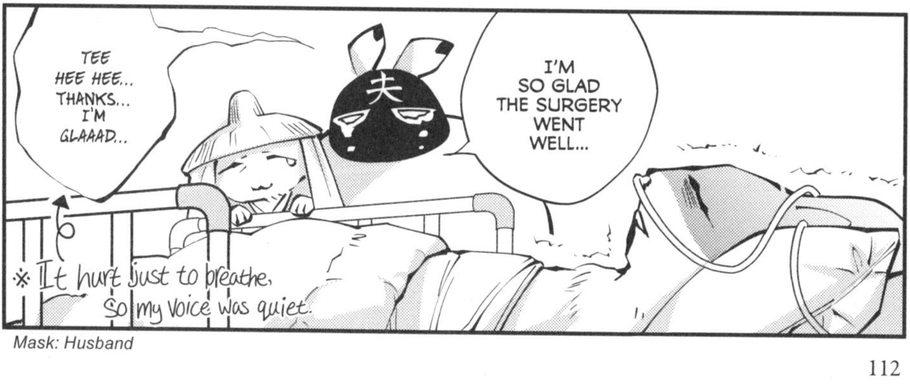
I'M SO GLAD THE SURGERY WENT WELL...
夫
TEE HEE HEE... THANKS... I'M GLAAAD...
※ It hurt just to breathe, so my voice was quiet.

Mask: Husband

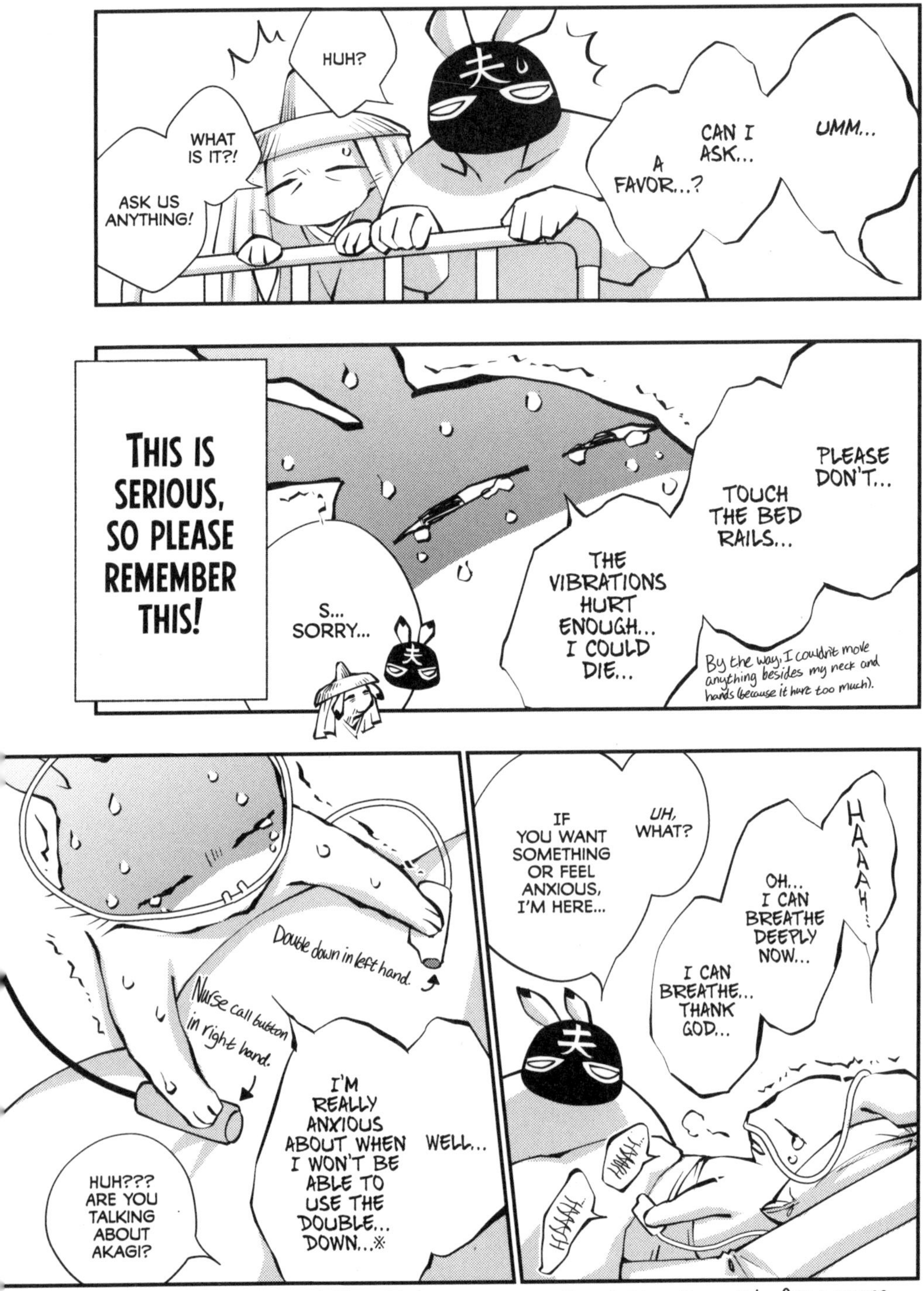
UMM...
CAN I ASK... A FAVOR...?
HUH?
WHAT IS IT?! ASK US ANYTHING!
PLEASE DON'T... TOUCH THE BED RAILS...
THE VIBRATIONS HURT ENOUGH... I COULD DIE...
By the way, I couldn't move anything besides my neck and hands (because it hurt too much).
S... SORRY...
THIS IS SERIOUS, SO PLEASE REMEMBER THIS!
HAAAH...
OH... I CAN BREATHE DEEPLY NOW...
I CAN BREATHE... THANK GOD...
UH, WHAT?
IF YOU WANT SOMETHING OR FEEL ANXIOUS, I'M HERE...
HAAAH...
HAAAH...
Double down in left hand.
WELL...
I'M REALLY ANXIOUS ABOUT WHEN I WON'T BE ABLE TO USE THE DOUBLE... DOWN...※
Nurse call button in right hand.
HUH??? ARE YOU TALKING ABOUT AKAGI?

※I decided to name the epidural button after a thing from a manga.

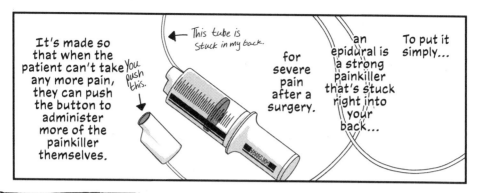

To put it simply...
an epidural is a strong painkiller that's stuck right into your back...
for severe pain after a surgery.
This tube is stuck in my back.
You push this.
It's made so that when the patient can't take any more pain, they can push the button to administer more of the painkiller themselves.
There wasn't much left, but...
Only one dose left!
Make sure you look at the measurements and figure out how much is left.
it still hurt too much.
Since this was my first time, I didn't know if that much pain was normal...
After all, my period cramps are really bad...
Maybe I'm just not good at dealing with pain.
So, I asked the nurse...
EVEN AFTER THE EPIDURAL IS FINISHED, YOU STILL HAVE YOUR IV, SINGLE-DOSE MEDICATION, AND SUPPOSITORIES, SO IT'S ALL RIGHT.
STUFF LIKE ACETAMINOPHEN OR IBUPROFEN.
Are you kidding me?
Aren't those just over the counter?
Plus, I couldn't talk much.
I couldn't really tell the nurse how anxious I was...
Ngh...
Ugh...
NOW I HAVE NO CHOICE...

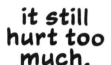

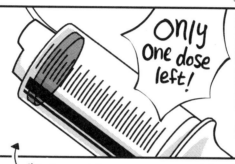

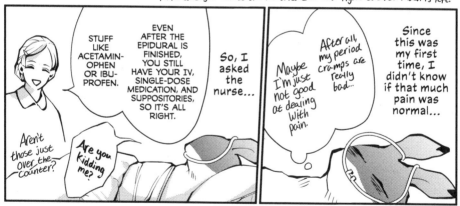

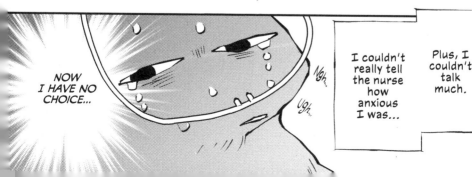

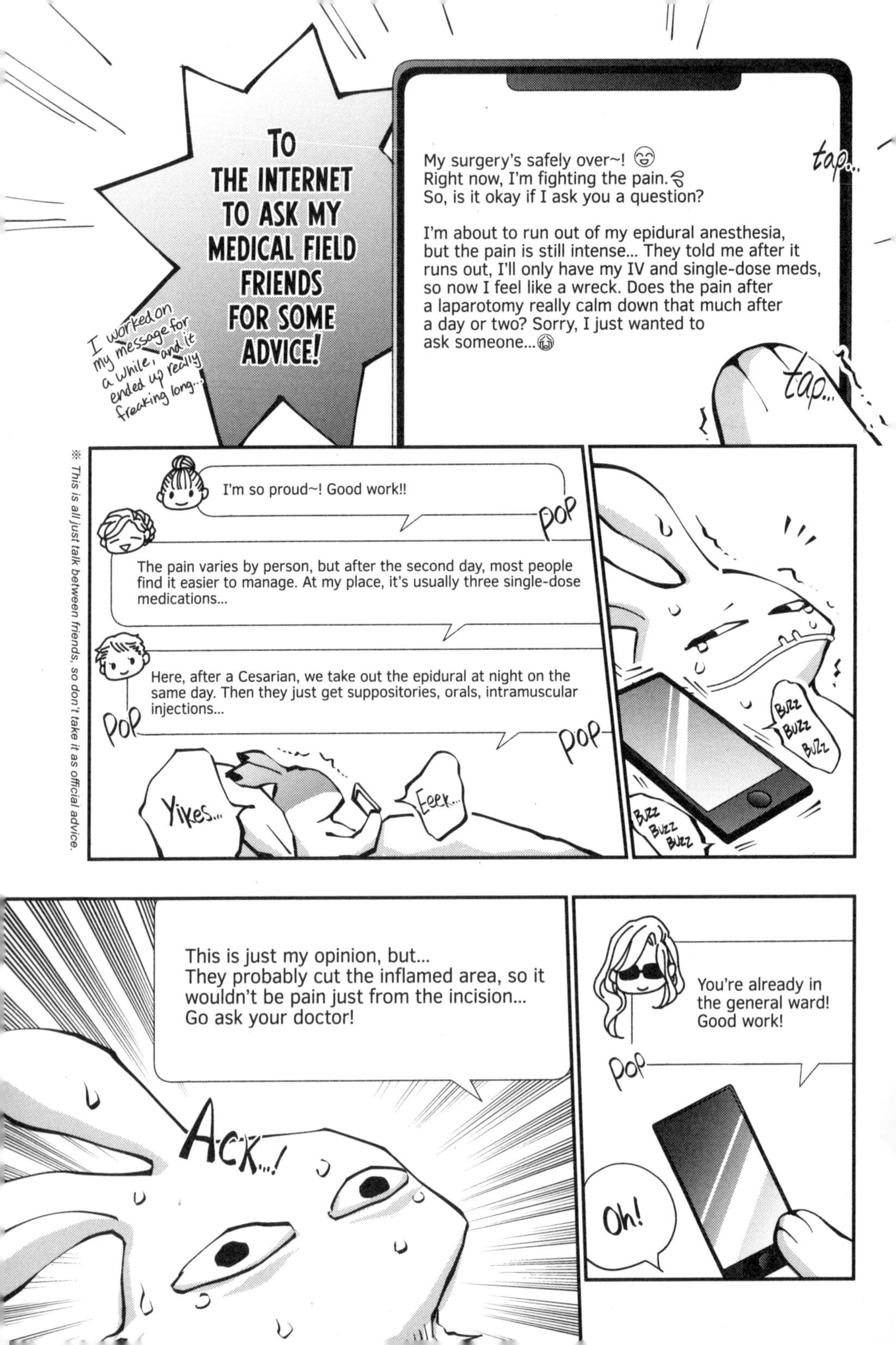
tap...
My surgery's safely over~! 😊
Right now, I'm fighting the pain.
So, is it okay if I ask you a question?
I'm about to run out of my epidural anesthesia, but the pain is still intense... They told me after it runs out, I'll only have my IV and single-dose meds, so now I feel like a wreck. Does the pain after a laparotomy really calm down that much after a day or two? Sorry, I just wanted to ask someone...
tap...
TO THE INTERNET TO ASK MY MEDICAL FIELD FRIENDS FOR SOME ADVICE!
I worked on my message for a while, and it ended up really freaking long...
BUZZ BUZZ BUZZ
BUZZ BUZZ BUZZ
I'm so proud~! Good work!!
POP
The pain varies by person, but after the second day, most people find it easier to manage. At my place, it's usually three single-dose medications...
Here, after a Cesarian, we take out the epidural at night on the same day. Then they just get suppositories, orals, intramuscular injections...
POP
POP
Eeek...
Yikes...
※ This is all just talk between friends, so don't take it as official advice.
You're already in the general ward! Good work!
POP
Oh!
This is just my opinion, but...
They probably cut the inflamed area, so it wouldn't be pain just from the incision...
Go ask your doctor!
ACK...!

NOW THAT SHE MENTIONS IT...
Staples
Belly button
ACCORDING TO THE EXPLANATION I GOT EARLIER, THERE'S ONLY ONE VERTICAL INCISION ON MY TORSO.
BUT THE PAIN RIGHT NOW...
IS A BURNING FEELING COMING FROM ALL OVER MY STOMACH.
IS...
IS MY COLON HURTING...?

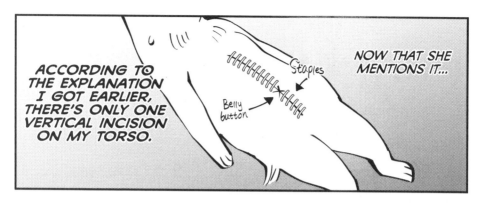

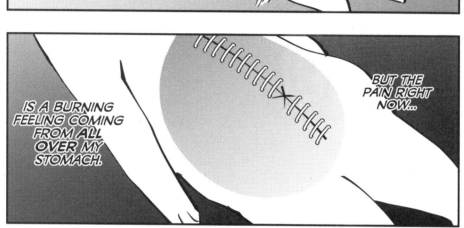

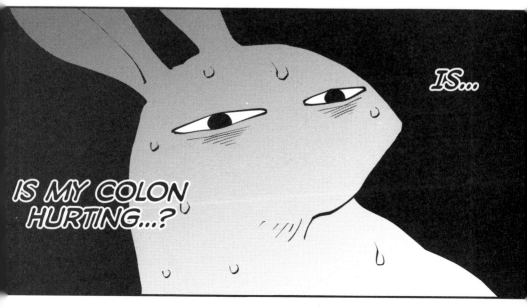

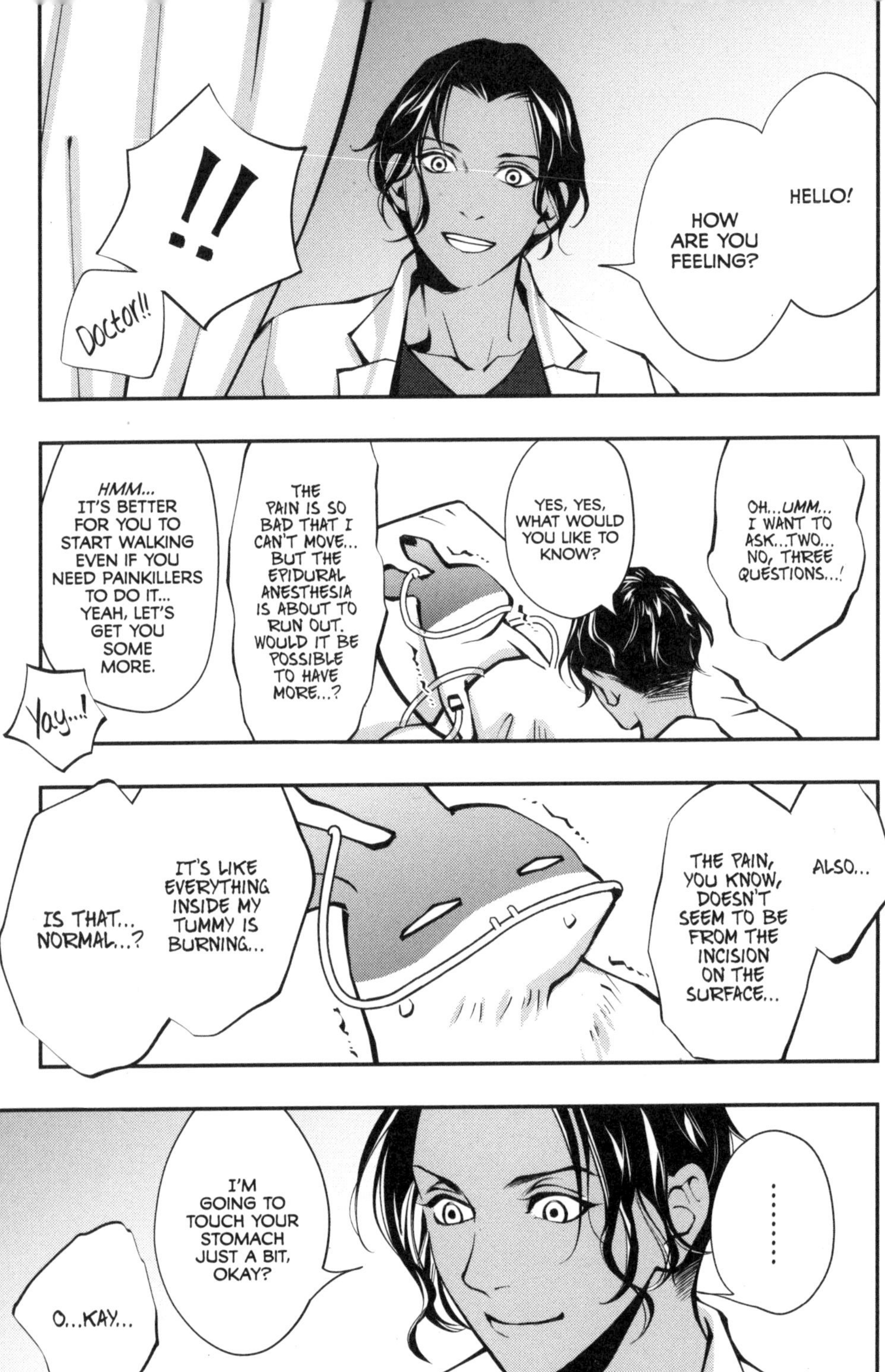
HELLO!
HOW ARE YOU FEELING?
!!
Doctor!!
OH...UMM... I WANT TO ASK...TWO... NO, THREE QUESTIONS...!
YES, YES, WHAT WOULD YOU LIKE TO KNOW?
THE PAIN IS SO BAD THAT I CAN'T MOVE... BUT THE EPIDURAL ANESTHESIA IS ABOUT TO RUN OUT. WOULD IT BE POSSIBLE TO HAVE MORE...?
HMM... IT'S BETTER FOR YOU TO START WALKING EVEN IF YOU NEED PAINKILLERS TO DO IT... YEAH, LET'S GET YOU SOME MORE.
Yay...!
ALSO...
THE PAIN, YOU KNOW, DOESN'T SEEM TO BE FROM THE INCISION ON THE SURFACE...
IT'S LIKE EVERYTHING INSIDE MY TUMMY IS BURNING...
IS THAT... NORMAL...?
....
I'M GOING TO TOUCH YOUR STOMACH JUST A BIT, OKAY?
O...KAY...

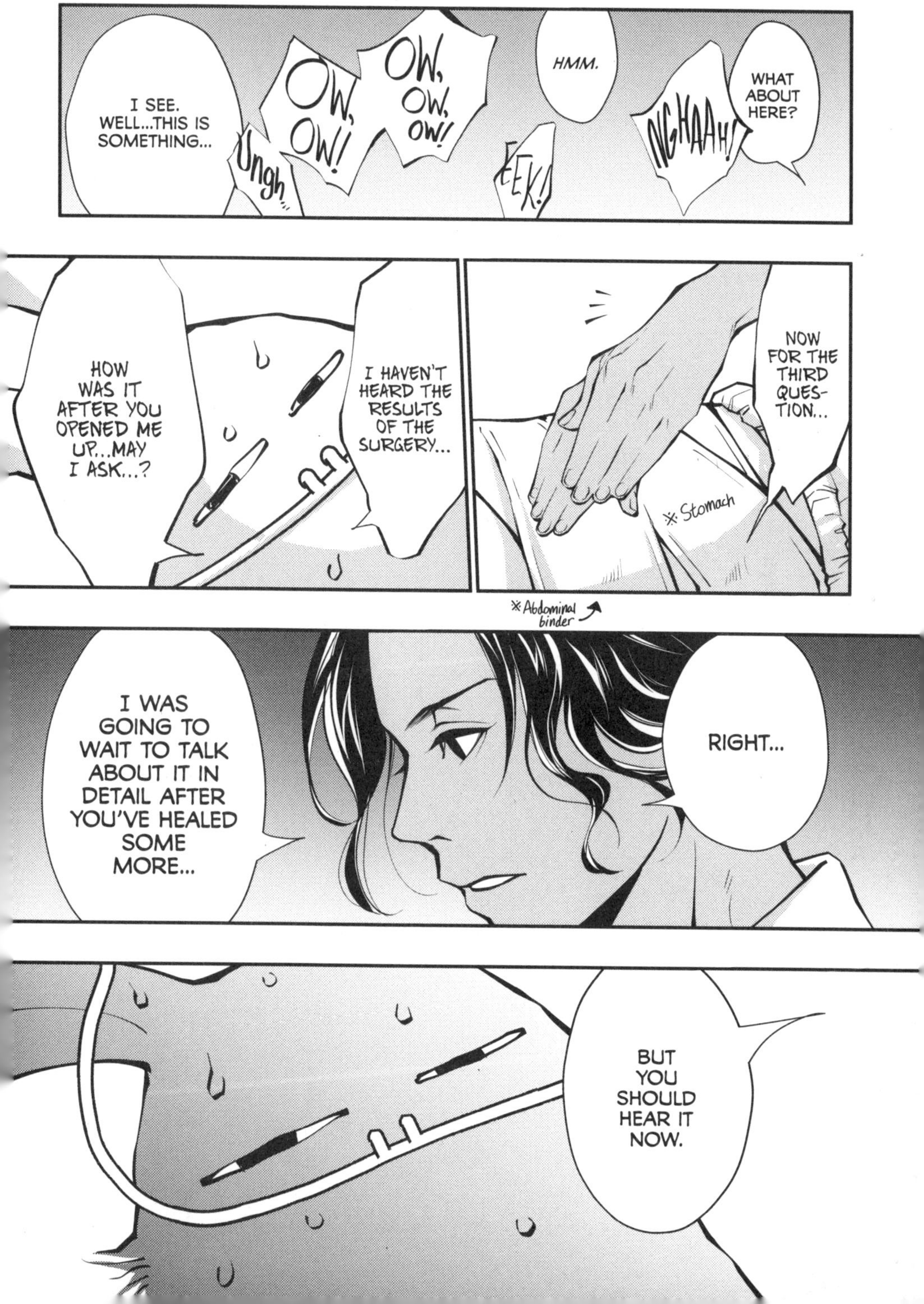
WHAT ABOUT HERE?
NGHAAAH!
EEK!
HMM.
OW, OW, OW!
OW, OW!
Ungh...
I SEE. WELL...THIS IS SOMETHING...
NOW FOR THE THIRD QUES-TION...
※ Stomach
I HAVEN'T HEARD THE RESULTS OF THE SURGERY...
HOW WAS IT AFTER YOU OPENED ME UP...MAY I ASK...?
※ Abdominal binder
RIGHT...
I WAS GOING TO WAIT TO TALK ABOUT IT IN DETAIL AFTER YOU'VE HEALED SOME MORE...
BUT YOU SHOULD HEAR IT NOW.

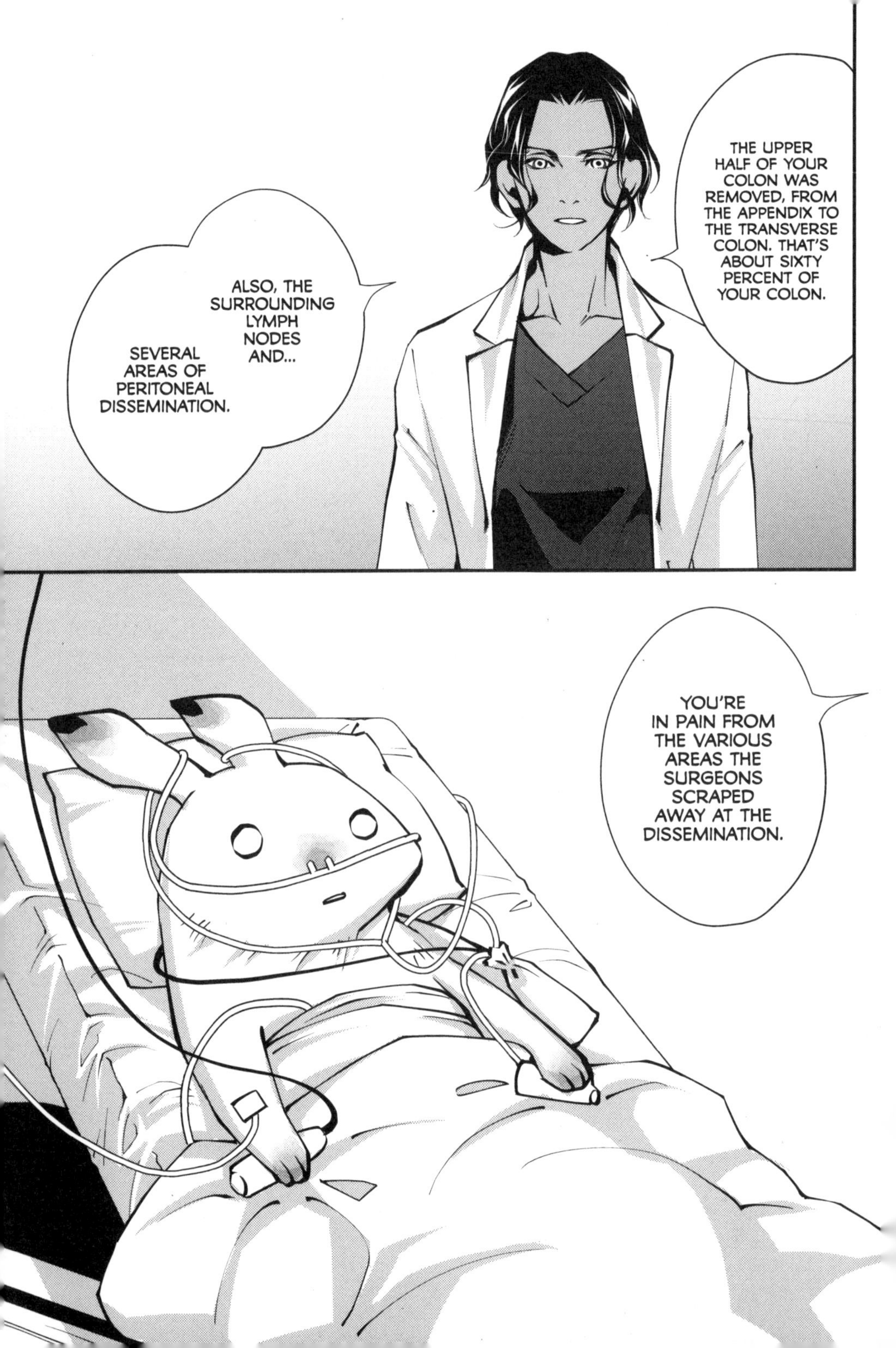
THE UPPER HALF OF YOUR COLON WAS REMOVED, FROM THE APPENDIX TO THE TRANSVERSE COLON. THAT'S ABOUT SIXTY PERCENT OF YOUR COLON.
ALSO, THE SURROUNDING LYMPH NODES AND...
SEVERAL AREAS OF PERITONEAL DISSEMINATION.
YOU'RE IN PAIN FROM THE VARIOUS AREAS THE SURGEONS SCRAPED AWAY AT THE DISSEMINATION.

PERITONEAL

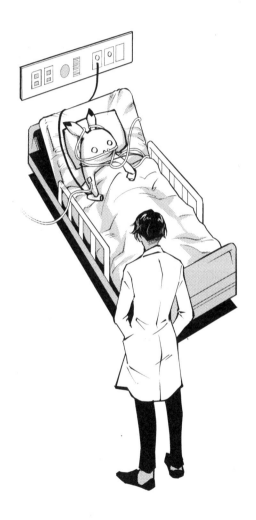

DISSEMINATION...?

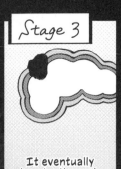

Peritoneal dissemination is a form of metastasis.
Stage 0
Muscular Layer
Mucous membrane
It's the colon cancer that forms on the inside of the colon.
Stage 1
It slowly advances and invades the structures of the colon.
Stage 3
It eventually breaks through the colon...
and spreads cancer throughout the abdominal cavity, like it's sowing seeds.
Then it sticks to the peritoneum, and when it grows large enough to see, it's called peritoneal dissemination.
Stage 4
Liver
Stomach
Peritoneum
Colon
Magnified
(This is a really big membrane. Stuff like your stomach and intestines are wrapped up in here.)
Abdominal Cavity
Greater Omentum
Small Intestine
※This is a really crude diagram!
It's really hard to completely remove peritoneal dissemination with surgery.
It's impossible to find peritoneal dissemination in the early stages when it's small enough to be invisible to the eye. It can't always be detected with an ultrasound or a CT scan, either.
Relapses often happen, and the prognosis is poor. Complete recovery is difficult.

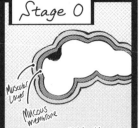

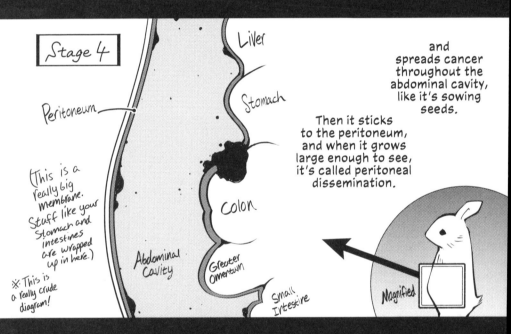

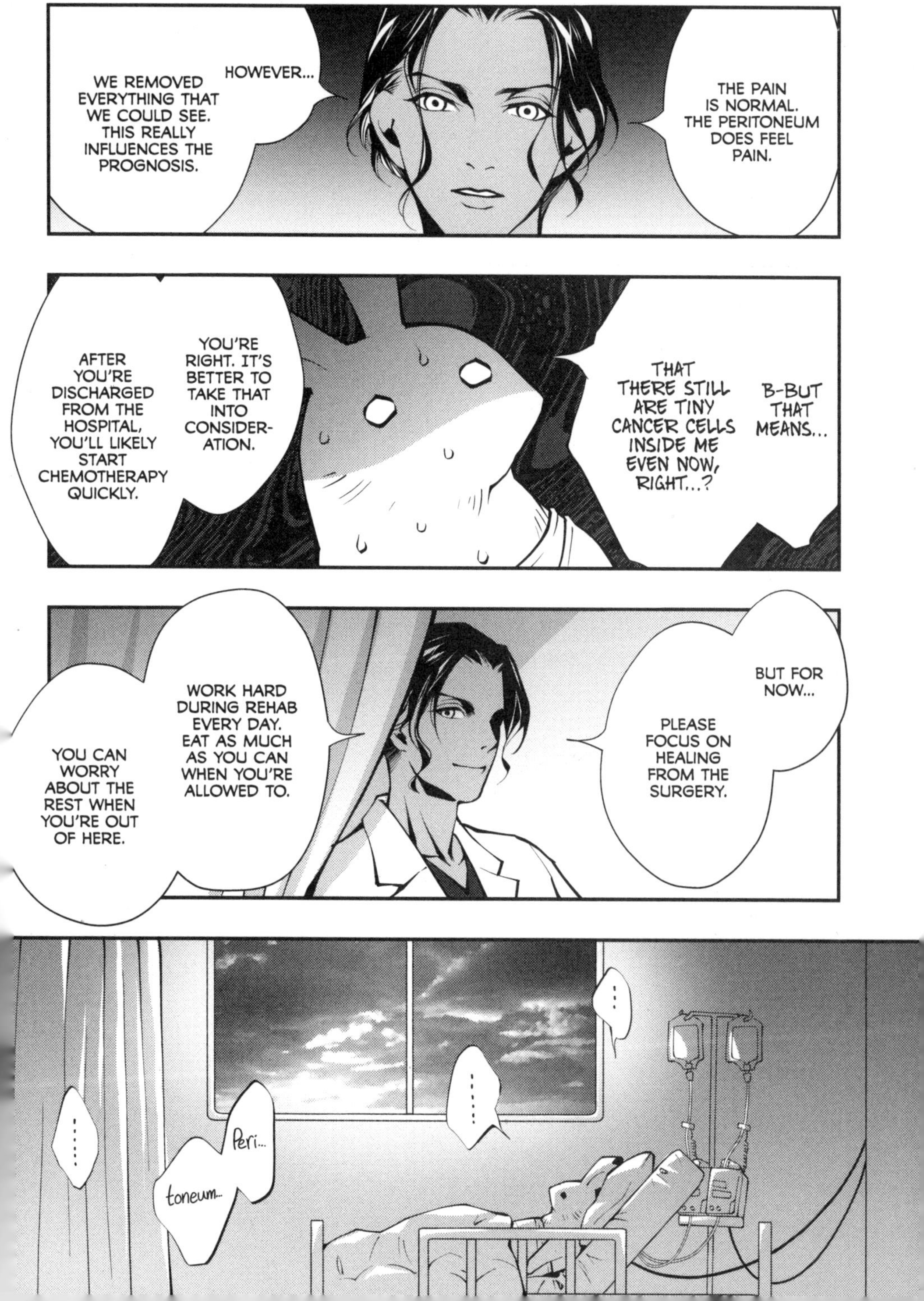
THE PAIN IS NORMAL. THE PERITONEUM DOES FEEL PAIN.
HOWEVER...
WE REMOVED EVERYTHING THAT WE COULD SEE. THIS REALLY INFLUENCES THE PROGNOSIS.
B-BUT THAT MEANS...
THAT THERE STILL ARE TINY CANCER CELLS INSIDE ME EVEN NOW, RIGHT...?
YOU'RE RIGHT. IT'S BETTER TO TAKE THAT INTO CONSIDER-ATION.
AFTER YOU'RE DISCHARGED FROM THE HOSPITAL, YOU'LL LIKELY START CHEMOTHERAPY QUICKLY.
BUT FOR NOW...
PLEASE FOCUS ON HEALING FROM THE SURGERY.
WORK HARD DURING REHAB EVERY DAY. EAT AS MUCH AS YOU CAN WHEN YOU'RE ALLOWED TO.
YOU CAN WORRY ABOUT THE REST WHEN YOU'RE OUT OF HERE.
...
......
Peri...
toneum...
......

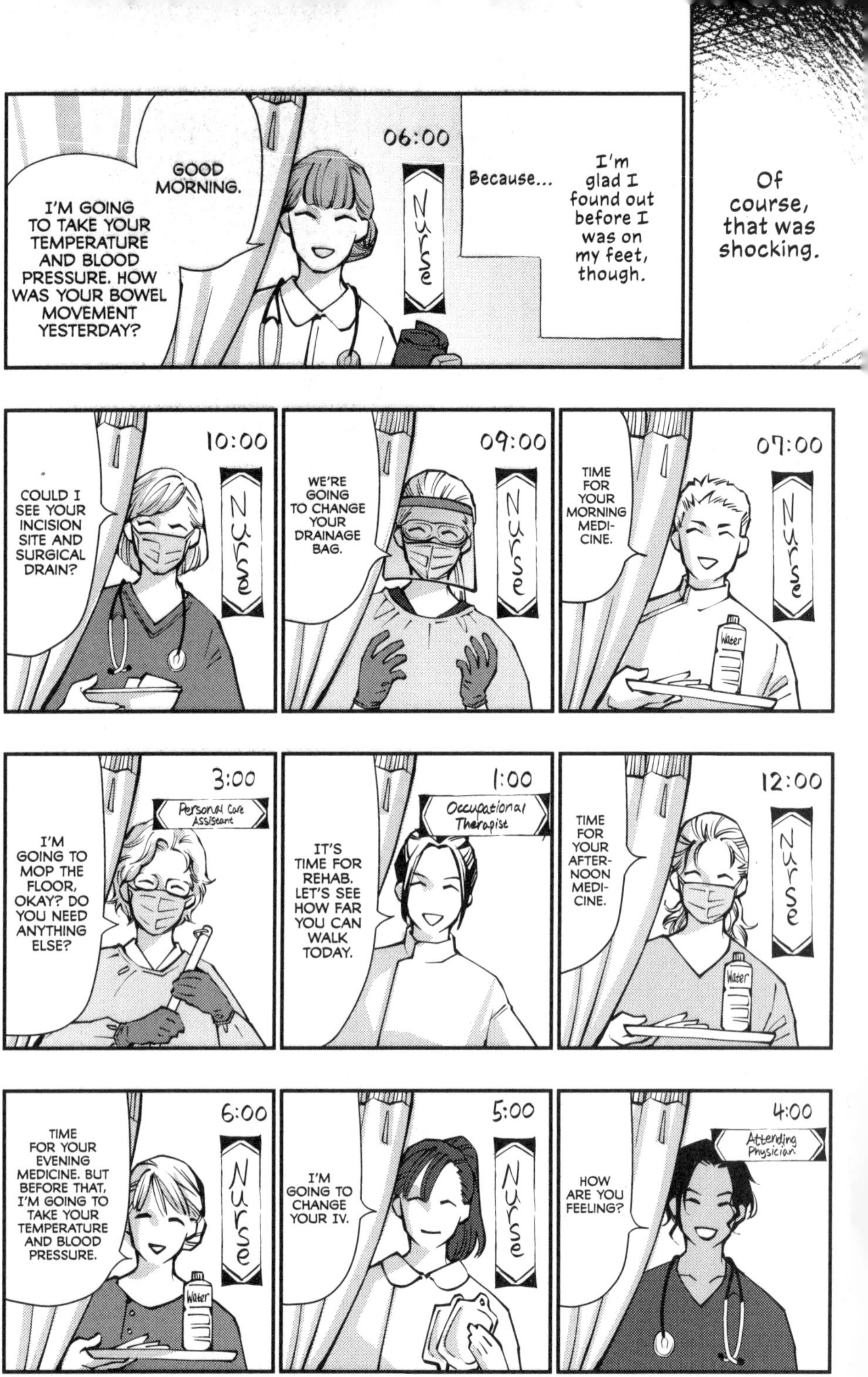
Of course, that was shocking.
I'm glad I found out before I was on my feet, though.
Because...
06:00
Nurse
GOOD MORNING.
I'M GOING TO TAKE YOUR TEMPERATURE AND BLOOD PRESSURE. HOW WAS YOUR BOWEL MOVEMENT YESTERDAY?
07:00
Nurse
TIME FOR YOUR MORNING MEDI-CINE.
Water
09:00
Nurse
WE'RE GOING TO CHANGE YOUR DRAINAGE BAG.
10:00
Nurse
COULD I SEE YOUR INCISION SITE AND SURGICAL DRAIN?
12:00
Nurse
TIME FOR YOUR AFTER-NOON MEDI-CINE.
Water
1:00
Occupational Therapist
IT'S TIME FOR REHAB. LET'S SEE HOW FAR YOU CAN WALK TODAY.
3:00
Personal Care Assistant
I'M GOING TO MOP THE FLOOR, OKAY? DO YOU NEED ANYTHING ELSE?
4:00
Attending Physician
HOW ARE YOU FEELING?
5:00
Nurse
I'M GOING TO CHANGE YOUR IV.
6:00
Nurse
TIME FOR YOUR EVENING MEDICINE. BUT BEFORE THAT, I'M GOING TO TAKE YOUR TEMPERATURE AND BLOOD PRESSURE.
Water

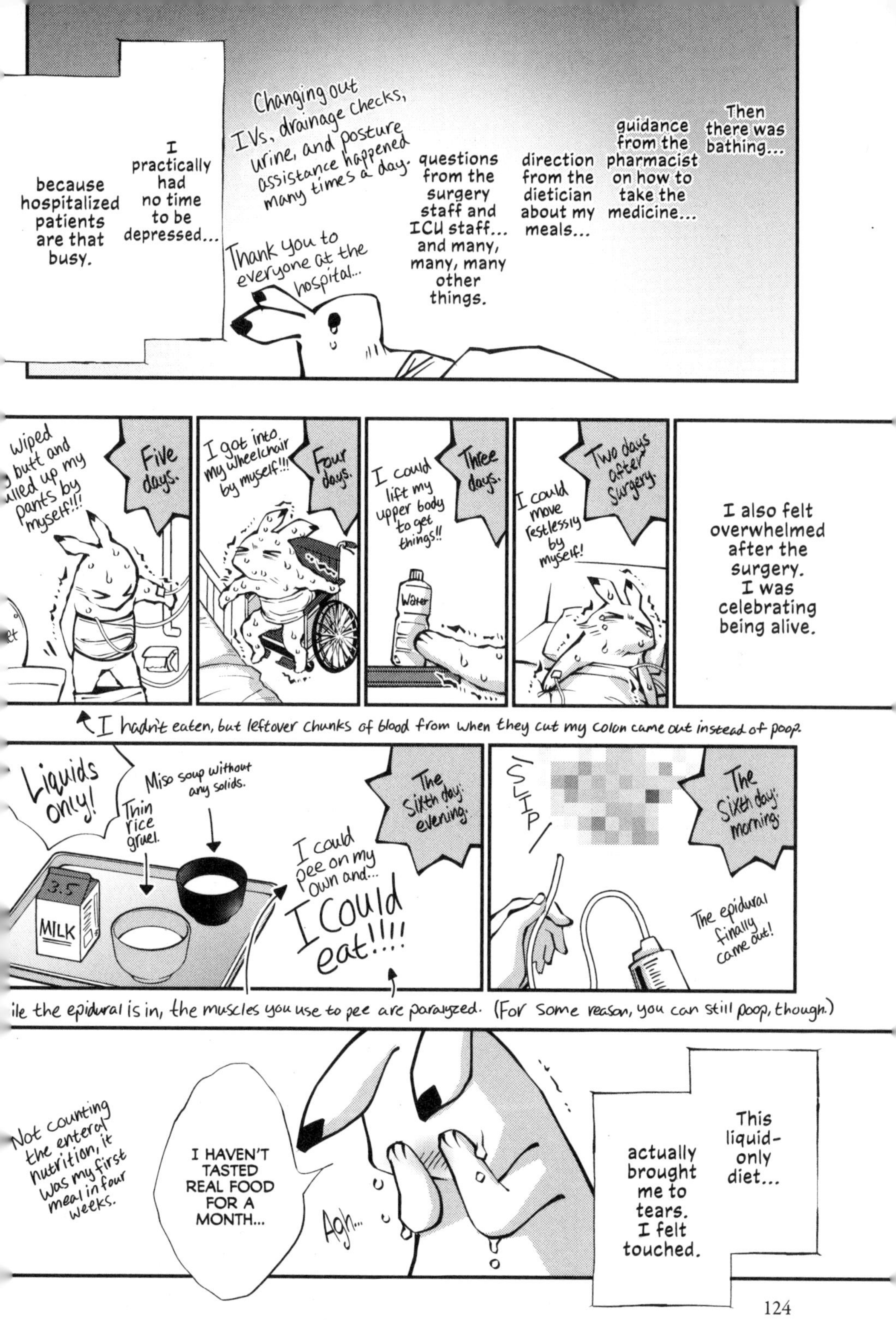
Then there was bathing...
guidance from the pharmacist on how to take the medicine...
direction from the dietician about my meals...
questions from the surgery staff and ICU staff... and many, many, many other things.
Changing out IVs, drainage checks, urine, and posture assistance happened many times a day.
Thank you to everyone at the hospital...
I practically had no time to be depressed...
because hospitalized patients are that busy.
I also felt overwhelmed after the surgery. I was celebrating being alive.
Two days after surgery.
I could move restlessly by myself!
Three days.
I could lift my upper body to get things!!
Water
Four days.
I got into my wheelchair by myself!!!
Five days.
wiped butt and ulled up my pants by myself!!!
I hadn't eaten, but leftover chunks of blood from when they cut my colon came out instead of poop.
The sixth day: morning.
SLIP
The epidural finally came out!
The sixth day: evening.
I could pee on my own and...
I could eat!!!!
Liquids only!
Miso soup without any solids.
Thin rice gruel.
3.5
MILK
ile the epidural is in, the muscles you use to pee are paralyzed. (For some reason, you can still poop, though.)
This liquid-only diet...
actually brought me to tears. I felt touched.
Agh...
I HAVEN'T TASTED REAL FOOD FOR A MONTH...
Not counting the enteral nutrition, it was my first meal in four weeks.

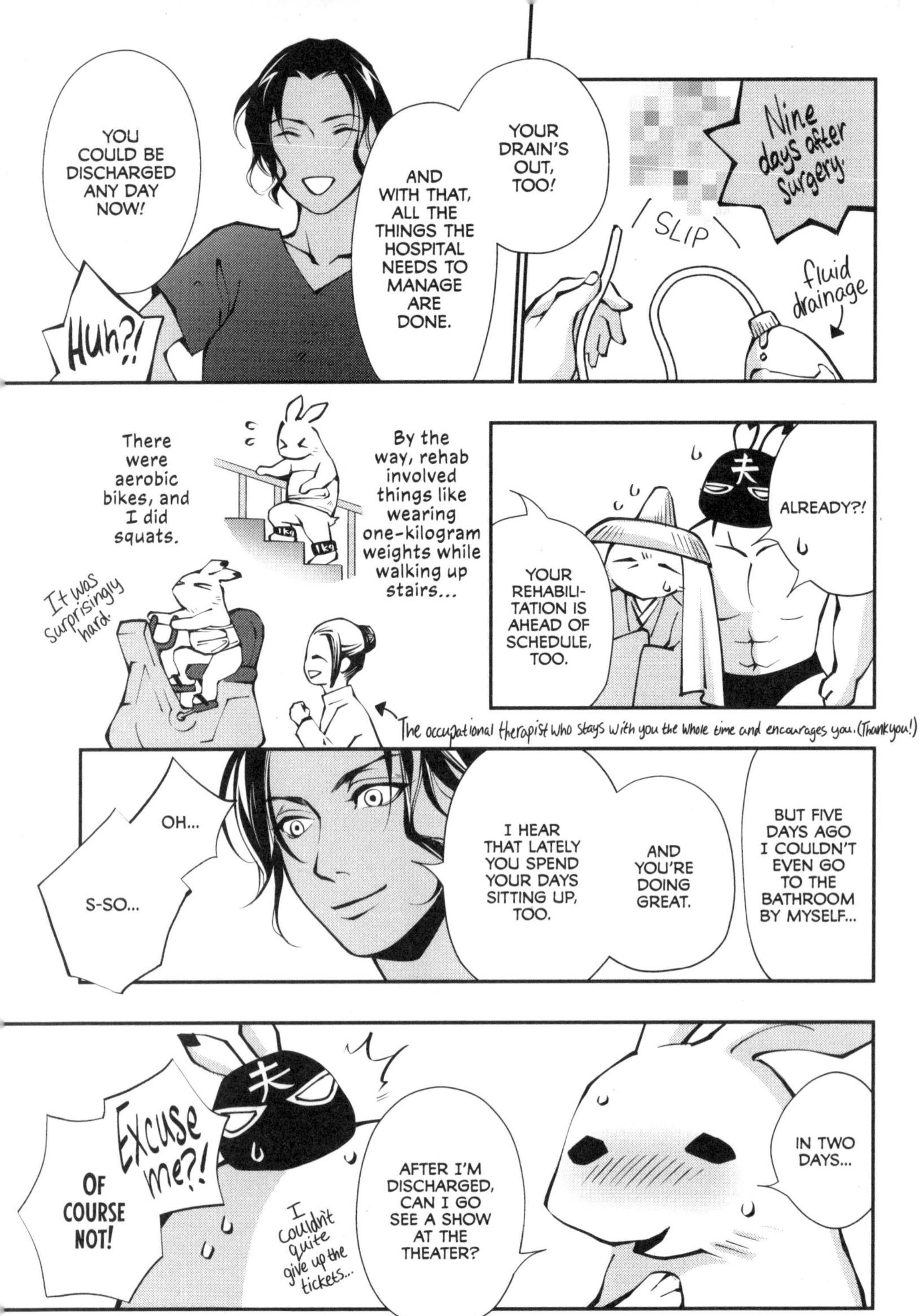
Nine days after surgery
SLIP
fluid drainage
YOUR DRAIN'S OUT, TOO!
AND WITH THAT, ALL THE THINGS THE HOSPITAL NEEDS TO MANAGE ARE DONE.
YOU COULD BE DISCHARGED ANY DAY NOW!
Huh?!
ALREADY?!
YOUR REHABILITATION IS AHEAD OF SCHEDULE, TOO.
By the way, rehab involved things like wearing one-kilogram weights while walking up stairs...
There were aerobic bikes, and I did squats.
It was surprisingly hard.
The occupational therapist who stays with you the whole time and encourages you. (Thank you!)
BUT FIVE DAYS AGO I COULDN'T EVEN GO TO THE BATHROOM BY MYSELF...
AND YOU'RE DOING GREAT.
I HEAR THAT LATELY YOU SPEND YOUR DAYS SITTING UP, TOO.
OH...
S-SO...
IN TWO DAYS...
AFTER I'M DISCHARGED, CAN I GO SEE A SHOW AT THE THEATER?
I couldn't quite give up the tickets...
Excuse me?!
OF COURSE NOT!

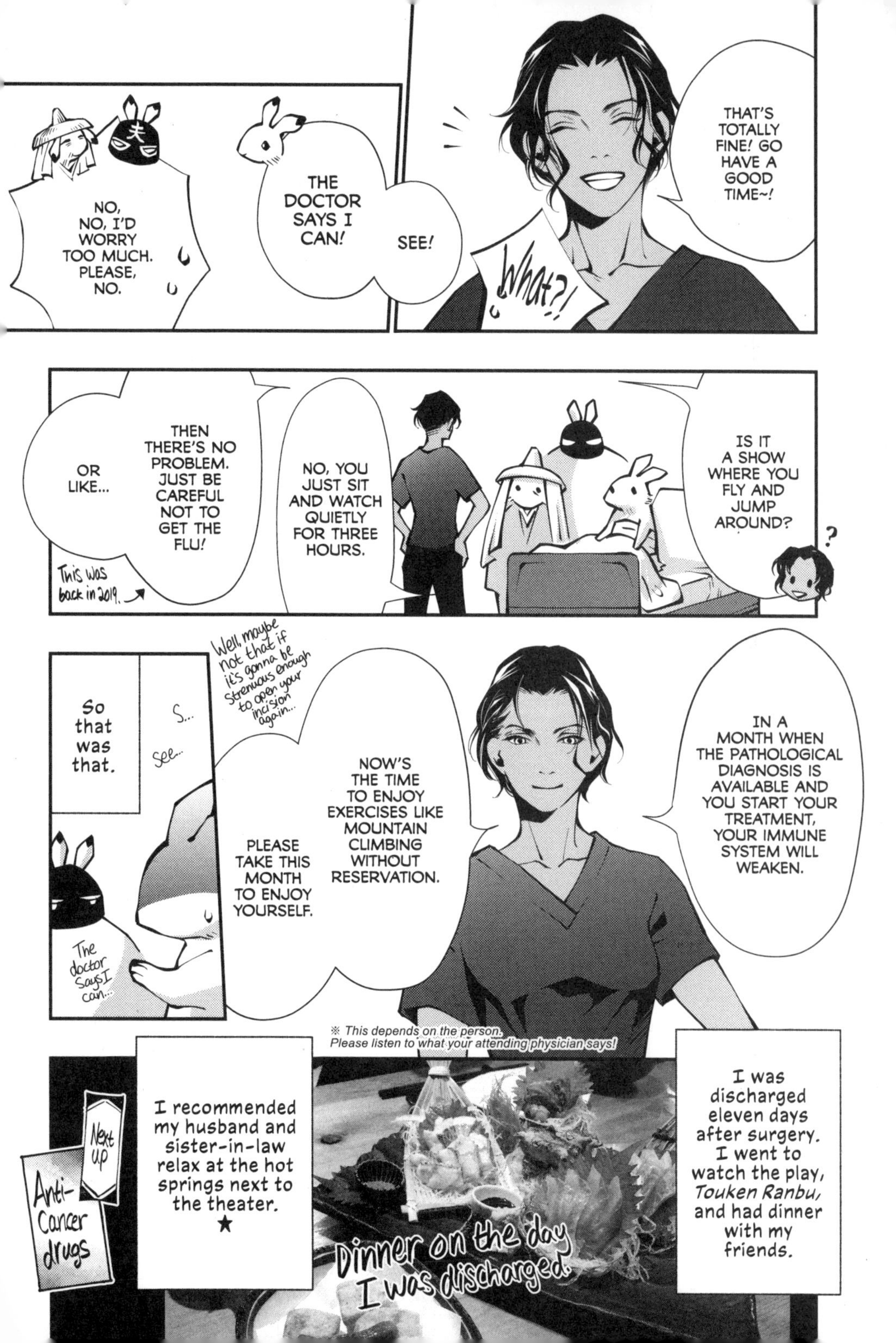
THAT'S TOTALLY FINE! GO HAVE A GOOD TIME~!
What?!
THE DOCTOR SAYS I CAN!
SEE!
NO, NO, I'D WORRY TOO MUCH. PLEASE, NO.
IS IT A SHOW WHERE YOU FLY AND JUMP AROUND?
?
NO, YOU JUST SIT AND WATCH QUIETLY FOR THREE HOURS.
THEN THERE'S NO PROBLEM. JUST BE CAREFUL NOT TO GET THE FLU!
OR LIKE...
This was back in 2019.
IN A MONTH WHEN THE PATHOLOGICAL DIAGNOSIS IS AVAILABLE AND YOU START YOUR TREATMENT, YOUR IMMUNE SYSTEM WILL WEAKEN.
NOW'S THE TIME TO ENJOY EXERCISES LIKE MOUNTAIN CLIMBING WITHOUT RESERVATION.
PLEASE TAKE THIS MONTH TO ENJOY YOURSELF.
Well, maybe not that if it's gonna be strenuous enough to open your incision again...
S...
see...
The doctor says I can...
So that was that.
※ This depends on the person. Please listen to what your attending physician says!
I was discharged eleven days after surgery. I went to watch the play, *Touken Ranbu,* and had dinner with my friends.
I recommended my husband and sister-in-law relax at the hot springs next to the theater. ★
Dinner on the day I was discharged.
Next up
Anti-Cancer drugs

I'm a Terminal
Cancer
Patient
BUT I'M FINE

I thought I had a stomachache, but it was terminal cancer. ⑨

This and that about anti-cancer drugs.

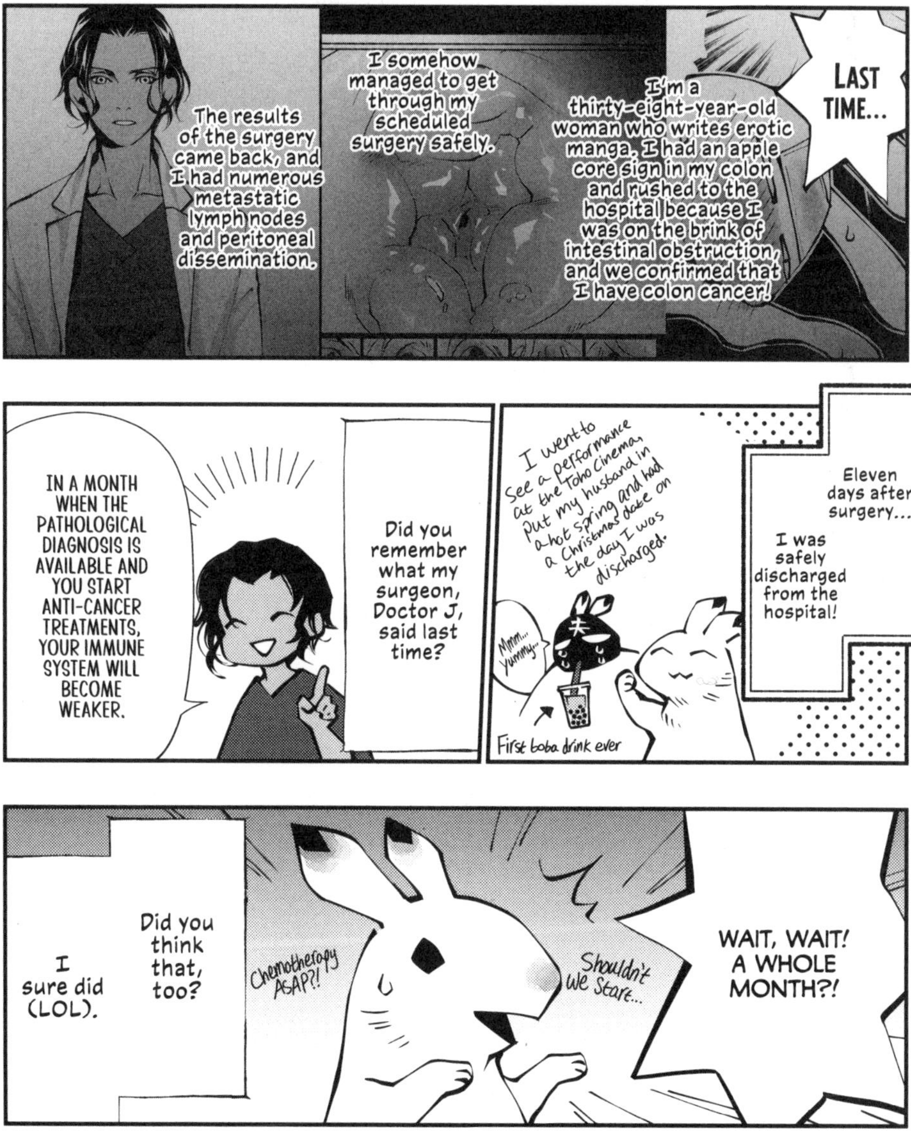
LAST TIME...
I'm a thirty-eight-year-old woman who writes erotic manga. I had an apple core sign in my colon and rushed to the hospital because I was on the brink of intestinal obstruction, and we confirmed that I have colon cancer!
I somehow managed to get through my scheduled surgery safely.
The results of the surgery came back, and I had numerous metastatic lymph nodes and peritoneal dissemination.
Eleven days after surgery...
I was safely discharged from the hospital!
I went to see a performance at the Toho Cinema, put my husband in a hot spring and had a Christmas date on the day I was discharged.
Mmm... yummy...
First boba drink ever
Did you remember what my surgeon, Doctor J, said last time?
IN A MONTH WHEN THE PATHOLOGICAL DIAGNOSIS IS AVAILABLE AND YOU START ANTI-CANCER TREATMENTS, YOUR IMMUNE SYSTEM WILL BECOME WEAKER.
WAIT, WAIT! A WHOLE MONTH?!
Shouldn't we start...
Chemotherapy ASAP?!
Did you think that, too?
I sure did (LOL).

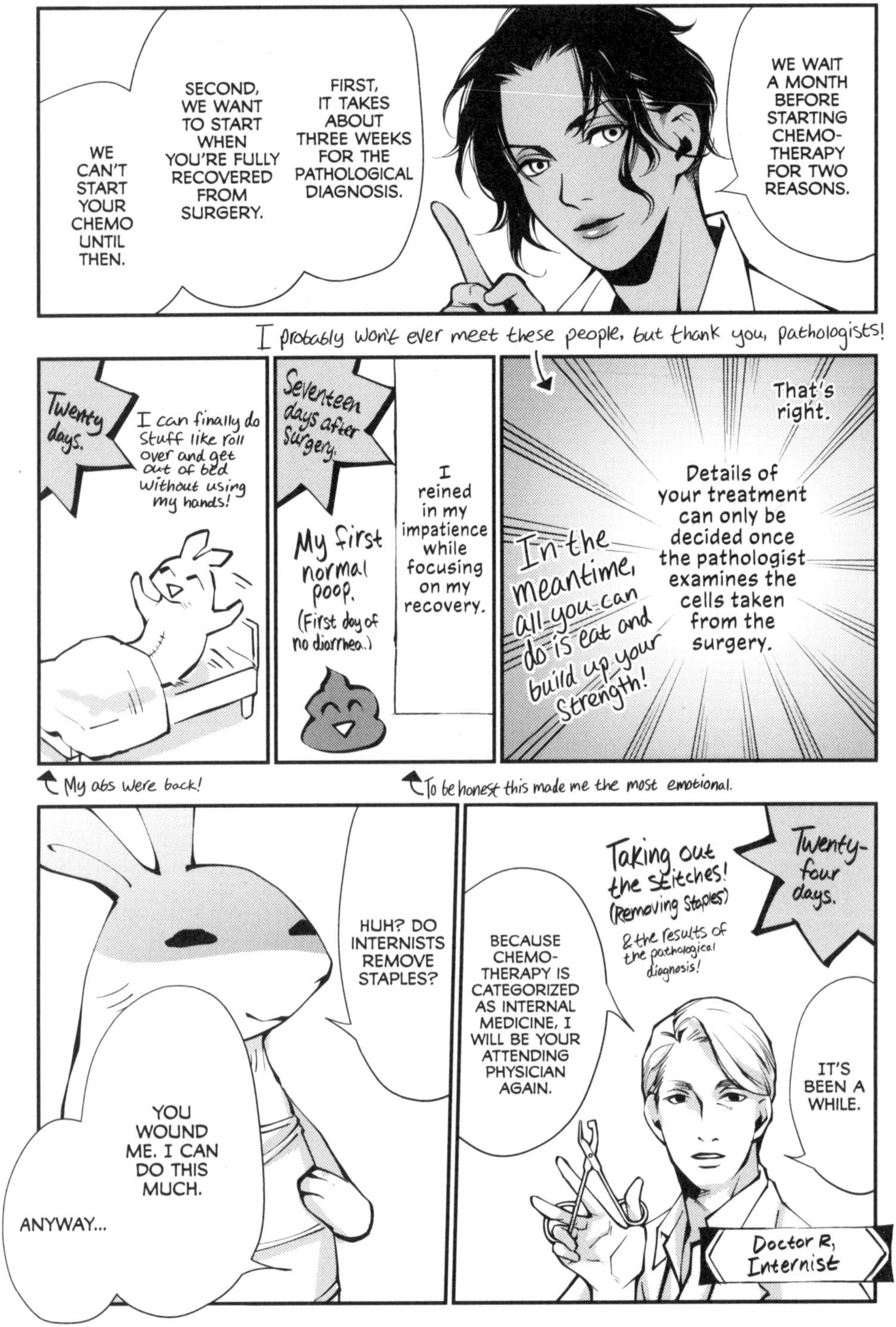
WE WAIT A MONTH BEFORE STARTING CHEMO-THERAPY FOR TWO REASONS.
FIRST, IT TAKES ABOUT THREE WEEKS FOR THE PATHOLOGICAL DIAGNOSIS.
SECOND, WE WANT TO START WHEN YOU'RE FULLY RECOVERED FROM SURGERY.
WE CAN'T START YOUR CHEMO UNTIL THEN.
I probably won't ever meet these people, but thank you, pathologists!
That's right.
Details of your treatment can only be decided once the pathologist examines the cells taken from the surgery.
In the meantime, all you can do is eat and build up your strength!
Seventeen days after surgery.
I reined in my impatience while focusing on my recovery.
My first normal poop.
(First day of no diarrhea.)
To be honest this made me the most emotional.
Twenty days.
I can finally do stuff like roll over and get out of bed without using my hands!
My abs were back!
Twenty-four days.
Taking out the stitches! (Removing Staples)
& the results of the pathological diagnosis!
IT'S BEEN A WHILE.
BECAUSE CHEMO-THERAPY IS CATEGORIZED AS INTERNAL MEDICINE, I WILL BE YOUR ATTENDING PHYSICIAN AGAIN.
Doctor R, Internist
HUH? DO INTERNISTS REMOVE STAPLES?
YOU WOUND ME. I CAN DO THIS MUCH.
ANYWAY...

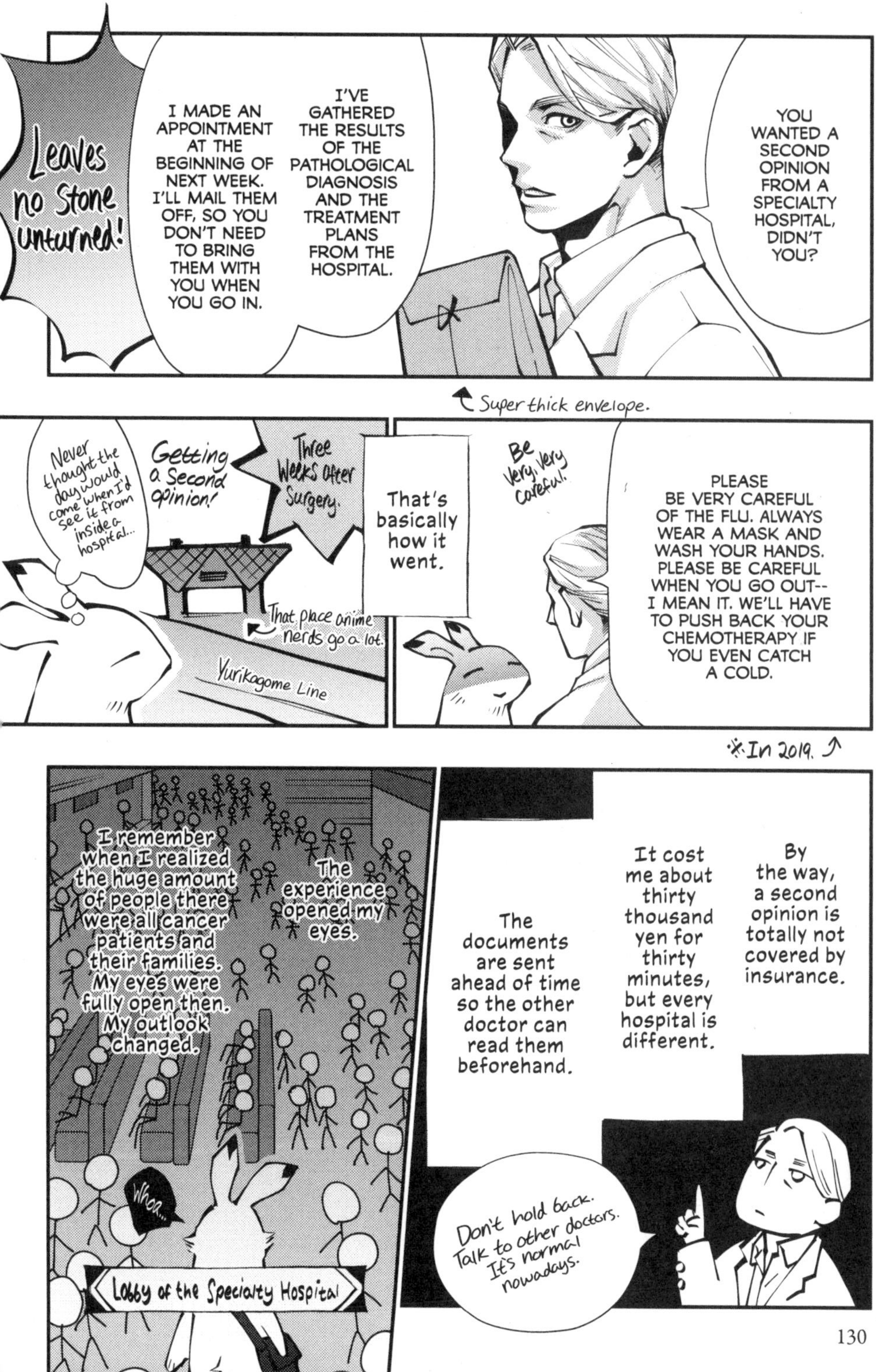
YOU WANTED A SECOND OPINION FROM A SPECIALTY HOSPITAL, DIDN'T YOU?
I'VE GATHERED THE RESULTS OF THE PATHOLOGICAL DIAGNOSIS AND THE TREATMENT PLANS FROM THE HOSPITAL.
I MADE AN APPOINTMENT AT THE BEGINNING OF NEXT WEEK. I'LL MAIL THEM OFF, SO YOU DON'T NEED TO BRING THEM WITH YOU WHEN YOU GO IN.
Leaves no Stone unturned!
Super thick envelope.
PLEASE BE VERY CAREFUL OF THE FLU. ALWAYS WEAR A MASK AND WASH YOUR HANDS. PLEASE BE CAREFUL WHEN YOU GO OUT-- I MEAN IT. WE'LL HAVE TO PUSH BACK YOUR CHEMOTHERAPY IF YOU EVEN CATCH A COLD.
Be very, very careful.
※In 2019.
That's basically how it went.
Three Weeks after Surgery.
Getting a Second opinion!
Never thought the day would come when I'd see it from inside a hospital...
That place anime nerds go a lot.
Yurikagome Line
By the way, a second opinion is totally not covered by insurance.
It cost me about thirty thousand yen for thirty minutes, but every hospital is different.
The documents are sent ahead of time so the other doctor can read them beforehand.
Don't hold back. Talk to other doctors. It's normal nowadays.
The experience opened my eyes.
I remember when I realized the huge amount of people there were all cancer patients and their families. My eyes were fully open then. My outlook changed.
Whoa...
Lobby of the Specialty Hospital

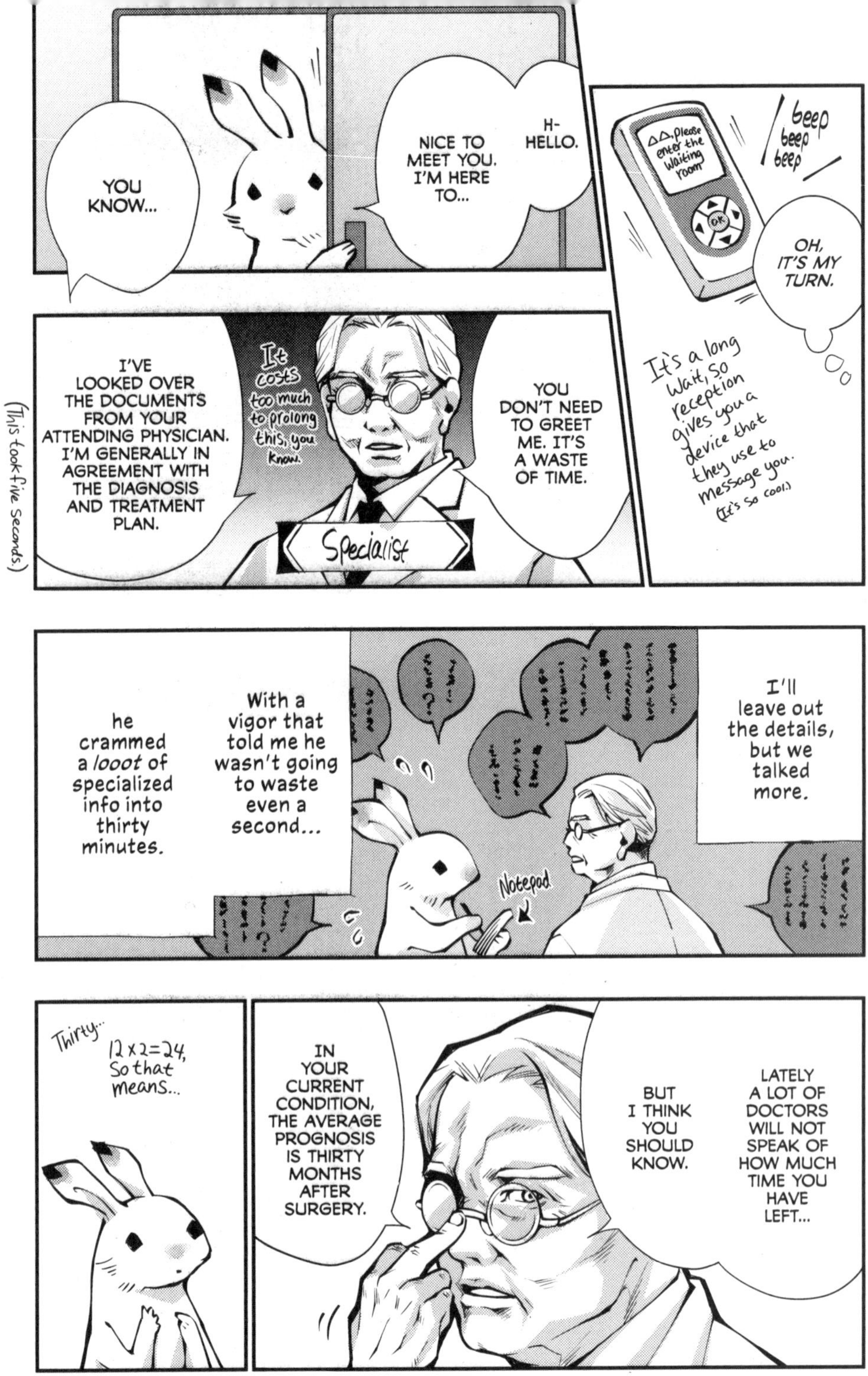
beep beep beep
△△, please enter the waiting room
OK
OH, IT'S MY TURN.
It's a long wait, so reception gives you a device that they use to message you. (It's so cool.)
H- HELLO.
NICE TO MEET YOU. I'M HERE TO...
YOU KNOW...
YOU DON'T NEED TO GREET ME. IT'S A WASTE OF TIME.
It costs too much to prolong this, you know.
Specialist
I'VE LOOKED OVER THE DOCUMENTS FROM YOUR ATTENDING PHYSICIAN. I'M GENERALLY IN AGREEMENT WITH THE DIAGNOSIS AND TREATMENT PLAN.
(This took five seconds.)
I'll leave out the details, but we talked more.
Notepad
With a vigor that told me he wasn't going to waste even a second...
he crammed a *looot* of specialized info into thirty minutes.
LATELY A LOT OF DOCTORS WILL NOT SPEAK OF HOW MUCH TIME YOU HAVE LEFT...
BUT I THINK YOU SHOULD KNOW.
IN YOUR CURRENT CONDITION, THE AVERAGE PROGNOSIS IS THIRTY MONTHS AFTER SURGERY.
Thirty...
12x2=24, So that means...

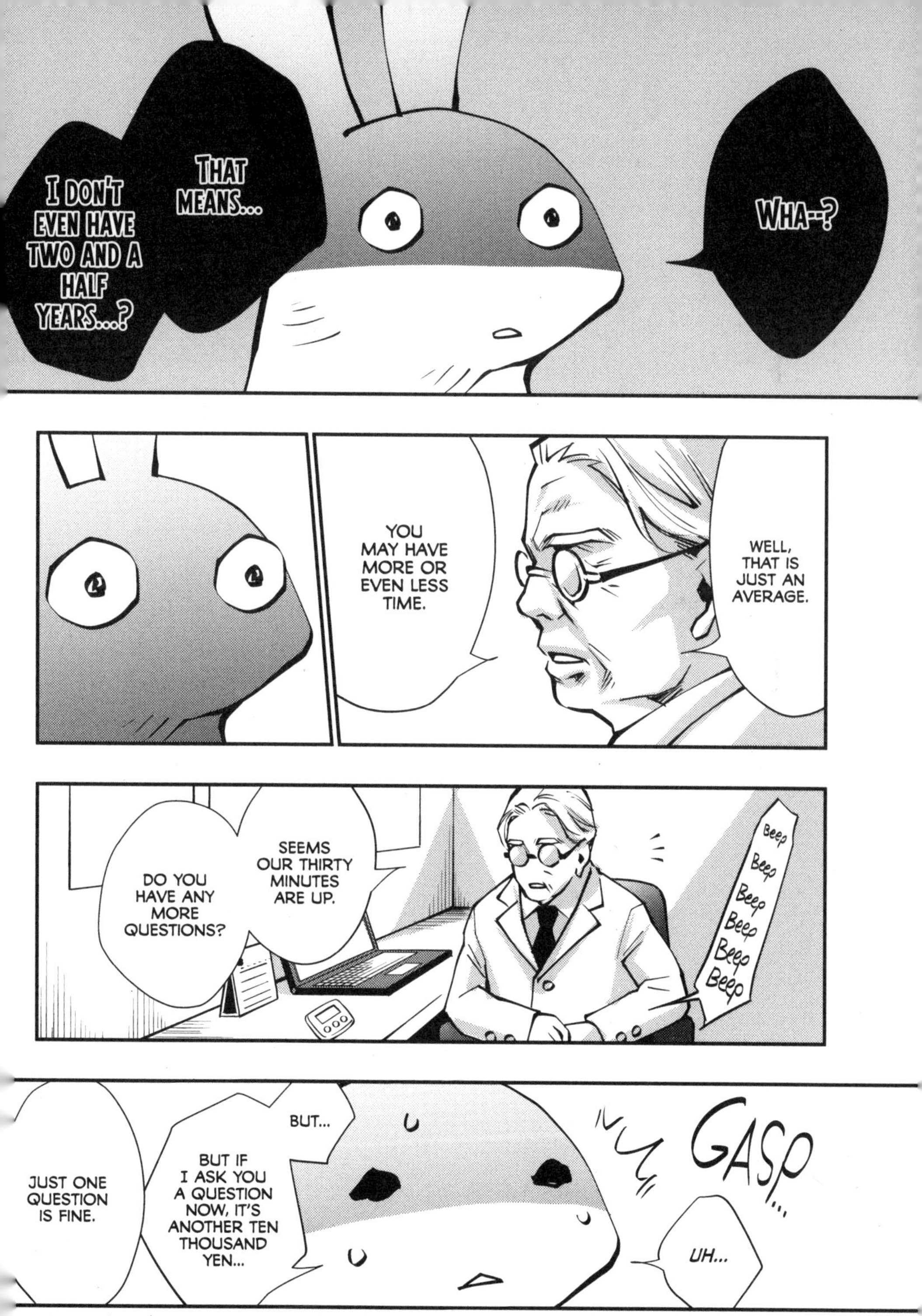
WHA--?
THAT MEANS...
I DON'T EVEN HAVE TWO AND A HALF YEARS...?
WELL, THAT IS JUST AN AVERAGE.
YOU MAY HAVE MORE OR EVEN LESS TIME.
Beep Beep Beep Beep Beep Beep
SEEMS OUR THIRTY MINUTES ARE UP.
DO YOU HAVE ANY MORE QUESTIONS?
GASP...
UH...
BUT...
BUT IF I ASK YOU A QUESTION NOW, IT'S ANOTHER TEN THOUSAND YEN...
JUST ONE QUESTION IS FINE.

fter thirty minutes have passed, you're billed ten thousand yen for every additional thirty minutes.

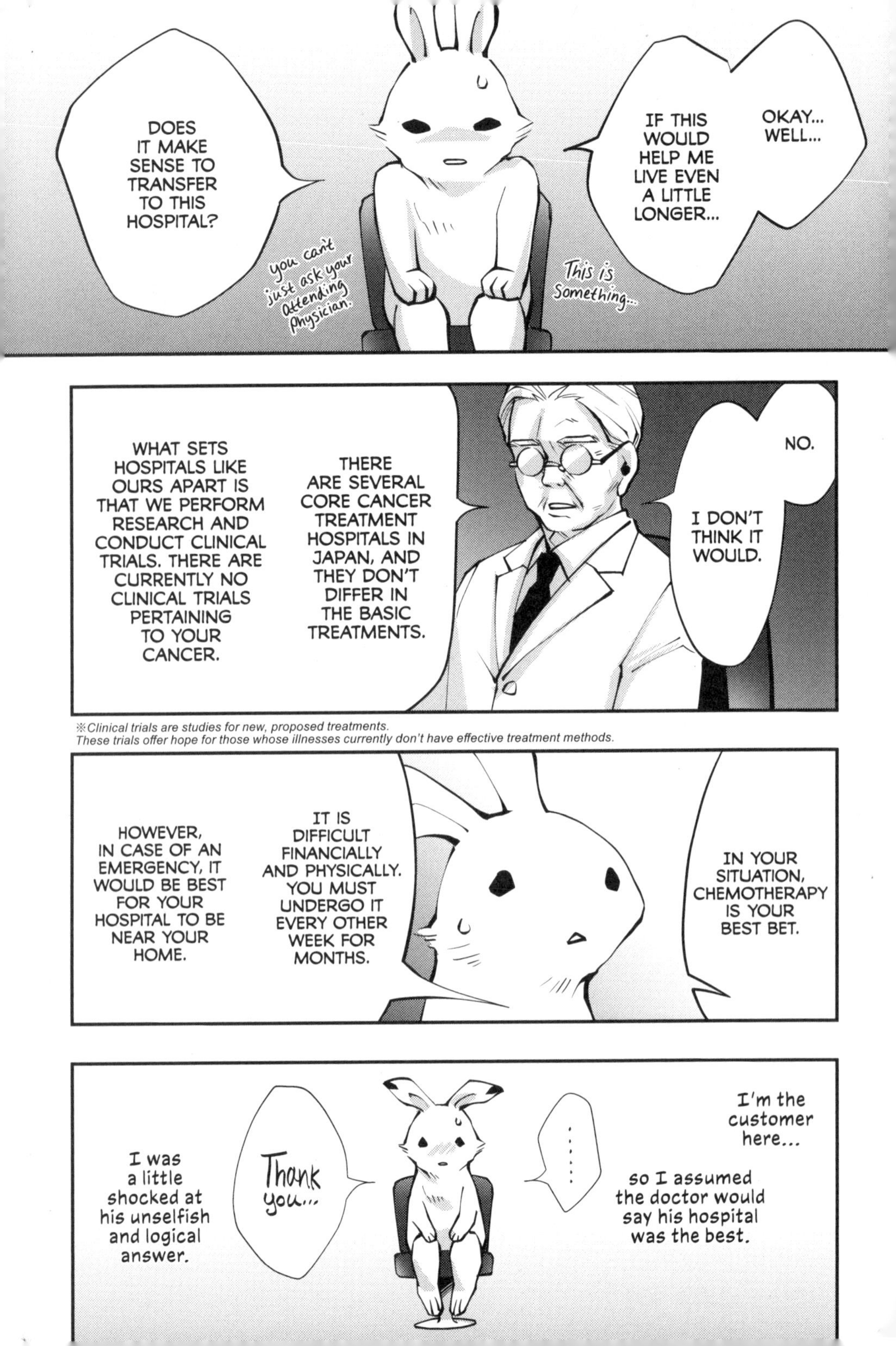
OKAY... WELL...
IF THIS WOULD HELP ME LIVE EVEN A LITTLE LONGER...
DOES IT MAKE SENSE TO TRANSFER TO THIS HOSPITAL?
This is Something...
you can't just ask your attending physician.
NO.
I DON'T THINK IT WOULD.
THERE ARE SEVERAL CORE CANCER TREATMENT HOSPITALS IN JAPAN, AND THEY DON'T DIFFER IN THE BASIC TREATMENTS.
WHAT SETS HOSPITALS LIKE OURS APART IS THAT WE PERFORM RESEARCH AND CONDUCT CLINICAL TRIALS. THERE ARE CURRENTLY NO CLINICAL TRIALS PERTAINING TO YOUR CANCER.
IN YOUR SITUATION, CHEMOTHERAPY IS YOUR BEST BET.
IT IS DIFFICULT FINANCIALLY AND PHYSICALLY. YOU MUST UNDERGO IT EVERY OTHER WEEK FOR MONTHS.
HOWEVER, IN CASE OF AN EMERGENCY, IT WOULD BE BEST FOR YOUR HOSPITAL TO BE NEAR YOUR HOME.
I'm the customer here...
so I assumed the doctor would say his hospital was the best.
......
Thank you...
I was a little shocked at his unselfish and logical answer.

※Clinical trials are studies for new, proposed treatments.
These trials offer hope for those whose illnesses currently don't have effective treatment methods.

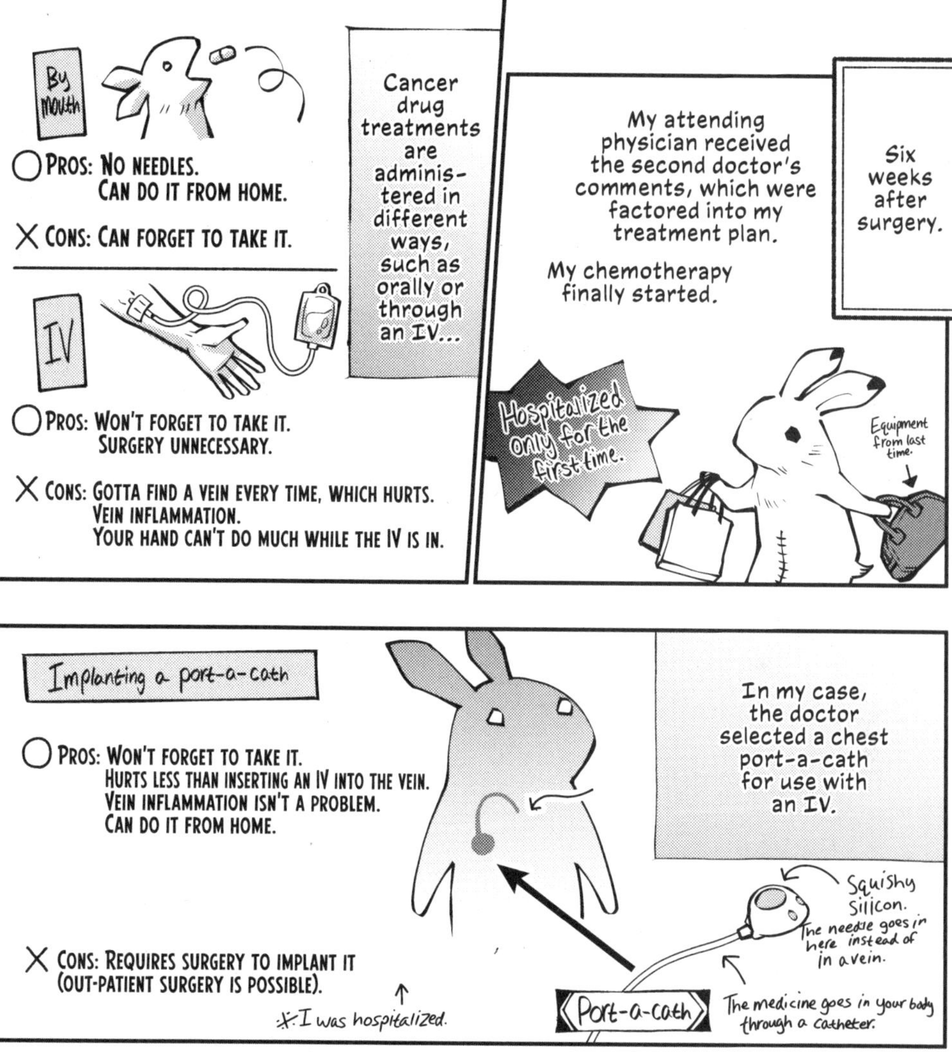

Six weeks after surgery.
My attending physician received the second doctor's comments, which were factored into my treatment plan.
My chemotherapy finally started.
Hospitalized only for the first time.
Equipment from last time.
Cancer drug treatments are adminis-tered in different ways, such as orally or through an IV...
By mouth
PROS: NO NEEDLES.
CAN DO IT FROM HOME.
CONS: CAN FORGET TO TAKE IT.
IV
PROS: WON'T FORGET TO TAKE IT.
SURGERY UNNECESSARY.
CONS: GOTTA FIND A VEIN EVERY TIME, WHICH HURTS.
VEIN INFLAMMATION.
YOUR HAND CAN'T DO MUCH WHILE THE IV IS IN.
In my case, the doctor selected a chest port-a-cath for use with an IV.
Implanting a port-a-cath
PROS: WON'T FORGET TO TAKE IT.
HURTS LESS THAN INSERTING AN IV INTO THE VEIN.
VEIN INFLAMMATION ISN'T A PROBLEM.
CAN DO IT FROM HOME.
Squishy silicon.
The needle goes in here instead of in a vein.
The medicine goes in your body through a catheter.
Port-a-cath
CONS: REQUIRES SURGERY TO IMPLANT IT (OUT-PATIENT SURGERY IS POSSIBLE).
※ I was hospitalized.

※ Port-a-cath: a port that is put under the skin to administer medicine.

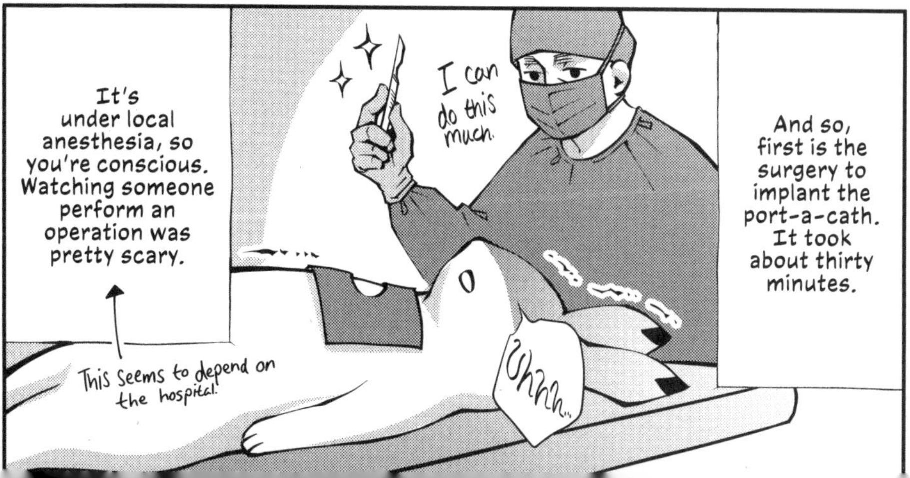

And so, first is the surgery to implant the port-a-cath. It took about thirty minutes.
I can do this much.
It's under local anesthesia, so you're conscious. Watching someone perform an operation was pretty scary.
Uhhh...
This seems to depend on the hospital.

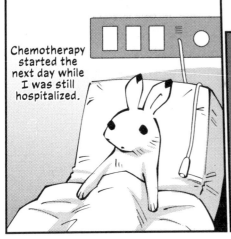

Chemotherapy started the next day while I was still hospitalized.

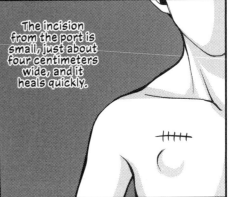

The incision from the port is small, just about four centimeters wide, and it heals quickly.

They give you a pamphlet.
↓

Your Drugs, Explanation, and Treatment Advice

PLEASE DO YOUR BEST TO MAKE A NOTE OF HOW YOU FEEL AND FOR HOW LONG THE SIDE EFFECTS LAST.

WE WILL SEE HOW MANY SIDE EFFECTS APPEAR, AND THAT WILL DETERMINE THE AMOUNT OF MEDICINE WE USE GOING FORWARD.

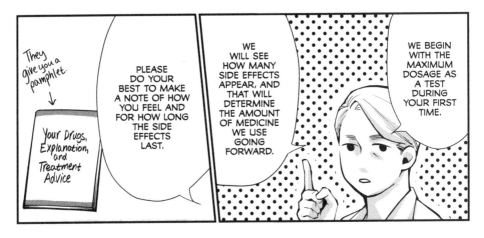

WE BEGIN WITH THE MAXIMUM DOSAGE AS A TEST DURING YOUR FIRST TIME.

But first!!

I'm going to explain the cancer drug treatments now.

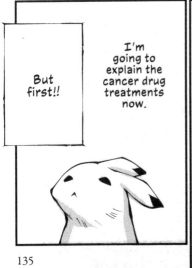

as well as how to manage the side effects and other advice.

The pamphlet also talked all about the drugs...

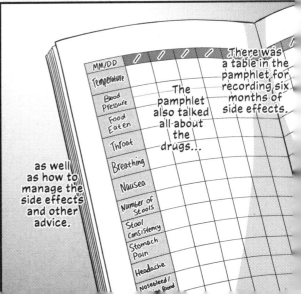

There was a table in the pamphlet for recording six months of side effects.

MM/DD				
Temperature				
Blood Pressure				
Food Eaten				
Throat				
Breathing				
Nausea				
Number of Stools				
Stool Consistency				
Stomach Pain				
Headache				
Nosebleed / Blood				

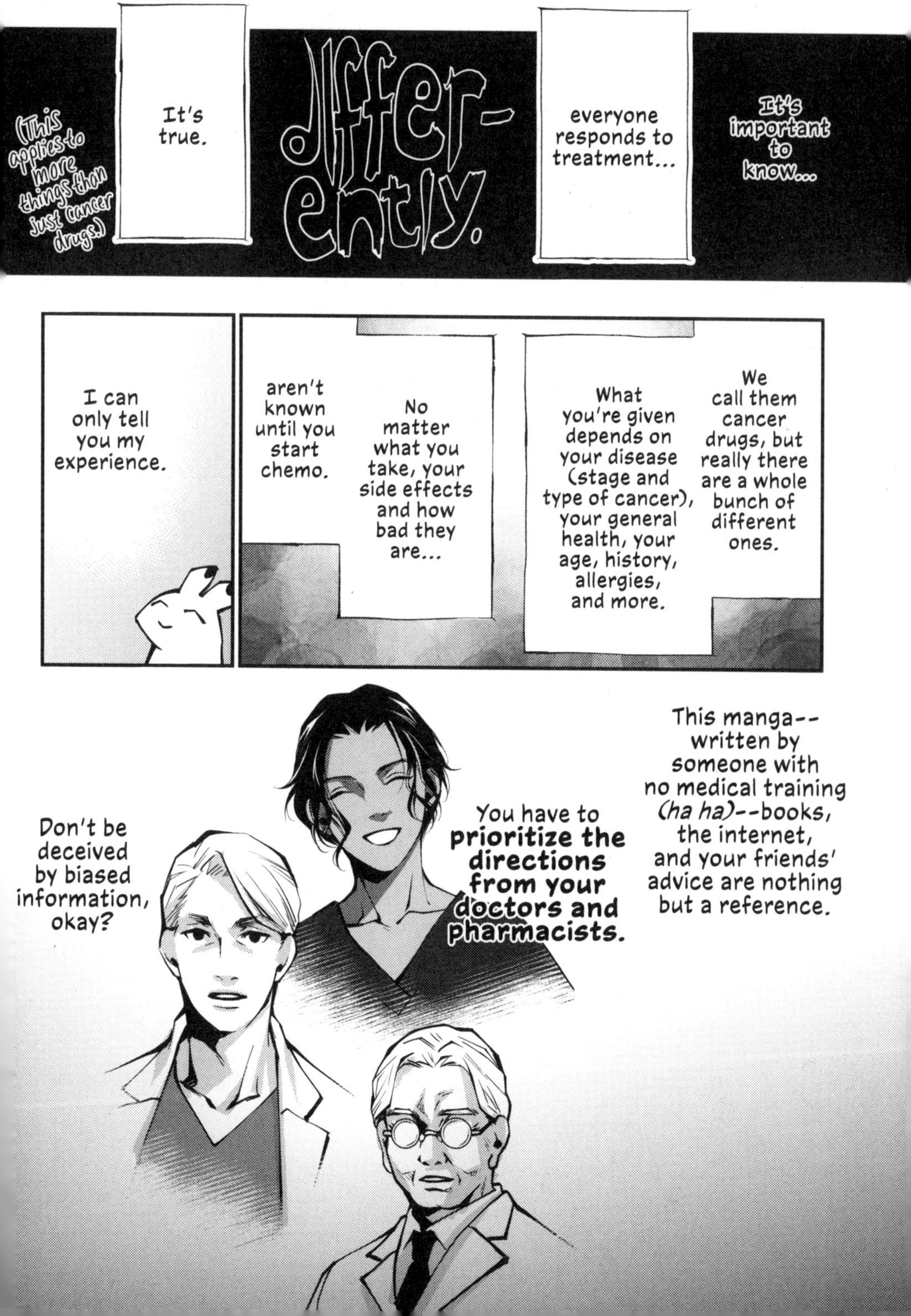
It's important to know...
everyone responds to treatment...
differently.
It's true.
(This applies to more things than just cancer drugs.)
We call them cancer drugs, but really there are a whole bunch of different ones.
What you're given depends on your disease (stage and type of cancer), your general health, your age, history, allergies, and more.
No matter what you take, your side effects and how bad they are...
aren't known until you start chemo.
I can only tell you my experience.
This manga--written by someone with no medical training (ha ha)--books, the internet, and your friends' advice are nothing but a reference.
You have to prioritize the directions from your doctors and pharmacists.
Don't be deceived by biased information, okay?

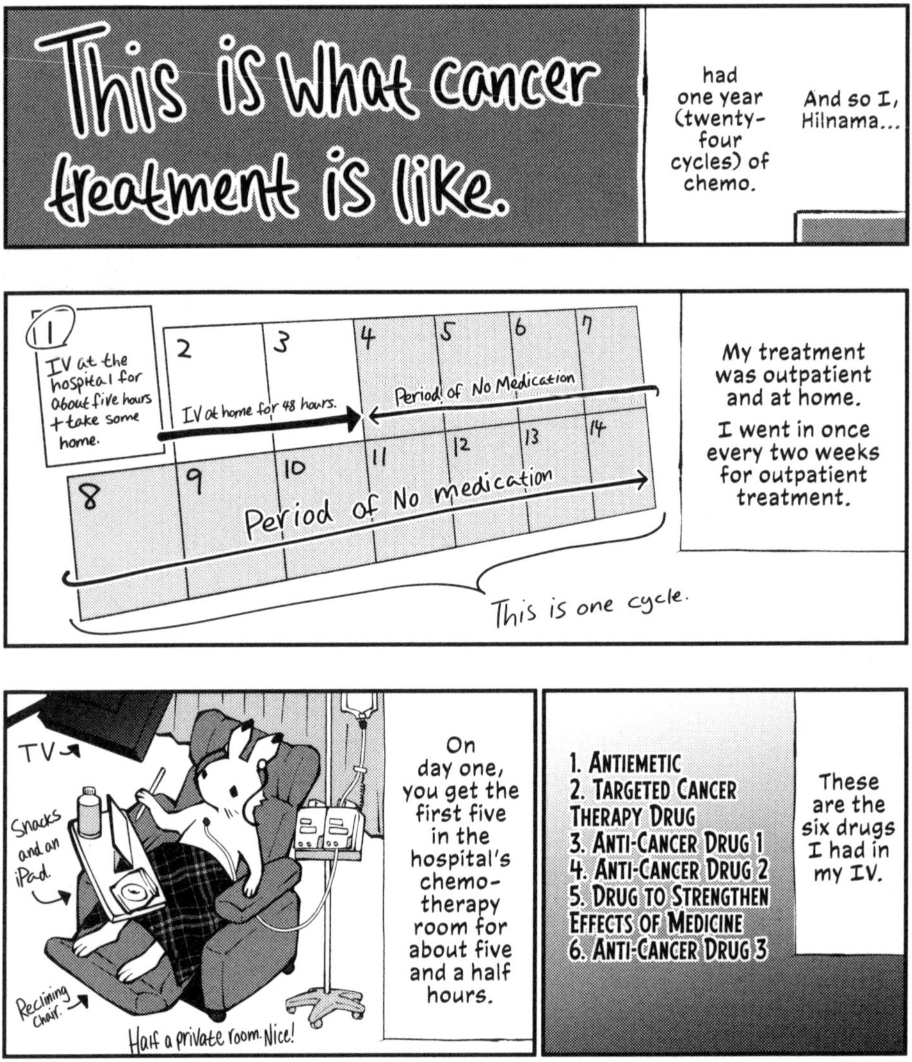

※ Pharmacotherapy includes cytotoxic chemotherapy (chemotherapy, in the narrow sense of the word), hormone therapy, and targeted cancer therapy. Different treatments are used for different kinds of cancer.

This is what cancer treatment is like.

And so I, Hilnama...

had one year (twenty-four cycles) of chemo.

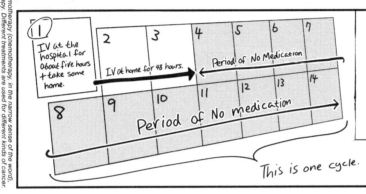

① IV at the hospital for about five hours + take some home.	2	3	4	5	6	7

IV at home for 48 hours.

Period of No Medication

8	9	10	11	12	13	14

Period of No medication

This is one cycle.

My treatment was outpatient and at home.

I went in once every two weeks for outpatient treatment.

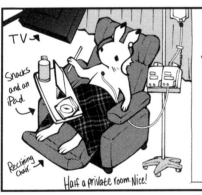

TV →

Snacks and an iPad. →

Reclining chair. →

Half a private room. Nice!

On day one, you get the first five in the hospital's chemotherapy room for about five and a half hours.

1. ANTIEMETIC
2. TARGETED CANCER THERAPY DRUG
3. ANTI-CANCER DRUG 1
4. ANTI-CANCER DRUG 2
5. DRUG TO STRENGTHEN EFFECTS OF MEDICINE
6. ANTI-CANCER DRUG 3

These are the six drugs I had in my IV.

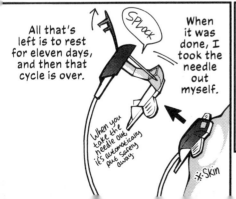

All that's left is to rest for eleven days, and then that cycle is over.

SPLACK

When it was done, I took the needle out myself.

When you take the needle out, it's automatically put safely away

※:Skin

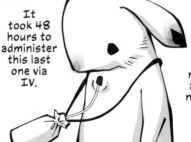

It took 48 hours to administer this last one via IV.

They hung a bottle of the sixth medication around my neck for me to take home.

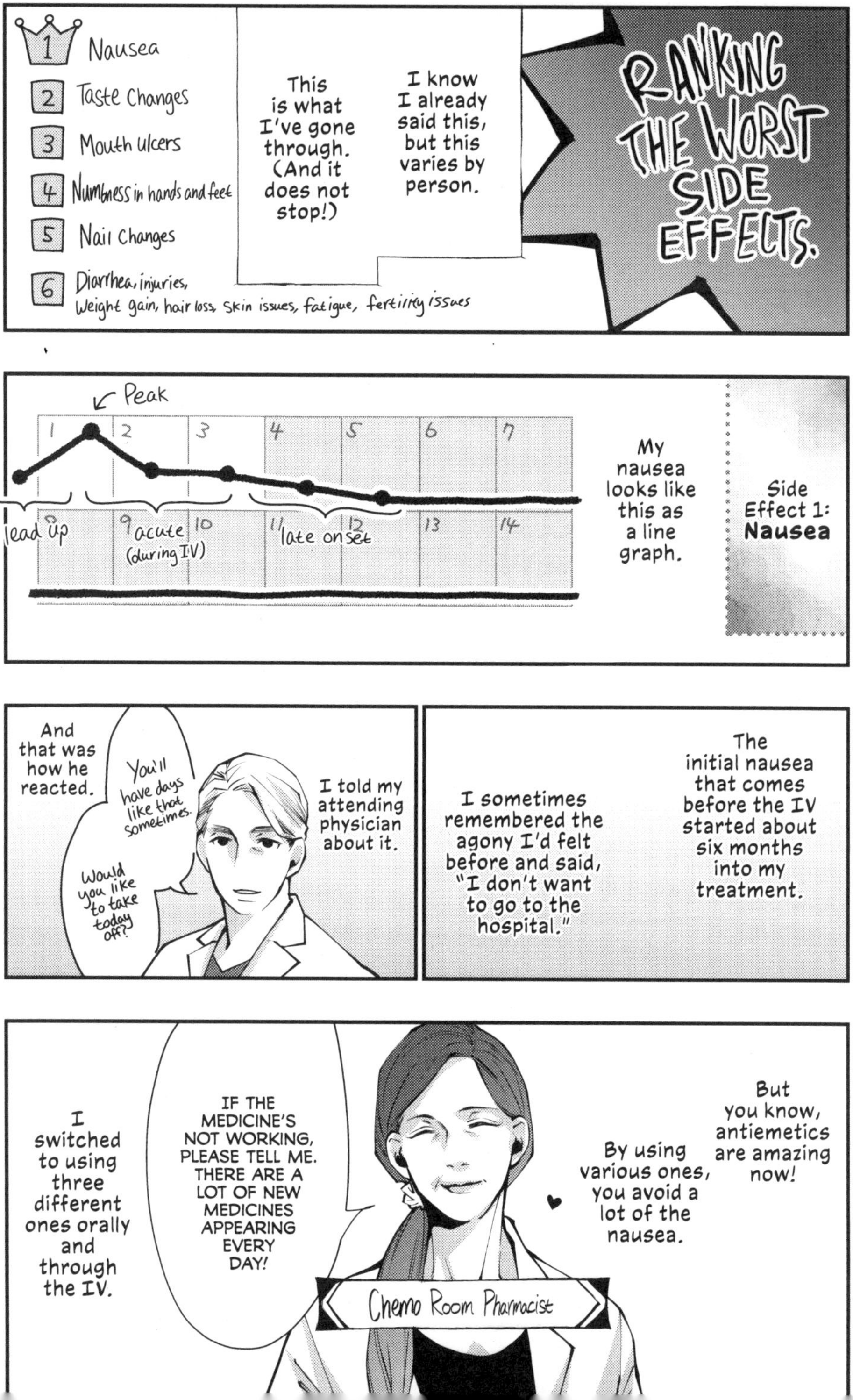
RANKING THE WORST SIDE EFFECTS.
I know I already said this, but this varies by person.
This is what I've gone through. (And it does not stop!)
1 Nausea
2 Taste Changes
3 Mouth ulcers
4 Numbness in hands and feet
5 Nail Changes
6 Diarrhea, injuries, Weight gain, hair loss, Skin issues, fatigue, fertility issues
Side Effect 1: **Nausea**
My nausea looks like this as a line graph.
Peak
1 2 3 4 5 6 7
8 9 10 11 12 13 14
lead up
acute (during IV)
late onset
The initial nausea that comes before the IV started about six months into my treatment.
I sometimes remembered the agony I'd felt before and said, "I don't want to go to the hospital."
I told my attending physician about it.
You'll have days like that sometimes.
Would you like to take today off?
And that was how he reacted.
But you know, antiemetics are amazing now!
By using various ones, you avoid a lot of the nausea.
Chemo Room Pharmacist
IF THE MEDICINE'S NOT WORKING, PLEASE TELL ME. THERE ARE A LOT OF NEW MEDICINES APPEARING EVERY DAY!
I switched to using three different ones orally and through the IV.

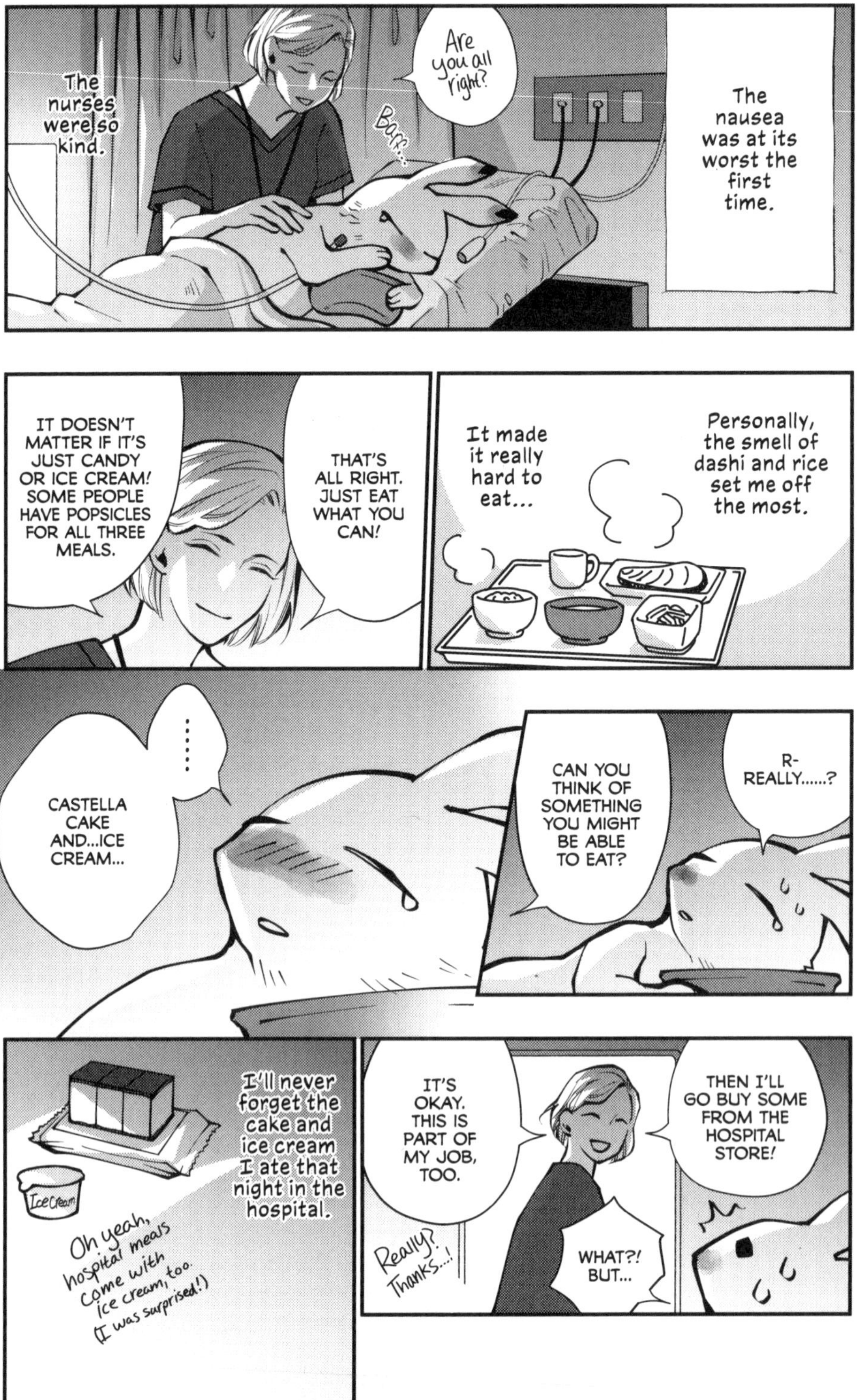
The nausea was at its worst the first time.
Are you all right?
Barf...
The nurses were so kind.
Personally, the smell of dashi and rice set me off the most.
It made it really hard to eat...
THAT'S ALL RIGHT. JUST EAT WHAT YOU CAN!
IT DOESN'T MATTER IF IT'S JUST CANDY OR ICE CREAM! SOME PEOPLE HAVE POPSICLES FOR ALL THREE MEALS.
R- REALLY......?
CAN YOU THINK OF SOMETHING YOU MIGHT BE ABLE TO EAT?
......
CASTELLA CAKE AND...ICE CREAM...
THEN I'LL GO BUY SOME FROM THE HOSPITAL STORE!
WHAT?! BUT...
IT'S OKAY. THIS IS PART OF MY JOB, TOO.
Really? Thanks...!
I'll never forget the cake and ice cream I ate that night in the hospital.
Ice Cream
Oh yeah, hospital meals come with ice cream, too. (I was surprised!)

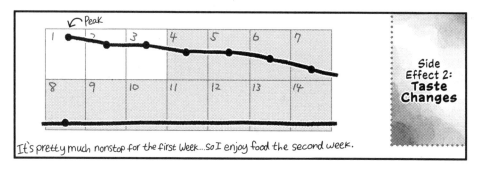

Side Effect 2: **Taste Changes**
Peak
1 2 3 4 5 6 7
8 9 10 11 12 13 14
It's pretty much nonstop for the first week...so I enjoy food the second week.
It wasn't that I couldn't taste things anymore.
More like some flavors got a bit weaker.
Normal
Sweet
Sour
Salty
Bitter
Umami
Peak
Sweet
Sour
Salty
Bitter
Umami
The worst part was...
my saliva felt like sand.
It's always there.
It feels like sand or dirt's stuck in there...
I think that causes some of my nausea...
I can taste sweet and sour things perfectly.
Orange Jello
Tomatoes and oranges are my saviors, but...
Orange Juice
Candy
Pickled Plums
eating them all the time wasn't fun.
I had tomatoes so often when I was sick that looking at them now makes me ill even though I'm not on medication.
BARF!
Why?!
It happened to a lot of foods. It's not good to rely on one thing too much, huh?

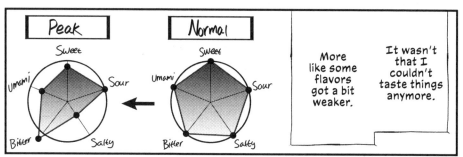

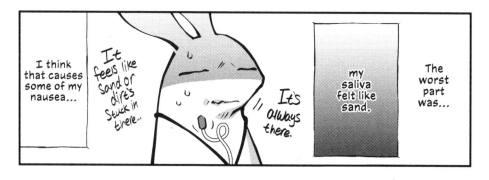

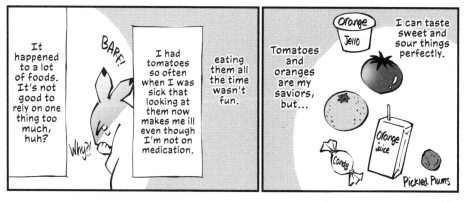

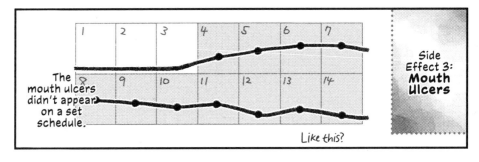

1	2	3	4	5	6	7
8	9	10	11	12	13	14

The mouth ulcers didn't appear on a set schedule.

Like this?

Side Effect 3:
Mouth Ulcers

They healed in a day.

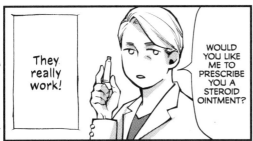

They really work!

WOULD YOU LIKE ME TO PRESCRIBE YOU A STEROID OINTMENT?

That made my time eating and relying on sour food difficult.

Once I got one, it took two weeks to heal.

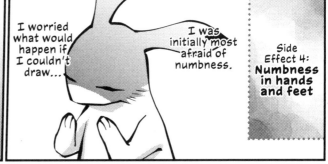

Anyway, I avoided heavy cleaning, cooking, and lifting heavy objects.

I needed help from the people around me for those.

I worried what would happen if I couldn't draw...

I was initially most afraid of numbness.

Side Effect 4:
Numbness in hands and feet

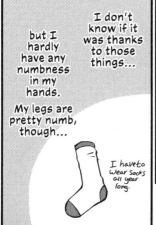

but I hardly have any numbness in my hands.

I don't know if it was thanks to those things...

My legs are pretty numb, though...

I have to wear socks all year long.

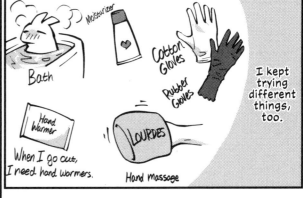

Bath

Moisturizer

Cotton Gloves

Rubber Gloves

Hand Warmer

When I go out, I need hand warmers.

LOURDES

Hand massage

I kept trying different things, too.

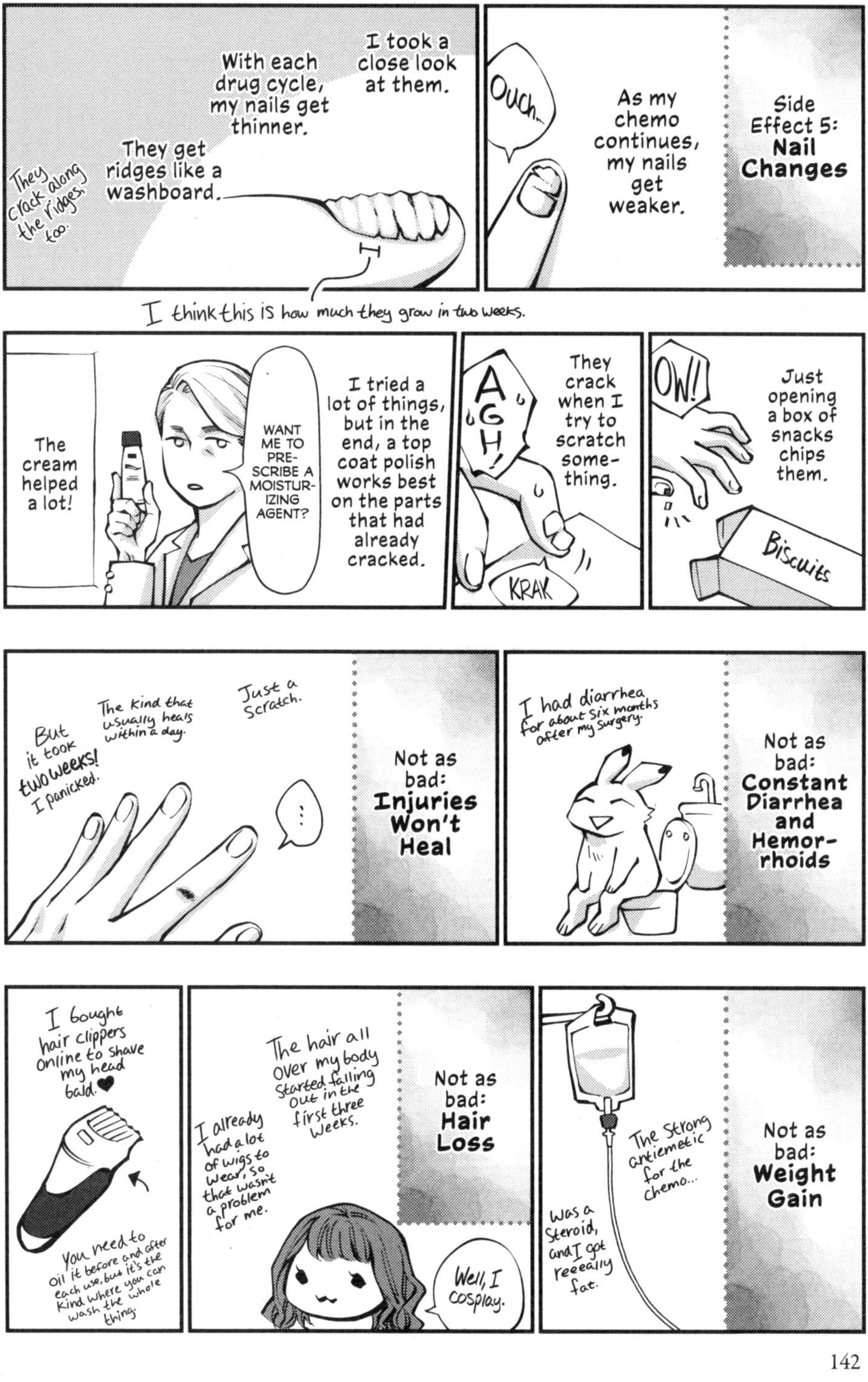

Side Effect 5: Nail Changes
As my chemo continues, my nails get weaker.
Ouch...
I took a close look at them.
With each drug cycle, my nails get thinner.
They get ridges like a washboard.
They crack along the ridges, too.
I think this is how much they grow in two weeks.
Just opening a box of snacks chips them.
OW!
Biscuits
They crack when I try to scratch some-thing.
AGH!
KRAK
I tried a lot of things, but in the end, a top coat polish works best on the parts that had already cracked.
WANT ME TO PRE-SCRIBE A MOISTUR-IZING AGENT?
The cream helped a lot!
Not as bad: Constant Diarrhea and Hemor-rhoids
I had diarrhea for about six months after my surgery.
Not as bad: Injuries Won't Heal
...
Just a scratch.
The kind that usually heals within a day.
But it took two weeks! I panicked.
Not as bad: Weight Gain
The strong antiemetic for the chemo...
Was a steroid, and I got reeeally fat.
Not as bad: Hair Loss
The hair all over my body started falling out in the first three weeks.
I already had a lot of wigs to wear, so that wasn't a problem for me.
Well, I cosplay.
I bought hair clippers online to shave my head bald ❤
You need to oil it before and after each use, but it's the kind where you can wash the whole thing.

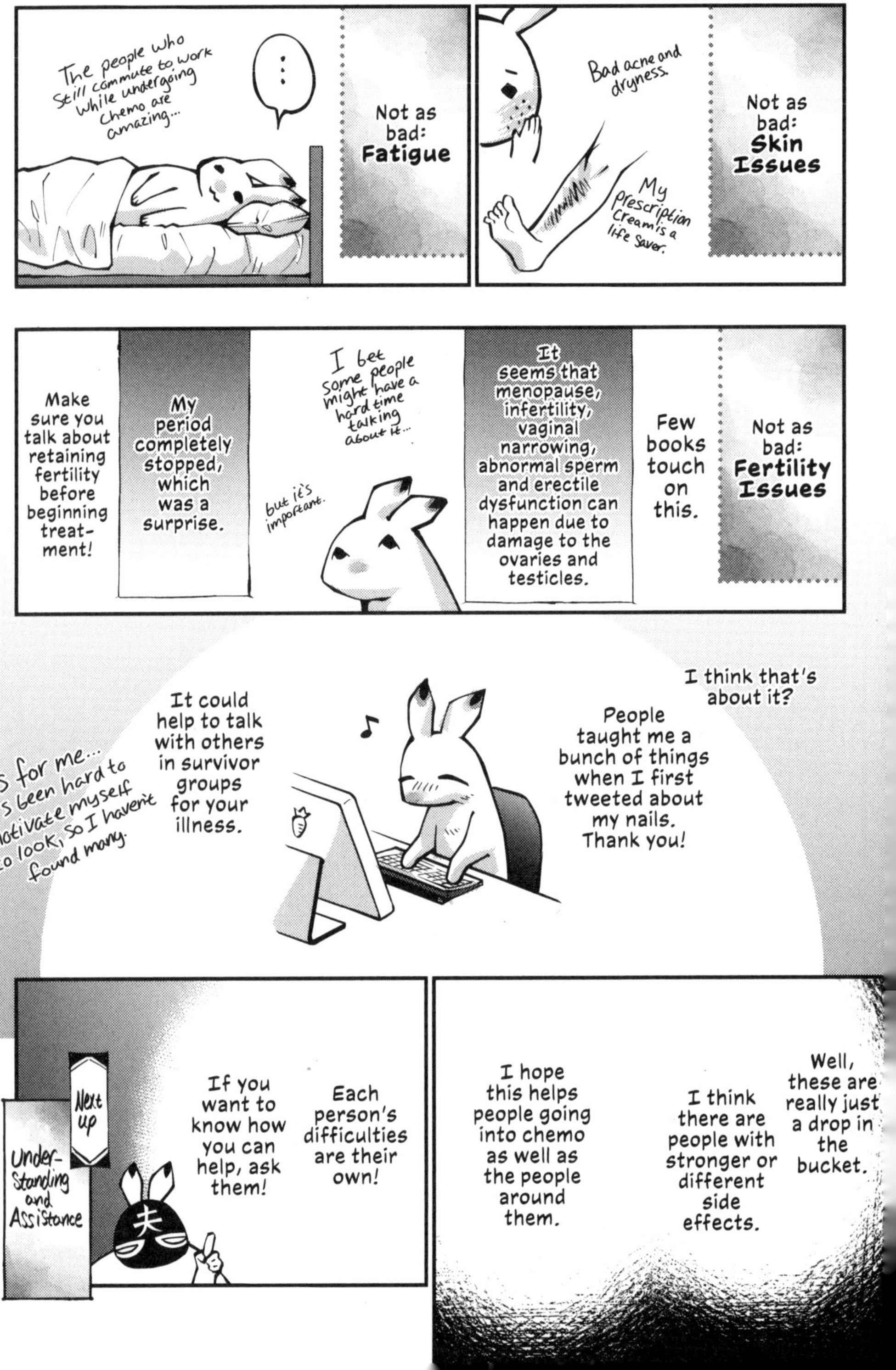

Not as bad: **Skin Issues**
Bad acne and dryness.
My prescription cream is a life saver.
Not as bad: **Fatigue**
...
The people who still commute to work while undergoing chemo are amazing...
Not as bad: **Fertility Issues**
Few books touch on this.
It seems that menopause, infertility, vaginal narrowing, abnormal sperm and erectile dysfunction can happen due to damage to the ovaries and testicles.
I bet some people might have a hard time talking about it...
but it's important.
My period completely stopped, which was a surprise.
Make sure you talk about retaining fertility before beginning treat-ment!
I think that's about it?
People taught me a bunch of things when I first tweeted about my nails. Thank you!
It could help to talk with others in survivor groups for your illness.
As for me... It's been hard to motivate myself to look, so I haven't found many.
Well, these are really just a drop in the bucket.
I think there are people with stronger or different side effects.
I hope this helps people going into chemo as well as the people around them.
Each person's difficulties are their own!
If you want to know how you can help, ask them!
Next up
Under-Standing and Assistance
夫

When I shared my cancer diagnosis online, one of
my medical friends said, "The advances in cancer
treatments are amazing. Knowledge grows, and
limitations from just a few years ago keep changing.
If you live even one or two years longer, your hope
will grow that much. Please don't give up, okay?"

I've been reading books about the history of cancer
research, and those words are *sooo* true!!

Thank you so much to those all around the world
 researching treatments and cures...I think there are a
lot of people who we don't get to see as patients, but
we should still be grateful for what you do. People like
from pathologists, researchers, and more. Thank you
also to the people whose positions I couldn't mention
because of my lack of knowledge.
Seriously, thank you!!!

Oh, I'm also grateful for Japan's healthcare system,
which allows for speedy preparations for treatment
and health insurance anywhere in Japan!

I'm a Terminal
Cancer
Patient
BUT I'M FINE

I thought I had a Stomachache, but it Was terminal cancer. ⑩
Time for the final Chapter.

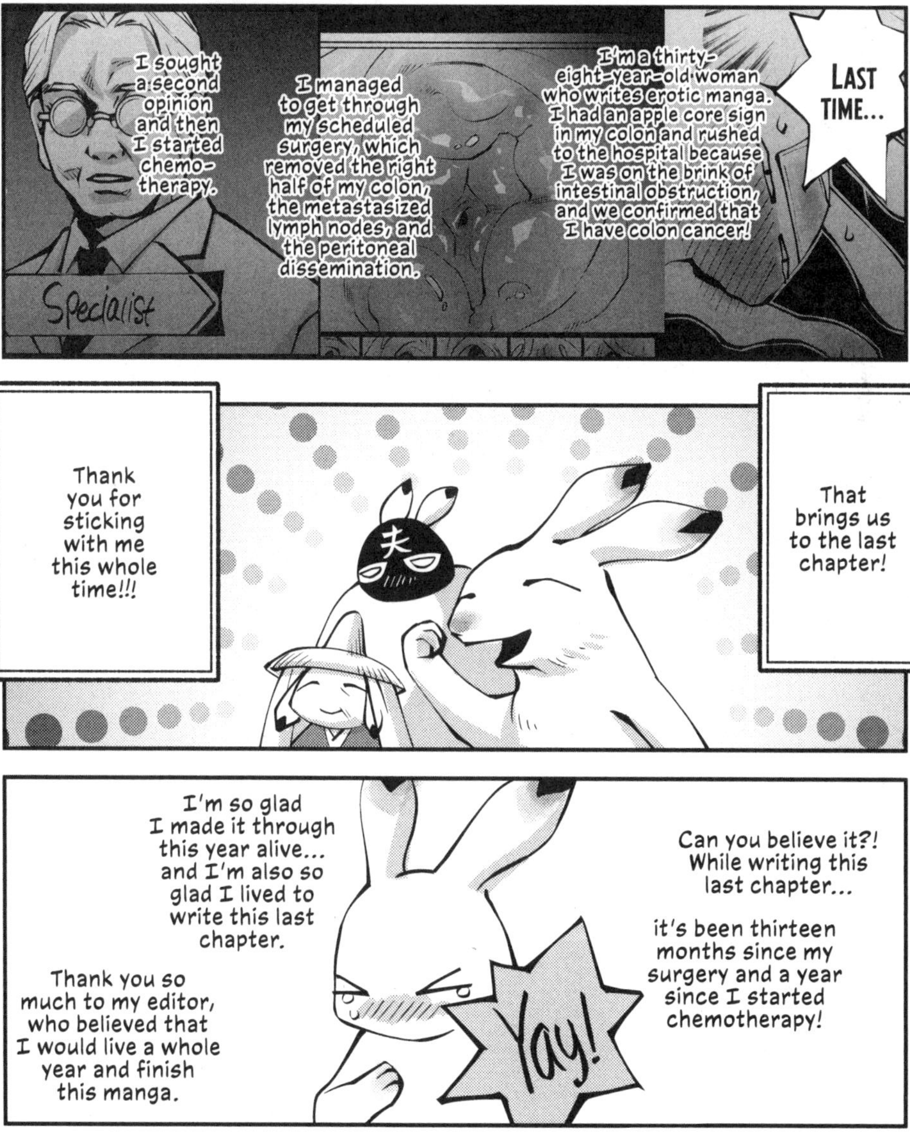
LAST TIME...
I'm a thirty-eight-year-old woman who writes erotic manga. I had an apple core sign in my colon and rushed to the hospital because I was on the brink of intestinal obstruction, and we confirmed that I have colon cancer!
I managed to get through my scheduled surgery, which removed the right half of my colon, the metastasized lymph nodes, and the peritoneal dissemination.
I sought a second opinion and then I started chemo-therapy.
Specialist
That brings us to the last chapter!
Thank you for sticking with me this whole time!!!
Can you believe it?! While writing this last chapter...
I'm so glad I made it through this year alive... and I'm also so glad I lived to write this last chapter.
it's been thirteen months since my surgery and a year since I started chemotherapy!
Yay!
Thank you so much to my editor, who believed that I would live a whole year and finish this manga.

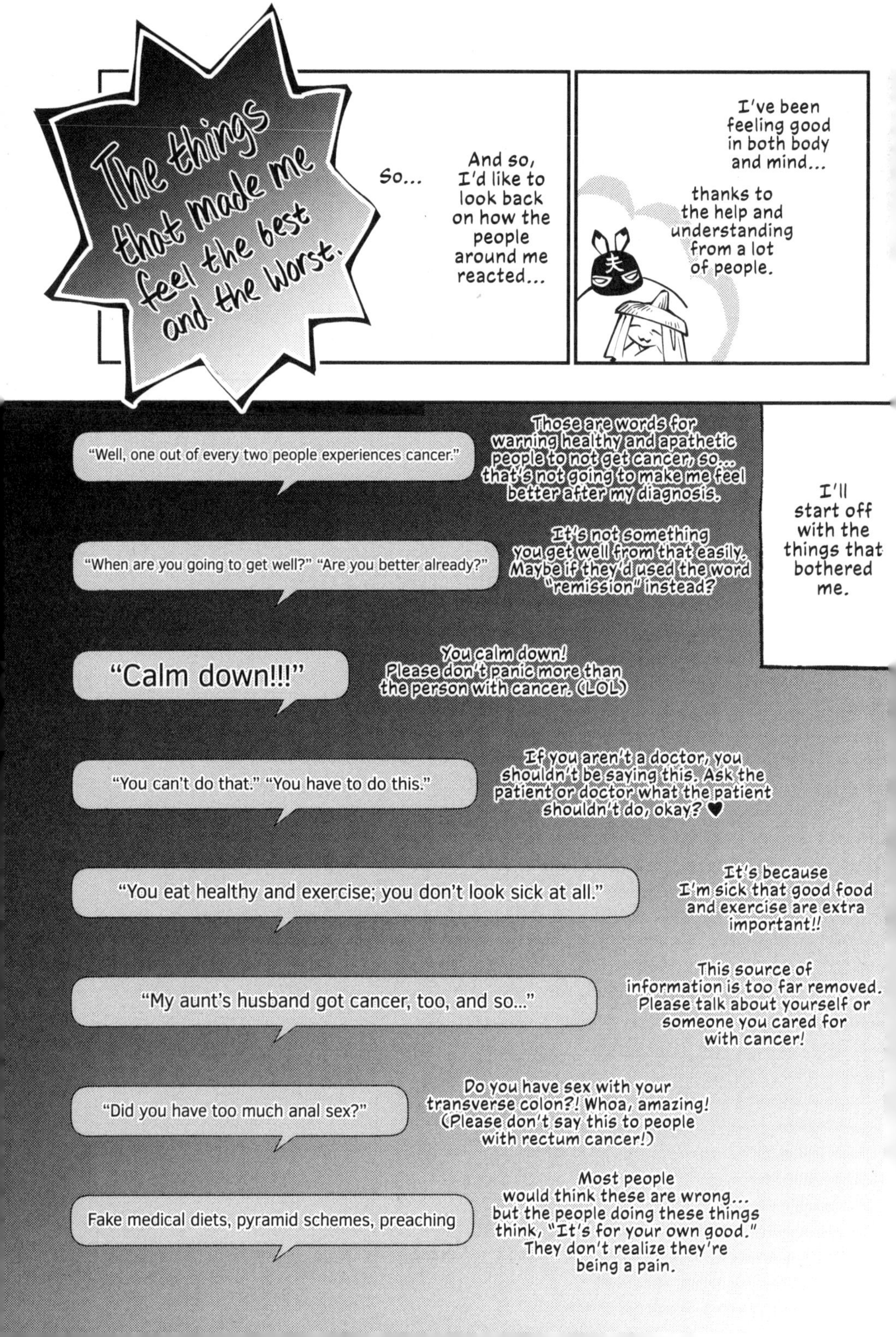
I've been feeling good in both body and mind...
thanks to the help and understanding from a lot of people.
And so, I'd like to look back on how the people around me reacted...
So...
The things that made me feel the best and the worst.
I'll start off with the things that bothered me.
"Well, one out of every two people experiences cancer."
Those are words for warning healthy and apathetic people to not get cancer, so... that's not going to make me feel better after my diagnosis.
"When are you going to get well?" "Are you better already?"
It's not something you get well from that easily. Maybe if they'd used the word "remission" instead?
"Calm down!!!"
You calm down! Please don't panic more than the person with cancer. (LOL)
"You can't do that." "You have to do this."
If you aren't a doctor, you shouldn't be saying this. Ask the patient or doctor what the patient shouldn't do, okay? ♥
"You eat healthy and exercise; you don't look sick at all."
It's because I'm sick that good food and exercise are extra important!!
"My aunt's husband got cancer, too, and so..."
This source of information is too far removed. Please talk about yourself or someone you cared for with cancer!
"Did you have too much anal sex?"
Do you have sex with your transverse colon?! Whoa, amazing! (Please don't say this to people with rectum cancer!)
Fake medical diets, pyramid schemes, preaching
Most people would think these are wrong... but the people doing these things think, "It's for your own good." They don't realize they're being a pain.

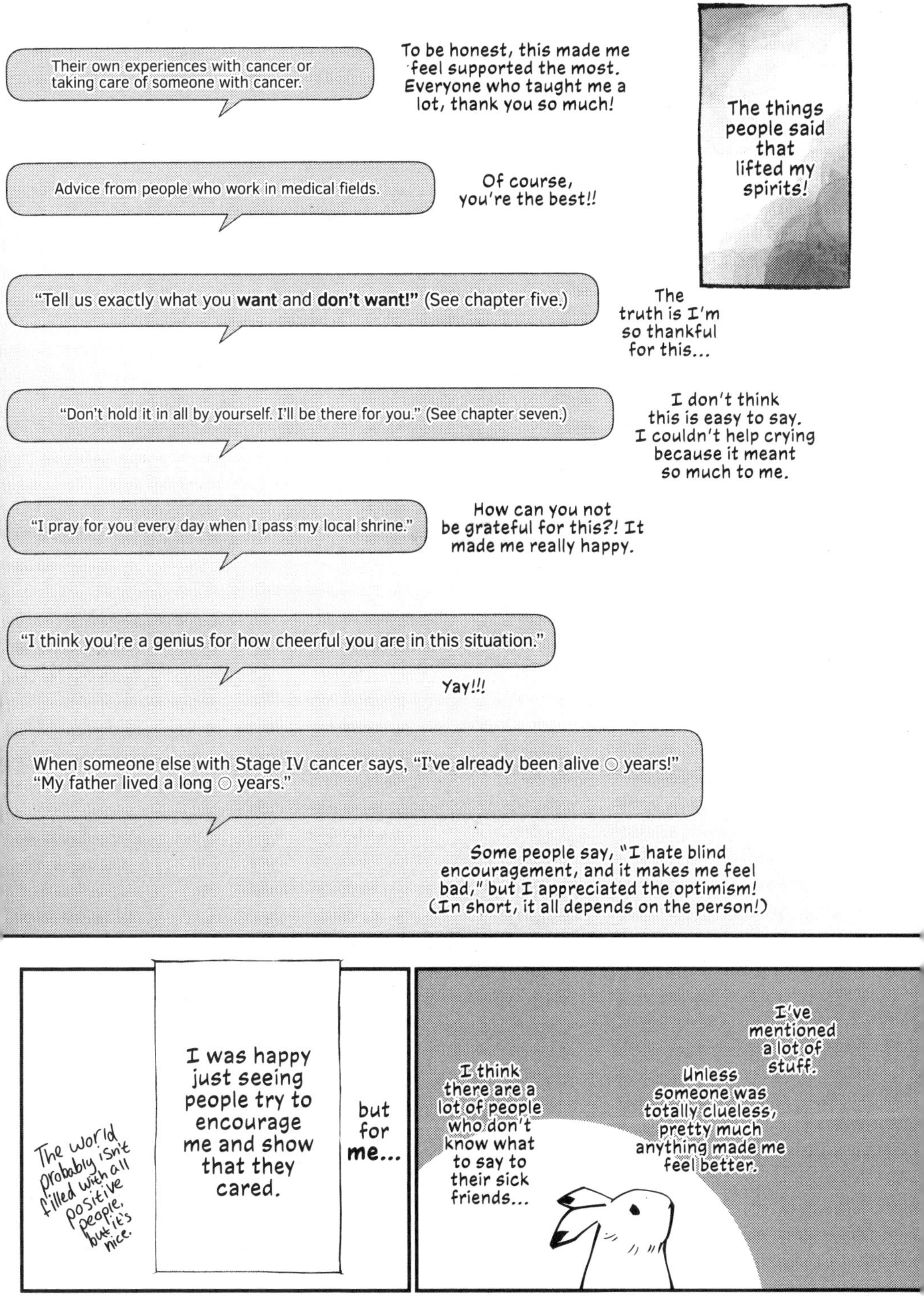
The things people said that lifted my spirits!
Their own experiences with cancer or taking care of someone with cancer.
To be honest, this made me feel supported the most. Everyone who taught me a lot, thank you so much!
Advice from people who work in medical fields.
Of course, you're the best!!
"Tell us exactly what you **want** and **don't want!"** (See chapter five.)
The truth is I'm so thankful for this...
"Don't hold it in all by yourself. I'll be there for you." (See chapter seven.)
I don't think this is easy to say. I couldn't help crying because it meant so much to me.
"I pray for you every day when I pass my local shrine."
How can you not be grateful for this?! It made me really happy.
"I think you're a genius for how cheerful you are in this situation."
Yay!!!
When someone else with Stage IV cancer says, "I've already been alive ◎ years!" "My father lived a long ◎ years."
Some people say, "I hate blind encouragement, and it makes me feel bad," but I appreciated the optimism! (In short, it all depends on the person!)
I've mentioned a lot of stuff.
Unless someone was totally clueless, pretty much anything made me feel better.
I think there are a lot of people who don't know what to say to their sick friends...
but for **me...**
I was happy just seeing people try to encourage me and show that they cared.
The world probably isn't filled with all positive people, but it's nice.

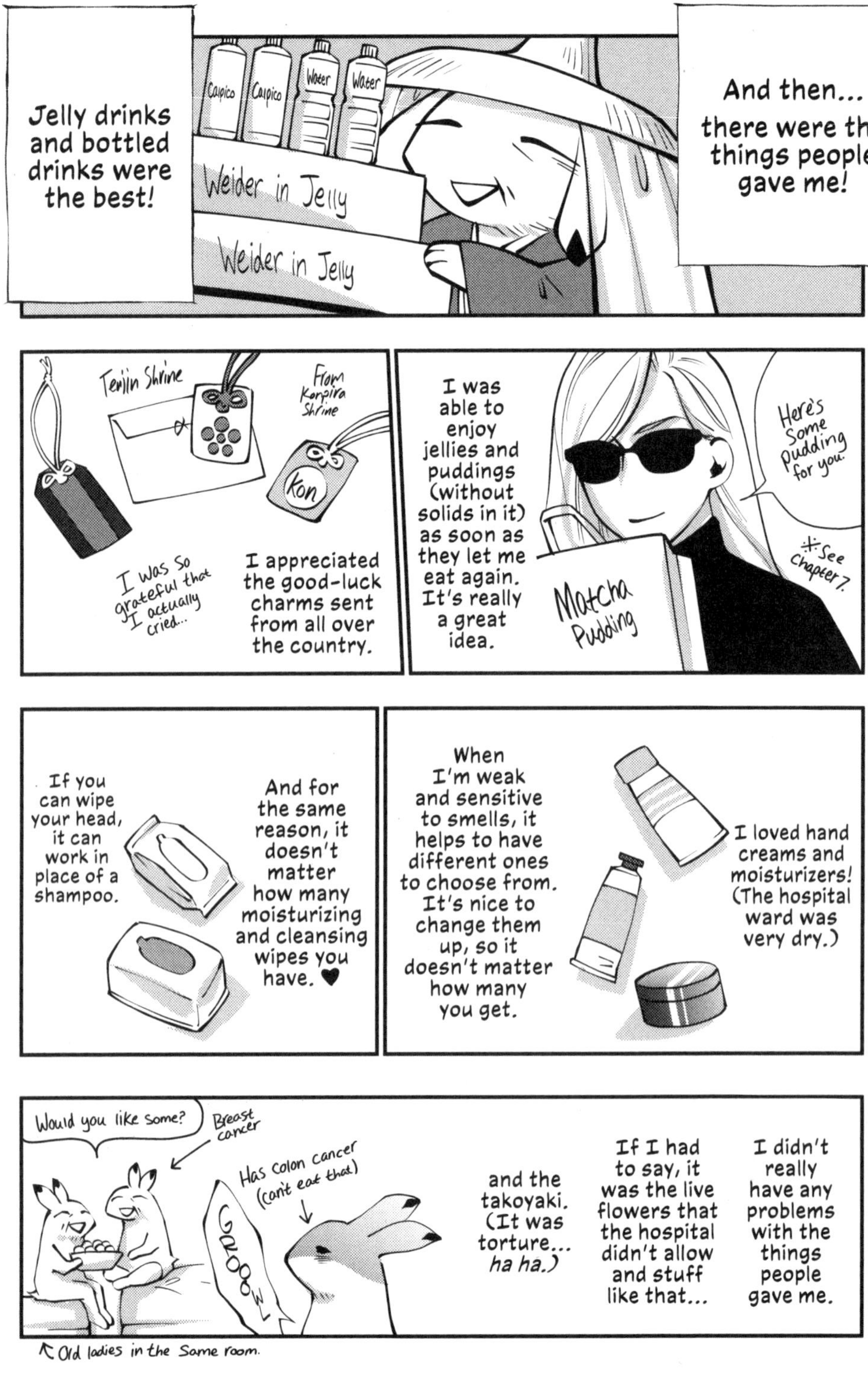

Jelly drinks and bottled drinks were the best!
Calpico
Calpico
Water
Water
Weider in Jelly
Weider in Jelly
And then... there were the things people gave me!
Here's some pudding for you.
※See Chapter 7.
I was able to enjoy jellies and puddings (without solids in it) as soon as they let me eat again. It's really a great idea.
Matcha Pudding
From Konpira Shrine
Kon
Tenjin Shrine
I appreciated the good-luck charms sent from all over the country.
I was so grateful that I actually cried...
I loved hand creams and moisturizers! (The hospital ward was very dry.)
When I'm weak and sensitive to smells, it helps to have different ones to choose from. It's nice to change them up, so it doesn't matter how many you get.
And for the same reason, it doesn't matter how many moisturizing and cleansing wipes you have. ♥
If you can wipe your head, it can work in place of a shampoo.
I didn't really have any problems with the things people gave me.
If I had to say, it was the live flowers that the hospital didn't allow and stuff like that...
and the takoyaki. (It was torture... ha ha.)
Has colon cancer (can't eat that)
GROOOWL
Breast cancer
Would you like some?
↖Old ladies in the same room.

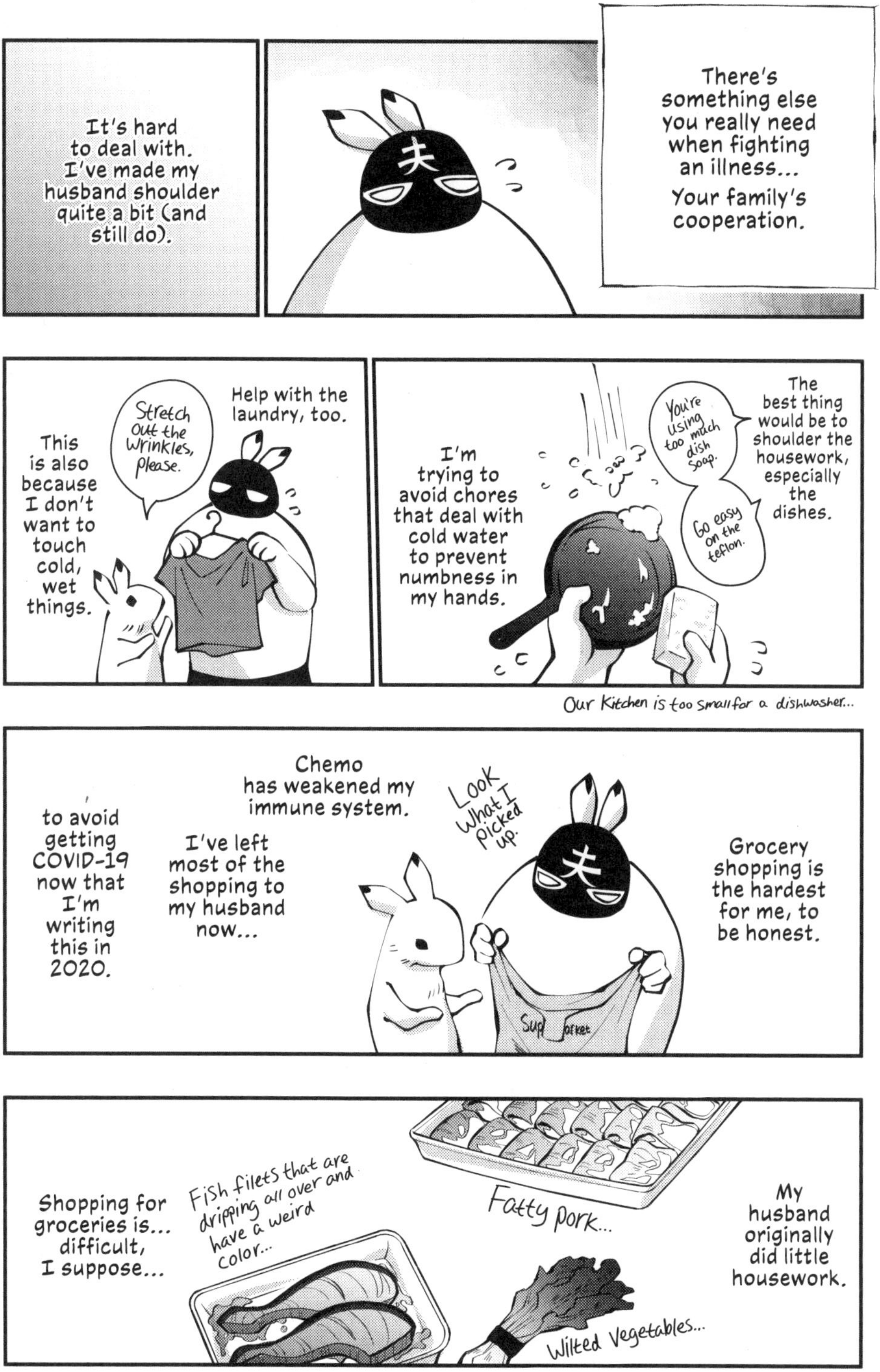

There's something else you really need when fighting an illness... Your family's cooperation.
It's hard to deal with. I've made my husband shoulder quite a bit (and still do).
The best thing would be to shoulder the housework, especially the dishes.
You're using too much dish soap.
Go easy on the teflon.
I'm trying to avoid chores that deal with cold water to prevent numbness in my hands.
Help with the laundry, too.
Stretch out the wrinkles, please.
This is also because I don't want to touch cold, wet things.
Our Kitchen is too small for a dishwasher...
Grocery shopping is the hardest for me, to be honest.
Look What I picked up.
Chemo has weakened my immune system.
I've left most of the shopping to my husband now...
to avoid getting COVID-19 now that I'm writing this in 2020.
My husband originally did little housework.
Fatty pork...
Wilted Vegetables...
Fish filets that are dripping all over and have a weird color...
Shopping for groceries is... difficult, I suppose...

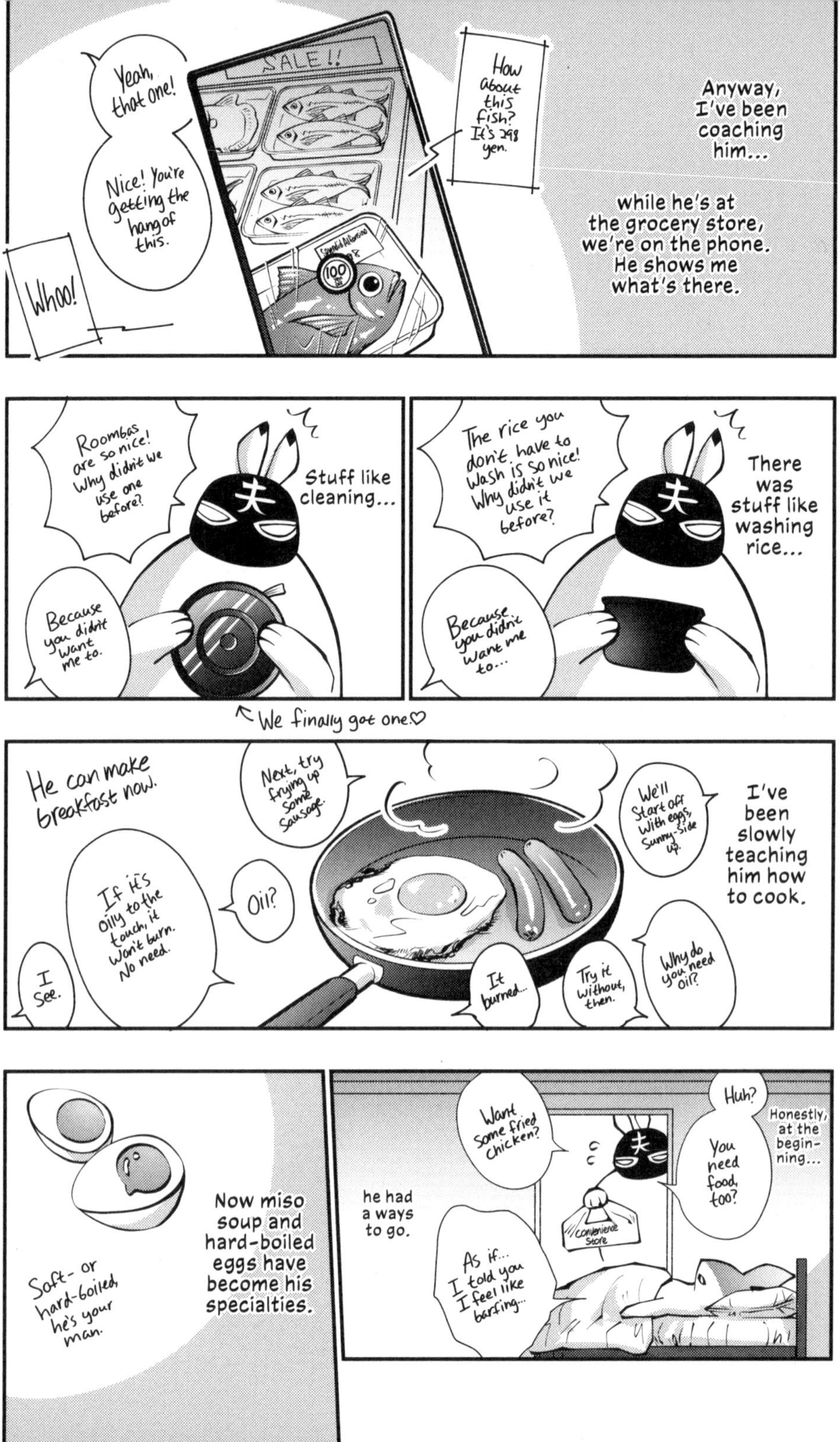
Anyway, I've been coaching him...
while he's at the grocery store, we're on the phone. He shows me what's there.
SALE!!
How about this fish? It's 298 yen.
Yeah, that one!
Nice! You're getting the hang of this.
Whoo!
There was stuff like washing rice...
The rice you don't have to wash is so nice! Why didn't we use it before?
Because you didn't want me to...
Stuff like cleaning...
Roombas are so nice! Why didn't we use one before?
Because you didn't want me to.
We finally got one♡
I've been slowly teaching him how to cook.
We'll start off with eggs, sunny-side up.
Why do you need oil?
Try it without, then.
It burned...
Next, try frying up some sausage.
Oil?
If it's oily to the touch, it won't burn. No need.
I see.
He can make breakfast now.
Honestly, at the beginning...
Huh?
You need food, too?
Want some fried chicken?
Convenience Store
he had a ways to go.
As if... I told you I feel like barfing...
Now miso soup and hard-boiled eggs have become his specialties.
Soft- or hard-boiled, he's your man.

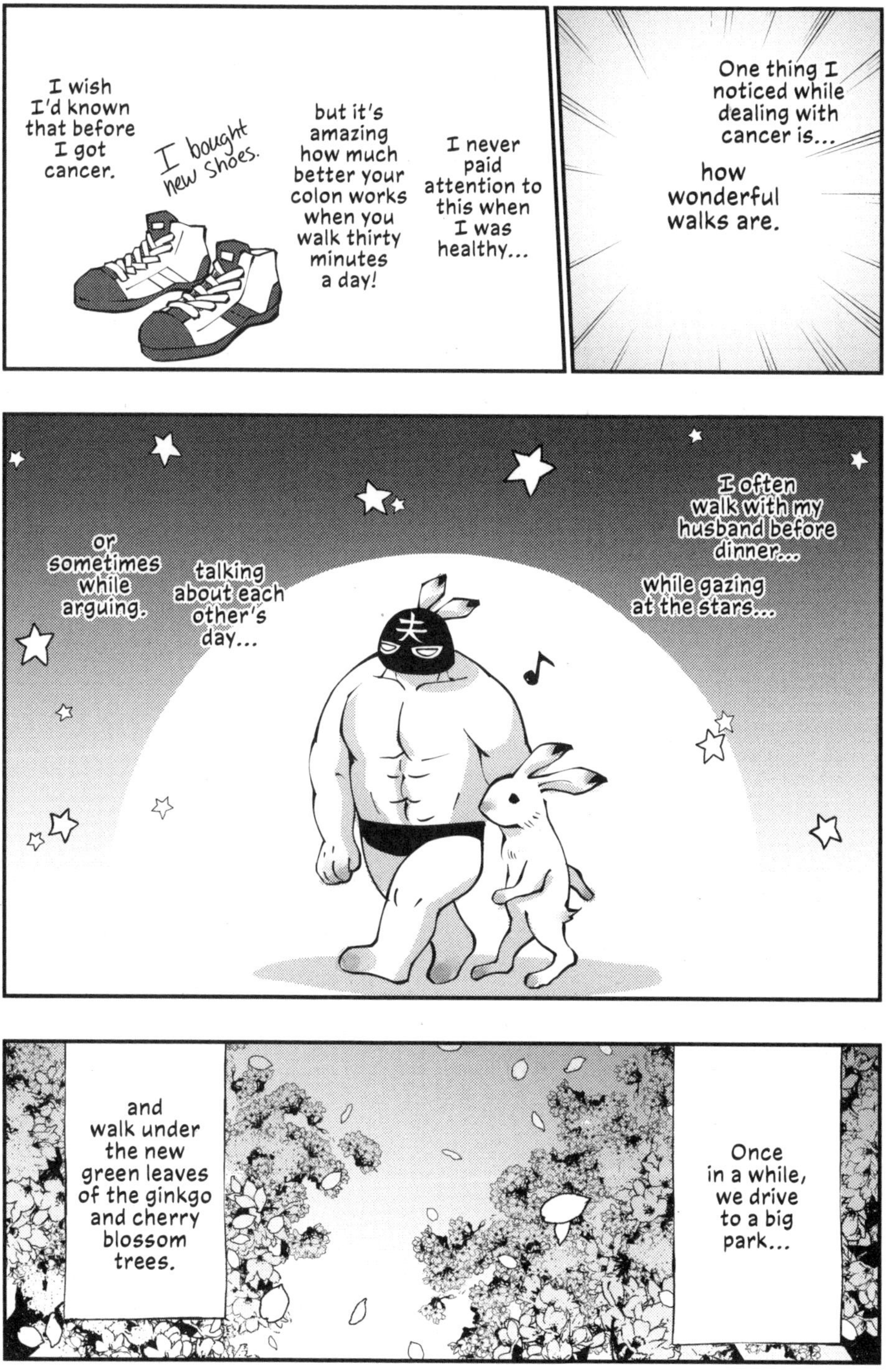
One thing I noticed while dealing with cancer is...
how wonderful walks are.
I never paid attention to this when I was healthy...
but it's amazing how much better your colon works when you walk thirty minutes a day!
I bought new shoes.
I wish I'd known that before I got cancer.
I often walk with my husband before dinner...
while gazing at the stars...
talking about each other's day...
or sometimes while arguing.
夫
Once in a while, we drive to a big park...
and walk under the new green leaves of the ginkgo and cherry blossom trees.

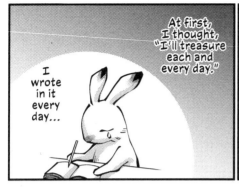

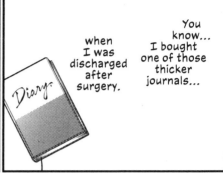

You know... I bought one of those thicker journals...
when I was discharged after surgery.
Diary.
At first, I thought, "I'll treasure each and every day."
I wrote in it every day...
but I only stuck with it for a month!!
Can't commit to projects.
I couldn't keep up the energy I had!! (LOL)
After a while I realized something.
Just because they told me how much longer I had to live with cancer...
doesn't mean I know exactly how long I'll live.
Might be next month, next year, or even ten years later.
It's not like my life is suddenly different in every way.
I really don't have a choice but to continue living every day like I always have.
I eat breakfast while working.

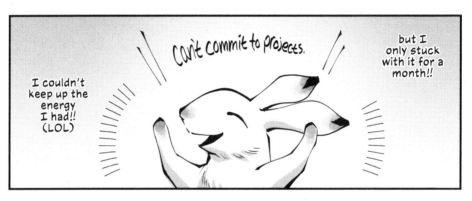

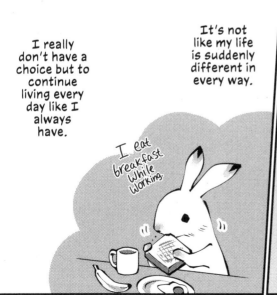

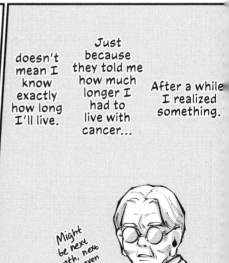

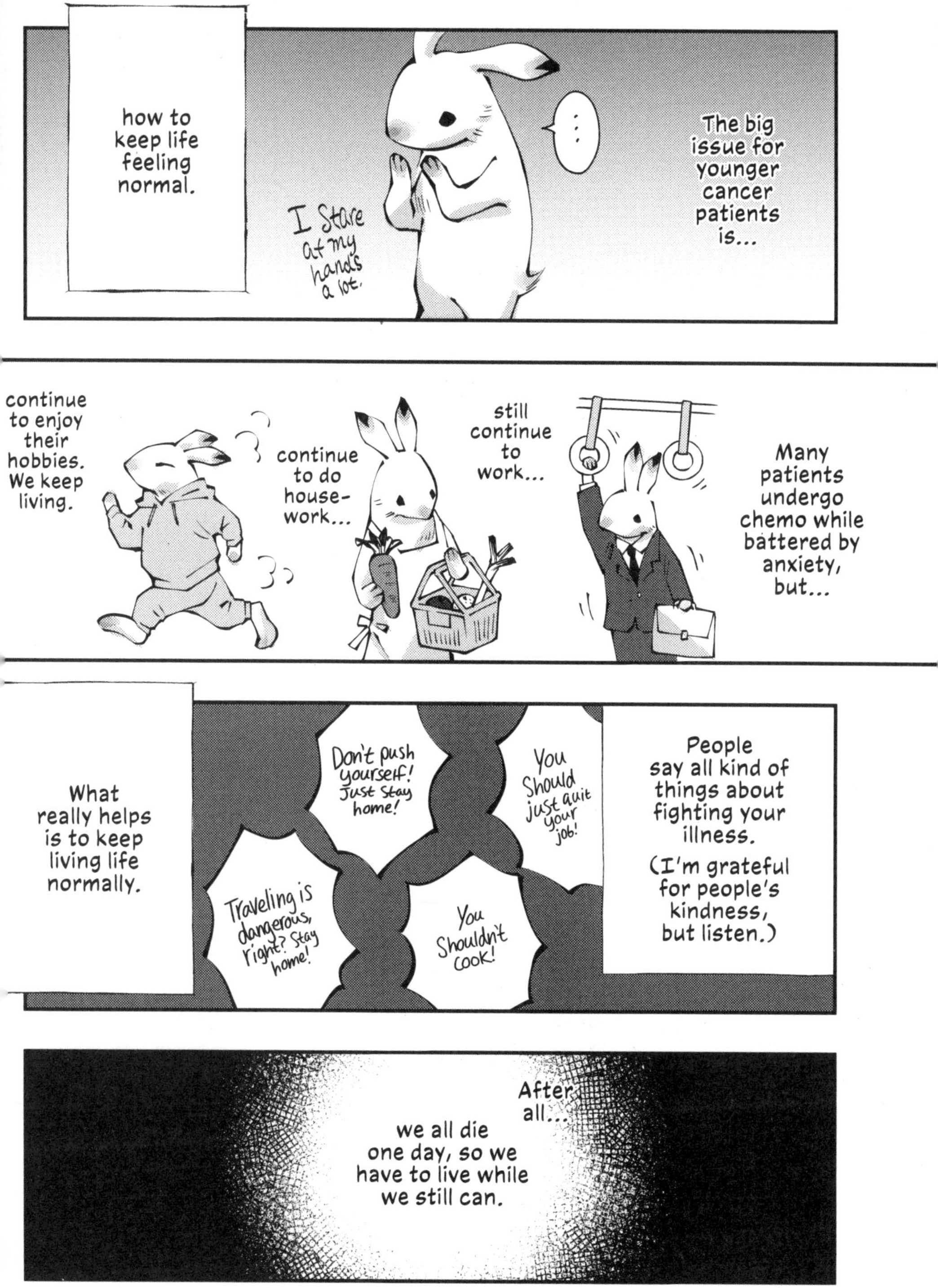
The big issue for younger cancer patients is...
. . .
I stare at my hands a lot.
how to keep life feeling normal.
Many patients undergo chemo while battered by anxiety, but...
still continue to work...
continue to do housework...
continue to enjoy their hobbies. We keep living.
People say all kind of things about fighting your illness.
(I'm grateful for people's kindness, but listen.)
You should just quit your job!
Don't push yourself! Just stay home!
You shouldn't cook!
Traveling is dangerous, right? Stay home!
What really helps is to keep living life normally.
After all...
we all die one day, so we have to live while we still can.

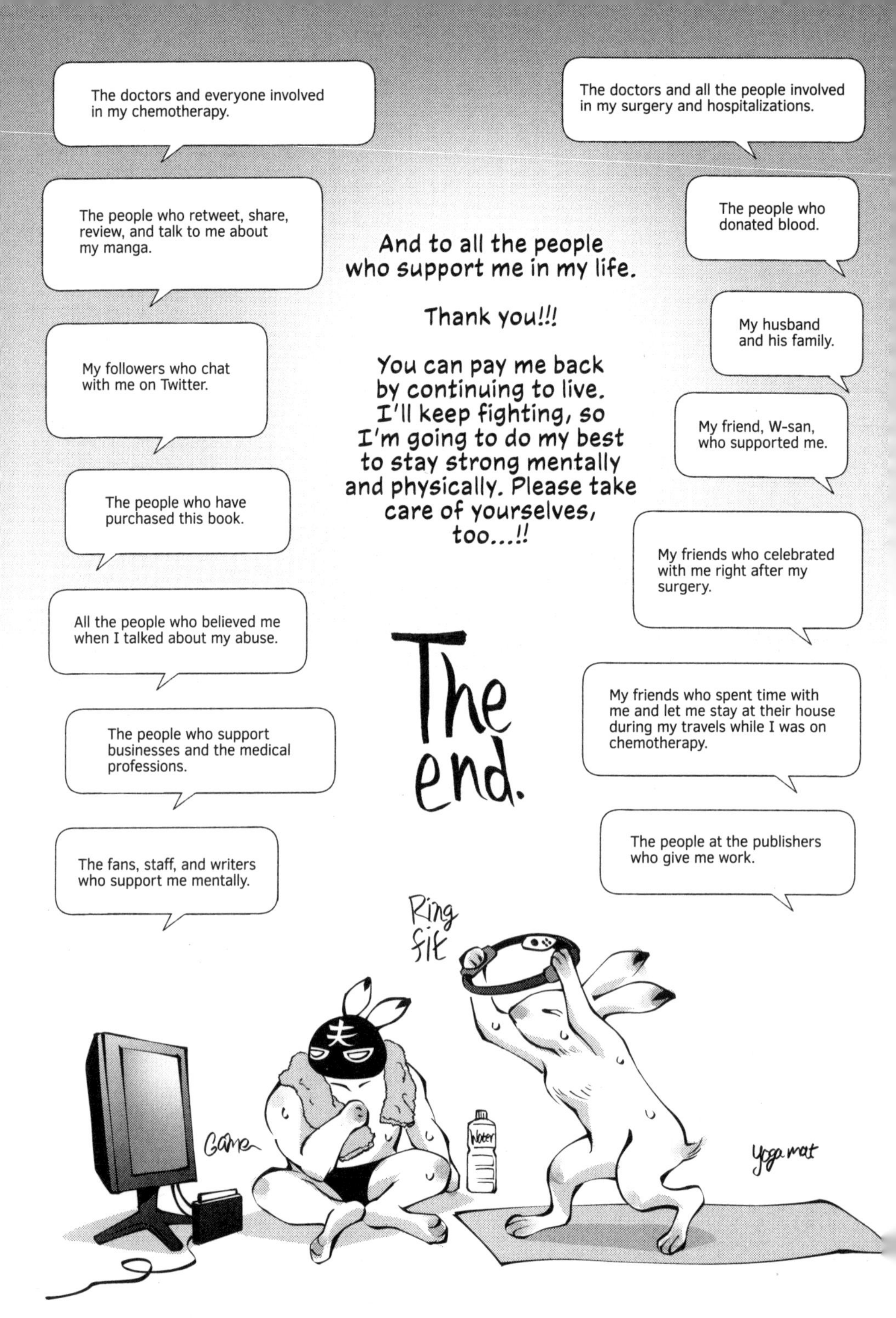

The doctors and all the people involved in my surgery and hospitalizations.
The doctors and everyone involved in my chemotherapy.
The people who donated blood.
The people who retweet, share, review, and talk to me about my manga.
My husband and his family.
My friend, W-san, who supported me.
My followers who chat with me on Twitter.
My friends who celebrated with me right after my surgery.
The people who have purchased this book.
And to all the people who support me in my life.
Thank you!!!
You can pay me back by continuing to live. I'll keep fighting, so I'm going to do my best to stay strong mentally and physically. Please take care of yourselves, too...!!
My friends who spent time with me and let me stay at their house during my travels while I was on chemotherapy.
All the people who believed me when I talked about my abuse.
The people at the publishers who give me work.
The people who support businesses and the medical professions.
The fans, staff, and writers who support me mentally.
The end.
Ring fit
Yoga mat
Water
Game

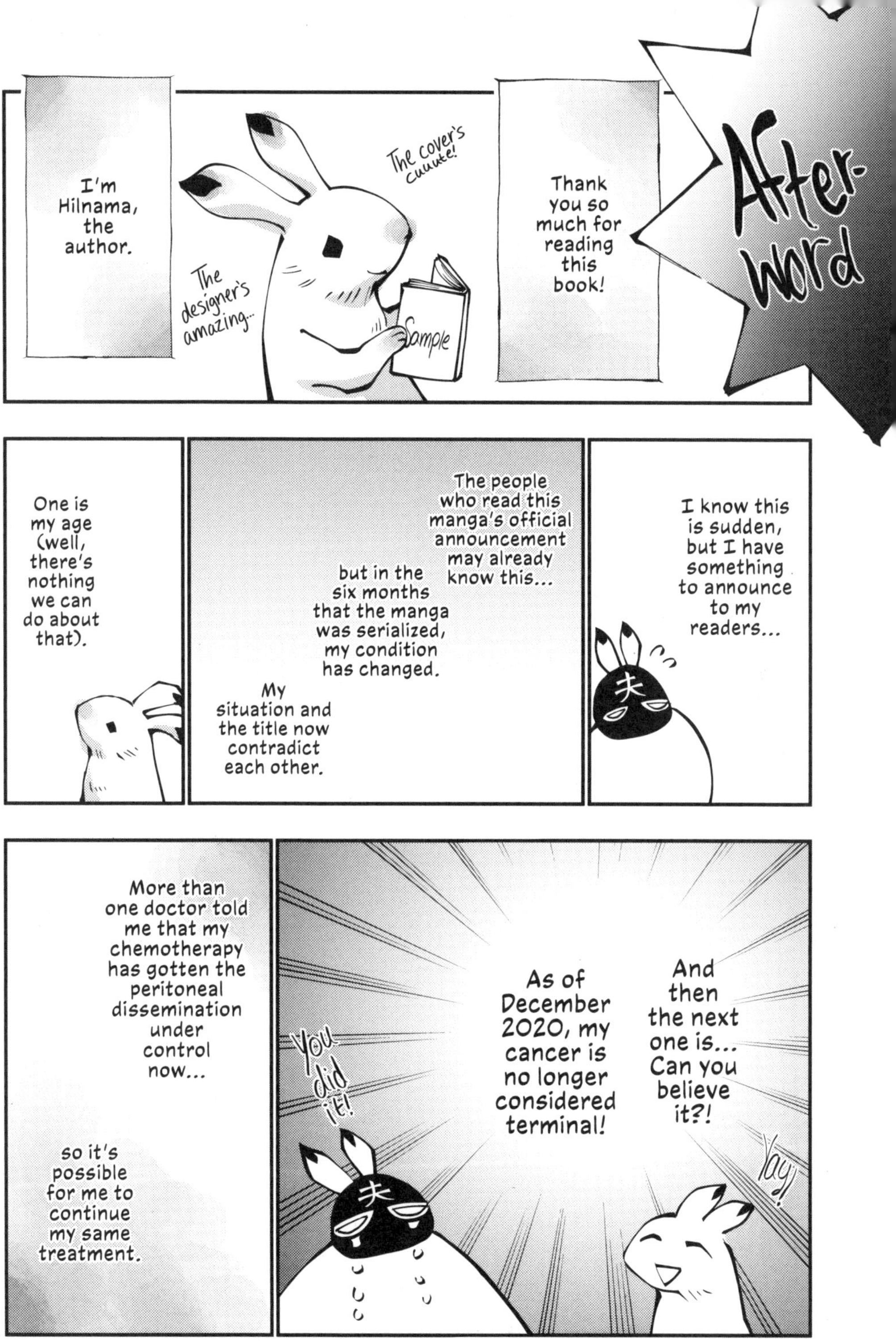

After-word
Thank you so much for reading this book!
The cover's cuuute!
The designer's amazing...
Sample
I'm Hilnama, the author.
I know this is sudden, but I have something to announce to my readers...
The people who read this manga's official announcement may already know this...
but in the six months that the manga was serialized, my condition has changed.
My situation and the title now contradict each other.
One is my age (well, there's nothing we can do about that).
And then the next one is... Can you believe it?!
As of December 2020, my cancer is no longer considered terminal!
Yay!
You did it!
More than one doctor told me that my chemotherapy has gotten the peritoneal dissemination under control now...
so it's possible for me to continue my same treatment.

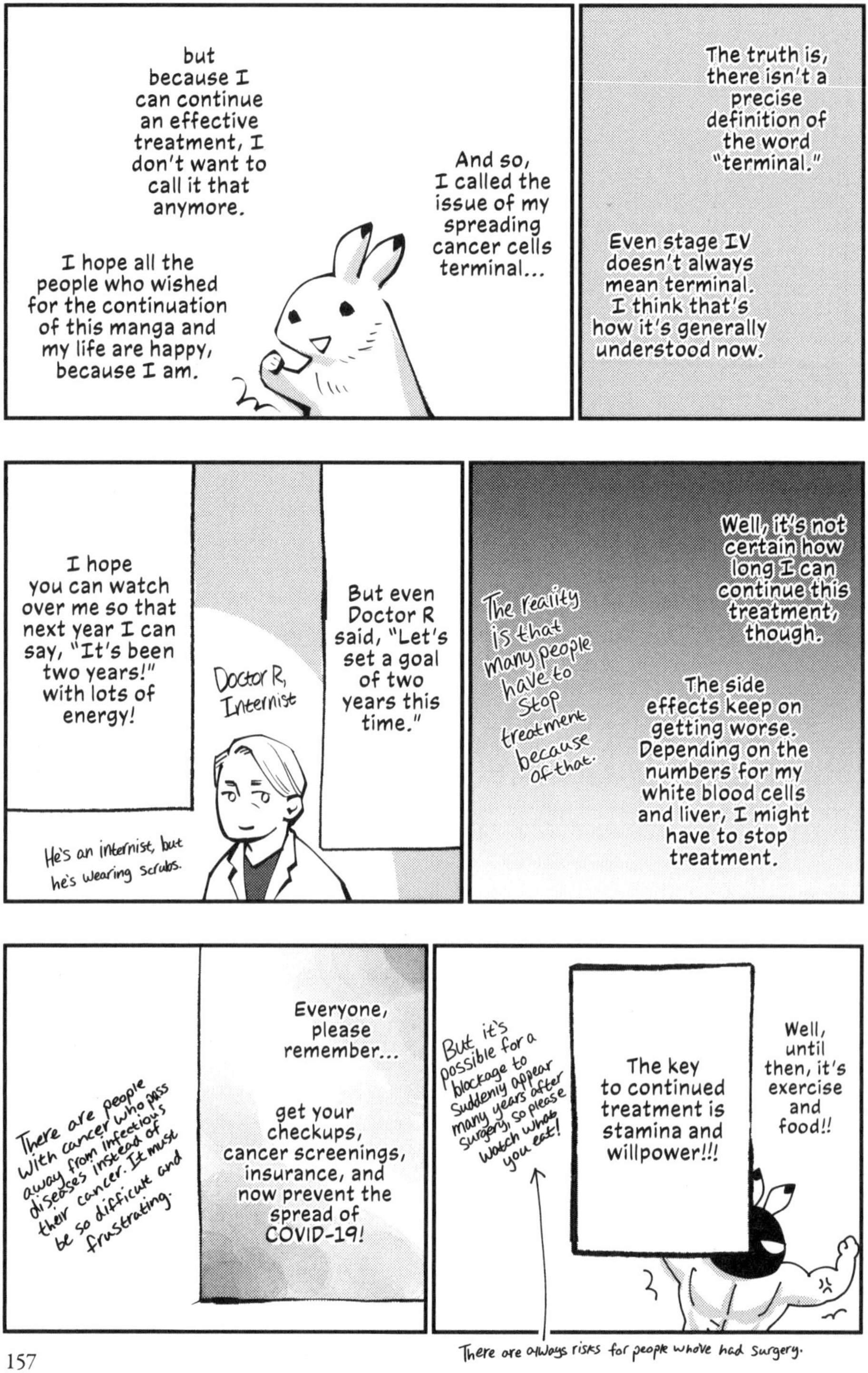
The truth is, there isn't a precise definition of the word "terminal."
Even stage IV doesn't always mean terminal. I think that's how it's generally understood now.
And so, I called the issue of my spreading cancer cells terminal...
but because I can continue an effective treatment, I don't want to call it that anymore.
I hope all the people who wished for the continuation of this manga and my life are happy, because I am.
Well, it's not certain how long I can continue this treatment, though.
The side effects keep on getting worse. Depending on the numbers for my white blood cells and liver, I might have to stop treatment.
The reality is that many people have to stop treatment because of that.
But even Doctor R said, "Let's set a goal of two years this time."
Doctor R, Internist
I hope you can watch over me so that next year I can say, "It's been two years!" with lots of energy!
He's an internist, but he's wearing scrubs.
Well, until then, it's exercise and food!!
The key to continued treatment is stamina and willpower!!!
But it's possible for a blockage to suddenly appear many years after surgery, so please watch what you eat!
There are always risks for people who've had surgery.
Everyone, please remember...
get your checkups, cancer screenings, insurance, and now prevent the spread of COVID-19!
There are people with cancer who pass away from infectious diseases instead of their cancer. It must be so difficult and frustrating.

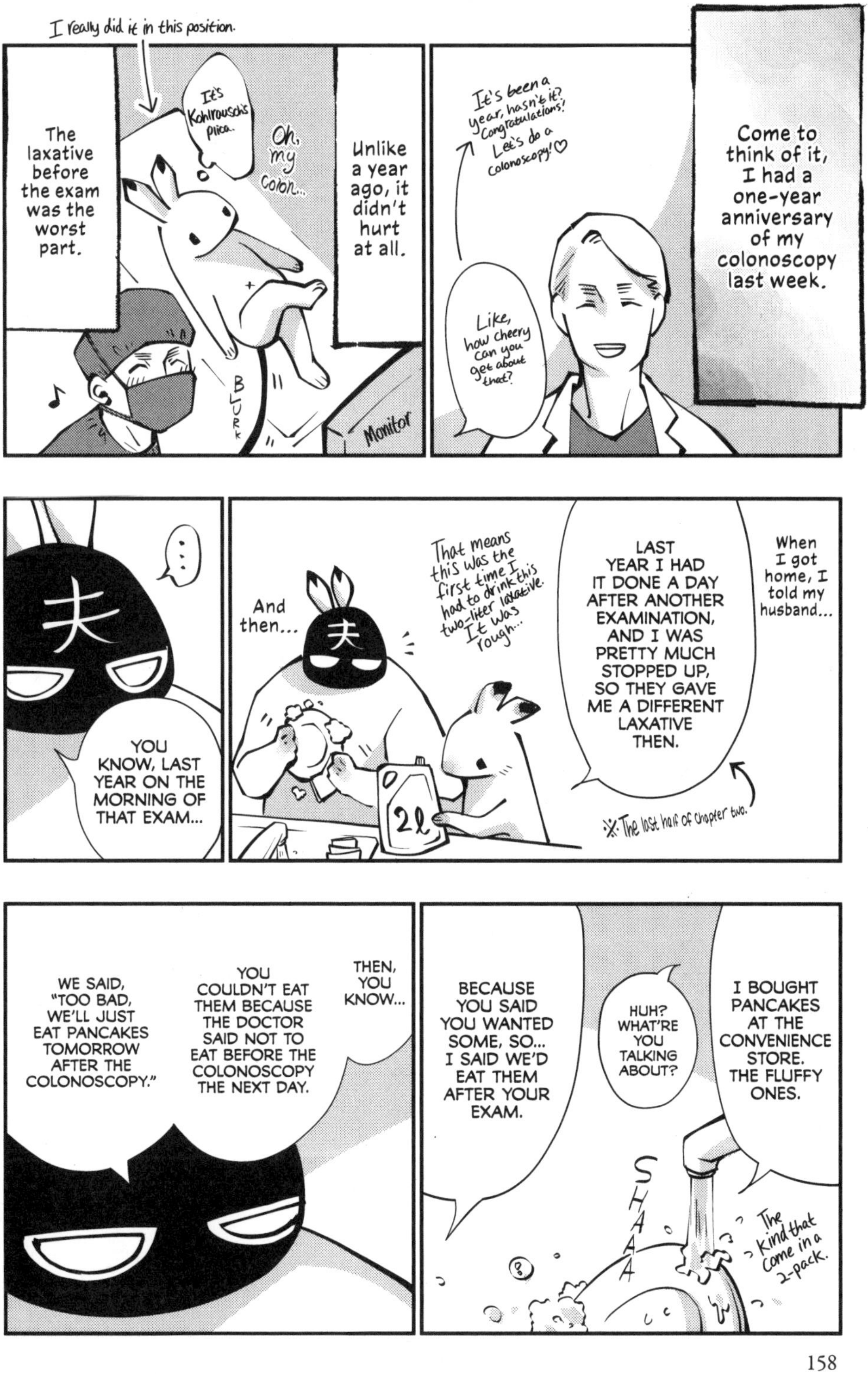

Come to think of it, I had a one-year anniversary of my colonoscopy last week.
It's been a year, hasn't it? Congratulations! Let's do a colonoscopy!♡
Like, how cheery can you get about that?
Unlike a year ago, it didn't hurt at all.
Oh, my colon...
It's Kohlrausch's plica.
I really did it in this position.
The laxative before the exam was the worst part.
BLURK
Monitor
When I got home, I told my husband...
LAST YEAR I HAD IT DONE A DAY AFTER ANOTHER EXAMINATION, AND I WAS PRETTY MUCH STOPPED UP, SO THEY GAVE ME A DIFFERENT LAXATIVE THEN.
※The last half of chapter two.
That means this was the first time I had to drink this two-liter laxative. It was rough...
And then...
2ℓ
...
YOU KNOW, LAST YEAR ON THE MORNING OF THAT EXAM...
I BOUGHT PANCAKES AT THE CONVENIENCE STORE. THE FLUFFY ONES.
HUH? WHAT'RE YOU TALKING ABOUT?
BECAUSE YOU SAID YOU WANTED SOME, SO... I SAID WE'D EAT THEM AFTER YOUR EXAM.
The kind that come in a 2-pack.
SHAAA
THEN, YOU KNOW...
YOU COULDN'T EAT THEM BECAUSE THE DOCTOR SAID NOT TO EAT BEFORE THE COLONOSCOPY THE NEXT DAY.
WE SAID, "TOO BAD, WE'LL JUST EAT PANCAKES TOMORROW AFTER THE COLONOSCOPY."

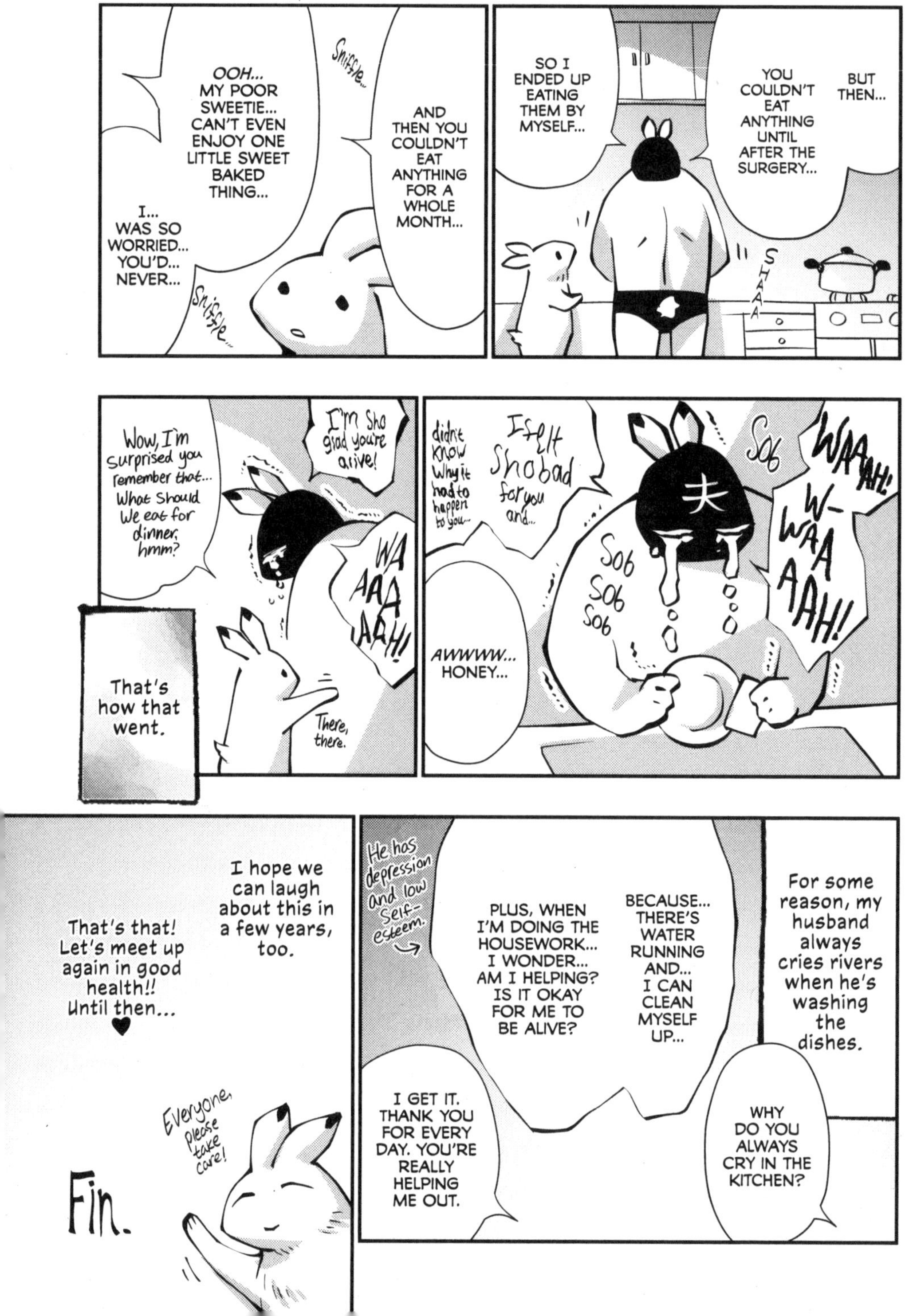
BUT THEN...
YOU COULDN'T EAT ANYTHING UNTIL AFTER THE SURGERY...
SO I ENDED UP EATING THEM BY MYSELF...
SHAA
AND THEN YOU COULDN'T EAT ANYTHING FOR A WHOLE MONTH...
Sniffle...
OOH... MY POOR SWEETIE... CAN'T EVEN ENJOY ONE LITTLE SWEET BAKED THING...
I... WAS SO WORRIED... YOU'D... NEVER...
Sniffle...
WAAAAH!
W-WAAAAH!
Sob
I felt sho bad for you and...
didn't know why it had to happen to you...
Sob Sob Sob
AWWWW... HONEY...
I'm sho glad you're alive!
Wow, I'm surprised you remember that... What should we eat for dinner, hmm?
WAAAAAH!
There, there.
That's how that went.
For some reason, my husband always cries rivers when he's washing the dishes.
WHY DO YOU ALWAYS CRY IN THE KITCHEN?
BECAUSE... THERE'S WATER RUNNING AND... I CAN CLEAN MYSELF UP...
PLUS, WHEN I'M DOING THE HOUSEWORK... I WONDER... AM I HELPING? IS IT OKAY FOR ME TO BE ALIVE?
He has depression and low self-esteem.
I GET IT. THANK YOU FOR EVERY DAY. YOU'RE REALLY HELPING ME OUT.
I hope we can laugh about this in a few years, too.
That's that! Let's meet up again in good health!! Until then... ♥
Everyone, please take care!
Fin.

SEVEN SEAS ENTERTAINME

CW00662473

I'm a Terminal Cancer Pa

(true) story and art by **Hilnama** BUT I'M FINE

TRANSLATION
Beni Axia Conrad

ADAPTATION
Carly Smith

LETTERING
Brendon Hull

COVER DESIGN
Nicky Lim

PROOFREADER
Leighanna DeRouen

SENIOR COPY EDITOR
Dawn Davis

MEDICAL READER FOR ENGLISH VERSION
Allyson Lieberman, MD, PhD

EDITOR
Kristiina Korpus

PRODUCTION DESIGNER
Christina McKenzie

PRODUCTION MANAGER
Lissa Pattillo

PREPRESS TECHNICIAN
Melanie Ujimori

PRINT MANAGER
Rhiannon Rasmussen-Silverstein

EDITOR-IN-CHIEF
Julie Davis

ASSOCIATE PUBLISHER
Adam Arnold

PUBLISHER
Jason DeAngelis

Seven Seas press and purchase enquiries can be sent to Marketing Manager Lianne Sentar at press@gomanga.com. Information regarding the distribution and purchase of digital editions is available from Digital Manager CK Russell at digital@gomanga.com.

ISBN: 978-1-63858-525-1
Printed in Canada
First Printing: November 2022
10 9 8 7 6 5 4 3 2 1

READING DIRECTIONS

This book reads from ***right to left***, Japanese style. If this is your first time reading manga, you start reading from the top right panel on each page and take it from there. If you get lost, just follow the numbered diagram here. It may seem backwards at first, but you'll get the hang of it! Have fun!!

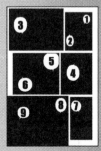

1
2
3
4
5
6
7
8
9